Interweaving myths in Shakespeare
and his contemporaries

Manchester University Press

Interweaving myths in Shakespeare and his contemporaries

Edited by Janice Valls-Russell, Agnès Lafont and Charlotte Coffin

Manchester University Press

Copyright © Manchester University Press 2017

While copyright in the volume as a whole is vested in Manchester University Press, copyright in individual chapters belongs to their respective authors, and no chapter may be reproduced wholly or in part without the express permission in writing of both author and publisher.

Published by Manchester University Press
Altrincham Street, Manchester M1 7JA
www.manchesteruniversitypress.co.uk

British Library Cataloguing-in-Publication Data is available

ISBN 978 1 5261 1768 7 hardback
ISBN 978 1 5261 1770 0 paperback

First published by Manchester University Press in hardback 2017

This edition first published 2020

The publisher has no responsibility for the persistence or accuracy of URLs for any external or third-party internet websites referred to in this book, and does not guarantee that any content on such websites is, or will remain, accurate or appropriate.

Typeset by Out of House Publishing

Contents

List of figures	*page*	vii
Notes on contributors		viii
Foreword/Forward: Mnemosyne – *Ruth Morse*		xi
Acknowledgements		xii
A note on the text		xiv

	Introduction: 'Ariachne's broken woof'	1
	Janice Valls-Russell, Agnès Lafont and Charlotte Coffin	
1	Shakespeare's mythological *feuilletage*: A methodological induction	25
	Yves Peyré	
2	The non-Ovidian Elizabethan epyllion: Thomas Watson, Christopher Marlowe, Richard Barnfield	41
	Tania Demetriou	
3	'This realm is an empire': Tales of origins in medieval and early modern France and England	65
	Dominique Goy-Blanquet	
4	Trojan shadows in Shakespeare's *King John*	86
	Janice Valls-Russell	
5	Venetian Jasons, parti-coloured lambs and a tainted wether: Ovine tropes and the Golden Fleece in *The Merchant of Venice*	109
	Atsuhiko Hirota	
6	Fifty ways to kill your brother: Medea and the poetics of fratricide in early modern English literature	128
	Katherine Heavey	
7	'She, whom Jove transported into Crete': Europa, between consent and rape	149
	Gaëlle Ginestet	

8 Subtle weavers, mythological interweavings and feminine
    political agency: Penelope and Arachne in early modern drama   173
    Nathalie Rivère de Carles
 9 Multi-layered conversations in Marlowe's *Dido, Queen of Carthage* 195
    Agnès Lafont
10 Burlesque or neoplatonic? Popular or elite? The shifting value
    of classical mythology in *Love's Mistress*   216
    Charlotte Coffin
11 Pygmalion, once and future myth: Instead of a conclusion   239
    Ruth Morse

Select bibliography   259
Index   276

Figures

1 'Europe ravie', from anon., *La métamorphose d'Ovide figurée* (Lyon: Jean de Tournes, 1557), p. 34. C189, fonds Cavalier, Médiathèque Centrale Emile Zola, Montpellier-Méditerranée-Métropole, France. © MCA-Montpellier. page 150
2 *The Rape of Europa* (mosaic). No. FAN.92.00.563, Musée départemental Arles antique, Arles, France. © R. Bénali, J.-L. Maby. 151
3 Veronese (Paolo Caliari) (1528–88), *The Rape of Europa* (oil on canvas). Palazzo Ducale, Venice, Italy. Bridgeman Images. 152
4 Titian (Tiziano Vecellio) (c. 1488–1576), *Europa*, 1559–62 (oil on canvas). Isabella Stewart Gardner Museum, Boston, MA, USA. Bridgeman Images. 153

Notes on contributors

Charlotte Coffin is senior lecturer at Université Paris-Est Créteil Val de Marne (France) and a member of the Institut des mondes anglophone, germanique et roman (IMAGER). She has published articles on classical mythology, the mythographers, Shakespeare and Heywood, and is preparing an edition of Heywood's *Golden Age*. She has contributed to the *Dictionary of Shakespeare's Classical Mythology* and is a member of the editorial board (www.shakmyth.org).

Tania Demetriou is lecturer at the Faculty of English at the University of Cambridge (UK). She works on the reception of classical texts in the early modern period, especially on literary responses to Homer. She co-edited *The Culture of Translation in Early Modern England and France, 1500–1660* (2015) together with Rowan Tomlinson, and two collections of essays together with Tanya Pollard: *Milton, Drama, and Greek Texts*, *The Seventeenth Century*, 31:2 (2016) (special issue) and *Homer and Greek Tragedy in England's Early Modern Theatres*, *Classical Receptions Journal*, 9:1 (2017) (special issue).

Gaëlle Ginestet teaches at the English Department of Université Paul-Valéry, Montpellier (France), and is a member of the Institute for Research on the Renaissance, the Neo-Classical Age and the Enlightenment (IRCL). She holds a Ph.D. on classical mythology in Elizabethan love sonnet sequences. She has published entries for *A Dictionary of Shakespeare's Classical Mythology* and edited Cantos VI and VII of Thomas Heywood's *Troia Britanica* both online (www.shakmyth.org).

Dominique Goy-Blanquet is professor emeritus at the Université de Picardie (France). Her works include *Shakespeare's Early History Plays* (Oxford University Press, 2003); *Shakespeare et l'invention de l'histoire* (Garnier, 3rd edn 2014); and *Côté cour, côté justice: Shakespeare et l'invention du droit* (Garnier,

2016); and the editions of Richard Marienstras's *Shakespeare et le désordre du monde* (Gallimard, 2012); of *Lettres à Shakespeare* (Marchaisse, 2014); and, with François Laroque, of *Shakespeare, combien de prétendants?* (Marchaisse, 2016).

Katherine Heavey is a lecturer in early modern English literature at the University of Glasgow (UK). Prior to this, she held a Leverhulme Early Career Fellowship at Newcastle University. Her first book, *The Early Modern Medea: Medea in English Literature 1558–1688*, was published by Palgrave Macmillan in 2015. She has published journal articles in *Literature Compass*, *Renaissance Studies*, *Translation and Literature* and the *Journal of the Northern Renaissance*.

Atsuhiko Hirota is an associate professor of English at Kyoto University (Japan). He is currently working on representations of Circe and Circe-like characters in Shakespeare, in connection with early modern discourses on the vulnerability of English identity. He has published essays on related topics for *The Shakespearean International Yearbook*, the Société française Shakespeare (http://shakespeare.revues.org) and *Cahiers élisabéthains*, and entries for *A Dictionary of Classical Mythology* (www.shakmyth.org).

Agnès Lafont is senior lecturer in early modern English literature at Université Paul-Valéry, Montpellier (France), and a member of the Institute for Research on the Renaissance, the Neo-Classical Age and the Enlightenment (IRCL). She is currently researching the reception of Ovidian Myrrha in sixteenth-century translations. She has published articles on mythology and edited *Shakespeare's Erotic Mythology and Ovidian Renaissance Culture* (Ashgate, 2013). She is a contributor to *A Dictionary of Shakespeare's Classical Mythology* (www.shakmyth.org).

Ruth Morse has taught at Paris-Diderot (Sorbonne Paris Cité); she spent a year at the National Humanities Center in the United States, where she completed *Imagined Histories: Fictions of the Past from 'Beowulf' to Shakespeare*. Among her books are *The Medieval Medea* (D. S. Brewer, 1996) and *Selected Poems of A. D. Hope* (Carcanet, 1986), as well as *Medieval Shakespeare: Pasts and Presents* (Cambridge University Press, 2013) and *Great Shakespeareans*, Vol. XVI (Continuum, 2013), in which she wrote the introduction and the chapter on Les Hugo.

Yves Peyré is emeritus professor of English literature at Université Paul-Valéry, Montpellier (France). He is general editor of the online *Dictionary of Shakespeare's Classical Mythology* and an online edition of Thomas Heywood's

Troia Britanica (www.shakmyth.org). He is the author of *La voix des mythes dans la tragédie élisabéthaine* (Paris, 1996); *William Shakespeare: 'Venus and Adonis'* (Didier-Erudition,1998); and essays on the classical reception, published in the UK, the USA and France.

Nathalie Rivère de Carles is senior lecturer at the University of Toulouse Jean-Jaurès (France). Her research focuses on theatre history, literary analysis of early modern plays, and cultural and political exchanges. She edited *Forms of Diplomacy* (Caliban: Presses Universitaires du Midi, 2015) and *Early Modern Diplomacy, Theatre and Soft Power: The Making of Peace* (Palgrave Macmillan, 2016). She is textual editor for the Norton Shakespeare, Third Edition (2015) and the author of several articles and chapters.

Janice Valls-Russell is a principal research associate of the French National Centre for Scientific Research (CNRS) at Université Paul-Valéry, Montpellier (France). The author of a Ph.D., and articles and chapters on classical mythology and the early modern world, she has edited Canto II of Thomas Heywood's *Troia Britanica*, and is project coordinator of *A Dictionary of Shakespeare's Classical Mythology* and the Early Modern Mythological Texts Series (www.shakmyth.org).

Foreword/Forward

Ruth Morse

Mnemosyne

ONE FINAL REFLECTION, READER, before we invite you to turn our pages. Scholars, too, have debts, and it is a rare privilege to be able to thank those to whom we owe them, as well as the usual duty to acknowledge their writing. Much in this volume pays homage to Yves Peyré, who has done so much to expand our knowledge of intertextual engagements between early modern writers and their classical reading. In the plenary lecture he gave at the 2013 European Shakespeare Research Association (ESRA) Conference in Montpellier (France), he selected a phrase – one just long enough to be identifiable – and then demonstrated its longevity through centuries of reuse. He has taught us to listen better, to attend to detail, and to read marginal notes and commentaries such as the moralised Ovids, some of which were not available in modern editions when he began his work. There was no line to be on, no search engines, no Wikipedia, none of those searchable texts that have so transformed our work. Early English Books Online was a dream for the future. Yves's example was simple: read the books, carefully, listening for echoes; remember. We would not have wanted to create this book without his presence. It is said that those who forget the past are doomed to repeat it, but it is just as true that without memory we *cannot* repeat it. Mnemosyne was the mother of the Muses; her name is inscribed above the door to the Warburg Institute of the University of London, a gift from a Hitler refugee and a library of delight. We confess, all of us, to keeping this whole project a secret, and for several years. Perhaps, Professor Peyré, you have thought yourself forgotten. Not while Memory lives and reads.

Acknowledgements

THIS VOLUME IS MORE than the sum of its parts. It is the result not only of individual research but also, to a great extent, of interactions and collaborative explorations that have grown and expanded over a number of years. Seminars on classical mythology in early modern England are organised on a regular basis in Montpellier's Institute for Research on the Renaissance, the Neo-Classical age and the Enlightenment (IRCL), a joint research unit of the French National Centre for Scientific Research (CNRS) and Université Paul-Valéry Montpellier 3. Several contributions grew out of keynote lectures and seminar presentations during the 2013 European Shakespeare Research Association (ESRA) Conference on Shakespeare and myth, which took place in Montpellier. Working versions of other contributions were first discussed in a panel during the Shakespeare 450 Conference in Paris in 2014, which was hosted by the Société française Shakespeare (SFS), and in a seminar at the International Shakespeare Conference in Stratford-upon-Avon, also in 2014.

Several of the contributors are involved in diverse roles in the IRCL's international, online projects, *A Dictionary of Shakespeare's Classical Mythology* and the Early English Mythological Texts Series (www.shakmyth.org). They have greatly benefited from the input of the two projects' other participants and editorial team.

We therefore wish to express our gratitude to the director of the IRCL, Nathalie Vienne-Guerrin, for her unfailing support. We are equally indebted to Créteil's Research Institute on Modern Languages and Cultures (IMAGER). Heartfelt thanks also to Ton Hoenselaars and Dominique Goy-Blanquet, then respective chairs of ESRA and the SFS, as well as the organisers of those two conferences, which provided a wonderful environment for so many of these fruitful and friendly exchanges. We are honoured and delighted to include Dominique among the contributors of this volume.

Acknowledgements

The enjoyment of working in libraries owed much to the helpful staff at the Bibliothèque nationale de France in Paris and its branch at Avignon, the Humanities Library of the Ecole normale supérieure (rue d'Ulm, Paris), the Shakespeare Institute Library, the Green Library at Stanford University and the Warburg Institute, as well as at the libraries of our respective institutions: Bibliothèque interuniversitaire de Montpellier and Bibliothèque du Campus Centre at Créteil. Most online resources would not be available without institutional support, which we gratefully acknowledge.

As general editor of *A Dictionary of Shakespeare's Classical Mythology* and the Early English Mythological Texts Series, Yves Peyré has impulsed work in this field, directing contributors towards new or under-explored sources and untiringly encouraging collaborative work and exchanges within and without the walls of the IRCL, in keeping with the agenda of the CNRS. Tania Demetriou helped with the Greek, and so much more besides. Ruth Morse provided feedback on the project, read early versions of parts of this volume, and invited us to look at the myth-making processes that underlie and condition afterlives. Her essay, which rounds off this volume, opens perspectives on post-Shakespeare reworkings and Shakespearian myths that were also explored during the ESRA conference and inspired a separate collection of essays, *Mythologising Shakespeare: A European Perspective*, edited by Florence March, Jean-Christophe Mayer and Nathalie Vienne-Guerrin, and published as a special issue of *Cahiers élisabéthains* (2016).

Above all, we wish to thank all our contributors for their enthusiasm and patience, especially in the final stages of completion.

The support and advice of Matthew Frost, Paul Clarke and everyone at Manchester University Press has greatly contributed to making this a stimulating and enjoyable journey.

And, of course, husbands, children and assorted pets have ensured that threads of love, laughter and fun get woven into the fabric.

A note on the text

UNLESS OTHERWISE STATED, SHAKESPEARE references are to G. Blakemore Evans with J. J. M. Tobin (gen. eds) *et al.*, *The Riverside Shakespeare*, 2nd edn (Boston, MA and New York: Houghton Mifflin, 1997). Chaucer references are to Larry D. Benson (ed.), *The Riverside Chaucer*, 3rd edn (Oxford: Oxford University Press, 2008 [1987]). References to Spenser's *Faerie Queene* are to A. C. Hamilton's edition (London: Longman, 1977).

All Greek and Latin references and their translations, when placed in quotation marks, are to the Loeb collection (Cambridge, MA: Harvard University Press and London: Heinemann), also available online at www.loebclassics.com. Translations in parentheses are by the authors themselves. Any other translations used are referenced in the endnotes.

When quoting from early modern texts, 'i', 'j', 'u', 'v' and long 's' have been silently modernised. Elided letters have been silently restored when the meaning is unchanged. Italics of names (gods, etc.) in early modern quotations have been removed and capitals retained only for proper names. Editors' decisions have been respected when quoting from modern editions.

The spelling of authors' names follows the *Oxford Dictionary of National Biography*. Unless otherwise stated, we follow the spellings of names of characters given in modern editions where they exist. One exception is Innogen, which we have considered more relevant to discussions in this volume than Imogen, since the name's origins can be traced back to the chronicles discussed by Dominique Goy-Blanquet in chapter 3.

Introduction:
'Ariachne's broken woof'

Janice Valls-Russell, Agnès Lafont and Charlotte Coffin

In *TROILUS AND CRESSIDA*, when Troilus sees Cressida yield to Diomede's advances, he reacts that his certainties 'are slipp't, dissolv'd and loos'd'. His references vacillate and fragment as he attempts to reconcile the Cressida he thought he knew in Troy and the one he has just observed in the Grecian camp. The effort required to rethink past knowledge in the light of present observation leads him to compress the mythological stories of Ariadne and Arachne:

> ... This is, and is not, Cressid!
> Within my soul there doth conduce a fight
> Of this strange nature, that a thing inseparate
> Divides more wider than the sky and earth,
> And yet the spacious breadth of this division
> Admits no orifex for a point as subtle
> As Ariachne's broken woof to enter.
> Instance, O instance, strong as Pluto's gates,
> Cressid is mine, tied with the bonds of heaven.
> Instance, O instance, strong as heaven itself:
> The bonds of heaven are slipp'd, dissolv'd, and loos'd,
> And with another knot, [five]-finger-tied,
> The fractions of her faith, orts of her love,
> The fragments, scraps, the bits and greasy relics
> Of her o'er-eaten faith, are given to Diomed.
>
> (V.ii.146–60)

Ariadne's clew, intended to guide the lover safely through labyrinths of danger provided it does not break, has become Arachne's woof, drawn through the warp to weave stories of love that a mere snapping of the yarn can disrupt. Yet, perhaps Troilus attempts to cling to the reassuring story of Ariadne as a saviour, even while the evidence clashes with the story he had believed in: the tracery of erstwhile bonds has been erased in a moment of cognitive dissonance. Starting from this instance of mythological texturing, this introduction sets the scene for the following chapters and their reinterpretations and explorations of the ways William Shakespeare and his contemporaries worked mythological material on their looms.

Yves Peyré's analysis of the resulting mythological cluster ('Ariachne's broken woof') shows how it brings together two Ovidian stories that Shakespeare suffuses elsewhere in his work with Petrarchan imagery of the beloved woman's hair as an imprisoning net and labyrinth.[1] In *Troilus and Cressida*, the resulting image of male dependence on and fearful fascination with female erotic agency carries intimations of self-destruction in the larger context of Troy's impending fall. It also encapsulates the dramatist's own art of creative interweaving. Shakespeare encases this enmeshed reference to *Metamorphoses* in epic material that he refashions by injecting the medieval tradition of Troy and its historical reverberations into the classical tradition. Cressida herself – her persona and her name – is an invention created by a misreading, conflating two figures from the *Iliad*, Briseis and Chryseis, given life by Boccaccio, by Geoffrey Chaucer, by Robert Henryson and, eventually, Shakespeare.[2] The 'overlapping' of texts and sources from different authors and different strata of cultural history combines the activities of a weaver's (Arachne's) production, with threads that suggest patterns and constitute guiding or teasing clews (Ariadne's) for the reader/spectator – a method that results in those tensions that Troilus finds so unsettling: 'this is, and is not'.

That classical mythology should be at the heart of this joint creative process between authors and their publics is not accidental. No myth exists in isolation, nor stands alone. 'Ariachne's broken woof' and the complex heritage of reception associated with Cressida's name exemplify the ways early modern authors make the most of classical mythology's lability, its potential for versatility and its inherent capacity to invite shifting interpretations: it simultaneously suggests analogy and tension between Arachne's enmeshing process within a web and Ariadne's liberating guidance out of the labyrinth, itself a stone web. Individually and collectively, readers and writers grasp allusion, identify or reinvent genealogies, retrace ramifications and recycle what they have inherited – as they understand or misunderstand, reinterpret or misinterpret. So doing, they engage in a process that a Franco-Flemish tapestry of the late fifteenth century captures in its depiction of Penelope, reproduced on the cover of this volume: as she weaves by day and unweaves by night, gaining a form of agency through her shuttle, which Nathalie Rivère discusses in Chapter 8, so her story – like other myths – travels through time, acquiring, shedding and refashioning content, and shifting in focus. Thus, in this design, a tapestry embraces medieval design and Renaissance perspective in its staging of a figure in the process of creating a tapestry, with yet another tapestry hanging as a backcloth in the background.

The contributors to this volume share Peyré's concentration on historically informed close reading in order to identify and understand the multiple layers that modify mythological texts from generation to generation. In their discussions of canonical texts alongside less frequently explored works, the following chapters offer fresh perspectives on classical mythology as it informed the writings of Shakespeare and his contemporaries over a period that ranges from the 1580s to the 1630s, from Christopher Marlowe to Thomas Heywood. Focusing on interweaving processes in early modern appropriations of myth, the chapters draw on a variety of approaches to ask how the uses of mythological stories enabled writers to play with representations of history, gender and desire. Building on recent research in different areas of early modern studies (classical reception, history of the book, medieval heritage, theatre history), this volume seeks to heighten awareness of multi-directional interactions in the perception and reappropriation of classical mythology in Elizabethan and Jacobean culture.

Reading and studying mythology: performative rhetoric and 'a tract of confusion'

Fascination with mythology enabled 'the survival of the pagan gods' (to borrow Jean Seznec's title) and offered a series of proxies to writers and artists otherwise constrained by censorship and self-censorship in what topics they could explore and what interests they could express.[3] As is well known, mythographers, from Boccaccio and Pictorius to Natale Conti and George Sandys, collated, referenced and glossed underlying meanings of myths, juxtaposing multiple interpretations. Across Europe, humanists used myths to explain the world and human activity. Classical mythology served both as a form of shorthand and as a springboard for invention, with poets, pedagogues and preachers drawing upon figures and tropes, reworking and reassembling them according to their aesthetic, rhetorical or ideological agendas. Thus, in his *Heptameron of Civill Discourses*, George Whetstone illustrates the ways love 'transgresseth every law' with 'Pigmalion [who] doted upon an image: Narcissus [who] was drowned in imbrasing his owne shadow: & mightie Jove, many times, [who] cast aside his divinitie, to dallie with simple country trulles'.[4] In a sermon preached in 1612, Thomas Adams explains God's legitimate desire to make man in his own likeness, 'as Apelles was delighted with his Tablets, Pigmalion with his Yvorie Statue, Narcissus with his forme in the Fountaine'.[5] The Apelles and Narcissus images resurface in Stephanus Luzvic's recusant *Devout Heart*, in a hymn in which Jesus is compared to Apelles and invited to paint a figure that the faithful 'may imitate, and love, / As did Narcissus'.[6]

John W. Velz and John Lewis Walker's annotated bibliographies show how much work has focused on the reception of the classics – more particularly of classical mythology – in early modern England, in and around the works of Shakespeare.[7] While it is well known that he and his contemporaries had direct access to Ovid as well as Seneca, Virgil, Horace and other classical authors, critics have more frequently considered the classics alongside each other, rather than through their interactions. Research on the reception of leading authors has left in the background the influence of others, such as Appian, Lucan, Lucian, Ausonius: the fact that they were not all readily available in English translation was no impediment to access. Students and scholars had access to Greek texts through primers and editions printed on the Continent: bilingual Latin–Greek editions and Latin translations of Euripides, Homer, Pausanias or Musaeus, whose *Hero and Leander* was one of the first texts printed in Greek, by the Aldine press in 1494. Gordon Braden has shown how Marlowe used one of these editions to write his own *Hero and Leander*.[8] In Chapter 2 Tania Demetriou shows how, like Musaeus' *Hero and Leander*, Colluthus's *Abduction of Helen* attracted interest as a pedagogical text, as well as inspiring poets. Ongoing research informing this volume confirms that the presence of Homer and other Greek sources in the early modern period was more important and influential than was once thought, nuancing the picture of classical reception and opening up new perspectives.[9]

The swift, cumulative diversification of texts broadened readers' and writers' horizons well beyond what they were exposed to in the classroom or at university.[10] Classical poetry and drama reached a widening audience through print: in Greek, in Latin and in vernacular translations. Ideas and texts circulated, and writers were very much aware of what was being produced in other countries, with Abraham Fraunce, for instance, as Demetriou recalls, presenting the Spanish poet Juan Boscán as a literary model alongside the Italian Torquato Tasso, and England's own Philip Sidney.

Links among learning, reading and orality remained strong, in keeping with a tradition of teaching in which texts were recited and exercises in rhetoric had a performative dimension: 'the study of books did not constitute a separate pedagogic sphere but one interwoven with their performance ... Those who could not perform what they knew, but knew it only from books, had no kind of learning at all.'[11] Marginalia and annotations framed source texts, offering interpretative guidance, drawing on (other) classical sources, mythographical commentaries or elucidations by Erasmus and others. Reciprocally, examples drawn from mythology illustrated adages and *sententiae*; and dictionaries provided encapsulated accounts of myths. All this catered for different levels of readership, and nourished readers' own handwritten annotations, and commonplace books, as they sought to make sense of interpretations that could at times appear confusing: in his dedicatory letter to the countess of Bedford, which precedes his masque *The Vision of Twelve Goddesses*, Samuel Daniel complains about 'the best Mytheologers, who wil make somewhat to seem anything, are so unfaithful to themselves, as they have left us no certain way at all, but a tract of confusion to take our course at adventure'.[12] Yet this 'tract of confusion' also contributed to the emergence of distinctive forms and voices; and it nourished readers' and audiences' receptivity to allusions and rewritings that could seem at once familiar and novel.

Texturing classical mythology, Roman politics and English history

The presence of classical mythology tends to be underplayed in religious texts such as those quoted above or in plays that dramatise the history of England. Yet, as essays in this collection analyse in detail, Shakespeare and his contemporaries converse – and are conversant – with sources and influences indiscriminately across the board: they invite classical texts into their writings along with medieval commentaries, Tudor refashionings and humanist glossings, reworking all this with and into material drawn from medieval chronicles, biblical writings, romances, Italian *novelle*, and the works of fellow poets and dramatists.

Let us briefly consider Suffolk's downfall in *2 Henry VI*, which provides a case study of overlapping uses of material, as Shakespeare draws from a variety of classical authors and genres, injecting them into a plot lifted from English chronicles.[13] Two moments are striking in the course of a scene where fighting and unnatural portents blur in the 'loud-howling wolves', 'misty jaws' of graves and bloodstained shore (IV.i.3, 6, 11). The Lieutenant insults Suffolk, punning on his name, William de la Pole:

LIEUTENANT. Poole! Sir Poole! lord!
Ay, kennel, puddle, sink, whose filth and dirt
Troubles the silver spring where England drinks.
Now will I dam up this thy yawning mouth
For swallowing the treasure of the realm.
...
And wedded be thou to the hags of hell,
...
By devilish policy art thou grown great,
And like ambitious Sylla, overgorg'd
With gobbets of thy [mother's] bleeding heart.

(IV.i.69–85)

The second moment occurs some thirty lines later, shortly before Suffolk is beheaded:

SUFFOLK. I charge thee waft me safely cross the Channel.
WHITMORE. Come, Suffolk, I must waft thee to thy death.
SUFFOLK. [Pene] gelidus timor occupat artus: it is thee I fear.

(IV.i.114–16)

This Latin phrase – which may be translated as 'Icy fear seizes my limbs almost entirely' – has been identified as a misquotation from Virgil and Lucan.[14] It also functions as a conflation. In the *Aeneid*, Virgil uses the phrase 'subitus tremor ocupat artus' (VII, 446) to describe Turnus's horror at the sight of Allecto, with her foaming mouth and hydra-like head of snakes, come from the underworld to wage war and death.[15] In Lucan's *Pharsalia*, an unfinished account of the civil wars of Rome, the inhabitants of Ariminum quake with fear on discovering that Caesar has crossed the Rubicon: 'deriguere metu, gelidos pavor occupat artus' (*Pharsalia*, I, 246), which Marlowe translated as 'They shooke for feare, and cold benumm'd their lims'. And thus we see English dramatists plundering Latin historical sources in order to lift their plays into something more than chronicle. Some spectators would have recognised the mythological references; others would not, but all would be aware of the hags of hell, Suffolk's arrogance and fear. These may suggest Virgil, in connection with the earlier evocation of portents of disaster, while intersecting with the *Pharsalia*, available in a Latin edition published in 1589 and read in schools.[16] In Marlowe's translation of the *Pharsalia*, Pompey is compared to 'arch-traitor Sulla' (I, 326), and depicted as 'having lickt /

Warm gore from Sulla's sword [and] yet athirst; / Jaws flesh'd with blood continue murderous' (330–2). Memories of the earlier civil wars fuse graphically with portents that are shot through with Senecan evocations of tyrants and ghosts: the sight of monstrous, 'prodigious births … appals the mother' (560–1); 'foul Erinnys stalk'd about the wals, / Shaking her snaky hair and crooked pine / With flaming top' (570–2); and in the 'black night' of Rome, 'Sulla's ghost / Was seen to walk, singing sad oracles' (579–80).[17]

In *2 Henry VI* Shakespeare transforms Sulla's dictatorship into monstrous jaws dripping with flesh and blood: Suffolk is a 'yawning mouth' (IV.i.72), 'ambitious Scylla' is 'overgorg'd / With gobbets of thy mother's bleeding heart' (84–5); feeding and ambition are a form of pregnancy – 'By devilish policy art thou grown great' (83) – which in turn harks back to 'sink'. Parallels between English and ancient history informed Elizabethan representations of civil strife. Written just before *2 Henry VI*, Thomas Lodge's *The Wounds of Civil War*, which dramatises Appian of Alexandria's account of the struggle between Marius and Sulla (variously spelled Sylla, Scilla and Scylla in early modern texts), carries its own share of bloodshed and portents. In the 1578 translation of Appian, a marginal note alerts the reader to the '[m]onstrous tokens' that announce Sulla's massacres.[18] Around the same time, Marlowe's Tamburlaine compares his tyranny to 'Jove's dreadful thunderbolts' (*1 Tamburlaine*, II.iii.6–24, 19) and himself to Jupiter (II.vii.12–29), a posture that Suffolk seeks to imitate when he is captured, without achieving his rhetorical one-upmanship: 'Jove sometime went disguised, and why not I?' (*2 Henry VI*, IV.i.48), 'O! that I were a god, to shoot forth thunder / Upon these paltry, servile, abject drudges' (103–4).[19] Reading this scene in the light of enmeshed source materials and the context of the London stage, one observes dramatists drawing on a common cultural background and reworking it in a shared environment, emulating and inspiring one another's dramatic and rhetorical effects even while sharing tricks of the trade, such as multiple beheadings. In a culture better at listening than today's audiences, a word or phrase that passed in a matter of seconds on stage might be remembered or recognised as echoes in subsequent plays or inserted into epic poems.

Fears of civil strife feed back into mythological narratives: in Lodge's *Scillaes Metamorphosis* (1589/90), which revisits *Metamorphoses*, XIII (898–968), Ate punishes Scylla by unleashing 'Furie and Rage, Wan-hope, Dispaire and Woe' (715), who chain her to the rocks while the waves echo her howls. Fury is war, '[h]is hands and armes ibathed in blood of those / Whome fortune, sinne, or fate made Countries foes' (719–20).[20] Considering the marine setting in *2 Henry VI*, the references to 'loud-howling wolves', the prophecy that Suffolk would die by water and '[a]gainst the senseless winds ... grin in vain', one may speculate that audiences received the homophony of Sulla the dictator and Scylla the transformed maid as a composite monster. This conflation might seem less far-fetched when one reads in Marlowe's translation of *Pharsalia* how, among the recorded portents, 'Coal-black Charybdis whirl'd a sea of blood; / Fierce Mastives howled' (I, 546–7). The texturing of material lifted from classical mythology, Roman history and medieval English chronicle releases a transformative process that has a generic impact: as Barbara Everett writes, '[i]n his history plays, Shakespeare turns chronicle into history, then history into drama, and then ... historical drama into something almost like myth: free-standing, undocumented and legendary works of art'.[21]

'Honest thefts', borrowings, blendings and recursions

As this case study illustrates, the underlying approach of this volume is to apply to the area of classical mythology practices of reading and writing that Robert S. Miola describes as thinking 'analogically, i.e. across texts, as well as logically' – the 'complex intertextual junction' Raphael Lyne traces in the Ovidian subtexts in *The Faerie Queene*.[22] It also builds on Oliver Lyne's notion of 'further voices' – of classical authors as receptors and crafters as well as models of multi-faceted figures and tropes – and explores the implications of this in early modern writing.[23] Translators, authors and scholars grew increasingly aware of this process as their knowledge of the classics expanded. Through Silver Age poets such as Lucan and Statius could be heard the voices of Virgil, Seneca and Ovid. In the fourth century CE, Ausonius admits his debt to Virgil in *Cupid Crucified* and Colluthus displays his own debt to Homer in the *Abduction of Helen*. The perceived direction of these interactions was not always predictable: Tania Demetriou recalls in Chapter 2 how early modern commentators thought that the fifth-century CE poet Musaeus taught Homer his craft. As Peyré notes in Chapter 1, when inviting Ovid into his writing, Shakespeare is also playing host to Virgil and, through him, Homer, thereby incorporating a subtle layering of meanings – an intertextual *feuilletage*, to use Roland Barthes's term – that reverberates through the text and beyond. And even when figures such as Europa or Pygmalion seem to derive from a single or predominant source (such as Ovid), or, in the case of Medea, a combination of classical sources (mainly Ovid and Seneca) and their early modern translations, similar processes are at work.[24]

From the late fifteenth century onwards, Elizabethans and Jacobeans accessed antiquity in the original text and in contemporary translation, alongside medieval texts, which provided printers with some of their earliest material, as A. E. B. Coldiron has shown. Circuits of penetration also included indirect channels via Italy, France and Spain.[25] Several chapters in this volume demonstrate how 'the persistent medieval' continued to shape readers' apprehensions of, say, the Troy story through the Renaissance reprint culture.[26] In *Reading the Medieval in Early Modern England*, Gordon McMullan and David Matthews underline a new 'sense of continuity and dependence' from the fourteenth to the seventeenth century, and invite 'reassessments of periodicity', which question traditional literary history and allow fresh insights into literary texts.[27] Curtis Perry and John Watkins warn of the dangers that lie in 'the lure of a neo-Burckhardtian idea of early modernity';[28] to the 'narratives of rupture' that developed in the wake of Burckhardt's study of the Italian Renaissance, Coldiron prefers 'narratives of continuity', 'the continuing presence of copious and vividly present pasts' in a 'reprint culture'.[29] Combining literary analysis and book history, she argues that literature of the fifteenth, sixteenth and seventeenth centuries changed in fluid, unpredictable ways, drawing on textual continuity even when asserting novelty. Even authors claiming to exhume an ancient past relied directly on a more recent past's texts.[30]

The contributors to this volume show how understanding modes of creativity and reception in the late sixteenth and early seventeenth centuries requires flexibility about timelines. While the availability of source texts in new editions and the humanist work they generated inspired diversified approaches to classical material and released new forms of aesthetics in the arts that cannot be minimised, the slate was not wiped clean of intermediary influences: 'medieval mediations' (to borrow Coldiron's phrase) were reactivated in the Tudor period, which looped back to earlier texts to usher them into the next decades through print and translation. Coldiron agrees with William Kuskin that '[t]exts do not emerge simply by linear means'.[31] She suggests combinations of patterns of production and circulation that interact in 'a vast, a very complex web', with implications for the mythological material under discussion here.[32] The linear organisation of transmission as *translation* is complicated by patterns that move forwards, backwards and sideways, across cultures and periods.[33] Kuskin's *Recursive Origins: Writing at the Transition to Modernity* is another contribution to this redefinition of periodisation. Imported from computer science, recursion designates the principle of reiterating one small operation again and again, gaining further complexity every time. An essentially dynamic process, it enables Kuskin to deconstruct illusory origins and identify the small 'loops' that have often been neglected in favour of huge leaps (as scholars addressed the relationship between Shakespeare and Chaucer, for instance, or Shakespeare and Ovid): 'the so-called moment of origins is less a comprehensive return to the classical past than a cycling through of local recursions on immediate precedents'.[34] Thus the medieval and Tudor heritages remained very much present, through chronicles, romances and mythological texts; through printed editions of Chaucer, William Caxton or Geoffrey of Monmouth; as well as translations of authors such as Christine de Pizan, whose portraits of exemplary ladies Brian Anslay translated and published under the title *Boke of the Cyte of Ladyes* in 1521.[35]

Recursive, relocated Troys

Classical mythology helped authors (and their publics) bend and challenge the genealogies of transmission and the boundaries of genre. This was particularly true of the 'matter of Troy', a supreme illustration of 'new narratives loosely based upon classical originals'.[36] Caxton's *Recuyell of the Historyes of Troye*, now famous for being the first book printed in English, in 1473–74, is itself a highly 'recursive' text, decisively contributing to the early modern fascination with Troy, which ranged across literary, historical and political agendas. The *Recuyell* loops back through an impressive number of texts. Caxton translated Raoul Lefèvre's *Recoeil des hystoires de Troyes*, completed a decade earlier, which adapts Boccaccio's fourteenth-century *Genealogia deorum gentilium* in the first two books; the third book follows Guido delle Colonne's late-thirteenth-century *Historia destructionis Troiae*, itself based on Benoît de Sainte-Maure's twelfth-century *Roman de Troie*, which adapts two sixth-century Latin texts that passed for eye-witness accounts of the Trojan conflict, Dares the Phrygian's *De excidio Trojae historia* and Dictys of Crete's *Ephemeris Belli Troiani*.

Caxton's *Recuyell* coexisted in print alongside universal chronicles, which interwove Trojan, Roman and 'English' matter, as well as more directly inspired narratives of Troy, and derivative romances and cautionary tales. Seventeen editions ensured its survival right into the eighteenth century. It influenced William Warner's *Albions England* and George Peele's *Tale of Troy*, and contributed to the dramatic texture and language of *Troilus and Cressida*. Around the same period, in the 1610s, Thomas Heywood drew on it as a major inspiration for *Troia Britanica* and his *Ages* plays, alongside classical sources, which he diversely accessed firsthand and through commentaries. In parallel, the Troy material acquired dramatic resonance with the translation of Seneca's tragedies in the 1560s and the availability of Euripides's Greek playtexts, as Tanya Pollard has shown through her study of *Hecuba*.[37]

The story of Troy provided examples of fluidity, linking mythological material with the matter of history and politics, which in turn justified and reinforced its centrality: the story runs through Roman and European history, or rather through chroniclers' (and kings') ongoing concern to fashion and legitimate their myths of origins. Just as Rome founded its legitimacy and ancestry in Troy, England rooted its royal genealogy in the continuity of the Roman-Trojan lineage – Troy rising phoenix-like from its ashes in Rome before being relocated to England and, more specifically, London as Troia Nova, Troynovant, or Troynovantum. This historico-political appropriation of the myth, initiated by, among others, Geoffrey of Monmouth's *Historia regum Britanniae*, was still current nearly 500 years later, in Thomas Dekker's 1612 pageant, *Troy Nova triumphans*.[38] It was further enriched by topical diplomatic and economic concerns: Andrew Duxfield argues that in the continuity of 'mytho-historical antecedents' that arch back to Rome and Virgil, Troy informed the legitimisation of Elizabethan England's colonial ventures, pointing to the example, in *Dido, Queen of Carthage*, of 'Aeneas's account of the fall of Troy'.[39]

There were, then, different ways of inviting the myth of Troy into the early modern world and onto the stage: in terms of setting and story, as in *Troilus and Cressida*; through the power of rhetoric, as Agnès Lafont demonstrates in her discussion of Marlowe's *Dido* in Chapter 9; as a clew running through the dramatised history of England, as Dominique Goy-Blanquet shows in Chapter 3; and, within that context, as a cultural capital shared by dramatists and spectators, as Janice Valls-Russell suggests in her discussion of *King John* in Chapter 4. The example of Troy encapsulates the fluidity noted by Coldiron in the ways literature evolved between the fifteenth and seventeenth centuries; the encounters between medieval-Tudor texts and the classics, through the Latin authors and increasingly, Homer; the malleability per se of the mythological material; and the flexibility of the Elizabethan stage, where 'time and place of action are in constant flux'.[40]

Whether directly accessed, or revisited by medieval and Tudor authors, this proteiform material was read and recycled alongside the early modern variations it inspired: epyllia, sonnets, sonnet sequences, epics, drama. Percolating through all levels of printing, Trojan material reached a widening range of readers, and the way it was packaged illustrates wider processes of reading and reception. Already in the Middle Ages, manuscripts by different authors were bound together, frequently revealing thematic correspondences. Paratexts also served to inflect reader response, such as the 'surprisingly vicious, misogynist Latin poem' that Caxton appended to his *Recuyell* and that was reprinted in most of the editions throughout the sixteenth century.[41] Similarly, Wynkyn de Worde added to his illustrated edition of Chaucer's *Troilus and Criseyde* (1517) stanzas that associate the mythological heroine with falsehood, undermining Chaucer's nuanced point of view with an openly negative condemnation of Criseyde.[42] And in 1532 Thynne printed Henryson's poem, *Testament of Cresseid*, as a sixth book added without attribution to Chaucer's poem, so that it reads as a sequel. Despite the differences between Henryson's (Scots) English and Chaucer's, his depiction of Cressida as a leprous whore influenced poets throughout the seventeenth century, who failed to remember that lepers were thought to have had their purgatory on earth, so that with death they went straight to heaven.[43] Such juxtapositions foreshadow, Lindsay Ann Reid argues, Shakespeare's open treatment of Cressida, which turns her into 'an interpretative amalgam', 'compounding all prior readings of her text'.[44] Thus he summons into the epic framework of the Troy story the non-classical tradition of the Cressida story, with its variations on her inconstancy and Troilus's constancy, to explore the interstices between ideals and 'reality' and question all forms of reception. Troilus anatomises this process in the speech that opened this introduction, and he later sums it up: 'Go, wind, to wind: there turn and change together' (V.iii.110). Love and heroism seem equally impossible, gesticulation and professions equally ineffectual.

Print and stage: growing up together and moving forward

Plays performed within a few years of each other reflect shared concerns, allusions and tropes. Authors parodied each other's works: John Marston openly pastiched Kyd's, Marlowe's and Shakespeare's plays; their action; rhetoric; and the way they were performed and staged.[45] Heywood had read and/or seen Shakespeare and Chapman, who had read and/or seen Marlowe and Lyly. They simultaneously engaged in 'acute intertextual manoeuvers' and indulged in intratextual self-referentiality, choosing to 'recollect' themselves.[46]

Translations of other European contemporary authors enriched the process. One instance of such lateral influences is the translation of Robert Garnier's Senecan drama, *Marc Antoine*, by Mary Sidney Herbert, countess of Pembroke, which was published under the title *Antonius* in 1592 and later reprinted as *The Tragedie of Antonie*. Garnier's play, written before 1575 and printed in 1578, is based on Jodelle's tragedy, *Cléopâtre*, and Plutarch's *Lives* (translated by Jacques Amyot), and is in itself an instance of interwoven influences: while the overall rhetoric is Senecan, the amplification of Cleopatra's lamentation recalls Virgil's Dido mourning Aeneas's departure. Antony (II.502–13) and the chorus (II.862–5) establish parallels between Egypt and Troy while recalling other tragic tales, mostly from Ovid's *Metamorphoses*.[47] Sidney translates faithfully, introducing subtle inflections by referring directly back to source material, essentially Plutarch, which she seems to have read in Amyot and Thomas North's translations.[48] Her blank verse amplifies Garnier's sympathetic characterisation of Cleopatra, which marks a break with the frequently derogatory medieval exemplum in emphasising her single-minded loyalty to Antony. Sidney thus introduced to the English cultural scene the dramatic potential of the Antony and Cleopatra story, which had inspired writers in Italy and France.[49] More widely, her contribution heightened interest in Senecan tragedy, with new emphasis on character through rhetoric, especially the use of soliloquy and the delineation of passions through mythological references. Responding to Sidney's influence as both translator and patron, Samuel Daniel produced a sequel, *The Tragedie of Cleopatra* (1594); Samuel Brandon opted for a different perspective in *The Tragicomedie of the Virtuous Octavia* (1598); and Fulke Greville wrote a play that he destroyed. Sidney's play also influenced Shakespeare's *Antony and Cleopatra*.[50]

Garnier's play 'generates unorthodox questions with respect to sexuality and political power'.[51] In France as in England, it was proof that politically inflected classical tragedies could become a medium through which it was possible to comment on the contemporary scene from a safer historical and generic distance – even though Fulke Greville's 'act of cautious self-censorship' suggests the 'potentially loaded topicality of the tradition of the Antony and Cleopatra plays and, particularly, their potential to interrogate issues relating to politics and sovereignty'.[52]

Such 'encounters' challenge the very notions of diachronic patterns, linearity or compartmentalised knowledge and culture, pointing rather to 'a creatively confused sense of literary chronology'.[53] Cross-fertilisation is synchronic, and accelerated by two complementary economic and cultural vectors, the book trade and the theatre: to quote J. S. Peters, 'The printing press had an essential role to play in the birth of the modern theatre at the turn of the fifteenth century. As institutions they grew up together.'[54] Colin Burrow shows how 'Shakespeare's references to classical authorities are theatrically motivated performances rather than scholarly citations': the classics are a 'changing and theatrically inflected resource'.[55] Illustrations of classical scenes in translations of Ovid also played their part in fashioning the representation of affect on stage, as did 'illustrated Terences and Plautuses ... their woodcuts copied again and again in dramatic editions'.[56]

Research into the economics, architecture and sociology of the theatre industry and the politics underpinning companies' agendas has cast fresh light on the conditions in which plays were written, staged, performed and received. All this helps us understand how creative habits were fashioned. If classical mythology left such marks on Shakespeare and his contemporaries, it is in part because the expanding availability of textual material occurred at a time of intense theatrical activity, with the development of outdoor and indoor playhouses, with their specific staging practices and targeted audiences. Not only was there fierce competition among the professional theatres, private patronage encouraged a wide range of cultural activities, within which women from aristocratic circles, such as Mary Herbert and Queens Anne of Denmark and Henrietta Maria, played a significant part. Whether performed in public playhouses or at court, plays and attendant genres such as masques provided an unrivalled arena for borrowings, blendings and parodies; for intergeneric experimentation and cross-generic transgressions; for a relocation of mythological narrative, topography and figures, to dramatic or seriocomic effect, as Charlotte Coffin shows in her discussion of Thomas Heywood's *Love's Mistress* in Chapter 10.

Interweaving processes

The nature of the early modern playhouse made it particularly well adapted to forms of writing that blend history; romance and classical mythology; epic scenes; and individual trajectories of quest, loss or transformation. Successive chapters in this volume propose close readings that reveal various forms of mythological interweaving, jacquarded motifs, plots and political agendas. While taking in ongoing processes of circulation, elaboration and reception, contributors to this volume invite us to return to the heart of the texts themselves. The interweaving that emerges is fluid, reflexive, self-regenerative, engendering new patterns that simultaneously retain familiar features. Writing of Bernardo Tasso's *Favola di Leandro e d'Hero* (1537) in his study of the Renaissance fortunes of Musaeus's *Hero and Leander*, Braden notes: 'Neither a translation nor a substantially new work, it weaves continually in and out of the Greek poem during its 679 lines, with numerous substitutions, rearrangements, and interpolations; but it always returns to some unmistakable feature from Mousaios.'[57]

What we term interweaving processes bring together complementary methods of investigation. Interactions, as we have seen, can travel back and forth in time, across cultures – radiate or come together. As previously discussed, they can be multi-layered – *feuilletage* – and entail proximity and displacement, overlayerings and palimpsests that are not quite so. Conflations of source materials, mythological stories, narrative conventions and symbolical motifs all have a liberating, expansive effect. When Ruth Morse analyses what she terms Shakespeare's 'deep imaginative collocations', which draw attention to textual and literary present absences, she shows how content can retain continuity while being remarkably malleable, expanding on the theory of memes. In the words of Helen Cooper, who has applied this theory to medieval romance, the meme is 'an idea that behaves like a gene in its ability to replicate faithfully and abundantly, but also on occasion to adapt, mutate, and therefore survive in different forms and cultures'.[58] Authors engage with their audiences through a play on familiarity and variation: 'The very familiarity of the pattern of the motif, the meme, alerts the reader to certain kinds of shaping and significance, and sets up expectations that the author can fulfil or frustrate. The same motif will not always mean the same thing, or in the same ways; on the contrary, what matters most is the variations on the ways it is used.'[59] Variations can be simultaneous within a text, interacting with other material, mythological or non-mythological – processes that Nathalie Rivère de Carles describes and analyses in Chapter 8 as internal and external forms of interweaving. In her discussion of the influence of the Greek epyllion, and the ways poems such as Marlowe's *Hero and Leander* deny all knowledge of the disaster to happen, Tania Demetriou draws attention to the 'recalibration of poets' classical interests', through which they play on generic affiliation, suggesting an intimate link with epic while also distancing themselves from it. All these approaches are dynamic; they stimulate experimentation with rhetoric and genre; encourage the emergence of new aesthetics; legitimise the revisiting of political, religious or historical contexts; involve reader and audience – then as now – in an ongoing process of collaborative recognition and reinvention that goes some way to accounting for the enduring success of so many of Shakespeare's and his contemporaries' productions.

Close readings

Starting from a timeless trope – blushing, more specifically the blushing of Hermaphroditus and Narcissus – Chapter 1 (Yves Peyré) draws on examples from Ovid, Homer, Shakespeare, Marlowe and Spenser. Travelling from Ovid back to Homer; forwards to Shakespeare, Marlowe, Spenser; and back again to Virgil, he sets the tone of the volume's investigation, organically evolving a methodology both from Roland Barthes's theory of *feuilletage* (multi-layering) and Shakespeare's own writing process. The dramatist's combined dynamics of trans-textuality and multi-textuality invites 'new types of dialogue ... beyond temporal and cultural differences' (p. 36). The purpose is not to track source ramifications for their own sake: it is to investigate their impact on various forms of writing.

Chapter 2 (Tania Demetriou) deconstructs assumptions about the so-called 'Ovidian epyllion', an amatory mythological narrative genre that emerged as a vibrant focus of creativity in late Elizabethan England. Demetriou demonstrates that alongside the pervasive influence of Ovid, this tradition owed much to the interaction between pastoral poetics and the precedent of a number of late Greek short epics that enjoyed widespread visibility in the early modern period. The mode of reading that these brief epics invite as a genre shaped the English poetic tradition in ways that have not been properly appraised before. Across the chapter, Demetriou proposes a revaluation of the contribution to 1590s poetic culture of Thomas Watson, avant-garde versifier and exceptional Hellenist. The influence of Watson's citation, translation and imitation of ancient Greek epyllia and especially Colluthus's *Abduction of Helen* reconfigures, she argues, the literary landscape that inspired Marlowe's *Hero and Leander*, and affords not only new ways of reading this poem, but also external evidence that it is finished.

Chapter 3 (Dominique Goy-Blanquet) considers the political use of foundational myths and explores the ambiguity of origins. As medieval France and England sought to assert a degree of autonomy from papal Rome, they used legends to sustain national pride and support their theories of empire. The chapter retraces the complex lineages that purportedly originated in Troy, in a context of competition among the respective courts and chroniclers of France, Burgundy and England. After recalling the increasing scepticism of early modern historians, Goy-Blanquet discusses Shakespeare's critical treatment of these tales of origins in his history plays, both classical and medieval. Their mythical background is one of mingled yarns – French and English, Celtic, Roman and Trojan – that Shakespeare further interweaves, sometimes with deliberate anachronisms, as he invites his public to find ways out of Britain's long and conflict-ridden involvement with continental culture.

Chapter 4 (Janice Valls-Russell) contends that in *King John*, the fall of Troy and the tragic fates of Andromache and Astyanax inform the staging of the siege of Angers, the rhetoric of conquest and destruction, the mother-and-child figures of Constance and Arthur, and the latter's death. Close readings suggest a rhetorical affinity with the translation of Seneca by Jasper Heywood, whose pathos is shown to derive from Homer via Euripides and Seneca. Stagings of the play provide instances of the way the audience is drawn into this cross-referentiality between an Elizabethan dramatist's depiction of medieval cities and the ruins of Troy.

Chapter 5 (Atsuhiko Hirota) shows how the myth of Jason and the Golden Fleece provides a subtext to *The Merchant of Venice*, where the staging of adventurous Venetians as Jasons, and rich daughters as either Medeas or coveted wealth, is fraught with ambivalence. The chapter shows how the myth gains additional layers of meaning in the economic context of sixteenth-century England, where the Golden Fleece is readily associated both with the exploitation of New World resources and with the all-important English wool trade. Hirota also shows how ovine metaphors are at the heart of a network of interactions between classical myth and biblical episodes, a syncretic combination that Shakespeare exploits to dramatic and symbolic effect.

Chapter 6 (Katherine Heavey) extends the discussion of the myth of the Golden Fleece, from the perspective of Medea's killing of her brother Apsyrtus. Shakespeare and his contemporaries knew the story through Ovid's *Tristia* and Seneca's *Medea* and their translations by Thomas Churchyard and John Studley, as well as Caxton's *History of Jason*. Heavey's discussion of various aspects of the myth (the brother–sister relationship, Apsyrtus's youth, Medea's repentance or lack thereof, Aeëtes's grief) shows how early modern translators and authors were sensitive both to her transgression of conventional gender roles and to the grief of Aeëtes. This led playwrights and poets to reshape the myth so as to express culturally specific anxieties about proper male behaviour and the expression of emotions. Looking at passages from Thomas Heywood, Richard Robinson, Robert Baron and Robert Herrick, Heavey also analyses the political implications of the myth. Her investigation shows how a myth is continually reshaped through combinations of sources and adaptation to new concerns.

Chapter 7 (Gaëlle Ginestet) focuses on another feminine figure – Europa – and the story of her abduction, which finds one of its earliest sources in a Greek epyllion by Moschus and was popularised by Ovid. Europa's ravishment by Jupiter in the guise of a bull provides an example of multiple rhetorical and aesthetic influences and readings in love sonnets and Shakespeare. Converging and conflicting depictions of Europa's rape in classical sources were available in the sixteenth century (Moschus, Ovid, Horace), alongside medieval (*Ovide moralisé*, Chaucer) and early modern revisitings (translators, mythographers and emblematists). Dipping into Horace, recovering elements that Ovid had left out from Moschus (to whom they had access in Latin translation), poets remetamorphosed the story into an erotic play of tensions between desire and rape.

Chapter 8 (Nathalie Rivère de Carles) turns to the ambivalent Penelopean and Arachnean palimpsests – discussed in this introduction to the volume – by exploring their impact on early modern English dramatic characterisation in plays retracing love and political conquests. The two myths connect the three 'lives' Aristotle defines as the components of the human quest for happiness: sensual enjoyment, political achievement and intellectual contemplation. Analysing classical and Renaissance sources alongside a corpus of Shakespearean and non-Shakespearean plays, and looking beneath the mythographical cloth of a silent exemplarity so as to retrieve the political 'voice of the shuttle', the chapter shows how the figures of Penelope and Arachne enable a debate on disobedience and the creation of representations of female agency on the stage.

Chapter 9 (Agnès Lafont) reinscribes Marlowe's Ovidian handling of the episode he draws from Virgil of Dido's fated encounter with Aeneas in a cultural context that includes medieval and Tudor revisitings of the mythological Dido. Her study of *Dido, Queen of Carthage* traces the transmission of references to her problematic exemplarity, from Chaucer's *Legend of Good Women* to Caxton's *Eneydos* and sixteenth-century pamphleteers such as Thomas Feylde, broadening the scope of possible intertextual echoes. In transferring the story to the stage Marlowe plays games with his sources, and this generic shift creates another reversal: as performed by boy actors, Dido's classical plight becomes a parody of aristocratic love concerns.

Chapter 10 (Charlotte Coffin) explores the reception of Thomas Heywood's *Love's Mistress*, which dramatises the story of Cupid and Psyche, from Apuleius's *Golden Ass*. Through comparison with emerging trends and contemporary genres Coffin contends that the play demonstrates the complex ways in which classical mythology could be received within a cultured audience in the 1630s. She connects Heywood's treatment of myth with the vogue for burlesque that was beginning to develop in France, and may have reached England through the influence of Queen Henrietta Maria and her courtiers. She also argues that Heywood at the end of his career was not so much going back to his mythological plays of the 1610s, as emulating the innovations of his young rival, James Shirley.

Rounding off the volume, Chapter 11 (Ruth Morse) takes as its starting-point a reference to Pygmalion in *Measure for Measure* to engage in a methodological discussion of influences. Enlarging on medieval and early modern reception, and on the ensuing accretion of significances attached to the figure (and to his statue), this chapter surveys critics' involvement with Pygmalion from a variety of perspectives, and the metamorphoses the myth undergoes in critical thought. Morse draws attention to the simultaneous continuity and malleability of references. The significance of the Pygmalion story is questioned afresh through relocations in new forms of popular culture, which evidence how Shakespeare's reworking in turn inspires later authors. Thus Shakespeare becomes part of the interweaving, allusive process, enriching the tapestry with his own 'displacements' and 'ruptures' and thereby adding his own layer to the ongoing work of *feuilletage*, on which the volume opened.

This *feuilletage* of sources and influences was made strikingly apparent in Melly Still's 2016 production of *Cymbeline* for the Royal Shakespeare Company: design, action and script gave physical and textual immediacy to the ways Shakespeare reshuffles myth, history and gender in the play to explore issues of origins and affiliation, tossing all the pieces in the air, as it were, to have them finally fall into place in a dizzying cascade of revelations. Illustrating the process that Morse describes in this volume and elsewhere, this production absorbed works produced in a 'world consequent upon, as well as subsequent to Shakespeare'.[60] This was a post-apocalyptic Iron Age Britain gone to ruin, ineffectually ruled by a queen wrapped in maternal grief. Memories of a former Golden Age were represented by a home video showing the royal family playing around a tree before the children's abduction, a tree stump centre stage, and graffiti on walls that read 'These were once trees' and 'Remember as it was'. The Roman legions were an orderly formation and Iachimo's Renaissance Italy was a bling, sexist world. Cymbeline's subjects wore cross-gendered clothes recycled from blankets, army surplus and lace tutus in a style loosely evocative of 'shabby chic' punk that suggested an inventive potential for renewal through the integration of diverse source materials. The script reflected a layering of influences: Latin, Italian and French were spoken, with the English text projected upstage. Attention was drawn to mythological imagery in the bedchamber scene, through a screen projection of the lines in which Iachimo compares himself to Tarquin entering Lucrece's chamber, and the passage on Philomel that Innogen (or Imogen) was reading before going to sleep.[61] Jupiter was flown down on the tree stump that had been uprooted earlier to reveal Belarius's grotto in the gaping hole left by the roots, which dangled overhead like a protective canopy; the god then morphed into a reinvigorated Posthumus. This production thus drew attention to cultural and textual hybridity, and the tensions underlying individual and collective trajectories of loss and recovery. The design also drew on the aesthetics of screen epics such as *Hunger Games*, which are influenced by Roman history and myth, as mediated to some extent by Shakespeare. Groping through scenes of darkness towards uncertain stability, this production showed that the interweaving of mythology and history within and with texts such as Shakespeare's is an ongoing creative process, one that remains deeply relevant to the expression of contemporary narratives.

Notes

1. Yves Peyré, 'Iris's "rich scarf" and "Ariachne's broken woof"': Shakespeare's mythology in the twentieth century', in Jonathan Bate, Jill L. Levenson and Dieter Mehl (eds), *Shakespeare and the Twentieth Century* (Newark: University of Delaware Press, 1998), pp. 280–93 (p. 284).
2. Roberto Antonelli, 'The birth of Criseyde – an exemplary triangle: "Classical" Troilus and the question of love at the Anglo-Norman court', in Piero Boitani (ed.), *The European Tragedy of Troilus* (Oxford: Clarendon Press, 1989), pp. 21–48, more especially 43–8.
3. Jean Seznec, *The Survival of the Pagan Gods: The Mythological Tradition and Its Place in Renaissance Humanism and Art*, trans. Barbara F. Sessions (Princeton: Princeton University Press, 1953 [1944]). See the select bibliography for further references.
4. George Whetstone, *An Heptameron of Civill Discourses* (London: Richard Jones, 1582), sig. Q2r. On the use of 'trulles', see Chapter 7 (Gaëlle Ginestet) in her discussion of Arthur Golding's translation of the myth of Europa and Perdita.
5. Thomas Adams, *Heaven and Earth Reconcil'd: A Sermon Preached at Saint Paules Church in Bedford, October 3 1612* (London: W. White, 1613), sig. B2r.
6. Stephanus Luzvic, *The Devout Hart or Royal Throne of the Pacificall Salomon* ([Rouen]: John Cousturier, 1634), p. 135.
7. John W. Velz, *Shakespeare and the Classical Tradition: A Critical Guide to Commentary 1660–1960* (Minneapolis: Minnesota University Press, 1968); John Lewis Walker, *Shakespeare and the Classical Tradition: An Annotated Bibliography, 1961–1991* (New York: Garland, 2002).
8. Gordon Braden, *The Classics and English Renaissance Poetry: Three Case Studies* (New Haven: Yale University Press, 1978), pp. 81–6, 126. See also Tanya Pollard, 'Greek playbooks and dramatic forms in early modern England', in Allison K. Deutermann and András Kiséry (eds), *Formal Matters: Reading the Materials of English Renaissance Literature* (Manchester: Manchester University Press, 2013), pp. 99–123. On Hero and Leander, see Chapter 2 (Tania Demetriou) in this volume.
9. On Greek studies in Renaissance Europe, see Anthony Grafton and Lisa Jardine, *From Humanism to the Humanities* (London: Duckworth, 1986), pp. 99–121.

On Greek texts and the early modern stage, see Tania Demetriou and Tanya Pollard, 'Homer, Greek tragedy, and the early modern stage: An introduction', in Tania Demetriou and Tanya Pollard (eds), *Homer and Greek Tragedy in England's Early Modern Theatres, Classical Receptions Journal*, 9 (2017) (special issue), 1–35.

10 T. W. Baldwin, *William Shakspere's Small Latine and Lesse Greeke*, 2 vols (Urbana: University of Illinois Press, 1944); Lynn Enterline, *Shakespeare's Schoolroom: Rhetoric, Discipline, Emotion* (Philadelphia: University of Pennsylvania Press, 2012).

11 Julie Stone Peters, *Theatre of the Book, 1480–1880: Print, Text and Performance in Europe* (Oxford: Oxford University Press, 2000), p. 114.

12 Samuel Daniel, *The Vision of the .12 Goddesses Presented in a Maske the .8 of January, at Hampton Court* (London: Simon Waterson, 1604), sig. A4r. Also quoted in Peters, *Theatre of the Book*, p. 121.

13 Unless otherwise indicated, the dating of plays follows Alfred Harbage, *Annals of English Drama: 975–1700*, 3rd edn, rev. S. Schoenbaum and Sylvia Stoler Wagonheim (London Routledge, 1989 [1964]).

14 See William Shakespeare, *King Henry VI Part Two*, ed. Andrew S. Cairncross, The Arden Shakespeare (London: Methuen, 1969 [1957]), p. 107, note to line 116: 'Possibly a confused and inaccurate recollection of *Aeneid*, 7. 446 (cf. 11. 424) and Lucan, *Pharsalia* 1. 246'. In his edition of The Norton Shakespeare (New York and London: Norton, 1997), Stephen Greenblatt notes that Shakespeare may be alluding to both Virgil and Lucan; p. 263n2. Richard Dutton does not comment this line in *Shakespeare, Court Dramatist* (Oxford: Oxford University Press, 2016), but he notes the wide range of classical references in both *2 Henry VI* and *3 Henry VI*, including at least one other Latin quotation, and he suggests that Shakespeare was 'writing for a more than usually educated audience, one which could be expected to rise to the challenge of sophisticated Latin references', such as that at court (pp. 208–9).

15 Turnus uses a similar phrase later: 'cur ante tubam tremor ocupat artus?' (XI, 424: 'why should our limbs quake before hearing the trumpet?').

16 George F. Butler, 'Frozen with fear: Virgil's *Aeneid* and act 4, scene 1 of Shakespeare's *The Second Part of King Henry VI*', *Philological Quarterly*, 79:2 (2000), 145–52; Lucan, *M. Annaei Lucani, De bello civili, libri decem argumentis illustrati …* (London: George Bishop, 1589). On Lucan in Shakespeare, see Baldwin, *Shakspere's Small Latine*, Vol. II, pp. 549–51.

17 References are to Christopher Marlowe, *The Poems*, ed. Millar MacLure (London: Methuen, 1968). Sulla's ghost reappears in the opening scene of Ben Jonson's *Catiline*.

18 Appian's *Roman History* was published in 1578, with title pages that variously carry the two imprints of Raulfe Newberrie and Henrie Bynneman, or simply Bynneman. The commentary and page reference (p. 50) are identical for the passage alluded to here in the three editions we consulted. References

are to Appian, *An Auncient Historie and Exquisite Chronicle of the Romane Warres, Both Civile and Foren. Written in Greeke by the Noble Orator and Historiographer, Appian of Alexandria ... Translated out of Divers Languages, and Now Set Forth in Englishe, According to the Greeke Text,* ... by W. B. ... (London: Ralph Newberrie and Henry Bynneman, 1578).

19 All references are to Christopher Marlowe, *Tamburlaine the Great*, ed. J. S. Cunningham (Manchester: Manchester University Press, 1981). The scene of Tamburlaine's chariot drawn by captive kings (Part II, IV.iii.0) parallels Sulla's arrival in Lodge's *Wounds of Civil War*, 'in his chair triumphant of gold, drawn by four Moors before the chariot' (III.iii.0): Thomas Lodge, *The Wounds of Civil War*, ed. Joseph W. Houppert (Lincoln: University of Nebraska Press, 1969), p. 43.

20 Nigel Alexander (ed.), *Elizabethan Narrative Verse* (London: Edward Arnold, 1967), pp. 33–55 (p. 53).

21 Barbara Everett, 'Shakespeare and the Elizabethan sonnet', *London Review of Books*, 30:9 (2008), 12–15, available at www.lrb.co.uk/v30/n09/barbara-everett/shakespeare-and-the-elizabethan-sonnet (accessed 17 October 2015).

22 Robert S. Miola, *Shakespeare's Reading* (Oxford: Oxford University Press, 2000), p. 4; Raphael Lyne, *Ovid's Changing Worlds: English 'Metamorphoses' 1567–1632* (Oxford: Oxford University Press, 2001), pp. 119–23 (p. 120).

23 R. O. A. M. Lyne, *Further Voices in Vergil's 'Aeneid'* (Oxford: Clarendon Press, 1987).

24 See Chapters 7 (Gaëlle Ginestet on Europa), 6 (Katherine Heavey on Medea) and 11 (Ruth Morse on Pygmalion).

25 James G. Clark, Frank T. Coulson and Kathryn L. McKinley (eds), *Ovid in the Middle Ages* (Cambridge: Cambridge University Press, 2011). See also Chapter 2 (Tania Demetriou).

26 A. E. B. Coldiron, *Printers without Borders: Translation and Textuality in the Renaissance* (Cambridge: Cambridge University Press, 2015), p. 59. More widely, this paragraph draws on the introduction and Chapter 1, as well as her earlier essay, 'The mediated "medieval" and Shakespeare', in Ruth Morse, Helen Cooper and Peter Holland (eds), *Medieval Shakespeare: Pasts and Presents* (Cambridge: Cambridge University Press, 2013), pp. 55–77.

27 Gordon McMullan and David Matthews (eds), *Reading the Medieval in Early Modern England* (Cambridge: Cambridge University Press, 2007), pp. 5–6.

28 Curtis Perry and John Watkins (eds), *Shakespeare and the Middle Ages* (Oxford: Oxford University Press, 2009), p. 3.

29 Coldiron, 'The mediated "medieval"', pp. 56, 55.

30 *Ibid.*, p. 56.

31 Coldiron, *Printers without Borders*, p. 20, quoting William Kuskin, 'Recursive origins: Print history and Shakespeare's *2 Henry VI*', in Perry and Watkins, *Shakespeare and the Middle Ages*, pp. 126–50 (p. 129).

32 Coldiron, *Printers without Borders*, p. 29.
33 *Ibid.*, pp. 20–30.
34 William Kuskin, *Recursive Origins: Writing at the Transition to Modernity* (Notre Dame: University of Notre Dame Press, 2013), p. 17.
35 Helen Cooper, *The English Romance in Time: Transforming Motifs from Geoffrey of Monmouth to the Death of Shakespeare* (Oxford: Oxford University Press, 2004); Morse et al., *Medieval Shakespeare*; Coldiron, *Printers without Borders*; Retha M. Warnicke, 'Anslay, Brian (d. 1536)', in *Oxford Dictionary of National Biography* (Oxford: Oxford University Press, 2004), available at www.oxforddnb.com/view/article/573 (accessed 10 October 2015).
36 Ruth Morse, *Truth and Convention in the Middle Ages: Rhetoric, Representation and Reality* (Cambridge: Cambridge University Press, 1991), p. 227. See pp. 92–4 on Troy as an instance of 'historical fictions', and pp. 233–42 on the *Aeneid* and medieval Trojan narratives.
37 Tanya Pollard, 'What's Hecuba to Shakespeare?', *Renaissance Quarterly*, 65:4 (2012), 1060–93.
38 See Chapter 3 (Dominique Goy-Blanquet). Chronicles include Robert Fabyan, *Fabyans cronycle* (London: Wyllyam Rastell, 1533); Thomas Lanquet, *An Epitome of Chronicles Conteining the Whole Discourse of the Histories, as Well of This Realme of England as All Other Countries* (London: Thomas Berthelet, 1549); and Raphael Holinshed, *Chronicles* (London: Henry Bynneman, 1577). Both Lanquet and Holinshed were expanded in successive editions. See also Heather James, *Shakespeare's Troy: Drama, Politics and the Translation of Empire* (Cambridge: Cambridge University Press, 1997).
39 Andrew Duxfield, '"Where am I now?": The articulation of space in Shakespeare's *King Lear* and Marlowe's *Dido, Queen of Carthage*', *Cahiers élisabéthains*, 88 (2015), 79–91 (p. 80). On Dido as a conflict of cultures and colonising powers, see Emily Bartels, *Spectacles of Strangeness: Imperialism, Alienation and Marlowe* (Philadelphia: University of Pennsylvania Press, 1993), pp. 29–52.
40 Stanley Vincent Longman, 'Fixed, floating and fluid stages', in James Redmond (ed.), *Themes in Drama: The Theatrical Space* (Cambridge: Cambridge University Press, 1987), pp. 151–60 (p. 157). See also M. C. Bradbrook, *Elizabethan Stage Conditions: A Study of Their Place in the Interpretations of Shakespeare's Plays* (Cambridge: Cambridge University Press, 1968 [1932]), pp. 30–2. Duxfield's 'Where am I now?' explores the implications of fluidity and flexibility.
41 Coldiron, *Printers without Borders*, pp. 59, 55–62 for a discussion of this paratext.
42 Lindsay Ann Reid, *Ovidian Bibliofictions and the Tudor Book: Metamorphosing Classical Heroines in Late Medieval and Renaissance England* (Burlington: Ashgate, 2014), pp. 84–6.
43 See, in Boitani (ed.), *The European Tragedy of Troilus*: C. David Benson, 'True Troilus and false Cresseid: The descent from tragedy', pp. 153–70, esp. 160–1;

Anna Torti, 'From "history" to "tragedy": The story of Troilus and Criseyde in Lydgate's *Troy Book* and Henryson's *Testament of Cresseid*', pp. 184–97.

44 Reid, *Ovidian Bibliofictions*, p. 105.
45 See Gary Bowman, 'Transformations of space and the collective enterprise in Marston's early plays for the Paul's Playhouse', *Cahiers élisabéthains*, 88 (2015), 47–62 (pp. 55–60).
46 Patrick Cheney, *Shakespeare's Literary Authorship* (Cambridge: Cambridge University Press, 2008), pp. 244, 238.
47 See introduction and notes in Robert Garnier, *Marc Antoine, Hippolyte*, ed. Raymond Lebègue (Paris: Les Belles Lettres, 1974).
48 For a comparison of Garnier and Mary Sidney's texts, see Mary Sidney Herbert, *The Collected Works of Mary Sidney Herbert Countess of Pembroke*, ed. Margaret P. Hannay, Noel J. Kinnamon and Michael J. Brennan, 2 vols, Vol. I: *Poems, Translations and Correspondence* (Oxford: Clarendon Press, 1998), pp. 139–51.
49 See Mary Morrison, 'Some aspects of the treatment of the theme of Antony and Cleopatra in tragedies of the sixteenth century', *Journal of European Studies*, 4:2 (1974), 113–25.
50 M. Sidney, *The Collected Works*, pp. 39–40.
51 Tina Krontiris, 'Mary Herbert: Englishing a purified Cleopatra', in S. P. Cerasano and Marion Wynne-Davies, *Readings in Renaissance Women's Drama* (London and New York: Routledge, 1998), pp. 156–66 (p. 163).
52 Daniel Cadman, '"Quick comedians": Mary Sidney, Samuel Daniel and the *theatrum mundi* in Shakespeare's *Antony and Cleopatra*', *Actes des congrès de la Société française Shakespeare*, 33 (2015), http://shakespeare.revues.org/3536 (accessed 18 May 2016).
53 Colin Burrow, *Shakespeare and Classical Antiquity* (Oxford: Oxford University Press, 2013), p. 38.
54 Peters, *Theatre of the Book*, p. 1.
55 Burrow, *Shakespeare and Classical Antiquity*, pp. 25, 30.
56 Peters, *Theatre of the Book*, p. 6. See also Ilaria Andreoli, 'Ovid's "meta-metamorphosis": Book illustration and the circulation of erotic iconographical patterns', in Agnès Lafont (ed.), *Shakespeare's Erotic Mythology and Ovidian Renaissance Culture* (Aldershot: Ashgate, 2013), pp. 19–39.
57 Braden, *The Classics and English Renaissance Poetry*, p. 94.
58 Cooper, *The English Romance in Time*, p. 3.
59 *Ibid.*, p. 15.
60 Ruth Morse, 'Tempests, magicians, movies: *The Tempest* and the final frontier', *Shakespeare Survey*, 53 (2000), 164–74 (p. 165).
61 For a discussion of this scene and of *Cymbeline*, see Chapter 3 (Dominique Goy-Blanquet).

1

Shakespeare's mythological *feuilletage*: A methodological induction

Yves Peyré

WHEN ROLAND BARTHES COMPARED a literary text to 'pâte feuilletée'[1] — pastry that puffs up into myriads of light, flaky, crisp layers, with multiple bubbles in the baked dough — he was not only reasserting what he called elsewhere 'la jouissance du texte' (the blissful experience of the text),[2] he was also defining the literary text as consisting of multiple layers branching off around countless interstices and alveoli, in opposition to what Maurice Blanchot had denounced as the totalitarian tendencies of a 'parole continue, sans intermittence et sans vide' ('a speech that is continuous, without intermittence and without blanks').[3] Turning his gaze far upstream, away from the literature of the 1960s and 1970s, Barthes might have taken as archetypal of such *feuilletage*, or multi-layering, the intertextual practices of classical antiquity. Just as Virgil's *Aeneid* constantly refers back to the *Odyssey* and the *Iliad*, through points of contact with, and departure from, Homeric epics, Ovid playfully invites Virgil and Seneca, as well as Homer, both directly and through Virgil, into his own compositions. Statius grounds his own creativity in Virgil, Ovid, Propertius and Catullus. Such texts can be best enjoyed not only when considered as independent, individual, autonomous creations in their own right, but, simultaneously, as belonging, each in its way, to a collective textual labyrinth: not an imprisoning one but an open, expanding structure, where all the pleasure consists in endlessly exploring back and forth, prospectively and retrospectively, blind alleys, nooks and corners, open vistas, as well as false perspectives, side-lanes and twisting paths. When Shakespeare plays host to Ovid, he is not inviting Ovid alone into his text, he is also welcoming in Ovid reading Virgil, himself reading Homer, with all the depth, freedom and delicious lightness this multi-layering engenders, as each text leaves a trace in the others, introducing an enriching leaven that expands the text.

An example of such multi-foliation may be found in the passage in Ovid where Salmacis approaches Hermaphroditus: the innocent boy blushes, his cheeks take on the same colour as apples hanging from the tree in the sun, 'hic color aprica pendentibus arbore pomis' (*Metamorphoses*, IV, 331). The comparison implicitly connects Hermaphroditus's story with Narcissus's despair in the preceding book. Enamoured of his own feminine beauty, with its mixture of blush and snowy white ('in niveo mixtum candore ruborem', III, 423), and frustrated not to be able to clasp his own reflection, the youth beats his bare breast: the blows colour his skin with the rosy glow of pain, 'roseum ... ruborem' (III, 482) that ironically mirrors the *rubor* on his cheeks and looks 'non aliter quam poma solent, quae candida parte, / parte rubent' (none other than apples do, part of which stays white, / while the other part reddens) (III, 483–4). In the stories of Hermaphroditus and Narcissus the reddening fruit expresses opposite facets of suffering and desire: Hermaphroditus's shyness as he vainly tries to avoid Salmacis's enterprising importunity; Narcissus's craving for what deludes and escapes him, and his ensuing anguished frustration. It is as if the game consisted in suggesting an underlying convergence between situations that seem to differ widely. The reverberations that Ovid's blushing apples create between the plight of Narcissus and that of Hermaphroditus are all the more powerful insofar as the intratextual echo within the *Metamorphoses* is reinforced by an intertextual reference to Sappho's poetry, where the apple reddening in the sun at the top of the tree, both coveted and out of reach, belongs to what is probably the remnant of a lost epithalamium; the fragmentary nature of this reference to a newly wedded bride[4] makes it indeterminate, wavering between promise and loss.[5] This uncertainty becomes ambivalence when the image is transferred from girl to boy as it passes from Sappho's epithalamium to Tibullus's *Elegies*, where it characterises Apollo's androgynous beauty, his snow-white skin tinged with a purple glow ('color in niveo colore purpureus', IV, iii, 30), an archetypal mixture of 'niveus' and 'purpureus' that makes him look 'ut juveni primum virgo deducta marito / inficitur teneras ore rubente genas / et cum contexunt amarantis alba puellae / lilia et autumno candida mala rubent' (like a newly wed virgin, her tender cheeks suffused with red, as when girls mix up lilies and amaranth, or when white apples grow red in autumn) (IV.iii.31–4). Through multiple transfers among Sappho, Theocritus[6] and Tibullus, the image naturally became a vector of mobile, fluctuating ambiguity, not only in Ovid's poetry, but also in Seneca's *Medea*, where the epithalamium in honour of Creusa describes the young bride reddening like snowy white steeped into blood-coloured dye[7] – not altogether without foreboding, since Creusa's modest blush is the harbinger of Medea's 'genae rubentes' (858), her reddening cheeks flushed in hatred and lusting for revenge.

Considered not as separate, independent images but as a coherent and logically connected poetic nexus, or as interdependent facets of the poetic imagination, the blushing apples in Sappho's fragment and in Tibullus's, Ovid's and Seneca's reworkings explore the nature of intertextual difference and consonance in relation to the problematic articulation of questionable opposites; these contradictions, which intertextuality both underlines and undermines, emphasise frustration and accomplishment, desire and fear, pain and pleasure. This, however, is but a small part of a wider process that opens onto further contradictions, as between the gender issues of masculinity and femininity suggested by Tibullus and Ovid, which are connected with generic differentiations, or between the epic and the erotic, or elegy and tragedy.

The gap seems unbridgeable. On the one hand, there is the temptation of delicious fruit blushing in the sun, superimposed onto blood rushing to the face as a result of different types of emotion; on the other, there is the blood that flows from a wounded, tortured, mangled body. Yet that is the leap, barely hinted at in Seneca's *Medea*, that Shakespeare might invite us to take in *Titus Andronicus*. It is a commonplace of criticism that the name of Lavinia comes from Virgil's *Aeneid*. As early as 1943, Robert Adger Law pointed out that Titus's consent to the marriage of his daughter Lavinia to the newly made Emperor Saturninus – even though she was already betrothed to Bassianus – recalls the plight of Virgil's Lavinia, 'who like Shakespeare's heroine, is promised by her father Latinus to Aeneas despite previous betrothal to King Turnus'.[8] Structurally, the link between the two situations combines symmetry and inversion. Aeneas has to take Lavinia from Turnus to fulfil the Fates' prediction that her union with a stranger (Aeneas) is a necessary step towards the foundation of Rome; when Saturninus takes Lavinia from Bassianus, who takes her back from him, this tug-of-war is one of the first signs that the empire founded by Aeneas has become 'a wilderness of tigers' (III.i.54) whose savagery vies with the barbarity of the Goths. Rather than dwell on the parallel predicaments of the two Lavinias, recent criticism has focused on Virgil's poetical evocation of Aeneas's promised wife. When she hears her mother beg Turnus not to fight Aeneas, Lavinia blushes:

> accipit vocem lacrimis Lavinia matris
> flagrantis perfusa genas, cui plurimus ignem
> subiecit rubor et calefacta per ora cucurrit.
> indum sanguineo veluti violaverit ostro

> si quis ebur, aut mixta rubent ubi lilia multa
> alba rosa, talis virgo dabat ore colores.
>
> (Virgil, *Aeneid*, XII, 64–9)
>
> Lavinia took in her mother's voice with burning tears bathing her cheeks, where an intense glow sent fire spreading on her burning face. As when one gives a violet colour to Indian ivory with blood-red purple, or as white lilies redden, when mixed with many roses, such colours the maiden's face showed.

Is it because she suffers at her parents' anguish, or is she is in love with Aeneas as some readers claim, or with Turnus as others assert? Is she in love at all? It is the nature of blushes to be open to interpretation, and Lavinia's blushing is the public expression of some violent emotion that, being voiceless, remains forever private. As Oliver Lyne has suggested, Virgil's vocabulary lends itself to double entendre and accompanies the epic voice with what he has called 'further voices'.[9] What attracts attention here, beyond the parallel with Tibullus's phrasing, is Virgil's original use of the verb *violare*. Considering the context, the verb, understandably, is often interpreted as meaning 'to alter the colour and give a purple hue, like that of a violet'; the verb *violare* also applies to the staining of an altar with the blood of sacrifice.[10] To detect such a subtext to Lavinia's blush would link the marriage that is imposed upon her with the marriage that Dido was denied, and designate her as one more victim in terms of feminine suffering, through a connection with Virgil's description of the mortally wounded warrior maid Camilla, whose 'virgineus cruor' (virgin blood) (*Aeneid*, XI, 804) has sometimes been viewed as superimposing a suggestion of defloration on the image of death.[11]

Ambrogio Calepino's *Dictionarium* defined *violo* as 'corrumpo, polluo, et quasi vim infero, quod propriè de virgine dicitur' (to soil, to defile, and so to say, to use force, said, strictly speaking, about a virgin).[12] John Florio's definition of the Italian word *violare*, with meanings modelled on those of the Latin, was 'to force, to ravish, to pollute, to defile, to marre, to spoil, to rape, to violate, to corrupt, to make fowle, to deflowre, to distaine, to hurt, to misuse, to wrong, to infringe, to do against, to transgress, as a man doth a law' – and, almost as an afterthought – 'Also, to adorn with violets, to dye violet'.[13] When confronted with the network constituted by the words 'violaverit', 'sanguineo' and 'virgo', Florio's definition, with its contiguity of brutality and delicacy, may suggest some hint of violence in the subtle texture of Virgil's poetry, which elsewhere associates the verb *violare* with the breach of integrity caused by a wound on a warrior's body[14] – what Thomas Cooper's *Thesaurus* (1565) referred to as '*corpus vulnere violare*: to wound'.[15]

Thus the combination of Senecan horror and Ovidian detachment that is prominent in *Titus Andronicus* is fused, as has been argued, with elegant Virgilian ambivalence.[16] One cannot rule out, of course, that we are reading Virgil's description of Lavinia's blush in the light of Shakespeare's treatment of her namesake in *Titus Andronicus*, thus projecting Shakespeare onto Virgil in what amounts to backward or retrospective interpretation. At the same time, in the *Aeneid*, Lavinia's blush itself sends one back, in the substructures of its literary construction, not only to the glowing beauty of Tibullus's effeminate Apollo, but also, simultaneously, to Homer's *Iliad* (IV, 141–2), where the image of ivory coloured in purple by Maionian or Karian women refers to the wound Menelaus received in battle. In his *Commentary (ad Aen.*, XII, 67), Servius noted that Virgil was borrowing his comparison from Homer, 'unde et "violaverit" transtulit: ille enim ait "μιηνη"' (from whom he imported 'violaverit': for Homer said 'μιηνη' [dyes, stains]). Homer uses the verb μιαινω (to stain) twice within five lines, to refer first to ivory being dyed purple (IV, 141), then to Menelaus's shapely, blood-stained thighs (IV, 146).[17] The lines on Menelaus's wound in the *Iliad* combine the elegant aestheticism of a stylistically elaborate description with an insistence on the resulting psychological impact that is expressed by the anaphoric repetition within two lines of the verb ριγεω (to shudder in terror) (IV, 148, 150). In *Titus Andronicus*, what also makes us shudder in terror is that male pleasure (at least Demetrius's and Chiron's) requires female mutilation, as if Shakespeare were stretching to its ultimate limits Virgil's remark that Turnus's desire for Lavinia was aroused when he saw her blush and tears roll down her cheeks (*Aeneid*, XII, 70).

In a different vein, intimations of eroticism in Lavinia's blush in the *Aeneid* were inevitably exploited by Ovid.[18] Acontius tells Cydippe how desirable she is when she blushes (*Heroides*, XX, 120); in the *Amores*, in the elegy entitled 'Ad amicam corruptam', shame makes a girl attractive to her lover, her eyes fixed on the ground are becoming, her face expressing grief is seductive (II, v, 43–4). Her most alluring feature, however, is her blush, rendered in a sophisticated palette of tinted similes:

> conscia purpureus venit in ora pudor,
> quale coloratum Tithoni coniuge caelum
> subrubet, aut sponso visa puella novo;
> quale rosae fulgent inter sua lilia mixtae,
> aut ubi cantatis Luna laborat equis,
> aut quod, ne longis flavescere possit ab annis,
> Maeonis Assyrium femina tinxit ebur.
>
> (*Amores*, II, v, 33–40)

[P]urple shame came over her self-conscious face, in the same way as the sky reddens with the colour of Tythonus's wife or a girl under the gaze of her new betrothed, in the same way as roses glow, mixed with lilies, or the moon losing strength, her horses held in enchantment, or as a Maeonian woman dyes Assyrian ivory, so that it does not yellow with the years.

In Marlowe's translation,

> A scarlet blush her guilty face array'd,
> Even such as by Aurora hath the sky,
> Or maids that their betrothed husbands spy;
> Such as a rose mix'd with a lily breeds,
> Or when the moon travails with charmed steeds,
> Or such as, lest long years should turn the dye,
> Arachne stains Assyrian ivory.[19]

Whether deliberately or not, Marlowe replaces Homer's Maeonian woman with Ovid's Maeonian Arachne,[20] thereby intuitively defining Ovid's and therefore his own text as a weaver's production that intertwines various literary strands. For Ovid elaborates a multi-layered text, almost a virtuoso literary game, in which the blending emotions of shame and desire are inseparable from the sheer enjoyment of a proliferating, embedded intertextuality: in a single sentence, he brings together Propertius's moon blushing in its eclipse[21] and Virgilian lilies and roses, which are predictably followed by Virgil's dyed ivory; the further addition of a Homeric detail that Virgil had dropped – the Maeonian woman – reinstates Homer behind Virgil in the construction of the Ovidian text; while Virgilian chronographic references to Aurora leaving the couch of old Tithonus (*Aeneid*, IV, 585; IX, 460; *Georgics*, I, 447), which Virgil was repeating from Homer's formulaic phrases (*Iliad*, XI, 1; *Odyssey*, V, 1), import their flagrant literariness into this new context of emotion.

When Britomart, who thought her disguise was efficient, finds that she has been discovered by Merlin,

> her pure ivory
> Into a cleare Carnation suddeine dyde;
> As faire Aurora rising hastily,
> Doth by her blushing tell, that she did lye
> All night in old Tithonus frosen bed,
> Whereof she seemes ashamed inwardly.
>
> (Spenser, *The Faerie Queene*, III.iii.20)

Spenser is writing two texts in one, in which conflicting moods jostle. The revelation of Britomart's identity suggests a deep poetic understanding of the blush as brutally laying bare the indefensive inner self to the gaze of the outside world,[22] as in some kind of psychological rape; while, interlaced with this story, the ironic interpretation of Aurora's blush is the expression of a young, lively woman's shame and frustration at sharing the bed of an old, impotent husband. To avoid being shamed by their disability, enfeebled old men, Montaigne advised, should leave sexual desire to tender youths, who blush like Virgil's Lavinia when they discover an awakening of their senses;[23] in Spenser, it is the frustrated younger wife who blushes, perhaps recalling playfully Statius's elaboration of the chronographia that balances Aurora's blush between her husband's implied iciness and the sun's ardour:

> et iam Mygdoniis elata cubilibus alto
> impulerat caelo gelidas Aurora tenebras,
> rorantes excussa comas multumque sequenti
> sole rubens.
>
> (*Thebaid*, II, 134–8)
>
> Already, Aurora, rising from the Mygdonian's bed, had pushed out of high heaven the icy shades of night, shaking dew-drops from her hair and blushing deep as the sun pursued her.

The literary game Spenser is playing here consists not merely in reformulating a topos in an unexpected way, but in making it jar subtly with its new context.

In Shakespeare's transformation, 'the sun with purple-coloured face', triumphantly abandoning a disconsolate lover, 'takes his last leave of the weeping morn' (*Venus and Adonis*, 1–2) instead of pursuing with his flames an Aurora who blushes with shame and desire. In the ambiguous environment of *Venus and Adonis*, 'Rose-cheeked Adonis' (*Venus and Adonis*, 3) is not a pale reflection of the powerful 'purple-coloured' sun, but a new version of Hermaphroditus, who blushes at Salmacis's advances – 'pueri rubor ora notavit' (a glow marked the boy's face) (*Metamorphoses*, IV, 329) – in the same way as Daphne, who desires to preserve her virginity: 'pulchra verecundo suffuderat ora rubore' (her beautiful face was flooded with a glow of modesty) (I, 484).[24] Like Hermaphroditus, Shakespeare's Adonis, who 'burns with bashful shame' (*Venus and Adonis*, 49), 'nescit, enim, quid amor; sed et erubuisse decebat' (did not know what love is; and yet his blush made him attractive) (*Metamorphoses*, IV, 330). Hermaphroditus's cheeks are not only the colour of ripening apples in the sun (330), they are also the hue of dyed ivory ('aut ebori tincto est', 331), a Virgilian echo that, when set alongside Sappho's fragment, seems to invite Lavinia into Shakespeare's poem. The 'maiden burning' of Adonis's cheeks (*Venus and Adonis*, 50) announces the blood that fascinates, almost hypnotises Venus, when she gazes on 'his soft flank, whose wonted lily white / With purple tears that his wound wept was drenched' (1053–4). What she sees is the result of the rape that she imagines she herself might have committed, had she 'been toothed' like the boar (1117–18). In other words, Adonis, who borrowed features from Hermaphroditus at the beginning of the poem, has become another version of Shakespeare's Lavinia. Or rather of Lucrece, perhaps, since Shakespeare's twin narrative poems could be read as a single one, with the two parts folding upon each other in near symmetry. While a feminised Adonis finds his counterpart in a Lucrece whom Ovid had endowed with a virile soul, 'animi matrona virilis' (*Fasti*, II, 847), Lucrece's 'rosy cheek' (*The Rape of Lucrece*, 386) echoes 'rose-cheeked' Adonis, and the boar's tusk is reduplicated in Tarquin's aggression, which is itself both repeated and cancelled out by Lucrece's knife. In *The Rape of Lucrece*, as in *Venus and Adonis*, the blood of blushing shame contrasts with the fire of lust, a disjunction that is cancelled out in the representation of the fall of Troy, which blends devouring flames and rivers of blood. The Troy picture is not only a projection of Lucrece's emotions, it works as a representation of the poem as a work of art. In its design, 'the red blood' is there not so much to figure a wound as 'to show the painter's strife' (1377) – a visual comment that might allow us to imagine in parallel that the red blood in the two poems may be working as a metapoetic intertextual marker. Repeatedly, 'the red blood' emphasises a tension between divergence and similarity that gives rise to converging differences.[25] The same glow on Adonis's and Venus's cheeks expresses opposite emotions, shame and desire (*Venus and Adonis*, 35–6), or 'pudor' and 'furor'. The same harmony of white and red is a feature both of loyal Lucrece and of treacherous Sinon (*The Rape of Lucrece*, 1510). The ambiguity climaxes in the confrontation between Lucrece and a young messenger she is sending to Collatine. Full of 'bashful innocence', the boy receives her message 'blushing on her with a steadfast eye' (1339–41). Seeing him blush, she imagines he knows her shame and she blushes in turn, which further heightens his blush: 'His kindled duty kindled her mistrust, / That two red fires in both their faces blazed' (1352–3). Like literary allusions, blushes are communicative and transmissible, although they may – or may not – acquire different meanings in the process. Two types of discourse engage in a dialogue in *The Rape of Lucrece*, one exploring non-differentiation at the cost of misinterpretation, the other insisting on the sharp contrasts that oppose white and red, or black blood and red blood; they blend in the emphatic over-determination of red upon red when the blood that flows from Lucrece's wound blushes at its own corruption (1749–50). One discourse emphasises separation between neat categories, while the other simultaneously undermines divisions, erases and blurs differences.

Halfway through the *Aeneid*, Virgil calls not on Calliope, the muse of epic poetry, as might have been expected, but on Erato, the muse of lyric and erotic poetry, as if suggesting the interlacing of the two strains in his poem.[26] More specifically, it has been argued that Statius's blending of elegiac and epic voices in the *Thebaid* transposes onto young warriors' dying bodies the *purpureus* and the *niveus* of a young girl's blushing skin, with the effect of eroticising and feminising a young man's death on the battlefield as an image of defloration.[27] In his unfinished *Achilleid*, it is in the story of Achilles's transvestism that Statius blends Virgilian epic, Ovidian witty playfulness and Pindaric lyricism. When the Greeks declare war upon Troy, Achilles is still at an age when a new down has not yet transformed his youth: 'Necdum prima nova lanugine vertitur *aetas*' (I, 163). His beauty is feminine: 'niveo natat ignis in ore / purpureus' (a fiery purple swims on his snowy face) (I, 161–2). It recalls his mother's face: 'plurima vultu / mater inest' (his mother is wholly in his face) (I, 164–5). Thetis dresses Achilles up as a girl, refashioning in all bad faith Ovid's and Propertius's accounts of Hercules's feminisation at Omphale's court, to encourage her son to walk in the steps of the great hero: 'Lydia dura / pensa manu mollesque tulit Tirinthius hastas' (In Lydia, the Tirynthian held his share of wool and effeminate spindles) (I, 260–1).[28] At the very moment when his mother offers him women's clothes, Achilles catches sight of Deidamia, King Lycosthenes's beautiful daughter, and what had started as a blush of shame at the idea of transvestism (I, 272) transforms itself into a blush of sudden desire: love sends an intense glow to his clear face, like milk mixed up with blood, 'vel ebur corrumpitur ostro' (or ivory corrupted by a purple dye) (I, 308). In his fifteenth century commentary, Francesco Maturanzio (Franciscus Maturatius) quoted Virgil's evocation of Lavinia's blush and explained the word 'corrumpitur': 'corrumpi videtur et violari quoniam propriam et naturalem amittit pulchritudinem' (it seems to be corrupted and defiled because it loses its proper and natural beauty).[29] At the same time as Virgil's 'violaverit', Statius's 'corrumpitur' echoes his former remark, 'nullo temeratus pectora motu' (no passion had ever yet soiled his heart) (I, 302), with Francesco Maturanzio's explanation of 'temeratus' as 'violatus prius, nam nunquam amaverat motu amoris' (for the first time sullied, for never before had he known love's passion).[30] Seen in the perspective of Maturanzio's commentary, the poetic nexus of blushes as markers of the first awakening, in various guises, to an awareness of sexuality is associated with the image of staining and pollution, a correlation that seems indicative of an ideological construction of the first signs of acquaintance with sexuality perceived as a kind of blemish – in the same way as Ambrogio Calepino merged *pueritia* (childhood) and *puritas* (purity).[31] It is some sort of virginity that Statius's Achilles loses. Yet, although he is wearing girl's clothes, the young hero is not to be the victim but the author of rape, since his disguise enables him to approach Deidamia and deflower her. He totally accedes to virility when he discards his girl's outfit and, from a heap of jewels and trinkets, seizes and claims for his own a blood-stained shield and a spear (II, 178–211), thus stepping out of his mother's controlling fiction of Omphale and Hercules.[32]

The story of a young hero leaving the world of women and infancy to enter war and maturity finds its inverted mirror, in *Antony and Cleopatra*, in the decline of a mature hero who is distracted from the battlefield by a love affair with an experienced woman, who is herself the inverted mirror of a blushing maiden. The disjunction between Mars's epic battlefield and Venus's erotic boudoir is emphasised by the gender inversion of Hercules and Omphale, which Shakespeare owes both to Plutarch and to Ovid. While Antony was dressed in Cleopatra's 'tires and mantles', she 'wore his sword Philippan' (II.v.22–3). But unlike Achilles, who grasps his new spear, a defeated Antony is led to realise that Cleopatra 'has robbed [him] of [his] sword' (IV.xv.23). The soldier's transfer to the world of Eros is completed with Cleopatra's celebrated appearance in the role of Venus:

> On each side her,
> Stood pretty dimpled boys, like smiling Cupids,
> With divers-coloured fans whose wind did seem
> To glow the delicate cheeks which they did cool,
> And what they undid did.
>
> (II.ii.208–12)

The picture reworks Plutarch's account, according to which 'on either hand of her, pretie faire boyes apparelled as painters doe set forth god Cupide, with litle fannes in their hands, with the which they fanned wind upon her'.[33] What Shakespeare adds is the glow. This is not a mere, insignificant variation on Plutarch. The play emphatically draws attention to Cleopatra's blush, just as the Cupids' 'divers-coloured fans' ironically refer back to Antony's description as 'the bellows and the fan to cool a gipsy's lust' (I.i.9–10); and the unexpected union of bellows and fan is itself reformulated in the paradoxical phrase 'what they undid did', which endlessly turns the satisfaction of sexual desire into further stimulation, in the same way as the fans seem 'To glow the delicate cheeks which they did cool'. The fire implied by the bellows is brought into prominence in the description of the barge, which, 'like a burnished throne / Burned on the water' (II.ii.198–9), with its reflection of 'burned' into 'burnished' and its paradoxical union of fire and water. The barge as fire on water is no more Plutarchan than the glow on Cleopatra's cheeks. But it is not new either. In *Jerusalem Delivered*, Torquato Tasso described the palace where Armida keeps Rinaldo under her charm. Over the entrance, two medallions constitute a warning against the dangers of lust. One of them, unsurprisingly, represents Hercules's subjection to Omphale, or rather, here, Iole (XVI, 3); next to it, the other one shows two boats, around which 'D'oro fiammegia l'onda',[34] which Edward Fairfax translated into English as 'The waters burnt around their vessels good, / Such flames the gold therein enchased threw'.[35] In this description of Antony and Cleopatra's ships at the battle of Actium, Tasso imitates Virgil's representation of the same scene, which is finely chiselled on Aeneas's shield: 'videres / fervere Leucaten auroque effulgere fluctus' (One could see Cape Leucate on fire and the sea aflame with gold) (VIII, 676–7). In the vicinity of the verb 'fervere' (to burn), the continued alliteration of 'effulgere fluctus' underlines the paradox of water shining like a flash of lightning.

Two possibilities are therefore offered. One may very well consider that Enobarbus's set-piece is no more than North's Plutarch rewritten by Shakespeare. Or a theory of multi-textuality might suggest that somehow other texts, which include Virgil's *Aeneid*, insinuated themselves into the act of rewriting. This would mean an interacting of Cleopatra's epiphany on the Cydnus with Antony's defeat at Actium, together with an ironic correspondence between the flame of desire and the fire of war. The two interlaced texts, Plutarch's and Virgil's, would not only arch between the opposite waterscapes of Cydnus and Actium; they also join in a common ekphrastic movement: in Virgil, the flashing light of the sea is the gold of which Aeneas's shield is made, while Plutarch's Venus, 'commonly drawn in picture', becomes an example, in Shakespeare, 'where we see / The fancy outwork nature' (207–8) – a converging interest in the nature of representation that suggests that the paradox of 'what they undid did', beyond drawing together cooling and fuelling, becomes a fitting hallmark for the creative act of simultaneous unwriting and rewriting, or, more accurately perhaps, unweaving and interweaving.

Such readings tend to consider Shakespeare's works as combining the complementary processes of what might be called 'trans-textuality' and 'multi-textuality'. They perceive Shakespeare's text as composite, growing out of the interaction of multiple texts, which never constitute a smooth, continuous, uniform, 'totalitarian' discourse (in Blanchot's sense) but, on the contrary, speak with polyphonic freedom as several discourses interlace, branch off, overlap or clash. Classical allusions woven into Shakespeare's text do not wholly belong to the text(s) they are summoned from, nor to the text into which they are invited, while they also belong to both. In Charles Martindale's words,

> When Shakespeare alludes to Ovid, is the result the same or different, Ovidian or Shakespearean or neither or both? A suitable figure for this paradox might be Ovid's hermaphrodite, the union or fusion of Salmacis and Hermaphroditus: 'nec duo sunt et forma duplex, nec femina dici / nec puer ut posit, neutrumque et utrumque videntur' (*Met.* iv.378–9; 'they are no longer two but a double shape, nor such as could be called woman or boy, but they seem neither and yet both').[36]

As figures of transience, fleetingly poised between white and red, purity and pollution, intactness and injury, as well as shame and desire or pain and pleasure, blushes, which also mediate between inner, secret depths and open, public surfaces, are privileged vectors for textual transmission. Textual transfers create an aesthetics of the in-between that challenges the 'neither ... nor' and the 'both ... and', or rather that combines overlapping and discontinuity, thus producing a theoretical space where all transformations are possible, and customary distinctions are questioned, as one element is changed into or superimposed onto its opposite. Trans-generic textual transfers not only favour an exploration of gender assumptions, they trigger off a wider process that approaches categories through their permeability. As it plunges its roots into the multi-layered, contrasted textual system of antiquity, Shakespeare's text develops its own all-inclusive, non-discriminatory vision, which enables it to be relevant in different climes and times. Based on textual dialogues, it calls for new types of dialogue. The forms of integration that it operates, beyond temporal and cultural differences, favour hybridisation, variegation and contamination in open configurations that emphasise the fluidity of frontiers, whether textual or cultural – so that it might be at least partly thanks to its multi-textuality, itself based on trans-textuality, that Shakespeare's text has become and remains essentially multi-cultural.

Notes

1 Roland Barthes, *Roland Barthes par Roland Barthes* (Paris: Seuil, 1975), p. 73.
2 Roland Barthes, *Le plaisir du texte* (Paris: Seuil, 1973), p. 84; *The Pleasure of the Text*, trans. Richard Millar (New York: Farrar, Straus and Giroux, 1975), p. 52. Millar

translates *jouissance*, which recurs throughout the book, as bliss – even though Richard Howard, in his foreword, acknowledges that the English word falls short of the erotically charged French word. Hence my phrase, 'blissful experience'.

3   Maurice Blanchot, *L'entretien infini* (Paris: Gallimard, 1969), p. 233; *The Infinite Conversation*, trans. Susan Hanson (Minneapolis: University of Minnesota Press, 1993), p. 155.

4   R. Drew Griffith, 'In praise of the bride: Sappho Fr. 105 (A) L-P. Voigt', *Transactions of the American Philological Association*, 119 (1989), 55–61.

5   It became a sign of hope, when Longus later developed it into a short narrative symbolising the fruitfulness of incipient pastoral love between Daphnis and Chloe. Angel Day, *Daphnis and Chloe* (London: Robert Waldegrave, 1587), sigs Dr and Nv.

6   Before Tibullus, Theocritus had transferred Sappho's reddening apple from the cheeks of a young bride onto those of little Cupids; *Idylls*, VII, 115. Tibullus fuses Sappho and Theocritus.

7   Seneca, *Medea*, 97–100: '<en rubor / perfudit subito purpureus genas> [F. Leo's hypothetical addition in his edition (Berlin: Weidmann, 1878–79)]; ostro sic niveus puniceo color / perfusus rubuit' (a red blush suddenly spreads over her cheeks, similar to the red colour spreading over the whiteness of snow dyed in violaceous purple).

8   Robert Adger Law, 'The Roman background of *Titus Andronicus*', *Studies in Philology*, 40:2 (1943), 145–53 (p. 146).

9   R. O. A. M. Lyne, *Further Voices in Vergil's 'Aeneid'* (Oxford: Oxford University Press, 2001 [1987]).

10 By extension, to defile and profane the altar: 'violavit et aras / caelicolum' ('he profaned the gods' altars'); Silius Italicus, *Punica* (XVII, 129–30), ed. and trans. J. D. Duff (Cambridge, MA: Harvard University Press, 1961), Vol. II, p. 448 – an example given by Robert Estienne in his *Dictionarium latinogallicum* (Paris: Estienne, 1546), and repeated by Thomas Cooper, *Thesaurus linguae Romanae et Britannicae* (London: Berthelet, 1565). In his commentary on the *Aeneid*, Jacobus Pontanus felt the need to explain that although *violare* is more often taken *in malam* as a synonym of *inficere* and *conspurcare*, it should be taken here *in bonam*; *Symbolarum libri XVII, quibus P. Virgilii Maronis Bucolica, Georgica, Aeneis* (Augsburg: Praetor, 1599), col. 2227.

11 Claire Jamset, 'Death-loration: The eroticization of death in the *Thebaid*', *Greece & Rome*, 51:1 (2004), 95–104 (pp. 97–8). Claire Jamset's argumentation bases itself on the work of D. P. Fowler, 'Vergil on killing virgins', in Michael Whitby, Philip R. Hardie and Mary Whitby (eds), *Homo viator: Classical Essays for John Bramble* (Bristol: Bristol Classical Press, 1987), pp. 185–98; and of Philippe Heuzé, *L'image du corps dans l'œuvre de Virgile* (Rome: Ecole française, 1985).

12 Ambrogio Calepino, *Ambrosii Calepini Bergomatis eremitani dictionarium* (Rhegii Lingobardiae [Reggio]: Dionysius Bertochus, 1502). The dictionary was

regularly reissued throughout the sixteenth century. In the editions printed between 1502 and 1522, this definition was completed by a quotation from Augustine's *Confessions*, III, 8: 'Violatur quippe ipsa societas, quae cum Deo nobis esse debet, cum eadem natura, cujus ille auctor est, libidinis perversitate polluitur' (It does violate the alliance we should keep with God because it defiles with the debauchery of lust the nature that he has created). Originally, Augustine was writing about sodomy, but taken out of context in Calepino's dictionary it had a more general scope. In editions published after 1522, the quotation from Augustine was dropped and replaced by examples of *violare* used in the figurative sense.

13   John Florio, *A Worlde of Wordes* (London: Edward Blount, 1598), p. 450.
14   Virgil, *Aeneid*, XI, 277, 591, 848; XII, 797: as noted by Lyne, *Further Voices*, pp. 120–1.
15   In the same entry, Thomas Cooper translated Virgil's phrase, 'Ebur ostro violare', as 'To mix ivory with purple', which he took over from Estienne's *Dictionarium latinogallicum*, where 'violare', in Virgil's description of Lavinia's blush, is translated as 'mêler, mélanger' (to mix), another way of avoiding embarrassment.
16   Charles Martindale, 'Shakespeare and Virgil', in Charles Martindale and A. B. Taylor (eds), *Shakespeare and the Classics* (Cambridge: Cambridge University Press, 2004), p. 98.
17   It is always used elsewhere with the idea of being defiled, sometimes in blood, often in dust: Homer, *Iliad*, XVI, 795, 797; XVII, 439; XXIII, 732.
18   On Ovid's manipulations of the Virgilian metaphor in the *Metamorphoses*, see Julia T. Dyson, 'Lilies and violence: Lavinia's blush in the song of Orpheus', *Classical Philology*, 94:3 (1999), 281–8.
19   Christopher Marlowe, *All Ovids Elegies*, II.v.34–40, in *Christopher Marlowe: The Poems*, ed. Millar Maclure (Manchester: Manchester University Press, 1968), p. 152.
20   As noted by Maclure in his edition of Marlowe's poems (p. 152n40), Arachne has the epithet 'Maeonia' in Ovid's *Metamorphoses*, VI, 5.
21   Ovid, *Amores*, II, v, 37 seems to be an echo of Propertius, *Elegies*, II, xxxiv, 52; see A. Allen, 'The Moon's horses', *The Classical Quarterly*, 25:1 (1975), 153–5.
22   Britomart's blushes are analysed by Theresa M. Krier in *Gazing on Secret Sights: Spenser, Classical Imitation, and the Decorums of Vision* (Ithaca, NY: Cornell University Press, 1990), pp. 157–67.
23   Michel de Montaigne, *Essays*, III, v: 'Sur des vers de Virgile' ('On some lines of Virgil'). While Montaigne transfers Lavinia's blush onto 'quelque enfance' (meaning tender youths), John Florio associates Virgil's lines with femininity and mistakenly translates 'some tender, irresolute and ignorant girle'; Michel de Montaigne, *Montaigne's Essays Translated by John Florio*, ed. L. C. Harmer (New York: Dutton, 1965 [1910]), Vol. III, p. 117.

24 Ovid's phrase seems ironically to superimpose upon Daphne's face, when Apollo pursues her, the glowing face of Virgil's moon (*Georgics*, I, 430): '[luna] si virgineum suffuderit ore ruborem' (if a virginal glow spreads over her face). Later in the *Metamorphoses*, the phrase describing Hermaphroditus's shame is used to refer to Arachne's pride (VI, 46).
25 See Dominique Goy-Blanquet, Chapter 3 in this volume, for a discussion of Lucrece and Troy, with rape as a foundational act for empires and nations.
26 The Muses' several roles were not clearly defined before the imperial epoch, which allows Paul Veyne to argue that the address to Erato (VII, 36) is a mere *captatio benevolentiae*: Virgil, *L'Enéide*, ed. and trans. Paul Veyne (Paris: Albin Michel and Les Belles Lettres, 2012), p. 214n3. Erato, however, whose name is coined on Eros, was associated with lovers (as Terpsichore was with dancing) by Plato in *Phaedrus*, 259; for Propertius, Erato plaits wreaths of roses – appropriate for lovers (*Elegies*, III, 3). Virgil might also have remembered that Apollonius Rhodius starts the story of the love of Jason and Medea with an address to Erato (*Argonautica*, III, 1–5). It has sometimes been argued that the address to Erato looks forward to the wedding of Aeneas and Lavinia; see Dorothea Clinton Woodworth, 'Lavinia: An interpretation', *Transactions and Proceedings of the American Philological Association*, 61 (1930), 175–94. One of the *Aeneid*'s 'further voices' might suggest an interweaving with the story of Nisus and Euryalus in Book IX.
27 Jamset, 'Death-loration'.
28 The story is developed by Ovid, *Fasti*, II, 305–26; some of the phrasing comes from Propertius, *Elegies*, III, xi, 17–20, especially 'tam dura traheret mollia pensa manu' (drew out soft wool with her tough hand) (III, xi, 20).
29 Statius, *Statii Sylvae ..., Thebais ..., Achilleis cum Maturantii commentariis* (Venice: Bartholomaeus de Zanis, 1494), fo. 187r.
30 *Ibid.*
31 Calepino, *Dictionarium*, s.v. 'Pueritia'.
32 For an extensive study of the crossing of boundaries in the *Achilleid*, see Carole E. Newlands, *Statius, Poet between Rome and Naples*, Bristol Classical Press (London: Bloomsbury Publishing, 2012), pp. 61–71. This scene is the subject of one of the tapestries in the Ulysses series, *The Discovery of Achilles by Ulysses* ('Niclaes', fl. 1562), at Hardwick Hall: Achilles, dressed in women's clothes, plunges a muscular, male arm into the chest to lift out a bow and arrows, while two similarly dressed young women view him with puzzled alarm, with Ulysses watching the scene.
33 Plutarch, 'Life of Marcus Antonius', translated by Thomas North from Jacques Amyot's French, quoted from Geoffrey Bullough, *Narrative and Dramatic Sources of Shakespeare* (London: Routledge and Kegan Paul, 1964), Vol. V, p. 274.

34 'e par, che tutto / D'incendio marcial Leucate auampi'; Torquato Tasso, *Gerusalemme liberata* (Parma: Erasmo Viotti, 1581), XVI, 4.
35 Edward Fairfax, *Godfrey of Bulloigne; or, The Recoverie of Jerusalem* (London: A. Hatfield for J. Jaggard and M. Lownes, 1600), p. 281.
36 Charles Martindale, 'Shakespeare's Ovid, Ovid's Shakespeare: A methodological postcript', in A. B. Taylor (ed.), *Shakespeare's Ovid* (Cambridge: Cambridge University Press, 2000), pp. 198–215 (p. 209).

2

The non-Ovidian Elizabethan epyllion: Thomas Watson, Christopher Marlowe, Richard Barnfield

Tania Demetriou

I like short poems, but I want them to be epic.

Alice Oswald[1]

Prologue or preludium: Richard Barnfield's *Hellens Rape*

ONE OF THE MOST riotous mythological narrative poems of the Elizabethan 1590s is Richard Barnfield's *Hellens Rape* (1594), an experiment in hexameter verse, alliteratively subtitled 'A light Lanthorne for light Ladies'.[2] The rape of Helen is narrated by Barnfield like never before:

> Adulterous Paris (then a Boy) kept sheepe as a shepheard
> On Ida Mountaine, unknown to the King for a Keeper
> Of sheep, on Ida Mountain, as a Boy, as a shepheard:
> Yet such sheep he kept, and was so seemelie a shepheard,
> Seemelie a Boy, so seemelie a youth, so seemelie a Younker,
> That on Ide was not such a Boy, such a youth, such a Younker.
>
> (sig. G3v)

Miraculously, given this narrative pace, Paris manages to make himself known to King Priam, and persuade him that he ought to bring back his aunt 'Hesyone' from Greece. On his laddish outing across the Aegean, he is escorted by 'Telamour', 'lust-bewitched Alexis' and 'eyefull ... Argus', companions who prove predictably keen on a detour to 'Lacedaemon', where they are hosted by Helen in Menelaus's absence. This is how the disaster happens:

> First they fell to the feast, and after fall to a Dauncing,
> And from a dance to a Trance, from a Trance they fell to a falling
> Either in others armes, and either in armes of another.
> ...

> ... Each one hies home to his own home
> Save Lord and Ladie: ...
> ...
> Well to their worke they goe, and bothe they jumble in one Bed:
> Worke so well they like, that they still like to be working:
> For Aurora mounts before he leaves to be mounting:
> And Astraea fades before she faints to be falling:
> (Helen a light Huswife, now a lightsome starre in Olympus.)
>
> (sig. G4v)

Helen is pleasurably ravished in her own bed and the poem ends here. Of her abduction to Troy, we hear not a word. With this pun on the titular 'rape', Barnfield mocks his readers' expectations of an epic story, to give them instead an erotic narrative romp. His carefree prequel to the Trojan War denies any knowledge of an epic catastrophe to ensue from Helen's extramarital 'jumble'. Barnfield toys not just with epic, but with moral readings of classical texts: his subtitle suggests that his poem will serve as 'a light Lanthorne for light ladies', yet by skipping the Trojan War, and concluding with this 'light Huswife's' transformation into a 'lightsome starre', Barnfield offers the reader a radically different 'lanthorne' from the one promised.[3]

Barnfield's little poem does, nevertheless, engage closely with epic. It name-checks various epic manoeuvres, as in this epic catalogue of the feast: 'Briskets and Carawayes, Comfets, Tart, Plate, Jelly, Ginge-bread, / Lymons and Medlars: and Dishes moe by a thousand' (sig. G4v); or this *ekphrasis* of Helen's rich palace:

> Flowers were framd of flints, Walls Rubies, Rafters of Argent:
> Pavements of Chrisolite, Windows contriv'd of a Christall
> Vessels were of gold, with gold was each thing adorned:
> Golden Webs more worth than a wealthy Souldan of Egypt
>
> (sig. G4r)

This is the same palace in which Telemachus and Nestor's son Peisistratus are welcomed and feasted in *Odyssey*, IV. Some readers will note that Barnfield translates Telemachus's exclamation there – 'Ζηνός που τοιήδε γ' Ὀλυμπίου ἔνδοθεν αὐλή' (The courts of Olympian Zeus must look like this ...) (*Odyssey*, IV, 74) – into his unique idiom: 'so stately a building, / Never ... / ... was to be seene, if nere to be seene was Olympus' (sig. G4r). In the deliciously inane comparison to a 'wealthy Souldan of Egypt', such readers may also spot an allusive frolic on the gold gifted to Homer's Helen and Menelaus by King Polybus in Egypt, 'ὅθι πλεῖστα δόμοις ἐν κτήματα κεῖται' (where households are wealthiest) (*Odyssey*, IV, 127). It is such epic-literate readers who will get the most out of the poem's final turn. These echoes invoke an arc that begins with these 'younkers'' merry-making, and ends twenty years later with the melancholy Telemachus in search of news of the long-lost Odysseus; yet this is an arc Barnfield's poem provocatively claims to know nothing of. Inviting a particular mode of reading, the epyllion's generic proximity to epic enables it to assert the mythical, aesthetic and ethical separateness of its own world. This interaction with the matrix of epic is crucial to its poetic work.

Barnfield's epyllic poetics is important because it hints at literary and classical effects we do not associate with English narrative poetry of this time. *Hellens Rape* displays an allusive fluency in Greek material, and a well-developed reflection on the resources of the literary prequel and of the little epic as a genre. This chapter argues that this constellation of interests was there in the poetic culture of the early 1590s and that they offer a new perspective on Christopher Marlowe's *Hero and Leander* and the development of the poetic tradition known as Elizabethan or 'Ovidian' epyllia. To understand this we need to reappraise the impact of the Greek epyllion on this period's poetic activities, not least through the innovative and popular classicism of Thomas Watson. This is the exploration I propose in this chapter, taking Richard Barnfield's mid-1590s perspective on English poetics as our guide.

Shepherds and lovers: remembering Watson in 1594

Barnfield's epic idiom repays closer attention. Playing with contemporaries' attempts to write in English hexameters, it strongly recalls the work proposed by Thomas Nash in 1589 as a beacon to such 'high-witted indeavours': Abraham Fraunce's 'excellent translation of Maister Thomas Watson's sugred *Amyntas*'.[4] This is Fraunce's bucolic Amyntas, remembering life before the death of Phyllis:

> Under a beech many times wee sate most sweetely together,
> Under a broade beech tree that sunbeames might not anoy us,
> Either in others armes, stil looking either on other:
> Both, many rimes singing, and verses both many making,
> And both so many woords with kisses so many mingling.[5]

Appearing in 1587, fast on the heels of Watson's 1585 Latin poem, this astonishingly popular work was reprinted in 1588, 1589, 1591 and 1596. But by 1593, the fruits of such poetic endeavours (and their association with Gabriel

Harvey) had left Nash much less impressed: 'the Hexamiter ... goes twitching and hopping in our language like a man running upon quagmiers up the hill in one Syllable and down the dale in another'.⁶ Barnfield agreed, judging from one of his contributions to *Greenes Funeralls*. Though some, he pens in 'Sonnet VII', consider poetry a waste of time:

> Yet I appeale to the pen of piereless Poet Amyntas,
> Matchles Amintas minde, to the minde of Matchles Amintas
> Sweete bonny Phillis love, to the love of sweete bonny Phillis,
> Whether pen, or minde, or love, of Phillis Amintas
> Love, or minde, or pen, of pen-love-minder Amintas [etc.]⁷

No waste of time at all. Barnfield is probably in witty repartee here with Ferdinando Stanley, a literary patron who adopted the Amyntas persona at this time in like-minded burlesque of Fraunce's repetitive poetics.⁸ Stanley's verses were circulating in late 1593, with Watson and Fraunce both recently dead, and *Greenes Funeralls* was published in early 1594. Barnfield's *Affectionate Shepherd*, the collection that contains *Hellens Rape*, appeared later that year, and featured a further tribute to 'Amintas' – most likely the by-then also dead Stanley – in which the poet identified himself as a beneficiary of his 'Love' and 'pure affection'.⁹ The title poem, structured as two complaints on successive days in the emotional career of the central pastoral figure, paralleled Watson's (and Fraunce's) *Amyntas*. Barnfield's collection, then, with this allusion, the homage to Amintas, and the facetious hexameters of *Hellens Rape*, was partly about English poetics in the early 1590s, in particular poetics in the wake of the tremendous influence of Watson's poem.

It was not just the English hexameter that gave hostages to fortune. The Greek hexameter, when its parataxis and patterns of iteration were rendered word-for-word into utilitarian Latin, could be equally entertaining. This is Paris keeping his flocks in Colluthus's *Abduction of Helen*, a short epic from the fifth–sixth century CE, in the widely available *ad verbum* translation of Michael Neander:

> Paris vero adolescens (adhuc) *pascebat* paternas oues
> *Pascens* (eas) seorsum ad fluenta Anauri.
> Seorsum quidem gregem agrestium taurorum *pascebat*,
> Seorsum etiam *pascebat* greges, *pascentium* (se) ouium ...

> Young Paris herded his father's flocks. On either side of the mountain torrent's stream he tended his herds, numbering separately the herd of thronging bulls, separately counting the droves of feeding flocks.¹⁰

In Colluthus's Greek, this elaborate description of Paris's shepherding logistics is an erudite game in versifying synonyms for sheep-keeping: νομεύω, ποιμαίνω, πεμπάζομαι, διαμετρέω, βόσκομαι.[11] Standing in for all of them, Neander's useful 'pasco' quickly transforms the passage into epic parody. Watson published a paraphrase of the poem in elegant Latin hexameters in 1586, a year after his *Amyntas*. He probably used Neander's crib, and probably learnt from it to avoid repetition at this point.[12] Watson, the most accomplished Latin poet of his generation according to Nash, was Nash's confederate in the mockery of Harvey and the English hexameter, as well as a poetic innovator in the vernacular, a popular dramatist and a constitutional rogue.[13] Colluthus's epyllion, and its link via Watson to the roguish literary community Barnfield was joining with this poetic volume, could well have inspired *Hellens Rape*.

In one of the many editions of Neander's Colluthus, intended for educational use, Barnfield and Watson could have found a dedicatory epistle ripe for a send-up. In it, Neander argued that adolescents would learn from this author not just the Greek language, but also other useful things, to wit:

> ab ipso Deo, qui … impuritatem … punit gravissime, excitari magistratus, & mitti exercitus militares, qui raptus, adulteria, nuptias prohibitas, & quascunque alias foedas & turpes libidines puniant, bellis, caedibus, terrarum ac imperiorium etiam potentissimorum eversionibus.[14]

> that God himself, who … severely punishes impurity … raises up magistrates and sends armies to punish rapes, adulteries, forbidden marriages, and all other foul and base lusts through wars, slaughters and the razing of countries and even most powerful kingdoms.

This is probably wishful thinking. Colluthus's tonally rich poem contains little invitation to moralise. It describes, for instance, a freshly bathed Paris approaching Helen's palace with a circumspect gait, lest the wind dishevel his hair or 'μὴ πόδες ἱμερόεντες ὑποχραίνοιντο κονίης' (his sexy feet get fouled by dust) (line 232). Watson loved this bit: his own, wittily contrived 'golden' hexameter – 'Ne niveas turpi foedaret pulvere plantas' (lest he soil his snow-white feet with foul dust) (line 241) – smeared, by verbal proximity, 'niveas' (snow-white) with 'turpi' (foul), and 'plantas' (feet) with 'pulvere' (dust). Earlier on, Colluthus imagines the clinching moment in the Judgement of Paris – the defining event of the poem and of the myth of Troy – as a surprise striptease by Aphrodite:

Ἡ δ'ἑανὸν βαθύκολπον, ἐς ἠέρα γυμνώσασα
κόλπον, ἀνηώρησε καὶ οὐκ ᾐδέσσατο Κύπρις.

Χειρὶ δ'ἐλαφρίζουσα μελίφρονα δεσμὸν Ἐρώτων
στῆθος ἅπαν γύμνωσε καὶ οὐκ ἐμνήσατο μαζῶν.

(lines 154–7)

And the Cyprus-born lifted her deep-folded fine robe, baring her chest to the open air, and felt no shame. Loosening with her hand the band of desires that brings delight to the mind, she bared her bosom entirely, and was not mindful of her breasts.

Colluthus's readers have already been introduced to this 'band'. Nervous before the contest, Aphrodite puts faith in her weapon: 'μελίφρονα δεσμὸν Ἐρώτων / ... / κεστὸν, ὅθεν φιλότητος ἐμῆς ἐμὸν οἶστρον ἑλοῦσαι ... γυναῖκες' (the band of desires that brings delight to the mind ... the *cestos* which makes women feel my sting, the frenzy of my passion ...) (lines 94–6). Homer's *cestos* is the bewitching embroidered band Hera borrows from Aphrodite in the celebrated, extraordinary episode of her seduction of Zeus in *Iliad*, XIV. In it, says Homer, lie all charms, 'ἔνι μὲν φιλότης, ἐν δ' ἵμερος, ἐν δ' ὀαριστὺς / πάρφασις, ἥ τ' ἔκλεψε νόον πύκα περ φρονεόντων' (passion, desire, love-talk, and persuasion, which seduces the mind even of those who are prudent) (*Iliad*, XIV, 215–16). Colluthus engages this Homeric object in narrating her victory. But, having prepared us to see its magic in action, he humorously literalises it, concentrating its powers in the distinctly unmetaphorical act of its removal: in conversation with Colluthus, the seduction of Zeus in the *Iliad* seems startlingly graphic. Mischievously casting the Judgement as Hera's first lesson in the efficacy of the *cestos*, Colluthus's imitation brings out the difference and the unlikely similarity between the world of his dreamy erotic epyllion and the universe of Homer's martial epic. The gap becomes a gulf as Colluthus multiplies verbal guises in which to dwell on Aphrodite's breasts as much as possible: κόλπος, στῆθος, μαζοί. Watson took good note. Instead of attempting to shadow the Greek's play on synonyms, he recreated its powerful visuality with a descriptive flourish:

> [Cypria] Blandius exhibuit nudato pectore mammas,
> Nec puduit quicquam turgentes mollibus ipsas
> Pandere flaminibus.

(lines 163–5)

The Cyprus-born showed her breasts more seductively having bared her chest, nor was she at all ashamed to lay them open, swelling in the soft breeze.

Not quite the shameless erotic frolic that is Barnfield's *Hellens Rape*, Colluthus's poem could certainly have pointed the way to it, not least in Watson's hands.

The epyllion and its discontents: classical, early modern, Ovidian

Barnfield's short, irreverent mythological epic spoof, with its amatory content and exuberant language, has never been described as a late Elizabethan epyllion, though these works are marked by very similar characteristics. Neither has Watson's version of Colluthus's short mythological epic. This goes back to how the term 'epyllion' became relevant to this moment of English literary culture. What scholars tend to refer to as the Elizabethan epyllion comprises a relatively fixed canon of poems, first proposed in Paul W. Miller's 1958 article 'The Elizabethan minor epic' and embodied as a corpus in 1963 in Elizabeth Story Donno's influential anthology, *Elizabethan Minor Epics*.[15] This canon starts with Thomas Lodge's *Scillaes Metamorphosis* (1589/90), and continues some three years later with Marlowe's *Hero and Leander* (entered posthumously in the Stationers' Register on 28 September 1593 but published in 1598); Shakespeare's *Venus and Adonis* (published in 1593, after being entered on 18 April); and such works as Thomas Edwards's *Cephalus and Procris* and *Narcissus* (entered 22 October 1593, published 1595), and Thomas Heywood's *Oenone and Paris* (1594). It stretches to as late as Francis Beaumont's *Salmacis and Hermaphroditus* (1602). It was Miller who proposed to call this genus of works 'epyllia'. The family resemblances among them had been noted earlier, with critics often referring to them as 'Ovidian poems'.[16] Miller, however, believed that new light could be shed on their genre by classical studies. Marjorie Crump had recently argued – more extensively than anyone before – that the 'epyllion' was a distinct classical genre. Invented by the Alexandrians in the third century BCE, it was a 'short narrative poem' (of variable length), concerned (most commonly) with a love story; it was (sometimes) 'decorated with descriptive passages' and (often) employed 'the dramatic form'; but its most distinctive constitutive feature was the digression, which could overshadow the frame tale.[17] Her examples included some of Theocritus's *Idylls* and Callimachus's fragmentary *Hecale* in Greek, and Catullus 64 and the pseudo-Virgilian *Ciris* in Latin; importantly, Crump argued that epyllic techniques had influenced Ovid's epic of short stories and dizzying digressions, and for her, this was the genre's last ancient incarnation. Key to the 'epyllion' bequeathed to Miller, then, was a particular narrative aesthetic. Its classical instances did not include mock epic, nor did they include late Greek epic narratives such as Colluthus's *Abduction of Helen* and its near contemporary, Musaeus's *Hero and Leander*, neither of which features a digression.

To Miller, the 'Ovidian poems' of the 1590s all seemed to display some of these characteristics as well as fulfilling the length criterion. His approach to genre was taxonomical, not historical. Based on it, Marlowe's *Hero and Leander*, with its lavish *ekphrases*, its dramatic speeches and above all its startling digression on Mercury, was the Elizabethan epyllion par excellence. Understood thus, the epyllic exemplarity of Marlowe's work owed much to Ovid but, paradoxically, nothing to the short epic of Musaeus, which was one of its sources. More generally, this 'classical epyllion' offered nothing to the English tradition that is not already there in Ovid, save a precedent for brevity. Even this was soon challenged, as classicists contested the view that the features enumerated by Crump added up to a genre. One, Walter Allen, hastened to alert the English scholar who had been misled. In his resoundingly entitled 'The non-existent classical epyllion', which appeared in the same journal and year as Miller's essay, he wrote: 'I fear that Mr. Miller has caught a tiger in his Classical comparison ... [T]here never was such a literary genre.'[18] In response to this disconcerting news, Renaissance critics agreed to adopt the tiger. They continued to use 'epyllion', now void of a classical referent, apologetically and heuristically, for its suggestion of something more formally distinctive about these poems than their Ovidian resemblances.[19] The classical term, having disowned any link to a classical form almost from the start, has given English scholars a way of referring to the poems as a distinct, new 1590s genre. In so far as their classical inspiration is concerned, these works, first grouped together as 'Ovidian poems' and now often referred to as 'Ovidian epyllia', have continued to be seen entirely as a chapter in the afterlife of Ovid.[20] But the term 'epyllion' has made a difference. It has emphasised, and arguably intensified and calcified, perceived affinities among these specific works – affinities that may seem more exclusive to us when we view all of them together than they did as this proposed new genre took shape. When Georgia Brown, for instance, writes that John Marston's *Metamorphosis of Pigmalions Image* (1598) is 'the most characteristic of all epyllia', she is clearly looking back on the tradition with Marston.[21] Yet it is useful to try and imagine this same tradition instead from the perspective of Barnfield in 1594, a year after the epyllia of Shakespeare and Marlowe, formative for the 'new genre', are brought to the press. Barnfield's *Affectionate Shepherd* borrows the stanza of Shakespeare's *Venus and Adonis*, more than a shade of its mature wooer's desperation and its Ovidian texture of psychological tragicomedy; it builds on the homoerotic sensuality of Marlowe's *Hero and Leander*, its descriptive exuberance and its Ovidian digression; but it also echoes the same poet's 'Passionate Shepherd', and, thinking on the threshold between pastoral and epic, alludes – as we have seen – to *Amyntas* by Marlowe's friend Watson; finally, it plays with the English hexameter in which the *Amyntas* had had such huge success, and experiments with a form that scales down epic, and that may have been associated with Watson. Looked at from this perspective, English poets at this time are indeed thinking about narrative poetry through the *Metamorphoses*; but they are also reflecting, with and without Ovid, on how to write small poems but get them to be epic. This ambition is rooted in their familiarity with, and creatively angled positioning in relation to epic; it is part of experimenting with the boundaries of pastoral; but it also has to do with a number of short, primarily Greek, ancient poems in the epic mode that were far more prominent in the Renaissance than today. Appraising the influence of this group of poems alters our sense of the classical energies in play in late Elizabethan poetry, and the place of Greek literature within them. But it can also shift our perspective on the poetic landscape out of which the 'Elizabethan epyllia' emerged, and the horizon of expectations we might bring to them. Barnfield's perspective in 1594, I suggest, reconfigures the place of both Watson and the Greek epyllion at this watershed moment for 1590s narrative poetry.

Most classicists today would say that reports of the classical epyllion's non-existence have been greatly exaggerated. Whatever the truth of Crump's arguments, short poems written in the distinctive idiom of epic do survive from Greek and Roman antiquity; such works articulate their poetic statement in conversation with epic, and their scale is necessarily part of that conversation. Colluthus's *Abduction of Helen* and Musaeus's *Hero and Leander* are works of this kind; so is the pseudo-Virgilian mythological *Ciris*, the pseudo-Virgilian parodic pastoral-epic *Gnat*, and the pseudo-Homeric mock epic *Battle of the Frogs and Mice* (*Batrachomyomachia*). Largely the province of specialists today, these works had an altogether different visibility in the Renaissance. The pan-European popularity of *Hero and Leander* is well documented.[22] Held in high esteem because its author was conflated with the mythical inventor of poetry, it was one of the first Greek texts to see print, and was published and republished in the sixteenth century in multiple cities and editions. Its commonest incarnation was probably as a primer in the Greek hexameter, alongside other suitably chosen texts for linguistic practice.[23] Often rendered into Latin, including in England by the talented William Gager in 1578/80,[24] it also drew the interest of some key vernacular poets before Marlowe: Bernardo Tasso and Clément Marot produced versions in the first half of the century, in 1537 and 1541 respectively, as did Juan Boscán, whose 1543 *Leandro* was admired by Fraunce.[25] Less well documented is the early modern life of Colluthus's *Abduction of Helen*.[26] This poem, too, could have a pedagogical function: Neander taught it at the Reformed gymnasium at Ilfeld, before editing it for similar use across Europe. But it would have been best known in connection with Homer's epics, since it was often printed in Homeric editions, and mentioned in paratexts as a prequel to the *Iliad*. These editions circulated in England and put Colluthus on the literary map for anyone exploring Homer's epics. For instance, in an annotated copy of Homer in St John's College, Cambridge, which does not print this poem, a reader noted: 'Qui cupit historiam integram trojanam cognoscere legat ... narrationem de pomo Eridis, de judicio Paridis, profectione in Graeciam, ac raptu Helenae apud Coluthum poetam Homeri nonnunquam in decimosexto adjectum' (Whoever wants to become acquainted with the full story of Troy, may read ... the narrative of the apple of Discord, the Judgement of Paris, the expedition to Greece, and the rape of Helen in Colluthus, often appended to Homer in *decimosexto*).[27] Jean de Sponde, editor of the magisterial 1583 commentary on the epics that was crucial to George Chapman, similarly sketched the 'Argumentum' of the *Iliad*, meaning the whole story of the Trojan War, referring his readers to the very elegant poem ('eleganti sane poemate') of Colluthus for its origins.[28] And precisely because the reception of the *Iliad* was intertwined with the *Abduction of Helen*, many early modern Homeric translators also translated Colluthus, making the poem available in Latin and the vernaculars.[29] An English translation and commentary was printed in 1651, where it was presented as 'a Prologue or Preludium' to the *Iliad*; and it is a mark of the sharp change in the poem's fortunes after this period that the next English version would be the one in the Loeb edition of 1928.[30] A very different work from these two, the mock epic *Batrachomyomachia*, shared the reception trajectories of both. Ascribed to Homer, it was seen as a satirical flourish written for recreation, or else 'is pueris, quos in Graecia passim docebat' (for the children Homer taught throughout Greece).[31] An inseparable part of the Homeric canon, it appeared with the epics even more regularly than Colluthus; and as an ideal text for readying aspiring scholars to approach the Greek hexameter in its more serious guises, it formed part of the collection of educational texts that also included Musaeus.[32] Homer's *Batrachomyomachia*, translated more often than any other ancient epyllion, was probably the most famous example of the epic register taking a light break.

Epic was the generic lens through which these poems were often viewed. All three form part of Henri Estienne's 1566 landmark edition of Greek 'heroic poetry', i.e. epic.[33] J. C. Scaliger, commenting in his 1561 *Poetice* on Aristotle's assumption that epic is long compared to tragedy, observes that epics do indeed tend to be long, 'non tamen semper cujusmodi vides apud Musaeum' (yet not always, as you see in Musaeus).³⁴ Lodovico Castelvetro, in his 1570 exposition of Aristotle's *Poetics*, echoes his view that *Hero and Leander* disproves the theory that epic needs to be long.³⁵ Building on this tradition, Alonso López Pinciano likewise presents *Hero and Leander* as the key example of 'epica ... breve', and insists elsewhere that the subject of an epic can be a love story, as for instance in the case of Musaeus.³⁶ Both these critics consider epic 'magnitude' in ways that impinge on these works. In the same discussion where he brings in Musaeus, Castelvetro argues that it is not the duration of epic that needs to have magnitude but its action; specifically, just like the action of a tragedy, it needs to involve a reversal. Elsewhere, Pinciano reflects on the 'concepto' of a literary work or one's idea of the subject ('la noticia que el hombre de la cosa concibe'). The 'concepto' of the *Batrachomyomachia* is great and lofty ('magnifica y alta') just like that of the *Iliad* or the *Aeneid*, he argues, for it treated its lowly matter ('lo baxo') loftily ('altamente').³⁷ Scaliger, on the other hand, sets out the narratological norms for composing epic and ends by justifying Musaeus for not following them, on the grounds that even though he is writing an epic, his subject matter is 'quasi tragoedia'.³⁸ What is striking is the way all these early modern critics defend these works as liminal cases of epic, so that they come to define the genre's contours. Interestingly, editors and scholars often referred to them as 'ποιημάτια', or 'poematia' (little poems).³⁹ The word could apply to any short poem, such as an epigram;⁴⁰ yet these long works are most likely to seem notably brief if they are species of epic.

Beginning his 1581 lectures on the *Batrachomyomachia*, Martinus Crusius announced that having sailed through the vast sea ('magno ... mari') of the *Iliad* and the *Odyssey*, he was now about to turn into a clear river ('limpidum quondam rivum declinabo').⁴¹ A sense of direction, of positioning in relation to epic, is crucial to these poems. They are always looking to epic – ambitiously forward, disenchantedly back, calmly sideways, playfully aslant. This idea of direction was reflected in the personal experience of them by those exploring Greek literature. These were works that made the epic idiom available for linguistic training, for translation and imitation, before or without taking on the epic's full challenges. Marco Girolamo Vida's advice to budding poets was 'not to venture to compose long *Iliads*' before they could 'tell in verse of the fearsome fates of a gnat, or of how in boundless battle the thundering mouse dealt death to the croaking troops of marsh-loving frogs'.⁴² But as Jessica Wolfe stresses, even with the *Batrachomyomachia*, this was far from the only imaginable positioning. Unlike the poems in the *Appendix Virgiliana*, none of these Greek epyllia were seen primarily as juvenilia, but rather as accomplished works that 'offer[ed] up competing ... treatments of epic values and norms'.[43] In an epigram often printed with *Hero and Leander*, Marcus Musurus contrasts martial epic with the poem of Musaeus, which inscribed on some puny pages how much Cupid could do by trifling with his little hands ('μικρῆσιν ... σελίδεσσιν / ὅσσ' ὀλίγαις παίζων χερσὶν ἔοργεν ἔρως'): amatory subject and small scale are cast in a competitive relation to epic, not as a step towards it.[44] Crucial to establishing that relation is the fact that in their tone and expressive capabilities, these poems are in dialogue with epic. Early modern commentators were aware of these works' energetic allusiveness, whether they thought of Homer as reworking Musaeus, or of Colluthus as drawing on Homer. They saw, for instance, that Aphrodite's victory performance in Colluthus is in conversation with the *Iliad* – that it recycles and creatively repositions a Homeric invention, so that the 'prelude' relies on intimate knowledge of that great work.[45] In this allusion they may have seen a demonstration of the epyllion's ability to mobilise and twist the literary expectations of epic-literate readers. Barnfield's *Hellens Rape* certainly suggests they saw such possibilities in the brief epic, and that the prequel possessed its own distinctive capacities for deploying them. His perspective, I believe, opens up a different view of this period's micro-poetics.

Watson, the Greek epyllion, and the prequel

Watson's 1585 *Amyntas* is written in playfully allusive Latin hexameters. It is a series of lamentations by the shepherd Amyntas on the death of Phillis, which grow more desperate the less he sleeps over ten days, and culminate on the eleventh in his suicide and metamorphosis into the amaranth. This, Watson narrates in strongly Ovidian accents. Watson described his *Amyntas* as a light poetic project like Homer's *Batrachomyomachia* or Virgil's *Gnat*, on account of its shallow subject matter.[46] He probably got to explore Homer's mock epic at an impressionable moment as a student at Winchester College, where the headmaster, Christopher Johnson, devoted ample class time to his own version of it in erudite Latin hexameters.[47] The parallel with *Amyntas* may have thus felt stronger to Watson than it does to us. As Staton once observed, Watson's wildly popular frivolous poem is an overlooked but key precursor of the 'Ovidian epyllia' of the next poetic generation.[48] In 1595, William Covell, one of Shakespeare's first admirers, referred to 'Wanton Adonis' as 'Watson's heyre'.[49] The poem definitely anticipates the witty eroticism of those works. Amyntas's memories of Phillis – of which we have already had a taste in Fraunce's translation – continue:

> Ejus et interdum tangebam mollia colla,
> ...
> ... dum tractabat eburno
> Pollice quas habui sparsas lanugine malas.
> Forsan et ausus eram teretes quandoque papillas
> Indigna mulcere manu, placideque movere.
>
> (I, 34–40)

> Sometimes I would touch her soft neck ... while she handled with her ivory thumb what sparse hairs I had on my downy cheek. And sometimes perhaps I would dare to touch her round breasts lightly with my undeserving hand, and gently stir them.

Watson's next literary venture was his 1586 Colluthus. A mini-epic in Latin hexameters in which a shepherd finds himself digressing into an amatory epic adventure, it was anything but worlds apart from the *Amyntas*. This poem too – now a bibliographical rarity – may have had an instant appeal, for Thomas Coxeter gives us notice of a lost Colluthus by Marlowe in 'English rhime', dating to 1587.[50] It would have made a fitting successor to what was probably Marlowe's first work of erotic classicism, his version of Ovid's *Amores*. And if it was inspired by Watson – with whom Marlowe was close by 1589 – we have here the beginnings of an innovative amatory poetics in which pastoral, Greek epyllion and the influence of Ovid all have a role.

By 1592, these connections assume a concrete expression, as Marlowe sees to print his friend's *Amintae gaudia*, or *The Joys of Amyntas*, shortly after Watson's death. This series of epistles and eclogues narrates the young wooing and cooing of Amyntas and Phillis with gracefully sparkling erudition. The last eclogue hints at Phillis's impending death, but only in a prophecy the lovers nonchalantly ignore. Watson's 'prequel' clearly bears the stamp of another work. Its fourth eclogue digresses into what is effectively an inset epyllion, four times as long as any other part of the poem, in which Amyntas narrates a dream, all about Venus's preparations for the occasion of Philip Sidney's transformation into the star Astrophilus. The epyllion, which is even set off from the rest of the text by a subtitle ('Amintae insomnium'), is the heart of the poem's appeal to its dedicatee, the countess of Pembroke. Amyntas's dream is not wholly unlike the vision revealed to another famous shepherd. In it, Venus is seized by the same competitive urge as when she stole the golden apple of the Hesperides from the rival goddesses by the boy's judgement ('Hesperidumque deis rivalibus abstulit aurum / judicio pueri') (*AG Ecl.*, IV, 58–9); even more tellingly, she wants to appear no less beautiful than when she fed the burning eyes of wanton Paris ('lascivi Paridis flagrantia lumina pavit') (line 57). This is, unmistakably, Colluthus's goddess. This time, she keeps her clothes on, but does send Mercury on an epic mission to fetch Juno's casket filled with a pink mist of allure, 'rosea ... pixida plenam / Nube venustatis' (lines 76–7), in an allusion to the *cestos* she herself once lent Juno, while she goes to find the actual *cestos*, mislaid, apparently, somewhere on Cyprus. Aligned with the festive mood of the gods, Watson's inset epyllion turns Sidney's death into an occasion for poetic and erotic celebration. As it does so, it reflects the joyful mode of *Amintae gaudia* as a whole, which pointedly shuts out tragedy from its universe. Or rather, it shields its characters – whether it is the deathless Olympians feasting Sidney, or the blissfully unsuspecting lovers – from the tragedy and loss that are foremost in the readers' thoughts. Watson may have seen something incipiently like this artful double perspective in Colluthus, whose prequel to the *Iliad* focuses on the comedy and drama of the abduction, only hinting at the great war as yet unthought of in its world. This is the particular literary capital the prequel can make out of the epyllion's capacity to assert its distinctiveness from the better-known world of epic.

At least one close contemporary seems to have made a link between *Amintae gaudia*, Colluthus and the prequel. 'J. T.', translator of part of the *Amintae gaudia* in 1594, was probably the John Trussell who published in 1595 *The First Rape of Faire Helen*, yet another Elizabethan narrative poem outside the epyllic 'canon'.[51] In other sources of this myth, a young Helen is abducted by Theseus, and restored after her brothers raise an army and destroy a small town in Attica.[52] In Trussell's poem, by contrast, Helen's ghost confesses to being raped and abandoned by the craven Athenian before she was married off to a haplessly unsuspicious Menelaus.[53] With this risqué emphasis on scandal and concealment, Trussell invites unkind connections between this story and the notorious outcome of Helen's marriage. Though not chronologically situating itself in ignorance of the known catastrophe, this epyllion, too, makes use of the prequel's literary resource of being automatically read in relation to the known. An eminently topical version of the known in this case was Barnfield's 1594 *Hellens Rape*, which similarly – as Trussell, perhaps, would have the reader note – is no trans-national *casus belli*, but a sexual escapade. Yet Trussell's Latin title page, *Raptus I Helenae*, seems to allude instead to Colluthus's or Watson's *Helenae raptus*, grandly announcing an epyllic prequel to a celebrated epyllic prequel.

Marlowe's *Hero and Leander*: 'desunt nonnulla'?

All of this changes the horizon of generic expectations relevant to that archetypal Elizabethan epyllion, *Hero and Leander*. In one of the poem's high points, Marlowe's Leander, 'rude in love, and raw' (line 545), begins to suspect that for all the greedy 'kisses' and 'sweet … embracements' (line 513) of his first time together with Hero, 'some amorous rites or other were neglected' (line 548).[54] Musaeus's epyllion was probably playing on Marlowe's mind here, for in his great wooing speech, Musaeus's Leander urges Hero to embrace the rite (*thesmos*) of desires that brings delight to the mind: 'μελίφρονα θεσμὸν Ἐρώτων' (line 147). Coming across this elegant metaphor, Marlowe may have realised that, by means of the softest letter-change, Colluthus had turned it into a euphemism for Aphrodite's erotic accessory: the band (*desmos*) of desires that brings delight to the mind ('μελίφρονα δεσμὸν Ἐρώτων') (line 156).[55] Certainly, if Marlowe's epyllion keeps circling back (as Gordon Braden has shown) to the haunting language of Musaeus's amatory piece, its creative energy is also indebted, at least indirectly, to the protean tone, fleeting mischief and double perspective of Colluthus's *Abduction*.[56]

Marlowe's biographer Patrick Honan sees *Hero and Leander* as a late work, as most critics do, and links it to *Amintae gaudia*, in that both poems celebrate 'young lovers who know almost nothing of love'.[57] The parallel, however, is perhaps even stronger. Marlowe refers in his poem to the 'tragedy divine Musaeus sung' (line 52). In doing so, he could be differentiating Musaeus's epyllion from his own, which, at least as it stands, ends on the delightfully gauche consummation of the pair's love, omitting the reversal of Musaeus's 'quasi tragoedia'. This would make Marlowe's poem a sort of prequel that, like Watson's *Amintae gaudia*, denies any knowledge of the disaster to happen. Looking at English poetics from Barnfield's vantage point in 1594 suggests that alongside Ovid's pervasive influence, the Greek epyllion and the prequel were vividly present and closely intertwined in the poetic microculture most pertinent to Marlowe at this time. This constitutes external evidence that the poem is finished. This early testament is particularly suggestive, given that our basic evidence to the contrary dates to 1598, five years on from Marlowe's death, in one of the most swiftly metamorphosing decades in English poetics.[58] Moreover, this same recalibration of these poets' classical interests and generic investments can make visible powerful internal testimony to the same effect. In imitating the double perspective of Watson's *Amintae gaudia*, Marlowe's *Hero and Leander* makes, I argue, agile and sophisticated use of the little epic's perfidious generic affiliation: its intimate connection to epic and simultaneous capacity to declare a rebellious and idiosyncratic discreteness from it.

Take the turning-point to the story as Marlowe tells it: Cupid's suit to the Fates on the behalf of the lovers at lines 385–482. When Cupid wounds Hero in a fit of pique, he is immediately gripped by remorse, and visits the Destinies to 'ma[k]e request / Both might enjoy each other, and be blest' (lines 379–80). They answer not in words, but with a withering look. Here, Marlowe embarks on his labyrinthine digression into a tale that explains the Fates' hostility to Cupid, and upon re-emerging, recaps: 'Then muse not Cupid's suit no better sped' (line 483). But what does 'no better' mean, and for whom? Just before Musaeus's Leander drowns, the poet says, abstractly: '"Ερως δ' οὐκ ἤρκεσε Μοίρας' (Cupid could not stay the Fates) (line 322). Yet the reader who read one text into the other would be doing so on their own initiative. To interpret the Destinies' scowl as a prophecy of the ending we know from other sources is to admit into the poem something Marlowe has deliberately left out. Marlowe, that is, makes the reader alone guilty of any thought of that fatal ending. Epic-literate readers are doubly guilty. For in epic, two-part wishes like Cupid's have a bad history. When, in the *Iliad*, Achilles prays to Zeus that Patroclus may win glory and come back safe, 'τῷ δ' ἕτερον μὲν ἔδωκε πατήρ, ἕτερον δ' ἀνένευσε' (one part the father granted him, and the other denied) (*Iliad*, XVI, 250); and when Arruns in the *Aeneid* prays that he may kill Camilla and return home, Phoebus 'voti … succedere partem / mente dedit, partem volucris dispersit in auras' (granted half the prayer, but half upon the passing breeze he threw) (*Aeneid*, XI, 794–5). The carefully constructed two-part wish is a silent allusion that prompts the readers' epic memory, involving them in the challenge of telling this story differently. All the more so as Cupid's wounding of Hero comes just after he 'beats down her prayers with his wings, / [and] Her vows above the empty air he flings' (lines 369–70). Tiptoeing around the epic answer, Marlowe makes the matrix of epic activate the threat of death, even as the poem itself manages to escape it, and remain innocent of anything other than the giddy drama of youthful desire.

Something similar happens when Leander takes his clothes off to swim to Hero. Marlowe may have noticed that Musaeus's Leander ties his clothes around his head before jumping in (lines 251–2), and may have remembered that swimming with one's clothes on is not a good omen in the *Odyssey*. When Odysseus almost drowns, the nymph Leucothea advises him to abandon his raft and clothes, and swim instead with just her 'κρήδεμνον' (veil) (*Odyssey*, V, 346) tied around him. This is how he makes it to Nausicaa's land. Marlowe's memory of the incident may have been triggered by the fact that, as Musaeus's salt-encrusted Leander emerges on Sestos, the sequence (at lines 264–71) redistributes elements from Nausicaa's reception of Odysseus. An earlier moment in Musaeus brought Odysseus and Nausicaa to other readers' minds. Hero's yielding protestation to Leander's wooing – Englished by Marlowe as 'Who taught thee rhetoric to deceive a maid?' (line 338) – reminded Crusius of the 'naufragus … & nudus & supplex' (shipwrecked, naked and supplicant) Odysseus who wins over Nausicaa by means of rhetoric.[59] And to Scaliger, Odysseus's celebrated supplication speech to Nausicaa seemed merely an insipid imitation of Leander's wooing.[60] For whichever reason, this part of the *Odyssey* does become reactivated in Marlowe's writing. His Leander, as unaware of epic danger as he is mindless of social niceties, simply takes his clothes off and jumps in, unwittingly placing himself in a well-omened position. Comically, his nakedness does win him the (not un-self-interested) tender good will of Neptune, and we know that this Leander will make it, when Neptune 'put Helle's bracelet on his arm, / And swore the sea should never do him harm' (lines 663–4); this is after all the Hellespont, named after Leucothea's niece, Helle. To the reader with an epic subconscious, the bare-bodied swimmer with just the bracelet tied around his arm is an Odyssean allusion. Unbeknownst to him, Leander is swimming in safety. This same reader, however, also knows that the sense of danger has all along been theirs, not the text's – it is activated by the matrix of epic and that is where Marlowe leaves it.

Had Leander read *Odyssey*, VI, he would have known that when a man washes up ashore with no clothes on, delicacy is of the essence in approaching a maiden. Innocent as he is of epic, he simply knocks on Hero's door, 'Where seeing a naked man, she screeched for fear, / Such sights as this to tender maids are rare, / And ran into the dark herself to hide' (lines 721–3). Compare Nausicaa's handmaidens, faced with the stark-naked Odysseus: 'σμερδαλέος δ' αὐτῇσι φάνη … / τρέσσαν δ' ἄλλυδις ἄλλη' (he seemed terrible to them … and they fled in fear, one here, one there) (*Odyssey*, VI, 135–8). Hero's comical 'screech' shows her thoroughly lacking in the presence of mind that differentiates Nausicaa from her maids and helps her resolve a tightrope social situation with almost immaculate decorum. Yet neither Leander's nor Hero's failures with decorum lead to failure in the end. In differing from their Homeric predecessors, this couple only heighten the text's refusal to acknowledge what there is to fear. The *Odyssey* gives Marlowe a very erudite joke about a naked youth and a maiden, but also a language for distancing and sheltering Hero and Leander from society and danger, leaving them to tussle with desire alone.

The epyllion's conversation with epic, then, strengthens the link between nakedness, innocence and success. Here, we come to the last two lines of the poem, where Night, 'o'ercome with anguish, shame, and rage, / Danged down to hell her loathsome carriage' (lines 817–18). Night's irritation arises from the fact that she is mocked by Hesperus, about to usher in dawn. Just before this, the naked Hero blushes as she faces Leander, Marlowe famously likening her 'ruddy cheek' to a 'kind of twilight' or a 'false morn' (lines 807, 803, 805). Pushing under these lines is an epic convention: rosy-fingered Dawn rising from the bed of her superannuated mate. Here she is, in one of Spenser's versions: 'faire *Aurora* from the deawy bed / Of aged *Tithone* gan her selfe to reare, / With rosie cheekes, for shame as blushing red' (*Faerie Queene*, I.xi.51, lines 2–3). Warren Boutcher brilliantly points out that the final lines of *Hero and Leander* recall the end of the *Aeneid*: 'vitaque cum gemitu fugit indignata sub umbras' (his life, full of rage, fled down to the shades with a moan) (*Aeneid*, XII, 952). But they do not, I believe, 'conflate the shamed figure of Hero with that of Night', as he suggests.[61] In contrast to Spenser, Marlowe studiedly detaches the word 'shame' from Hero's dawn-like blush and gives it to dawn's opponent, Night. Though Hero 'sigh[s] to think upon th' approaching sun' (line 786), the poem sees things differently: down to the its precipitous, last extant line, the only view we get of the exposed Hero is through the unashamedly admiring eyes of Leander. All other thoughts are the readers'. Boutcher's comment does however point to the conscious knottiness of these lines.[62] In sending Night to hell, Marlowe is also sending to hell a hefty weight of convention that aligns pleasure with shame, night and death. This is where his poem ends, with that entirely unconventional figuration of the break of day as the demise of night, and Hero in naked splendour by her callow lover. Marlowe's reference to dawn before night makes it as difficult to grasp this ending, as it is not to read beyond his poem to the death that catches up with these lovers in other versions of the story, 'as the night the day'. Yet by alluding to the end of the *Aeneid*, I think Marlowe tells his readers that this *is* where the poem ends. The *Aeneid*'s conclusion is sudden, ambivalent and difficult. In its refusal to look forward to the glory of Rome and marriage with Lavinia, it seemed spurious to many early modern readers, hence the popularity of supplements to the epic.[63] To read Marlowe's *Hero and Leander* as an 'Ovidian epyllion' is similarly to find, along with its 1598 publishers and completers, that 'Desunt nonnulla' ('A part is missing'). To read it with an epic subconscious is to feel the difficulty and the thrill of narrating erotic experience as Marlowe has done. In 1594 Barnfield was, I think, such a reader, if the shameless finale of his own epyllion is something to go by:

> For Aurora mounts before he leaves to be mounting:
> And Astraea fades before she faints to be falling:
> (Helen a light Huswife, now a lightsome starre in Olympus.)
>
> (sig. G4v)

Notes

I am grateful to the editors for the various occasions out of which this essay emerged, and for their judicious responses and touching generosity. Colin Burrow, Terence Cave, Stephen Harrison, Charles Martindale, Subha Mukherji, Chloe Preedy and Matthew Reynolds offered especially helpful comments on different versions. Janice Valls-Russell and Yves Peyré have been an inexhaustible source of support and mythological inspiration.

1. Poetry reading, 1 July 2016, University of York, in the context of *Poetic Measures: A Variable Measure for the Fixed*. Quoted with Alice Oswald's permission.
2. Richard Barnfield, *The Affectionate Shepheard* (London: John Danter for T. G[ubbin] and E. N[ewman], 1594), sigs G3v–G4v. For biographical information on Barnfield, see Andrew Worrall, 'Biographical introduction: Barnfield's feast of "all varietie"', in Kenneth Borris and George Klawitter (eds), *The Affectionate Shepherd: Celebrating Richard Barnfield* (Selinsgrove: Susquehanna University Press, 2001), pp. 25–40. The poem receives no extended discussion in this collection of essays – the only one dedicated to Barnfield to my knowledge – but see Richard Barnfield, *The Complete Poems*, ed. George Klawitter (Selinsgrove: Susquehanna University Press, 1990), p. 34; Harry Morris, 'Richard Barnfield, *Amyntas*, and the Sidney circle', *Proceedings of the Modern Language Association*, 74 (1959), 318–24 (pp. 322–4); and Walter F. Staton and Harry Morris, 'Thomas Watson and Abraham Fraunce', *Proceedings of the Modern Language Association*, 76 (1961), 150–3.
3. The myth of Helen's catasterism is told in Natale Conti, *Mythologia* (Venice: [Comin da Trino], 1567), p. 248v (VIII, ix).
4. Thomas Nash, 'To the gentlemen students of both universities', in Robert Greene, *Menaphon* (London: T[homas] O[rwin] for Sampson Clarke, 1589), sigs **r–A3r (sig. Ar).
5. Abraham Fraunce, *The Lamentations of Amyntas* (London: John Wolfe for Thomas Newman and Thomas Gubbin, 1587), sig. Ar.
6. Thomas Nash, *The Apologie of Pierce Pennilesse: or, Strange Newes* (London: John Danter, 1593), sig. G3r.
7. Ronald B. McKerrow (ed.), *Greenes Newes Both from Heaven and Hell (1593) and Greenes Funeralls (1594)* (London: Sidgwick and Jackson, 1911), p. 79; on the similarity between this sonnet and *Hellens Rape*, see p. ix.

8   On Barnfield and Stanley, see Leo Daugherty, 'The question of topical allusion in Richard Barnfield's pastoral verse', in Borris and Klawitter, *The Affectionate Shepherd*, pp. 45–61. On Stanley's parody, see Steven May, 'Spenser's "Amyntas": Three poems by Ferdinando Stanley, Lord Strange, fifth earl of Derby', *Modern Philology*, 70 (1972), 49–52. The strongest argument in favour of Stanley as Amintas (rather than Fraunce or Watson) is that 'Sonnet IV' in *Greenes Funeralls* suggests he is alive: see McKerrow, *Greenes Funeralls*, p. 75.
9   Barnfield, *The Affectionate Shepheard*, sig. E4v.
10 Colluthus, *Helenae raptus*, trans. and ed. Michael Neander (Basel: J. Oporinus, 1559), p. 35. Emphasis mine. On Neander's Colluthus, see Ángel Ruíz Pérez, 'Historia editorial del *Rapto de Helena* de Coluto', in Ignacio J. García Pinilla and Santiago Talavera Cuesta (eds), *Charisterion Francisco Martín García oblatum* (Cuenca: Universidad de Castilla-La Mancha, 2004), pp. 339–61 (pp. 340–2).
11 See Colluthus, *L'enlèvement d'Hélène*, trans. and ed. P. Orsini, repr. edn (Paris: Les Belles Lettres, 2002), lines 103–6; but also Lucia Prauscello, 'Colluthus' pastoral traditions: Narrative strategies and bucolic criticism in the *Abduction of Helen*', in Katerina Carvounis and Richard Hunter (eds), *Signs of Life? New Contexts for Later Greek Hexameter Poetry*, *Ramus*, 37 (2008) (special issue), 173–90, for a superb account of why Paris keeps such multifarious flocks.
12 References to all of Watson's works will be to line numbers in Thomas Watson, *The Complete Works*, ed. Dana F. Sutton (2011), www.philological.bham.ac.uk/watson/ (accessed 25 January 2016). In his 'Introduction' to *Helenae raptus*, Sutton argues that Watson used René Perdrier's crib, based on two shared mistakes in the Greek; in fact, these 'errors' correspond to textual problems at lines 67b and 242 common to all early editions, and Watson more often has Neander's frequently reprinted translation at the back of his mind.
13 Thomas Nash, *Have with You to Saffron Walden* (London: John Danter, 1596), sigs T3v–T4r. On Watson, see Michael J. Hirrel, 'Thomas Watson, playwright: Origins of modern English drama', in David McInnis and Matthew Steggle (eds), *Lost Plays in Shakespeare's England* (Basingstoke: Palgrave Macmillan, 2014), pp. 187–207.
14 Colluthus, *Helenae raptus*, pp. 15, [3].
15 Paul W. Miller, 'The Elizabethan minor epic', *Studies in Philology*, 55 (1958), 31–8; Elizabeth Story Donno (ed.), *Elizabethan Minor Epics* (New York: Columbia University Press, 1963). Donno's was the basis for later important anthologies, such as Sandra Clark (ed.), *Amorous Rites: Elizabethan Erotic Verse* (London: Everyman, 1994).
16 See Miller, 'The Elizabethan minor epic', p. 31; and e.g. Hallett Smith, *Elizabethan Poetry: A Study in Conventions, Meaning, and Expression* (Cambridge, MA: Harvard University Press, 1952), pp. 64–101; Walter F. Staton, 'The influence of Thomas Watson on Elizabethan Ovidian poetry', *Studies in the Renaissance*, 6 (1959), 243–50 (p. 243). For Douglas Bush, *Hero and Leander* and *Venus and*

Adonis represented the 'twin peaks of the Ovidian tradition in England', a tradition of 'spicy amorous poems'; *Mythology and the Renaissance Tradition in English Poetry*, rev. edn (New York: Norton, 1963), p. 137.

17   Mary Marjorie Crump, *The Epyllion from Theocritus to Ovid* (Bristol: Bristol Classical Press, 1997 [1931]), pp. 22–4.

18   Walter Allen, 'The non-existent classical epyllion', *Studies in Philology*, 55 (1958), 515–18 (p. 515). This was a recapitulation, for the benefit of English scholars, of his views in 'The epyllion: A chapter in the history of literary criticism', *Transactions and Proceedings of the American Philological Association*, 71 (1940), 1–26.

19   Always with a caveat about its ancient pedigree. See Donno, *Elizabethan Minor Epics*, p. 6; Clark, *Amorous Rites*, pp. xxvii, l; William Keach, *Elizabethan Erotic Narratives: Irony and Pathos in the Ovidian Poetry of Shakespeare, Marlowe and Their Contemporaries* (Sussex: Harvester, 1977), pp. xvi–xvii; Clark Hulse, *Metamorphic Verse: The Elizabethan Minor Epic* (Princeton: Princeton University Press, 1981), p. 22; Jim Ellis, *Sexuality and Citizenship: Metamorphosis in Elizabethan Erotic Verse* (Toronto: University of Toronto Press, 2003), pp. 4, 241n6; Georgia E. Brown, *Redefining Elizabethan Literature* (Cambridge: Cambridge University Press, 2004), p. 111n19.

20   Including in all of the studies mentioned in the previous note. A notable recent exception is William P. Weaver, *Untutored Lines: The Making of the English Epyllion* (Edinburgh: Edinburgh University Press, 2012), which discusses this tradition of poems in connection with Aphthonius's *Progymnasmata*.

21   Brown, *Redefining Elizabethan Literature*, p. 152.

22   Most recently and comprehensively in Roland Béhar, '*Musæum ante omnes ...*: la fortune critique de Musée dans la théorie poétique espagnole du *Siglo de Oro*', *e-Spania*, 2015, http://e-spania.revues.org/24615 (accessed 2 July 2016), but as early as Bush, *Mythology*, pp. 123–4. See also Warren Boutcher, '"Who taught thee rhetoricke to deceive a maid?": Christopher Marlowe's *Hero and Leander*, Juan Boscán's *Leandro*, and Renaissance vernacular humanism', *Comparative Literature*, 51 (2000), 11–52; and Gordon Braden, *The Classics and English Renaissance Poetry: Three Case Studies* (New Haven: Yale University Press, 1978), pp. 81–118.

23   First published as Aesop et al., *Aesopi Phrygis vita et fabellae* ... (Basel: J. Froben, 1517/18). As well as Aesop's fables and Musaeus, this often-reproduced collection contained the *Battle of the Frogs and Mice* and the mock-tragedy *Battle of the Cats and Mice* by Theodoros Prodromos (twelfth century CE).

24   Gager's translation is extant as London, British Library, Additional MS 22583, pp. 41–56.

25   See e.g. Abraham Fraunce, *The Arcadian Rhetorike* (London: Thomas Orwin, 1588), where he often quotes Boscán's *Leandro*.

26   With the exception of Pérez, 'Historia editorial', who nevertheless overlooks the interrelated reception of the *Iliad* and Colluthus.

27 St John's College, Cambridge, MS Cc.16.11, flyleaf, part of a fuller chart. The reader could be referring to Homer, *Ilias et Odyssea: secunda editio*, ed. F. Portus ([Geneva]: J. Crispinus, 1570), the first Homeric edition to print the poem, or any of the many subsequent ones, in this highly portable format.

28 Jean de Sponde (ed.), *Homeri quae extant omnia*, 2 vols (Basel: E. Episcopius, 1583), Vol. I, p. 43.

29 Helius Eobanus Hessus, *Coluthi ... De raptu Helenes... Epithalamion Helenes ex Theocrito. Moschi Amor fugitivus* (Erfurt: Melchior I Sachse, 1534); Paolo La Badessa, *Il rapimento di Helena* (Messina: heir of Petruccio Spira, 1571); Sieur Du Souhait, *L'Iliade d'Homere ... ensemble le Ravissement d'Helene* (Paris: Pierre Chevalier, 1620); Federico Malipiero, *L'Iliada d'Omero ... il Ratto d'Elena* (Venice: Paolo Baglioni, 1642).

30 E. Sherburne, *Salmacis ... The Rape of Helen, a Comment Thereon* (London: W. Hunt for T. Dring, 1651), p. [44].

31 George Chapman, *The Crowne of all Homers Workes* (London: John Bill, 1624), sig. [¶4]r; Philipp Melanchthon, *Opera omnia*, ed. K. G. Bretschneider and H. E. Bindseil, 28 vols (Halle an der Saale/Braunschweig: C. A. Schwetschke, 1834–60), Vol. XI, p. 118.

32 On the poem's pedagogical function, see Paul Botley, *Learning Greek in Western Europe, 1396–1529* (Philadelphia: American Philosophical Society, 2010), p. 85; see also Jessica Wolfe, *Homer and the Question of Strife from Erasmus to Hobbes* (Toronto: University of Toronto Press, 2015), pp. 112–75.

33 Homer et al., Οἱ τῆς ἡρωϊκῆς ποιήσεως πρωτεύοντες ποιηταί, ed. Henri Estienne ([Geneva]: H. Estienne, 1566).

34 Julius Caesar Scaliger, *Poetices libri septem*, ed. Luc Deitz, G. Vogt-Spira and M. Fuhrmann, 5 vols (Stuttgart–Bad Cannstatt: Frommann–Holzboog, 1994–2003), Vol. I, p. 132 (I, vi, 12a).

35 Lodovico Castelvetro, *Poetica d'Aristotele vulgarizzata, et sposta* (Basel: Pietro de Sedabonis, 1576), p. 533.

36 Alfonso López Pinciano, *Philosophia antigua poetica* (Madrid: Thomas Junti, 1596), pp. 297, 470; see Béhar, '*Musæum ante omnes ...*', §31.

37 Pinciano, *Philosophia*, pp. 273–4.

38 Scaliger, *Poetices*, Vol. III, p. 24.

39 All of the Aldine editions of *Hero and Leander*, starting with Musaeus, Ποιημάτιον τὰ καθ' Ἡρώ καὶ Λέανδρον (Venice: Aldus Manutius, 1495–97), refer to it as a 'ποιημάτιον'. Froben describes the *Batrachomyomachia* as a 'poemation' in [Homer], *Batrachomyomachia* (Basel: J. Froben, 1518), p. 3 (in Aesop et al., *Aesopi Phrygis vita et fabellae ...*). Martinus Crusius and Henri II Estienne both refer to the *Abduction of Helen* and the *Batrachomyomachia* as 'poematia': see Martinus Crusius, *Commentationes in primum librum Iliados Homeri ... [(1594). In Homerum Prolegomena (1581)]* ([Heidelberg]: Gotthardus Voegelinus, 1612),

sig. **6r; 'In *Batrachomyomachiam* Homeri … praefatio', in *Philologiae Barbaro-Graecae pars altera*, ed. J. M. Lang (Altdorf: J. W. Kohles, 1707), pp. 42–60 (p. 53); Homer, *Homeri poemata duo, Ilias et Odyssea, sive Ulyssea. Alia item carmina ejusdem* ([Geneva]: [Henri II Estienne], 1588), sigs ¶iir, ¶iiir.

40   E.g. Sponde uses 'poemation' to refer to epigrams ascribed to Homer on the title-page of his edition.
41   Crusius, 'In *Batrachomyomachiam*', p. 42.
42   Quoted in David Scott Wilson-Okamura, *Virgil in the Renaissance* (Cambridge: Cambridge University Press, 2010), p. 89.
43   Wolfe, *Homer and the Question of Strife*, p. 124. See also Colin Burrow, 'English Renaissance readers and the *Appendix Vergiliana*', *Proceedings of the Virgil Society*, 26 (2008), 1–16.
44   Musaeus, Ποιημάτιον, sig. αv.
45   Neander and Sherburne both explain the *cestos*'s Homeric origins in their commentaries: Colluthus, *Helenae raptus*, p. 64; Sherburne, *Salmacis…*, p. 73.
46   In the poem's dedicatory epistle to 'Henrico Noello'.
47   On Johnson's teaching of the *Batrachomyomachia*, see Tania Demetriou and Tanya Pollard, 'Homer, Greek tragedy, and the early modern stage: An introduction', in Tania Demetriou and Tanya Pollard (eds), *Homer and Greek Tragedy in England's Early Modern Theatres, Classical Receptions Journal*, 9 (2017) (special issue), 1–35. Watson was probably at the school *c.* 1563–70: see Ibrahim Alhiyari, 'Thomas Watson: New biographical evidence and his translation of *Antigone*' (Ph.D. dissertation, Texas Tech University, 2006).
48   Staton, 'The influence of Thomas Watson'.
49   William Covell, *Polimanteia* (Cambridge and London: John Legate and J. Orwin, 1595), sig. R3r.
50   Charles Nicholl, 'Marlowe, Christopher (bap. 1564, d. 1593)', *Oxford Dictionary of National Biography* (Oxford: Oxford University Press, 2004), www.oxforddnb.com/view/article/18079 (accessed 25 July 2016).
51   See Robert F. W. Smith, '*John Trussell: A life (1575–1648)*' (Ph.D. dissertation, University of Southampton, 2013), pp. 27–8.
52   E.g. Conti, *Mythologia*, pp. 199r, 219r; and see Laurie Maguire, *Helen of Troy: From Homer to Hollywood* (Chichester: Wiley-Blackwell, 2009), p. 4.
53   When Theseus disappears after the rape (lines 223–8), Helen decides to hide her situation (301–12) but betrays herself to her maids, one of whom recommends concealment, based on the happy precedent of Helen's mother, Leda (529–666). Finally, Leda herself comes up with the solution of the marriage to Menelaus (715–38), and Helen's 'obloquy' is successfully 'metamorphosed' on the wedding night (853–64). References to John Trussell, *The First Rape of Faire Hellen*, in M. A. Shaaber, '*The First Rape of Faire Hellen* by John Trussell', *Shakespeare Quarterly*, 8:4 (1957), 407–48.

54 Christopher Marlowe, *The Collected Poems*, ed. Patrick Cheney and Brian J. Striar (Oxford: Oxford University Press, 2006); references are to the continuous line-numbering system in this edition.
55 Cf. Nonnus, *Dionysiaca*, XLII, 271: 'μελίφρονα θεσμὸν Ἐρώτων'.
56 For the argument that the poem draws directly on Colluthus, see Pamela Royston Macfie, 'Allusion as plunder: Marlowe's *Hero and Leander* and Colluthus's *Rape of Helen*', *Renaissance Papers* (2013), 31–42.
57 Patrick Honan, *Christopher Marlowe: Poet and Spy* (Oxford: Oxford University Press, 2005), p. 305.
58 See Marion Campbell, '"Desunt nonnulla": The construction of Marlowe's *Hero and Leander* as an unfinished poem', *English Literary History*, 51 (1984), 241–68, for a critical discussion of the arguments in favour of the poem's incompleteness, and p. 246 for her assessment of the 'external evidence' as 'unreliable'. Campbell does not discuss Richard Carew's reference to '[M]arlowe's fragment' in 'The excellency of the English tongue' (British Library, MS Cotton Julius F XI, fo. 267v), which is earlier: i.e. *c.* 1595–96. While the fact that Carew misspells Marlowe as 'Barlowe' suggests no closeness to the poet's circle, it is also interesting that when he twins Marlowe's poem and Shakespeare's *Venus and Adonis*, he compares them not to Ovid's poem, but to an ancient epyllion, Catullus 64. For a fascinating link between Marlowe's deferred ending and Colluthus, see the conclusion of Macfie, 'Allusion as plunder'.
59 Martinus Crusius, *Poematum Graecorum libri duo ... Orationum liber unus*, 3 vols (Basel: J. Oporinus, 1567), Vol. III, p. 30; Cf. Musaeus's 'τίς σε πολυπλανέων ἐπέων ἐδίδαξε κελεύθους;' (Who taught you the devious paths of eloquence?) (line 75).
60 Scaliger, *Poetics*, Vol. IV, pp. 54–5 (V, ii, 215b).
61 Boutcher, '"Who taught thee rhetoricke ...?"', p. 47.
62 The inverse dynamics of night and day throughout the poem are discussed in Braden, *The Classics and English Renaissance Poetry*, pp. 150–3; on shame and the epyllion, see Brown, *Redefining Elizabethan Literature*.
63 See Wilson-Okamura, *Virgil in the Renaissance*, pp. 237–47 on Maffeo Vegio's continuation, and p. 239n174 for bibliography on others.

3

'This realm is an empire': Tales of origins in medieval and early modern France and England

Dominique Goy-Blanquet

READING HOLINSHED'S EFFORTS TO place Samothes or Brutus on England's family tree, or Nicole Gilles's juggling with Paris the Trojan and the renaming of Lutèce, one feels sorry for those chroniclers who had to reconcile a variety of founding tales and defend mutable causes. The historian Marc Bloch recommends caution with the word 'origin': 'In popular usage, an origin is a beginning which explains. Worse still, a beginning which is a complete explanation. There lies the ambiguity, there the danger!' For history has frequently been put to the service of value judgements, 'whether the subject was the German invasions or the Norman conquest of England'. He concludes his section on 'The Idol of Origins' by quoting an Arab proverb: 'Men resemble their times more than they do their fathers.'[1]

The problem is that they *want* to resemble their fathers. Founding myths, as Colette Beaune has shown, need a renowned ancestor, warlike feats, identification with a territory, continuity, purity of blood – and someone to tell the story: fame must be recorded by pen if it is to survive marble monuments.[2] Too little has been written about the high deeds of early French kings, notes the Prologue to *Croniques et annales de France depuis la destruction de Troye*: 'leur vertu, vaillance, & prouesse … surmonteroit les faictz des Atheniens, Grecz, Troyens, & autres nations & mesmes ceulx des Rommains, qui plus ont fait de langue que d'espee' (their virtue, valour and prowess would be remembered above the feats of the Athenians, Greeks, Trojans and other nations, and even above those of the Romans, who did more with their tongues than their swords).[3] To the features listed by Beaune, one should add language, as did the Prussian ideologues whose heirs would ultimately cause Bloch's death.[4] Their first source on the purity of German blood was Tacitus, who adhered to the opinion 'that in the peoples of Germany there has been given to the world a race unmixed by intermarriage with other races, a peculiar people' (*Germania*, IV). These and other complex mixtures of myths, legends and biblical elements helped rival chroniclers to fashion tales of origins that Shakespeare would revisit, exploring alternatives of cultural and family hybridity.

Family trees

French and English medieval monarchs were one large family, divided by common sources, territories and ancestors. Chroniclers and poets supported their respective claims with millenarian or messianic themes, mythological epics and popular legends, often using the same ones: Gautier (Walter) Map for the Plantagenets, the monk Hélinand de Froidmont for the Capetians, tell the story of the Mesnie Hellequin, an incarnation of the Celtic god Herne from whom the kings of France and England inherited their power to heal scrofula.[5] The royal miracle, to quote Bloch again, expressed above all 'a particular concept of supreme political power', in competition with the ecclesiastical authorities.[6] The resistance to papal intrusions in temporal affairs required delicate handling of his representatives. Where English kings fought losing battles with their religious counsellors, the French constructed a cult of sacred monarchy through a steady alliance with the Church, in the footsteps of their founding couple, Clovis and Bishop Rémi, who christened the Frankish ruler and his kingdom sometime between 496 and 506. Louis IX's canonisation in 1297 did not just reward his singular virtues, it crowned two centuries of joint dynastic effort on the part of the monarchy and the Church. In England, the construction of a central power met far more checks. British history since time immemorial was one of repeated conquests and usurpations. Pressed to justify frequent dynastic changes, English chroniclers often urged their kings to emulate the French monarchs, St Louis or Charles V the Wise. Richard II, a declared admirer of both, modelled his huge works of embellishment in Westminster on the Palais de Justice, which featured statues of all the French kings since Pharamond.[7]

An even better pupil, Henry V was Louis's direct heir, as he loudly reminded everyone on presenting his claim to the French throne.[8] Even if he hadn't read Joinville, Prince Hal could still have found plenty of material in Matthew Paris's *Chronica majora*.[9] In comparison with Louis, Matthew finds the English king, Henry III, too weak with the pope's legates, those foreigners 'who seek the milk from the sheep of the Lord's fold, pluck the wool and scrape away the flesh from them, flay and disembowel them'.[10] Louis had suffered no encroachments on his sovereignty when the papacy's financial demands raised complaints throughout Europe. The jurists who advised his grandson Philip the Fair argued that 'Li rois est souverains en choses temporeix' (the king is sovereign in matters temporal).[11] France, they claimed, had never been part of the Constantine Donation – which formed the basis of papal theocracy – and therefore stood outside the pope's authority: submission to Rome was only temporary, and illegitimate, being based on force and born from murder.[12] Their thugs brought it down with one blow at Anagni in 1303, plundering the papal court and imprisoning Boniface VIII. John Foxe's *Actes and Monuments* relates Boniface's ordeal with this marginal note: 'Here may all kings by the French king learne how to handle the pope.'[13] In Dante's *Inferno*, Boniface is committed to the third circle of hell, with the popes guilty of simony: 'Ah Constantine! what ills were gendered there – / No, not from thy conversion, but the dower / The first rich Pope received from thee as heir!' (XIX, 115–17). But Dante, with equal indignation, also condemns the attack on the pope in *Purgatorio*: 'I see the Lily storm Alagna's paling / And in Christ's Vicar, Christ a captive made' (XX, 85–6).[14]

Various imperial propagandists after Dante questioned the legitimacy of the Donation, until Lorenzo Valla established it was a fake, written in clumsy medieval Latin some 400 years after Constantine's death. His *De falso credita et ementita Constantini donatione declamatio* was first translated into English in 1525, before Henry VIII had any thoughts of divorce.[15] The payment of a tribute to Rome had long been a sore point. When Henry VIII declared to the world that 'this realm of England is an empire', there was nothing new in the statement.[16] The preamble to the Act in Restraint of Appeals simply echoed the old medieval maxim, *Rex in regno suo est imperator* (The king in his kingdom is an emperor).[17] The Roman legacy of *imperium* 'denoted independent authority; it described a territorial unit; and it offered an historical foundation for claims to both the authority and the territory ruled by Roman emperors'.[18]

Mother cities

In the *Aeneid* (I, 278–9), Jupiter promises the Romans *imperium sine fine*. Saint Jerome condemned the phrase *Roma aeterna* as blasphemy, but popes would use it to stress their legitimacy as heirs to the Roman empire. There are two versions of the city's origin: one Latin, told by Livy in *History of Rome* (I, iv–vii), of a vestal and her twins who grow up to commit regicide, fratricide, rape and other crimes; one Greek, told by Dionysius of Halicarnassus (*Roman Antiquities*, I, lxiv–lxxii), of a prince and princess who married and had many children. Dionysius sought to establish a common lineage among the cities of Greece – including Troy, which he claimed was originally Greek (I, lxii), and Rome.[19] The tensions between these two foundation myths inform their literary sequels. Livy (I, vi) imputes to 'avitum malum, regni cupido' ('the curse of their grandsires, the greed of kingly power') the fratricidal rivalry between Romulus and Remus, which Augustine makes the epitome of all civil wars.[20] At the end of the more irenic *Aeneid* Jupiter promises Juno the Italian people will keep their names, customs and languages but join their blood with the Trojans', whose name and identity must disappear: this union, sealed by the marriage of Aeneas and Lavinia, will give birth to a superior race. Jupiter had promised Venus that the Trojans would survive in the heroes' lineage: 'From this noble line shall be born the Trojan Caesar, who shall extend his empire to the ocean, his glory to the stars' (I, 286–7), Caesar drawing his name Iulius from the great Iule – Ascanius, son of Aeneas.[21]

From Euripides's *Trojan Women* to the early modern period, the 'matter of Troy' never ceased to exercise writers. The city's fall struck the medieval imagination as an emblem of extreme catastrophe: it was 'the first genocide durably imprinted on the European consciousness', Richard Marienstras notes.[22] Homer's Agamemnon wants the whole race destroyed to avenge his family's honour. Virgil's Aeneas recalls 'an orgy of killing': 'Down fell the fifty bedchambers with all the hopes for generations yet to come' (*Aeneid*, II, 503–4). Blending mythology, history and medieval legends, romances offered rich depictions of a luxurious and sophisticated Trojan society.[23] Not only beautiful people but a prosperous city had been erased from the earth, leaving only a few survivors to roam undiscovered lands.

Greek sources stated that although no son of Priam had survived, numerous Trojan princes escaped the disaster. Aeneas went on to found Rome. His friend Antenor founded Padua, Livy's homeland, and Antenoride, later Venice.[24] After years of wandering, Brutus landed in Albion. Francion and his companions reached the Danube valley, where they built Sycambria, some of them moving westwards to found Lutèce. Those who had remained in Sycambria rebelled against the Romans, took the name of Franks, and joined their relatives in Lutèce. One of the etymologies often invoked for the name Frank was *francus*, 'free', because having settled on the right bank of the Rhine, they stood outside the *limes*, the limits of the Roman empire.[25] In 396, their leader, Duke Marcomir, 'qui fut moult fort et hardi chevalier' (who was a very stout and hardy knight), began the 'mutation des noms':[26]

Gaul would henceforth be called France in memory of Francion; Lutèce was renamed Paris after the Trojan hero who ravished Helen – the fact he was the one responsible for the disaster was not a hindrance – and Marcomir's son, Pharamond, was elected as the Franks' first king.[27]

Claims to be descended from Priam were legion: 'en cest isle sommes Troiien' (on this island we are Trojans, all), Philippe Mouskes of Tournai stated in his thirteenth-century *Chronique rimée*, stressing the blood links that founded a national brotherhood beyond geographical and social differences.[28] Montaigne, writing in praise of Homer's creative power, notes that 'most nations seeke to derive themselves from his inventions' and recalls how the Turk 'Machomet, second of that name, Emperour of Turkes', wrote to Pope Pius II that he could not understand why 'the Italians will bandie against me, seeing we have our common off-spring, from the Trojans; and I as well as they have an interest to revenge the blood of Hector upon the Græcians, whom they favour against mee'.[29] This was a long-reverberating feud: Pope Pius II, who had initially accepted the Franks' Trojan origins, was much incensed by the Turks' similar claims.[30] Duke Philip of Burgundy, who shared his views, encouraged his chroniclers to advertise his own Trojan lineage.[31] While the French monarchs harped on their Carolingian origins, Burgundy tapped several sources, adding to his Trojan pedigree an affiliation to Jason and the Argonauts, which he proclaimed at the Feast of the Pheasant on 17 February 1454, when he created the Order of the Golden Fleece with the declared aim to reconquer Jerusalem. It was Burgundy, and Margaret of York's marriage with Philip's son Charles the Bold, that inspired the printer William Caxton's taste for romance: in the 1470s he translated works on Troy and Jason that the Burgundian Raoul Lefèvre had written a decade or so earlier.[32]

Despite the violence that surrounded their arrival in various parts of Europe, the exiled princes of Troy were reputed to have brought civilisation with them, and were held equal with the Greeks as models of western culture. Wherever they settled, they allegedly built new cities, taught courtesy and chivalry, and gave the people good laws.[33] French kings, who claimed a descent from Francion, encouraged cycles of Troy romances – *Le roman d'Aeneas, Le roman d'Alexandre* and *Le roman de Thèbes* – that made up the 'matter of Rome'. Benoît de Sainte-Maure composed *Le roman de Troie* at the request of Eleanor d'Aquitaine, while Geoffrey of Monmouth pleased the Norman monarchy by tracing the origins of British kings to Aeneas's grandson Brutus. Apologists strove to lodge both conquering and civilising virtues into their tales. In France, formerly Gaul, the Trojans were credited with having chased away the thieves that ruled the land, and with establishing peace. In Albion they freed the place from giants. Arthur's wars, which take up about a quarter of Monmouth's *Historia regum Britanniae*, received the support of Archbishop Dubricius: to die willingly for one's country, 'that in itself is victory and a cleansing of the soul'.[34] Between reports of bloody prowess, Monmouth dedicates a few momentous pages to a splendid feast at Caerleon, first source of the *matière de Bretagne*. The feast is broken up by the arrival of a letter summoning Arthur to Rome: he has disobeyed the empire by holding back the tribute of Britain. In a rousing speech, he argues that the tribute is illegal, for '[n]othing that is acquired by force and violence can ever be held legally by anyone'.[35] No-one reminds him of his own conquering wars, and they all march off cheerily against Rome, with God on their side.

Not only the blood but the language of those mythical ancestors runs in the Britons' veins: both Britain and Brittany claim to speak 'the language of the people ... up to then [having] been known as Trojan or Crooked [rough] Greek, [which] was called British'.[36] On the French side, Alain Bouchart, in *Grandes croniques de Bretaigne* (1514), confirms that 'le langage breton est le vray et ancient langage de Troye' (the Breton language is the true and ancient language of Troy), thereby justifying its emancipation from Latin culture.[37] The fierce rivalry between France and England over the Trojan ascendancy peaked during the Hundred Years' War, when it was invoked to prove that the English were a mongrel, inferior race.[38] According to Jean Juvénal des Ursins, 'when the Trojans came to France, there they made the Salic law', and Charles V would use the myth retroactively against English claims to his throne.[39] Lydgate's *Troy Book*, filled with references to the war in France, was presented to Henry V in the months following the Treaty of Troyes (1420), a treaty Charles VII sought to sap through Trojan references.[40] By the end of the fifteenth century, the Trojan legend was competing with other tales of origin. A rival tradition was setting up the Gauls as *the* privileged ancestors: being descended from Noah, they were closer to Christianity. In his *Illustration de Gaule et singularité de Troie* (1511), Jean Lemaire de Belges neatly solved several difficulties by making the Gauls ancestors of the Trojans who had migrated as far as Asia Minor. Thus the Franks' arrival was a return to their fatherland, not an invasion: two successive waves of migration reunited people of one blood. Clovis and the Holy Ampulla now figured on the family tree side by side with Pharamond and the Salic law.

Who, of the French and English kings, could legitimately claim to descend from Priam? Which of the two kingdoms best deserved honour for its pleasance, valiance and riches? Written near the end of the Hundred Years' War, the *Débat des hérauts d'armes de France et d'Angleterre* argued that English claims to the island rested neither on history nor law – and even less their claims to France.⁴¹ The line of British kings had been erased by internecine struggles, and replaced by Saxons, one of whom – Inglus, or Anglist – gave Britain his own name, Ingleterre. France's 'auld alliance' with Scotland was based on 'the Trojan origin common to both peoples',⁴² as was the traditional sympathy of the French for all the Celtic enemies of the English Crown.⁴³ The *Débat* arbitrated by Dame Prudence concludes that the 'Angloiz' are 'grans vantoires et mesprisent tout aultruy fait que le leur': braggarts who sneer at others' exploits.

England hit back nearly a century later, under Edward VI, with a symmetrical *Debate between the Heralds of England and France* (1550) by one John Coke, 'clarke of the statutes of the Staple of Westmynster', which vilified the French nation: their Fleur de luce comes from Satan, their holy oil is only good for salads, and their kings support schismatic popes with treasonous plots and money. The legendary British king Arviragus was baptised in 66, long before Clovis. Most of their heroes, Coke contends, are not even French: they have mistranslated into their vulgar tongue hundreds of untrue tales of Charlemagne, Lancelot and others to extol themselves. Every French writer of histories to this day 'devyseth a sondry petigrue for them'. All their sayings are feigned, down to their assumed name: they are not Franks but 'Frantyque men, a name propyce and mete for them'.⁴⁴

New scepticism

Coke's *Debate* comes at the end of a tradition, developed in war 'poems of scorns' that denounce the enemy's false tales. A more objective wave of scepticism had begun half a century earlier with Robert Gaguin, who was the first to cast doubt on his own country's mythology. In his *Compendium de Francorum origine et gestis* (1515), he writes that claims to a Trojan ancestry are dubious, given the contradictions in the sources, none of which date from antiquity: 'Mais voye le Chroniqueur combien loing de la verite il a honteusement escrit / Car au regard de moy ie nay point trouue la vraye source et generation des francoys' (But see the Chronicler, how far from the truth he shamefully wrote / For my own part, I could not find the true source and generation of the French).⁴⁵ His reservations about the Trojan ancestors of Europe greatly irritated French and English chroniclers alike.⁴⁶ Robert Fabyan, who draws heavily on Gaguin's *Compendium* in his *New Chronicles of England and France* (1516), quotes a story of Chilperic's reign 'which is for folys to believe', but expresses no such doubts when he unrolls Monmouth's list of British kings. His 'scepticism' focuses on one source: 'maister Robert Gagwyne, whiche levyth no thynge out of his boke that may sounde to the avauncement of the Frenshe nacyon'.[47] Polydore Vergil, who also drew on Gaguin, raises equally harsh protests when voicing his disbelief of Brutus and Arthur: 'Trulie ther is nothinge more obscure, more uncertaine, or unknowne then the affaires of the Brittons from the beginninge.'[48] This must have tasted particularly bitter, coming from a foreigner named after Priam's youngest son, Polydoros.[49] Thomas Cromwell's protégé John Bale accused Vergil of 'polutynge our Englyshe chronycles most shamefullye with his Romishe lyes and other Italyshe beggerye',[50] while John Caius charged him with having burnt old manuscripts to make sure they would not expose his falsifications.[51]

Vergil made his case worse by claiming that the Romans, not Brutus, brought literature and civility to Britain, in which he was following Tacitus. It was to counter Vergil's attack on the British founding myth, Catherine Lisak argues, that Tudor scholars wove together fragments of various tales in their attempt to present a consistent and honourable story of origins.[52] While this antiquarian interest was directly inspired by the political agenda, it was also motivated by the urgent need to save whatever records might risk destruction in the looting of monasteries. Instead of arguing with Vergil, John Bale and Caius did the kind of syncretic job Lemaire de Belges had done on the French genealogy a generation earlier.[53] In Lemaire, Gaul was first peopled by Samothes, fourth son of Japhet. Bale deftly inserted Samothes between classical and British mythology as the first post-Flood monarch, quoting as his authority 'Friar John Annius of Viterbe' who claimed to have found a list of kings of Celtica in fragments falsely attributed to Berosus the Chaldean.[54]

Like the early Tudor monarchs who collected all the dynastic legitimation they could claim, the chroniclers sought to reconcile Celtic and biblical sources to provide a suitable ancestry for Britannia. Thomas Elyot included Noah's son Japhet in his dictionary.[55] Bale and the anti-Vergilians went further, adopting Samothes as Japhet's descendant, and making him rule over the British Isles before Brutus. In his *Description of England*, which was published as the first part of Holinshed's *Chronicles*, William Harrison considers 'the testimony of Berossos is proof sufficient' that 'this our island ... seemed to be a parcel of the Celtic kingdom, wherof Dis, otherwise called Samothes, one of the sons of Japheth, was the Saturn or original beginner';[56] yet he warns his readers that 'I doo but onlie shewe other mennes conjectures, grounded neverthelesse uppon likelie reasons.'[57] Under the influence of Jean Bodin and other theoreticians historiography had begun to evolve, and in the 1587 edition Harrison is even more cautious: 'I thinke good to advertise the reader that these stories of Samothes, Magus, Sarron, Druis, and Bardus, doo relie onelie upon the authoritie of Berosus, whom most diligent antiquaries doo reject as a fabulous and counterfet author.'[58] The legend must have been wearing thin by the time Prince Hal refers to it: 'Nay, they will be kin to us, or they will fetch it from Japhet' (*2 Henry IV*, II.ii.111–12).

Earlier faith in the truth and utility of history was also wearing thin as a new generation of historians learnt to hone their tools. What Holinshed or Harrison actually believed is beside the point. Samothes ruled an ideal city, until ambition made the giant Albion cross the seas to invade his realm. A golden age was once again destroyed by the same *regni cupido* – desire to rule – that drives all conquerors. Harrison, like Holinshed, is primarily concerned with this spirit of conquest, a constant of English history that repeatedly upsets the initial order.[59] Their concern is both ethical and professional. Each new line erases all facts and traces of the former order, frustrating the historian in his quest for archaeological textual evidence on which to base a genuine history of origins. Samothes's laws and his days of 'excellent wisdom' are now unknown, Harrison writes, 'sith new lords use commonly to give new laws, and conquerors abolish such as were in use before them'.[60] Albion overthrew Samothes and changed the name of the island, which changed again when he in turn was overthrown by Brutus, whose own line ended with Gorboduc's sons. The Government was then 'divided betwixt five kings or rulers, till Dunwallon of Cornewall [Molmutius] overcame them all'. Few kings can be paralleled with this 'Dunwallo (King Henry the Fifth excepted)', for he 'brought the realm to good order, that long before had been torn with civil discord'.[61] His laws endured until the Saxons got the upper hand, and reduced him to the fate of Brutus: 'the certain knowledge so well of the one as of the other is perished and nothing worthy memory left of all their doings'.[62] A faint glimmer of hope remains, however: after doing all they could to abolish the British laws, the Saxons began to relent, '& not so much to abhorre and mislike of the lawes of Mulmutius', when they 'entered into amitie with the British nobilitie and after that began to join in matrimony with the British ladies, as the British barons did with the Saxon frowes'.[63] Once again, two inimical peoples were reconciled in mixed marriages.

However biased by ideology, new tools and methods were being applied to the study of the past. Even supporters of Geoffrey of Monmouth were beginning to distance themselves from his tales. His *Historia regum Britanniae* had done much service, supporting the Tudors' Welsh ancestry and their vision of English dominance over Britain's other components. The kingdoms of Scotland, Wales and Ireland had once been ruled with civility by Brutus's three sons, Locrine, Albanact and Camber, until discord caused the end of the empire and the loss of its name. As Armitage notes, the empire of Great Britain was an invention of Henry VIII's and Somerset's unionist pamphleteers to justify invasions by upholding a Roman image of Britain as the new *res publica*: a Protestant monarchy would restore the island's former political and religious unity. Spenser pursued the good work in *The Faerie Queene* with a line of British kings running from Brutus to Elizabeth I. His dedication to the Empress 'Queen of England France and Ireland and of Virginia' uniquely expanded the royal title to incorporate this new English province of North America in what was 'perhaps the most ambitious and hardline British imperial vision of its time'.[64]

Shakespeare's tongues

However respectful of 'our gracious Empress', young Shakespeare does not seem to have shared Dante's or Spenser's faith in the imperial model. His first and only depiction of empire, in *Titus Andronicus*, shows its decline into a barbarian tyranny that makes Astraea lose heart and forsake the earth – '*Terras Astraea reliquit*; / Be you remem'bred, Marcus, she's gone, she's fled' (IV.iii.4–5) – in direct reference to the iron age in *Metamorphoses* (I, 149–50): '*victa iacet pietas, et virgo caede madentis / ultima caelestum terras Astraea reliquit*' ('piety lay vanquished, and the maiden Astrea, last of the immortals, abandoned the blood-soaked earth'). The dismemberment of the common weal is practised on the mutilated bodies of the Andronici, and on the muted Lavinia, who suffers a far worse fate than her namesake in the *Aeneid*. Marcus Andronicus insists upon the continuity with Troy, the ancestor of both Rome and Shakespeare's London, as, seeing in Lucius a second Aeneas, he recalls 'that baleful burning night / When subtile Greeks surpris'd King Priam's Troy', and denounces the fatal engine '[t]hat gives our Troy, our Rome, the civil wound' (V.iii.83–4, 87).[65] Shakespeare's first image of empire, set up against the remains of the Republic, shows a decadent culture, whose very hero initiates the decadence.[66] Titus's human sacrifice, not on the battlefield, but on the altar of his gods, betrays a lack of faith in his own rituals, as if Roman deities relished human blood, like the ugly idols depicted by Augustine. What follows his transgression replicates not the tale of the murdering twins, but the foundational crime of the Republic: the rape of Lavinia re-enacts the rape of Helen, itself retaliation for the rape of Hesione, the nameless 'old aunt' repeatedly evoked in *Troilus and Cressida*, who was the original cause of the Trojan war; Hercules, who did not receive the promised reward for rescuing her, gave her to his follower Telamon.[67] When Paris was sent to free her from the Greeks, he brought back Helen instead. The Trojan War is itself the repeat of Hercules's earlier sack of Laomedon's kingdom in retaliation for his treachery. Of Laomedon's sons, only Priam was allowed to survive.[68]

Iachimo, on entering Innogen's (or Imogen's) bedroom, takes his own place in a line of rapists: 'Our Tarquin thus / Did softly press the rushes ere he waken'd / The chastity he wounded' (*Cymbeline*, II.ii.12–14). '*Tace, Lucretia*' – this is how Livy begins the tale in his *History of Rome* (I, lviii, 2): 'Shut up, Lucrece. I am Sextus Tarquin; here is a sword in my hand; you will die if you utter a sound'.[69] Ovid shows more sympathy for the heroine in *Fasti* (II, 721–852): she answered never a word. Voice and power of speech and thought itself fled from her breast (797–8). Shut up Lucrece, shut up Lavinia. But Tarquin's is generally deemed a happy fault, which brings about the fall of a tyrannical regime. The Argument to Shakespeare's *The Rape of Lucrece* recalls that the people, when told of this vile deed, were 'so moved, that with one consent and a general acclamation the Tarquins were all exiled, and the state government changed from kings to consuls' (lines 43–5). Yet the political drama has little room in the poem itself, where it is shown through the prism of feminine woe. The siege of Troy takes up one-ninth of the verse: an unnecessary digression, Sidney Lee complains, which 'delays the progress of the story beyond all artistic law'.[70] Though Lee praises the 'exceptional vividness' of the passage, he feels the young poet is showing off, correcting his sources' misapprehensions, to prove he had read widely on the subject. More fruitfully, the philosopher Michèle Le Dœuff points out that here Shakespeare is breaking with tradition, from Livy onwards, by allowing Lucrece an eloquent plea. As she admires the painter's portrayal of Hecuba, 'Lucrece swears he did her wrong, / To give her so much grief, and not a tongue' (lines 1462–3).[71]

While Shakespeare's plays rarely mention Arthurian lore or 'the dreamer Merlin',[72] they are peppered with allusions to Troy – even before the legend reached the height of its popularity on stage, in the last decade of Elizabeth's reign – with references to valiant Hector; wily Ulysses; false Aeneas; perjured Sinon; shallow, beautiful Helen. Maddened Hecuba is the epitome of extreme female woe, Nestor stands for age and wisdom, Troilus is a passionate lover, and Pandarus … a pandar. *Troilus and Cressida* reflects the evolution of the original tale through the Middle Ages, following the *Aeneid* in its preference for the noble Trojans over Homer's deceitful Greeks – there is no equivalent of Hector in the Greek camp, and no Trojan as abject as Achilles. This does not exonerate the Trojans from responsibility for their own destruction, and makes no promise of a blissful future – the foundation of Rome is a long four-and-a-half centuries away. How blissful remains a moot point, explored at length in the Roman plays.

There is no evidence anywhere that Shakespeare shares the notion of 'happy fault' so prominent in the nation's founding myths when he revisits and queries the chroniclers' themes. Henry V's imperial ambitions are framed between his father's advice to busy giddy minds, and the bishops' suspicious assurances that his will be a just war. Shakespeare does not show much interest in the genealogy of the French monarchy. Indeed, he contents himself with a metrical rearrangement of Archbishop Chicheley's speech in Holinshed, including an erroneous reference to 'King Lewis the tenth'.[73] He may have saved Edward Hall's more correct and more verbose oration for Polonius: 'In whiche realme, to reherse what noble persons, what beautiful cities, what fertile regions, what substancial marchantes and what plentifull riuers are conteigned and included, I assure you that time should rather faile then matter shoulde wax skant.'[74]

Whatever doubts might be raised about Pharamond's descent, the stage Henry is aware that the French king's title to France is far stronger than his own to England when he acknowledges 'The fault / My father made in compassing the crown' (*Henry V*, IV.i.290–1). Before him, Richard of Gloucester had stood on stage between two bishops, to court public opinion. The accuracy of records was severely tested in *Richard III*, not just by the wise child's asking wise questions about Julius Caesar, but by pert little York, who is caught spreading vile stories about his Uncle Richard. Hall, Shakespeare's main source for the early histories, does attempt to record varying accounts, most noticeably when he reports both Polydore Vergil's and Thomas More's versions of the reign of Richard III, but he imputes events impartially to pagan Fortune or divine justice.[75] Holinshed includes large extracts of Hall and More, copied verbatim. If Shakespeare learnt something more from Holinshed than Hall, it is not in their pious accounts of the last Plantagenets, but in Holinshed's problematised historiography of the Roman conquest, when admired historians of antiquity stood in critical comparison against the native breed of chroniclers.

True to tradition, Shakespeare's Henry V, like Richard III, alternates ruthless armed conquest and courtship in his attack on maiden cities.[76] The discordance is blatant between the epic tale told by the chorus and the facts performed on stage by Henry's orders. Even before the battle cements the national union he has successfully engineered, the *conditor alme* initiates the telling of his own legend 'from this day to the ending of the world'.[77] His supporters provide 'their conquering Caesar' with a full line of victorious ancestors, plus a sly reference to Alexander the Pig, who killed his friend, evoking Prince Hal's cruel rejection of Falstaff. The fact of conquest, Roman or Norman, had been subject to endless revisionism. Sir John Fortescue (c. 1395–c. 1477) ignored the Roman conquest in his drive to strengthen the myth of a common law born and bred on English soil, though he admitted the fact of the Norman invasion, which introduced the use of Law French in the English courts of justice.[78] In 1602, Edward Coke denied this and argued that William the Conqueror had transported 'the excellencie and equitie of the Lawes of England' back to Normandy.[79] To Bradin Cormack, *Henry V* and *Richard III* represent not the glory but the impermanence of conquest. We remember not an event, but a pattern, a history of invasion and counter-invasion since the Normans and the long history of English losses on the Continent: 'Put simply, 1485 is 1066.'[80] Englishness itself is a hybrid, a point echoed in *Cymbeline*.

Near the end of the canon, *Cymbeline* pithily sums up Shakespeare's survey of the British past. Most critics identify the Queen with retrograde isolationism, and note that her account of the Roman struggle to subdue Britain is confirmed by Caesar's *Gallic Wars*.[81] Actually she does not need the classics to feed her anger. Harping again on the theme of unity, Holinshed devotes several chapters to the hard time Caesar was given when he attempted to land, and found his enemies 'readie to resist him', for they 'had by general consent appointed the whole rule and order of all things touching the warre unto Cassivellane'.[82] A blueprint for Henry V's victorious incorporation of Welsh, Scottish and Irish captains into his English army, this Cassibellan, who 'had bin at continuall warre with other rulers, and cities of the land', was now elected 'chiefe governour of all their armie, permitting the order and rule of all things touching the defense of their countrie against the Romans onelie to him'.[83]

The legitimacy of the tribute to Rome, a central issue in the chronicle, was still highly sensitive in Jacobean England, as appears from the troubled history of John Selden's research into the origin of tithes.[84] It is treated on stage through a brilliant display of anachronism: early modern corrupt Italy in the guise of the villain Iachimo is defeated by Celtic Britain, whose victorious king now freely agrees to pay tribute to Augustan Rome. This neat way of settling cultural, as distinct from political, debts thinly disguises a critical view of their suppression in one sweep by the Welsh monarch Henry Tudor.[85] Shakespeare's Cymbeline, educated at the court of Augustus, seems to embody these opposites when his wife and stepson are determined to revive ancient British laws. His programme to repair the laws of 'our ancestor' Mulmutius is a lost cause. Cloten's claim that 'Britain's a world / By itself' (III.i.12–13), the Queen's argument for 'the natural bravery of your isle' (III.i.18), are obliquely answered by Cymbeline's lost sons. Belarius's idealised rustic abode is to them 'a cell of ignorance', a pinching prison: 'We have seen nothing: / We are beastly' (III.iii.33, 39–40). The fact that Guiderius goes disguised under the name 'Polydore', its only occurrence in the canon, may well be Shakespeare's payment of a personal debt to the first competent historian he read. The boys have no time for pastoral delights or archaic nostalgias: while Belarius sounds like Duke Senior in Arden, they do not wish to live happy secluded lives; they are bored in their low-roofed cave and crave for action. With their support, Cymbeline rejects insularity and offers a civilised way out of the narrow lane where Posthumus Leonatus and his Welsh brothers win the day, by paying tribute to the larger model of independence, Roman law and continental culture.[86]

At the end of the play, families and broken couples are reunited, but before this happy conclusion, a *polyanagnorisis* has rehearsed all the tragic possibilities of earlier plots.[87] The demons of jealous envy, ambition, conservatism, xenophobia are overcome. The Italian traitor is chastised and, best of all, his plot has failed. Innogen and Posthumus escape the double suicide that was the usual fate of thwarted lovers, not through any exceptional talent, but by a faith that wins against all odds. Innogen's victory over fate begins when she wakes up near a corpse dressed in her husband's clothes: instead of doing a Juliet, Thisbe or Cleopatra, she moves on to live and bring his murderer to justice. It is by disguise and error that she comes through, a tribute to the theatre as your only providential mythmaker. Thanks to an accumulation of mistakes, law is restored, and tragedy defeated. Old myths of insularity are laid to rest. The reunited characters can now piece out one nation with their layers of imperfections; native or imported customs; exotic tales; and that daunting enemy to purity of blood, mixed marriages.

So what is it that foundation myths need to found? Not brass, nor stone, nor earth, nor boundless seas, but some elusive, glamorous quality that must endlessly shift and transform meanings to adapt the tale to a new cause, in a newly changed world. Claims for territory and authority that used to be supported by brute force of arms had to be fought with other, more elaborate means such as diplomacy, proofs – true or fake – of time-honoured legitimacy, poetic narratives committing them to memory and recording them for future ages. The archaeology of England, of all Europe, showed layers of conquests and destructions that had erased from the earth splendid cities like Troy, their common ancestor elect. Virgil's replacement of the original wolfish twins' story by a tale of peaceful and prosperous marriage suggested an alternative to fratricidal rivalries. Centuries later, dreams of empire remained as potent as ever, but the chroniclers were turning into modern historians, growing more attuned to the collateral damages caused in the records by the conquerors' demands, lighting the way to Shakespeare's Dantesque journey through the ancient hells of history.

Notes

1. Marc Bloch's *Apologie pour l'histoire ou métier d'historien* was published posthumously in 1944; March Bloch, *The Historian's Craft*, trans. Peter Putnam (Manchester: Manchester University Press, 1992 [1954]), pp. 25–6 (29).
2. Colette Beaune, *Naissance de la nation France* (Paris: Gallimard, 1985), p. 39.
3. Nicole Gilles, *Les croniques et annales de France, depuis la destruction de Troye…*, Vol. I (Paris: Gabriel Buon, 1566), sig. A2r.
4. Johann Gottlieb Fichte published *Reden an die deutsche Nation* in 1808, after Prussia's defeat at Jena. Based on Tacitus, his text provided arguments for the *Blut und Boden* creed; Johann Gottlieb Fichte, *Addresses to the German Nation*, ed. Gregory Moore (Cambridge: Cambridge University Press, 2009).
5. Anne Lombard-Jourdan, *Aux origines de Carnaval* (Paris: Odile Jacob, 2005), pp. 261–7.
6. Marc Bloch, *The Royal Touch: Sacred Monarchy and Scrofula in England and France*, trans. J. E. Anderson (London: Routledge and Kegan Paul, 1973), p. 28.
7. In 1599 Thomas Platter counted fifty-eight statues: 'Description de Paris par Thomas Platter le jeune, de Bâle', *Mémoires de la Société de l'histoire de Paris*, 28 (1896), p. 180.
8. Jacques Le Goff, 'Saint Louis', in *Héros du moyen âge: le saint et le roi* (Paris: Gallimard, 2004), pp. 752, 846, 841.
9. Jean de Joinville's *Chroniques des croisades* (1309) offer narratives of Richard the Lionheart's crusade.
10. Matthew Paris, 'The King's letter of complaint to the Pope', in *Chronica majora*, trans. J. A. Giles, published as *Matthew Paris's English History from the Year 1235 to 1273*, 3 vols (London: Henry G. Bohn, 1852–54), Vol. II (1853), p. 400. Paris's *Chronica* pursues and amplifies Roger of Wendover's *Flores historiarum* (written c. 1201–34), which begins with the Creation.
11. Gérard Soulier, *L'Europe, histoire, civilisation, institutions* (Paris: Armand Colin, 1994), p. 48.
12. A theme developed in the *Songe du vergier*, attr. Evrard de Trémaugon (d. 1386), ed. Marion Schnerb-Lièvre, 2 vols (Paris: CNRS, 1982), Vol. I, pp. 53–7.

13   John Foxe, *Actes and Monuments* (London: John Day, 1570), Book IV, p. 443. Also known as *Foxe's Book of Martyrs*.

14   Dante Alighieri, *The Comedy of Dante Alighieri*, trans. Dorothy L. Sayers: *Cantica I Hell (L'Inferno)* and *Cantica II Purgatory (Il Purgatorio)* (Harmondsworth: Penguin, 1963–76 [1955–62]).

15   Lorenzo Valla, *On the Donation of Constantine* (1525), trans. G. W. Bowersock (Cambridge, MA: Harvard University Press, 2007). Cranmer included it in his *Collectanea satis copiosa* (1530) to prove the pope's usurpation of his sovereignty.

16   See Walter Ullmann, 'This realm of England is an empire', *Journal of Ecclesiastical History*, 30:2 (1979), 175–203 (p. 184).

17   See Mauro Sarti and Mauro Fattorini, *De claris archigymnasii bononiensis professoribus...*, 2 vols (Bologna: n.p., 1888), Vol. I, pp. 103–13.

18   David Armitage, *The Ideological Origins of the British Empire* (Cambridge: Cambridge University Press, 2000), p. 30.

19   See also Jacques Poucet, 'L'*Enéide* et la tradition prévirgilienne', *Folia electronica classica*, 4 (2002), http://bcs.fltr.ucl.ac.be/FE/04/tradition.html (accessed 21 April 2016).

20   Augustine of Hippo, *The City of God*, trans. John Healey, ed. and rev. R. G. V. Tasker (London: Dent, 1945), Vol. I, XV, 5, pp. 64–5.

21   Virgil, *The Aeneid: A New Prose Translation*, trans. David West (Harmondsworth: Penguin, 1991), p. 45. All references to the *Aeneid* in this chapter are to this edition.

22   Richard Marienstras, *Shakespeare au XXIe siècle: petite introduction aux tragédies* (Paris: Editions de Minuit, 2000), p. 105. Ben Kiernan also describes Virgil's account of the fall of Troy as a genocide in *Blood and Soil: A World History of Genocide and Extermination from Sparta to Darfur* (New Haven: Yale University Press, 2007), pp. 60–3.

23   A prose version of Benoît de Sainte-Maure's *Roman de Troie* (c. 1170) was integrated into the *Histoire ancienne jusqu'à César*, in its second version (c. 1340, Naples), replacing Dares Phrygius's *De excidio Trojae historia*. See the introduction to this volume on the medieval Trojan traditions and their enduring success.

24   See Jacques Poucet, 'L'origine troyenne des peuples d'Occident au Moyen Age et à la Renaissance: un exemple de parenté imaginaire et d'idéologie politique', *Les études classiques*, 72 (2004), 75–107.

25   The Franks, a group of Germanic tribes, lived on both sides of the Rhine. See Alain Bossuat, 'Les origines troyennes: leur rôle dans la littérature historique', *Annales de Normandie*, 8:2 (1958), 187–97 (p. 190).

26   Gilles, *Croniques et annales de France*, Vol. I, year iii.c.xxix, sig. ix. Marcomir is designated as a son of Priam in the *Gesta regum Francorum* (c. 727).

27   Gilles, *Croniques et annales de France*, Vol. I, sigs vii–viii, x–xii.

28   Philippe Mouskes chronicles the story of the Franks up to 1242, anchoring their origins in Troy, *Chronique rimée de Philippe Mouskes ... par le Baron de Reiffenberg*,

2 vols, Collection de chroniques belges inédites (Brussels: Hayez, 1836–45), Vol. I, p. 8, line 163.

29 Michel de Montaigne, *The Essays or Morall, Politike and Militarie Discourses of Lo: Michaell de Montaigne* …, trans. John Florio (London: printed by Val. Sims for Edward Bount, 1603), II, 36 (p. 432).

30 Aeneas Sylvius (Pope Pius II) limits this ascendancy to the Romans in his *Cosmographia*, in *Opera omnia* (Basel: Henricus Petri, 1551), esp. 'De Asia', lxvii, p. 349, and 'De Europa', xxxviii, p. 433. See Margaret Meserve, *Empires of Islam in Renaissance Historical Thought* (Cambridge, MA: Harvard University Press, 2008).

31 'Comment est descendus mon dit tres redoubté et tres puissant seigneur du hault, noble et excellent sang des Troyens' (Jean Wauquelin), and 'Second Hector' (Georges Chastellain), quoted in Wilma Keesman, 'Troje in de middeleeuwse literatuur: antiek verleden in dienst van eigen tijd', *Literatuur: tijdscrift over nederlandse letterkunde*, 4 (1987), 257–65 (p. 262).

32 See the introduction to this volume, and Dominique Goy-Blanquet, 'Shakespeare, Burgundy, and the design in the arras', in Jean-Christophe Mayer (ed.), *Representing France and the French in Early Modern English Drama* (Newark: Delaware University Press, 2008), pp. 49–67.

33 Bossuat, 'Les origines troyennes', p. 192.

34 Geoffrey of Monmouth, *The History of the Kings of Britain [Historia regum Britanniae]*, trans. and intr. Lewis Thorpe (Harmondsworth: Penguin, 1966), IX, iv.

35 *Ibid.*, p. 232.

36 *Ibid.*, p. 72. 'Curvum Graecum', rough Greek, is probably the Latin translation of Welsh 'Cam Roeg', a pun on 'Cym Raeg', the native word for the Welsh language. See A. O. H. Jarman, *Sieffre o Fynwy: Geoffrey of Monmouth* (Cardiff: Wales University Press, 1966), p. 29.

37 Alain Bouchart, *Grandes croniques de Bretaigne*, ed. Marie-Louise Auger and Gustave Jeanneau, 3 vols (Paris: CNRS, 1986–98), Vol. I (1986), I.ii.1, p. 82.

38 See Bossuat, 'Les origines troyennes', pp. 187–97.

39 Jean Juvénal des Ursins, *Ecrits politiques de Jean Juvénal des Ursins*, ed. Peter S. Lewis (Paris: Klincksieck, 1978–93), Vol. I (1978), p. 156. Beaune, *Naissance de la nation France*, pp. 269–73.

40 The treaty was signed on 21 May 1420; the *Troy Book* was completed in the summer or autumn of 1420. Lydgate followed Guido delle Colonne's *Historia destructionis Troiae* (1287), but expanded it to over 30,000 lines, incorporating many other Trojan tales in circulation: Walter F. Schirmer, *John Lydgate: A Study in the Culture of the XVth Century*, trans. Ann E. Keep (London: Methuen, 1961), p. 43.

41 Written between 1453 and 1461, authorship unknown; *Le débat des hérauts d'armes de France et d'Angleterre suivi de 'The Debate between the Heralds of England*

and *France' by John Coke*, ed. L. C. A. Pannier and Paul Meyer (Paris: Firmin Didot, 1877), pp. 7–11.

42 Philippe Contamine, 'Trojanerabstammung', in Liselotte Lutz *et al.* (eds), *Lexikon des Mittelalters*, 9 vols (Munich: Artemis, LexMa and Metzler, 1977–98), Vol. VIII (Munich: LexMa, 1997), col. 1041. The 'auld alliance' is the name later given to the 1295 treaty between Philip the Fair and John Balliol against Edward I.

43 Bossuat, 'Les origines troyennes', pp. 196–7.

44 John Coke, *The Debate between the Heraldes of England and France, Compiled by John Coke* (London: Rycharde Wyer, 1550). I am quoting Coke from *Le Débat des hérauts d'armes*, pp. 110–12.

45 Pierre Desrey, *Les croniques de France* (Paris: Galiot du Pré, 1515), Part I, p. 1, translated from Robert Gaguin's *Compendium de origine et gestis Francorum* (Paris: Pierre Le Dru, 1495) at the request of Charles VIII. Much of the *Compendium* was an abridged version of the *Grandes chroniques de France* that Primat, monk of the Abbey of Saint-Denis, wrote at the request of Louis IX, covering the history of the Franks from the Trojans to his own time. These chronicles were augmented under successive reigns. See Bernard Guenée, 'The *Grandes chroniques de France*: The *roman* of kings', trans. John Goodman, in Pierre Nora (ed.), *Rethinking France: Les lieux de mémoire*, 4 vols (Chicago: University of Chicago Press, 2001–10), Vol. IV (2010): *Histories and Memories*, pp. 205–30.

46 See Sylvie Charrier, *Recherches sur l'œuvre latine en prose de Robert Gaguin (1433–1501)* (Paris: Champion, 1996), pp. 454, 517.

47 Robert Fabyan, *The New Chronicles of England and France, in Two Parts; by R. F. (1516)*, ed. Henry Ellis (London: Rivington, 1811), pp. 91, 415.

48 Polydore Vergil, *Anglica historia* (1534), in *Polydore Vergil's English History* ..., ed. Sir Henry Ellis (London: Camden Society, 1846), p. 33.

49 In Homer, *Iliad*, XX, 407–20, Polydoros is stabbed in the back by Achilles.

50 John Bale, Preface, in *A Brefe Chronycle Concernynge the Examinacyon and Death of the Blessed Martyr of Christ Syr Iohan Oldecastell ...* (Antwerp: Hans Luft?, 1544), p. 5.

51 John Caius, *De antiquitate Cantebrigiensis Academiae ...*, published anonymously (London: Henry Bynneman, 1568), then under his name after his death, as *Historiae Cantebrigiensis academiae...* (London: John Daye, 1574); translated in Sir Henry Ellis (ed.), *Three Books of Polydore Vergil's English History* (London: Camden Society, 1844), p. xxiii.

52 Catherine Lisak, 'Shakespeare et la Cité de Samothès', in Dominique Goy-Blanquet (ed.), *Le poète dans la cité: de Platon à Shakespeare* (Brussels: In'hui/Le Cri, 2003), pp. 64–83. John Leland retorted with *Assertio inclytissimi Arturii regis Britanniae* (London: R. Wolfe, 1544), John Prise of Brecon with a *Fides Historiae Britanniae* (1546) and a *Historiae Brytannicae defensio* (published in 1573, after

'This realm is an empire' 83

his death, by Henry Bynneman), which were also refutations of Polydore Vergil's attacks.

53   See Jack P. Cunningham, 'England's Adam: The short career of the Giant Samothes in English Reformation thought', *Early Modern Literary Studies*, 16:1 (2012), http://extra.shu.ac.uk/emls/16-1/adam.htm (accessed 23 April 2016). Bale's version was accepted by Leland, Caius, Lambarde and Holinshed; questioned by Stow; and ignored by Camden: see Thomas D. Kendrick, *British Antiquity* (London: Methuen, 1950), pp. 59–76.

54   Giovanni Nanni, known as Annio da Viterbo, was the first to establish a direct link between Samothes and the history of the British Isles, in a work published in Rome in 1498, translated by Richard Linch, *An Historical Treatise of the Travels of Noah unto Europe: Containing the First Inhabitation and People Thereof ... Even until the First Building of Troy by Dardanus* (London: Adam Islip, 1601).

55   Thomas Elyot, *The Dictionary of Syr Thomas Elyot Knyght* (London: Thomas Berthelet, 1538). Juan Luis Vives had pointed out in his commentary to his edition of Augustine's *De civitate Dei* (Basel: Froben, 1522), VII, 4, that Samothes was nowhere mentioned in the Bible.

56   William Harrison, *The Description of England*, ed. Georges Edelen (Washington: Folger Shakespeare Library; New York: Dover Publications, 1994 [1968]), pp. 162–3. Unless otherwise stated, all references to Harrison are to this edition, which follows the 1587 edition as published in Raphael Holinshed's *Chronicles* (William Harrison, *The Description of England*, in Raphael Holinshed, *The First and Second Volumes of Chronicles* (London: Henry Denham, 1587), Vol. II: *The Historie of England*), omitting the historical and topographical books. See Edelen's introduction, pp. xvn1 and xxxiv–xxxv, on Harrison's *Description* and his extensive revisions between the 1577 and 1587 editions.

57   William Harrison, *The Description of England*, in Raphael Holinshed, *The Firste Volume of the Chronicles of England, Scotland and Ireland*, 2 vols (London: Henry Bynneman, 1577), Vol. I: *The Historie of England*, p. 1.

58   Harrison, *The Description of England* (1587), Chapter 3 ('Of the giant Albion'), p. 6.

59   Lisak, 'Shakespeare et la Cité de Samothès', pp. 73–8.

60   Harrison, *Description of England*, Chapter 9, p. 163.

61   *Ibid.*, Chapter 9, pp. 163–4; on Dunwallon, p. 163. Reprinted substantially in Holinshed, *The First and Second Volumes of Chronicles*, Vol. I, 'third book of the Description', Chapter 9 ('Of the lawes of England since hir first inhabitation'), pp. 176–7.

62   Harrison, *Description of England*, Chapter 9, p. 163.

63   *Ibid.*, p. 164. Holinshed, *The First and Second Volumes of Chronicles*, Vol. I, 'Of the lawes of England since hir first inhabitation', p. 177.

64   Armitage, *Ideological Origins*, p. 53; Spenser, *Faerie Queene*, II.x.5, 13–14. In his *View of the Present State of Ireland*, Spenser stresses the British ascendancy to

support his argument for the suppression of Gaelic Irish and reform of degenerated Old English settlers. Edmund Spenser, *A View of the Present State of Ireland*, ed. William Lindsay Renwick (Oxford: Clarendon Press, 1970), esp. pp. 48–68.

65 Eugene M. Waith attributes those lines to Marcus in his edition of the play (Oxford: Oxford University Press, 1984), as does the Riverside edition, used here. Jonathan Bate, in William Shakespeare, *Titus Andronicus*, ed. Jonathan Bate, The Arden Shakespeare (London: Routledge, 1995), attributes them to a Roman Lord, as do Stanley Wells, Gary Taylor et al. (eds), *The Oxford Shakespeare: The Complete Works* (Oxford: Clarendon Press, 1988).

66 Bate, in Shakespeare, *Titus Andronicus*, ed. Bate, p. 17, considers that Shakespeare 'collapses the whole of Roman history … into a single action'. Lodge's near-contemporary *Wounds of Civil War* shows how 'civill discords and domesticke broies' (I.i.302) destroy the Republic when Scilla begins to 'gape with murder for a monarchy' (V.iii.75); Thomas Lodge, *The Wounds of Civil War*, ed. Joseph W. Houppert (London: Edward Arnold, 1970).

67 On Hesione, see Atsuhiko Hirota, 'The memory of Hesione: Intertextuality and social amnesia in *Troilus and Cressida*', *Actes des congrès de la Société française Shakespeare, Shakespeare et la mémoire*, 30 (2013), 43–56.

68 See J. M. Scammell, 'The capture of Troy by Heracles', *Classical Journal*, 29:6 (March 1934), 418–28.

69 This has been discussed by Michèle Le Dœuff in a paper on 'Lucrèce et la République', presented on 19 March 2013 at a CRAL (EHESS/CNRS) symposium on philosophy, aesthetics and gender issues.

70 Sidney Lee (ed.), *Shakespeare's Lucrece* (Oxford: Clarendon, 1905), introduction, p. 8.

71 Le Dœuff, 'Lucrèce et la République'. See also Chapter 1 (Yves Peyré) on the imagery of blood and blushing that provides a further link between the plight of Lucrece and the embedded story of Troy.

72 Hotspur's ironical comment on Glendower's superstitious beliefs in *1 Henry IV*, III.i.148.

73 *Henry V*, I.ii.77, emended to 'Louis the ninth' in William Shakespeare, *King Henry V*, ed. T. W. Craik, The Arden Shakespeare (London: Routledge, 1995). Holinshed, *The First and Second Volumes of Chronicles*, 'Henrie the fift, prince of Wales', Vol. III, p. 545, has 'King Lewes also the tenth otherwise called saint Lewes'.

74 Edward Hall correctly mentions 'Lewes also the ninth whome the Frenchemen call Sainct Lewes'; Edward Hall, *The Union of the Two Noble and Illustre Famelies of Lancastre and Yorke. Hall's Chronicle*, ed. Henry Ellis (London: J. Johnson, 1809), p. 51.

75 Ibid., pp. 286–7. See Samuel Kinser (ed.), *Memoirs of Philippe de Commynes*, trans. Isabelle Cazeaux (Columbia: University of South Carolina Press, 1973 [1969]), IV, x, p. 283.

76 Janice Valls-Russell (Chapter 4) suggests that this is already present in the rhetoric of *King John*.
77 See Lydgate's 'Devotion of the fowls', in *A Selection from the Minor Poems of Dan John Lydgate*, ed. J. O. Halliwell (London: Percy Society, 1840), Vol. II, p. 78. According to Schirmer, *John Lydgate*, p. 275, 'Lydgate was probably *not* the author' of this poem.
78 John Fortescue, *On the Laws and Governance of England*, ed. Shelley Lockwood (Cambridge: Cambridge University Press, 1997), pp. 26–7, 66.
79 Edward Coke, 'To the reader', in *Le tierce part des reportes* (London: Thomas Wight, 1602), sig. E1r–v.
80 Bradin Cormack, *A Power to Do Justice: Jurisdiction, English Literature, and the Rise of Common Law, 1509–1625* (Chicago: University of Chicago Press, 2007), p. 204.
81 Julius Caesar, *Gallic Wars*, IV and V. See J. Clinton Crumley, 'Questioning history in *Cymbeline*', *Studies in English Literature, 1500–1900*, 41:2 (2001), 297–316.
82 Holinshed, *The First and Second Volumes of Chronicles*, Vol. II, 'third book of the historie of England', Chapter 14, p. 28.
83 *Ibid.*
84 See G. J. Toomer, 'Selden's "Historie of tithes": Genesis, publication, aftermath', *Huntington Library Quarterly*, 65:3–4 (2002), 345–78.
85 See Andrew Hadfield, *Shakespeare and Republicanism* (Cambridge: Cambridge University Press, 2005), pp. 165–6.
86 Leah S. Marcus, *Puzzling Shakespeare* (Berkeley: University of California Press, 1988), pp. 124–5. Cormack, *A Power to Do Justice*, pp. 243–53.
87 *Polyanagnorisis* is the term Philip Edwards uses in *Threshold of a Nation* (Cambridge: Cambridge University Press, 1979), p. 91.

4

Trojan shadows in Shakespeare's *King John*

Janice Valls-Russell

IN THE EARLY 1920S, the German scholar Alois Brandl suggested that Constance's speeches in III.iv of *King John* (1595–96) might be derived from the scene in which Andromache pleads with Ulysses on behalf of Astyanax in Seneca's *Troades*, though A. R. Braunmuller found Brandl's 'argument of influence ... unconvincing'.[1] Were there only that single scene, Brandl's suggestion might appear tenuous and Braunmuller's caution legitimate. I shall argue here that Andromache and her suppliant rhetoric stand at the heart of a wider Trojan presence in a play that Francis Meres described as a tragedy in 1598 and that critics have long accepted is not merely a 'history', but 'tragical-historical'. *King John*, I would suggest, is 'tragical-historical-mythological', a genre overlooked by Polonius (*Hamlet*, II.ii.396–402). I wish to discuss what does not seem to be there: I mean the Trojan matter of the play, which powerfully structures and textures the scenes of the siege of Angiers and, more specifically, the tragic fates of Constance and Arthur. Besides a close textual reading in the light of the Trojan material that was available to Shakespeare and his contemporaries, such as Seneca's *Troades* and Jasper Heywood's translation of the play, I shall also be referring to some directorial choices of Deborah Warner, Josie Rourke, David Giles, Gregory Doran and Laurent Pelly, since stagings are apt to generate a liberating energy that taps back into the dramatist's original process of creation and illuminates the text. Albeit that Troy is never mentioned, it is there, in the powerfully laden imagery and rhetoric: a presence that I term an aesthetics of shadows – hence the title of this chapter.

Polonius belonged to a culture in which 'mythological' material informed tragedy and the writing of national history, inscribing events and genealogies in a wider picture. Even though King John urges the Bastard to '[b]e Mercury, set feathers to thy heels' (IV.ii.174), he is no Jupiter, unable to control darker forces such as Ate, to whom his mother is compared, '[S]tirring [him] to blood and strife' (II.i.63). This reference anticipates the unleashing of uncontrollable events, a return to the Ovidian 'iron age' (IV.i.60), a period of strife that causes Astraea to abandon the earth, and that young Arthur remembers in the 'torture chamber' scene, in a multi-layered reference to Hubert's 'hot irons', to John's rule and, perhaps, to the canons' 'iron indignation 'gainst [the] walls' of Angiers (II.i.212).[2] As Agamemnon recalls in the *Iliad* (XIX, 85ff.), Ate's shadow hangs over the birth of Hercules, who provides the main explicit mythological motif in *King John*, with references anchored in the script – 'It [the lion-skin] lies as sightly upon the back of him / As great Alcides' [shows] upon an ass' (II.i.143–4) – and is visually confirmed by the presence on stage of a lion's skin, worn by the duke of Austria, as noted by the Bastard (136–46). Hercules is conflated with larger-than-life Richard the Lionheart, whose legacy is central to the play's family, dynastic and diplomatic conflicts. Richard's illegitimate son, the Bastard, links Hercules and Richard (I.i.261–7) and inscribes himself in that twofold lineage when he challenges Austria's usurpation of the heroic role, killing him (III.ii) and recovering the legacy (the lion's skin).[3] Austria's shallow parody of courage and values, as he forsakes his pledge to defend Arthur, also allows a link with the Omphale story, which is interwoven with the image of the Amazons, this classical reference being itself conflated with references to Roman history in the Bastard's contemptuous address to the English rebels:[4]

> And you degenerate, you ingrate revolts,
> You bloody Neroes, ripping up the womb
> Of your dear mother England, blush for shame;
> For your own ladies and pale-visag'd maids
> Like Amazons come tripping after drums,
> Their thimbles into armèd gauntlets change,
> Their needles to lances, and their gentle hearts
> To fierce and bloody inclination.
>
> (V.ii.151–8)

The play contains no explicit allusion to Troy, to Andromache or to any other character from the Trojan story. Yet Ate provides an entry-point, as does Salisbury's description of Britain as 'clippe[d] about' by 'Neptune's arms' (V.ii.34) – a danger-fraught embrace, when one remembers the sea-god's ambivalence towards Troy and his hostility to the Greeks on their homeward voyage. What I shall consider above all is a cumulative effect of contextual and internal evidence, approaching this as an instance of 'Shakespeare's deep imaginative collocations', the creative process Ruth Morse unravels in her discussion of Pygmalion in the closing essay of this volume and that, in *King John*, is both textual and spatial.[5]

Trojan collocations

Hercules and Neptune lead into Trojan territory via what A. E. B. Coldiron describes as 'medievally mediated' tropes of Troy that reached England both through Caxton's edition, in 1474/75, of a French version of Raoul Lefèvre's *Recoeil des hystoires de Troyes* (c. 1464), and through his own earlier translation of 1473/74.[6] This *Recuyell of the Historyes of Troye* was edited right into the seventeenth century and played a key role in establishing a tradition of transposing the Trojan story into a medieval ambience: gods became kings, kings vassals, Greek and Trojan heroes were depicted as knights, while the city of Troy was described as a medieval city – and illustrated as such in manuscripts and early editions.

The Trojan story has a way of forcing its way into scenarios of destruction and political violence, as in Thomas Lodge's Roman play, *The Wounds of Civil War* (1588), in a brief but powerful evocation of the city's destruction and the ensuing vulnerability of its female inhabitants.[7] Furthermore, Trojan material is resonant in a play that negotiates medieval dynastic, diplomatic and religious issues that still carried tricky implications during the reign of Elizabeth. As Dominique Goy-Blanquet demonstrates in Chapter 3, European myths of origins, particularly those of France, Burgundy and England, relied on genealogies that reached back to founding mythological epics, with the English monarchy claiming descent from Priam via Aeneas and Brutus the Trojan. Troy underlay universal and national chronicles, which were regularly updated, as the process of mythmaking combined with rhetorical historiography to fashion what Morse terms 'imagined pasts' that were politically acceptable, and enduring – Thomas Heywood pursued this in *Troia Britanica* (1609), albeit with tongue-in-cheek scepticism.[8] Trojan motifs weave their way through Arthurian and other monarchical romances without much explicit acknowledgement: the structural parallels are, however, a kind of acknowledgement for readers who recognised them. In *King John*, such processes include the Hercules/Richard analogies and are evident in the ways Shakespeare revisits the historical material he found in sources such as Holinshed's *Chronicles*, reworking setting, sequences and characters for dramatic effects and scenographic considerations. Mirabeau (in the chronicle) becomes Angiers; through stagecraft metonymy, the theatre's upper gallery and props such as banners and pennants invite the audience to see the playhouse simultaneously as a fortified city and as a venue from which a citizen may speak on behalf of a besieged population and challenge royal authority. From the outset, mother–child relationships are staged as central to the shaping of personal and collective destiny, with three mothers of three sons, all related, present in the opening act. Two of these mothers are powerful, political antagonists: Queen Eleanor, King John's influential mother, and Constance, a would-be queen or regent, whose husband, Geoffrey (John's elder brother), would have reigned but for his untimely death, making their son Arthur a claimant to the throne. (The third is Lady Falconbridge, a former mistress of Richard the Lionheart and mother of the illegitimate Bastard.) Family loyalties – or lack of them – are entangled with dynastic issues. The symmetry of the two queens' concerns and their attempts at political agency continue right up to their near-simultaneous deaths, which are announced in a single speech (IV.ii.119–24).

Shakespeare's approach is twofold. He reinforces the dramatic effects by compressing the action, highlighting the volatility of pledges and staging in rapid sequence John's march on Angiers, Louis and Blanche's betrothal, Louis's invasion of England, Constance and Eleanor's deaths, Arthur's tragic fall, and John's death.[9] Elsewhere, as Braunmuller points out, he 'elaborates certain emotional moments – especially Constance's grief in Act III, Scene iv and the dialogue between Arthur and Hubert in Act IV, Scene i'.[10] The dramatic intensity arises from this reworking of chronicle sources and *The Troublesome Raigne of King John* – if one accepts the chronology that places this play before *King John*:[11] Shakespeare pares away material here, expands it there, heightening contrasts and reinforcing the sense of isolation and drama to obtain sharply delineated visual and rhetorical moments that are more suggestive of mythological narratives than of messier historical accounts. Constance is no longer the historical remarried widow, but a solitary, tragic figure; Arthur is no troop-leading prince, no 'moralizing young man but a small boy crying out in his innocence ("Is it my fault that I was Geoffrey's son?")'[12] – a child, as in *The Troublesome Raigne of King John*, and he is perceived as such by Hubert – 'pretty child' (IV.i.129) – and the courtiers – 'sweet child', 'poor child', 'tender kinsman' (IV.ii.81, 97, 58).

Mother and son are framed by a picture of domination and discord, with the high walls in Acts II and IV recalling medieval military architecture and besieged Troy – which Thomas Heywood makes explicit in *1 Edward IV* (1599), when another Falconbridge stands outside London:

> Yet stand we in the sight of upreared Troy,
> And suck the air she draws. Our very breath

Flies from our nostrils, warm unto the walls.
We beard her bristling spires, her battled towers,
And proudly stand and gaze her in the face.

(Scene ix, 1–5)[13]

As in Heywood's play, the verbal and physical sense of towering verticality is key to the dramatic tension of a number of scenes in *King John*. Directors have conveyed this in a variety of designs, from ladders set up against a wall in Deborah Warner's minimalist production for the Other Place, in Stratford-upon-Avon, in 1988, to the use of the upper levels of the Swan Theatre, also in Stratford, in Gregory Doran's and Josie Rourke's productions, in 2001 and 2006. Breaking with the lavish, more or less accurately historicised sets of the nineteenth and early twentieth centuries, such productions forgo historical reconstruction and invite audiences to step back and engage with the play's mythical dimension. Laurent Pelly's 1998 production for Avignon made the most of the massive walls of the Papal Palace, but resolutely kept historical analogy at a distance through the use of steel platforms on wheels and present-day costumes. In any of those productions, the gates and battlements of Angiers, which structure much of Act II, could thus be those of any besieged city, from Troy onwards.[14] With the citizen up on the walls 'as in a theatre' (II.i.375) addressing the French and British kings who stand below, the scene recalls the fall of Troy in the *Iliad*, with its rhetoric of negotiation and threat, and its shifting of perspective from citizens to legacies and back again reminiscent of Homer's alternately showing the war from Trojan or Greek viewpoints. These 'walls' later become those of the prison, or castle ('*Enter Arthur on the walls*') (IV.iii.0), from which the young prince falls to his death, in much the same way as Astyanax is pushed or jumps from the walls of Troy, depending on the choice of narrative, cancelling out hopes of negotiation or compromise that early modern dramatists frequently signal by having characters move between the upper and lower levels. In Pelly's production, the upstage wall of the Papal Palace was essential to the design and dynamics of the production, 'a shadow theatre, the mirror reflexion of the acting area', as Pelly 'combined defocusing and refocusing techniques'.[15]

To use E. A. J. Honigmann's phrase,[16] the language associated with the setting of II.i is a rhetoric of excess and 'imagery of oppression', of the kind that Homer, Euripides, Virgil or Seneca used to describe the siege and ruin of Troy; the prospects of bloodshed that run through the long scene recollect Aeneas's account of the horror of the fall of Troy (*Aeneid*, II, 298–566). Acting as the play's conscience, as Hecuba, Cassandra and Andromache do in Troy,

Constance initially seeks to deflect the prospect of violence by inviting Philip to wait for his ambassador to return from England, ironically anticipating John's belated, Senecan clear-sightedness – which, in his case, may also be read as fudging indecisiveness:

> PHILIP. We'll lay before this town our royal bones,
> Wade to the market-place in Frenchmen's blood
> ...
> CONSTANCE. ... we shall repent each drop of blood
> That hot rash haste so indirectly shed.
>
> (II.i.41–9)
>
> JOHN. There is no sure foundation set on blood;
> No certain life achiev'd by others' death.
>
> (IV.ii.104–5)

Images of carnage jostle through a scene in which '[t]he cannons have their bowels full of wrath' (II.i.210), and lest one think my comparisons far-fetched, consider one reviewer who saw 'Trojan horses' in the mobile, tiered platforms that Pelly used for his Avignon production as war machines.[17] Like Ilium, Angiers defies diplomacy and embodies opposition. Hence the temptation to batter down the 'winking gates' (215) and dislodge the 'sleeping stones' (216) of 'old-fac'd' (259) 'saucy walls' (404).[18] In a joint act of royal one-upmanship, John would 'lay this Angiers even with the ground' (399) while Philip would enact Jupiter, who withdrew his help from Troy: 'Our thunder from the south / Shall rain their drift of bullets on this town' (412–13).

The complex interweaving of historical and mythological material I have suggested is clear here. The Bastard mordantly invites the two kings to join forces to bombard the town, until their cannons have 'brawl'd down / The flinty ribs of this contemptuous city ... till unfenced desolation / Leave them as naked as the vulgar air' (II.i.383–7). He turns to biblical history for historical legitimacy, invoking what was in fact an inverted situation, 'the mutines of Jerusalem' (378) – the Jews' uprising against the Romans. Above all, the momentary truce between the two kings recalls how the Greeks overcame their rivalries and united against Troy. The citizens of Angiers, however, prove as stubbornly resolute as the Trojans, reinforcing their 'gates against the world' (II.i.272) and determined to defend their city come what may; their imagery imitates Homer's and Virgil's metaphoric language:

> The sea enraged is not half so deaf,
> Lions more confident, mountains and rocks

> More free from motion, no, not Death himself
> In mortal fury half so peremptory
> As we to keep this city.
>
> (II.i.451–5)

In the vast *Cour d'Honneur* of Avignon's Papal Palace, open to the sky and the mistral wind, which plays tricks with acoustics, the citizen on the battlements became a disembodied voice that bounced off the walls above and behind the audience, travelling down the centuries, laden with memories of besieged cities. Shakespeare's text never takes us into Angiers, but directors can, and do. In Avignon, the two kings faced the audience as they threatened to raze the city, and suddenly spectators were no longer gazing at the city walls but trapped within them, as war machinery, metallic tiered platforms, ground slowly forwards across the stage. A similar sense of involvement was also felt in Doran's production, where Hubert addressed the king from the audience, recalling the way in which Hector is viewed in the *Iliad*, standing on the walls with other members of the Priam household and watching the fighting below.[19]

Although few battles are actually shown on stage in *King John*, imagery of violence and bloodshed runs through the play. Moments before discovering Arthur's broken body, Salisbury declares:

> The King hath dispossess'd himself of us;
> We will not line his thin bestained cloak
> With our pure honors, nor attend the foot
> That leaves the print of blood where'er it walks.
>
> (IV.iii.23–6)

Rhetoric is a weapon for coercion and blackmail, threatening the more vulnerable members of the community:

> KING PHILIP. With unhack'd swords and helmets all unbruis'd,
> We will bear home that lusty blood again
> Which here we came to spout against your town,
> And leave your children, wives, and you in peace.
> …
> Then, tell us, shall your city call us lord
> …
> Or shall we give the signal to our rage
> And stalk in blood to our possession?
>
> (II.i.254–66)

Here again, the fall of a besieged city evokes the final hours of Troy: the warriors are all killed, their women, children and old men reduced to chattels in the hands of the Greeks, just as Andromache had foretold (*Iliad*, VI, 406–39) and reiterated on hearing of Hector's death (XXII, 482–6; XXIV, 725–38). Cassandra-like, she had predicted her own enslavement and her son's violent death, moments that Euripides powerfully dramatized in *Hecuba* and *Trojan Women*, and that had struck root in European collective imagination through translations and adaptations. Like Euripides, Shakespeare brings centre-stage the women and children who are the casualties of war, concentrating the threats that collectively hang over them in the linked plights of Constance and Arthur.

Constance: sister to Andromache and daughter to Hecuba

The structural combination of threats against a besieged city and of focused maternal grieving further strengthens the Trojan analogy by establishing a kinship not only between Angiers and Troy but also between the fates of Constance and Arthur and those of Andromache and Astyanax, through a tradition that extends from Homer to Euripides to Seneca and Virgil.[20]

The Troy story was part of the cultural memory, the city's fall overshadowing later destructions, Hecuba and Andromache lamenting with later grieving widows and mothers. Constance shares her maternal solicitude with classical figures of mourning mothers, borrowing and adapting their rhetoric to fashion a mental and emotional state the audience could recognise and empathise with. Kelly Hunter, who performed the part of Constance in Gregory Doran's production, writes that 'every decision and feeling [Constance] has is experienced through her total obsession with being female: her marital status, her value as a child-bearing woman, and her success as a mother, specifically as the mother to the young and rightful heir to the throne'.[21] What emerges are similarities between the *personae* fashioned after characters depicted in the *Iliad*, dramatised in Euripides's *Trojan Women* and Seneca's *Troades*, and in Shakespeare's refashioning of Holinshed's Constance and Arthur. Close readings of the Constance and Arthur scenes suggest that Jasper Heywood's translation of Seneca's play (*Troas*) may be the foremost among possible mediators for the Greek sources that include translations into Latin of the *Iliad* and *Trojan Women*, as well as Seneca's own Latin text.[22] Heywood's 'Argument' expounds Andromache's distress and comments on the wresting of a child from its mother, drawing perhaps, as we shall see, on Erasmus's fashioning of her maternal exemplariness.

Shakespeare progressively isolates Constance and Arthur from the other historical agents, while ensuring that they retain a powerful onstage presence until the end of Act III for Constance, and Act IV for Arthur, who continues to haunt the play's and England's collective imagination as he moves from an onstage physical presence into the mythmaking process. When a messenger (Salisbury) is sent to inform Constance of the wedding between Louis and Blanche, his embarrassment and her distress offer another parallel with Andromache, who sat at work within her rooms (*Iliad*, XXII, 437–41), with no-one daring to inform her of Hector's death, then breaking down, grief-crazy, loosening her hair and lamenting her plight (XXII, 460–72), as Constance will do. Constance's championing of her son's cause is shot through with references to her widowed status, and the vulnerability she expresses is amplified when she realises that Philip and Austria have withdrawn their support:

> My name is Constance; I was Geffrey's wife,
> Young Arthur is my son; and he is lost.
>
> (III.iv.46–7)

Geoffrey, Constance and Arthur parallel Hector, Andromache and Astyanax through the widows' mourning, their concern for their sons and the political importance of their respective deaths. Constance's metonymic constancy in preserving Geoffrey's memory and legacy emphasizes her determination to reclaim the throne for her son and her attachment to him, so like 'in feature to his father Geffrey' (II.i.126) – a resemblance that is also noted by Philip (99–103) and taken as proof of illustrious descent (as for the Bastard, in I.i):

> Look here upon thy brother's Geffrey's face:
> These eyes, these brows, were moulded out of his;
> This little abstract doth contain that large
> Which died in Geffrey; and the hand of time
> Shall draw this brief into as huge a volume.
>
> (II.i.99–103)

Jasper Heywood's Andromache similarly draws attention to the likeness between father and son:

> O childe, O noble fathers broode and Troians only ioy,
> ...
> O ymage of thy father loe, thou lively bearst his face,
> This countenance to my Hector had, and even such was his pace.
> The pitch of all his body such, his handes thus would he beare.
>
> (*Troas*, fo. 108v)

Even when 'dismembered' and 'deformed' by death, Astyanax resembles Hector:

> Sic quoque est similis patri.
>
> (Seneca, *Troades*, 1117)

> An[dromache]. Loe herein doth he yet likewyse, his father represent.
>
> (*Troas*, fol. 117v)

Arthur's royal origins break through the 'ship-boy's semblance' (IV.iii.4) and live on in death:

> PEMBROKE. O death, made proud with pure and princely beauty!
> ...
> SALISBURY. Murther, as hating what himself hath done,
> Doth lay it open to urge on revenge.
> BIGOT. Or when he doom'd this beauty to a grave,
> Found it too precious-princely for a grave.
>
> (IV.iii.35–40)

Arthur was born to a high destiny (II.ii.49–54); he is feared as a rival, and rumours of his death, far from settling the issue, fan the flames of his legitimacy – until his alter ego, his young cousin Henry, succeeds John.[23] The Greeks feared that a living Astyanax would 'rebuild' Troy and perpetuate the dynasty – his replacement was Ascanius, Aeneas's son, as Andromache suggests in Thomas Phaer and Thomas Twynne's translation of the *Aeneid*:

> Than said she thus: take this of mee, mine owne hands hath it made,
> Take this my childe, that long with thee my love in minde may last.
> Of Hectors wife receive thy freends good will, and tokens last,
> O figure, nert Astianax, alone to me most deere,
> So he his eyes, so he his hands, so like he bare his cheere,
> And now alike in yeres with thee his youth he should have led.
> [Marginal note: She resembleth him to hir own son that was kild][24]

In Euripides's *Hecuba*, the eponymous, aged queen is outraged by the death of her son Polydorus, not only because he was her last living child but because he was betrayed by the person he had been entrusted to, Polymestor: the sacred laws of hospitality have been flouted. What makes it even worse in *King John*, as in *Richard III*, is that the threats to the widow and the child come from within the family circle, from uncle, grandmother, cousin; in Josie Rourke's production,

Arthur's 'death proved the pivotal moment in this production … the catalyst for … John's final descent from conscientious king into immoral tyrant'.[25] This is indeed the iron age: 'non hospes ab hospite tutus, / non socer a genero, fratrum quoque gratia rara est' ('Guest was not safe from host, nor father-in-law from son-in-law; even among brothers 'twas rare to find affection') (*Metamorphoses*, I, 144–5). Earlier, Eleanor's 'horrified look' and hasty exit had signalled that she understood what John had ordered Hubert to do; in this production, Arthur's death also revealed her failure, or inability, to prevent the deed.

Constance's combination of premonitory fears and wild reactions (III.i.83–95) recalls Andromache's; her words provide stage directions that transform her into a personification of lamentation:

> … my grief's so great
> That no supporter but the huge firm earth
> Can hold it up [*Throws herself on the ground.*]. Here I and sorrows sit.
>
> (II.ii.71–3)[26]

In the *Iliad*, Andromache seems at times another version of Cassandra – a duality Shakespeare stages in *Troilus and Cressida*, where wife and sister, on their knees, jointly appeal to Hector not to go out onto the battlefield (V.iii.7–24): she predicts what will befall her and her son in every passage in which she appears, and is described as grieving 'like a raving woman' and a fury (XXII, 460).[27] Constance's despair echoes that of the female characters in Euripides and Seneca. Just as Homer describes Andromache (and Hecuba) loosening their hair and tearing at it, Euripides's and Seneca's Hecuba encourages her daughters, daughters-in-law and their companions (those, at least, who have not yet had their heads shaved) to unbind their hair, bare their breasts and shed all modesty, since rank and ritual have become meaningless in the reversals of fortune that make slaves of queens and princesses, and concubines of wives (Seneca, *Troades*, 82–116). Mourning and excess are closely entwined, and Jasper Heywood renders this as follows:

> Untie thattyre, that on your heads ye weare,
> And as behoveth state of misery,
> Let fall aboute your woeful neckes your hayre.
> …
> For what wedlocke should you your bosomes hyde?
> Your garmentes loose, and have in readiness
> Your furious handes uppon your breast to knocke
> This habite well beseemeth our distresse,
> …

> Renew agayne your longe accustomde cryes,
> And more then earst lament your miseryes.
> We bewayle Hector.
>
> (*Troas*, fo. 99v)

Constance's 'distracted' grief is associated with her appearance. Text and stage directions draw attention to her hair, in a commonplace typology linking unkempt hair, uncontrolled behaviour and lamentation that similarly applies to Cassandra in *Troilus and Cressida* ('*Enter Cassandra, raving* [*with her hair about her ears*]', II.ii.sd after 100) and to Hecuba, who 'ran about with flaring hair … her pendant lockes she tare', in a poem Thomas Fenne published in 1590, 'Hecubaes mishaps, expressed by way of apparition…':[28]

> KING PHILIP. Bind up those tresses. O what love I note
> In the fair multitude of those her hairs!
>
> (III.i.61–2)
>
> KING PHILIP. Bind up your hairs.
>
> (III.i.67)
>
> CONSTANCE. I will not keep this form upon my head
> [*Tearing her hair*]
> When there is such disorder in my wit.
>
> (III.iv.101–2)

A mother's grieving, as Constance points out, is senseless to those who have not suffered loss:

> He talks to me that never had a son.
>
> (III.iv.91)

> Fare you well! Had you such a loss as I,
> I could give better comfort than you do.
>
> (III.iv.99–100)

This topos of maternal grief had been developed by Jasper Heywood in his introductory Argument:

> Her pinching pang of hart who may expresse,
> But such as of like woes, have borne a part?
> Or who bewayle her ruthful heavines
> That never yet hath felt therof the smart?
> Ful well they wot the woes of heavy hart.
> What is to leese a babe from mothers breast,
> They know that are in such a case distrest.
>
> (*Troas*, fo. 97v)

Immoderate manifestations of grief may have been considered excessive in early modern England, but they were dramatically effective – and acceptable – in poetry as on stage.[29] Furthermore, self-laceration and language are a woman's last weapons when male support has been withdrawn; refusing to be silenced is the final provocation, a form of empowerment. Kelly Hunter believes that Constance is anything but 'mad'.[30] Like Euripides's Hecuba in his eponymous play, her command of language rarely fails her, even in her more desperate moments. Similarly, Claire Bloom, Constance in David Giles's 1984 production for the BBC, saw her as a 'woman of tremendous intellect … no woman in Shakespeare has such complex language'.[31] Constance eloquently upholds the legitimacy of Arthur's claim, both to the characters on stage and to the audience and, through the audience, she ensures her son's right to the throne is anchored in the collective imagination.[32] Arthur may die on stage, but his mother ensures that he is successfully memorialised. In that respect, far from being reduced to helpless female inaction, she finds inspiration and strength in a rhetoric that draws both on political discourse and on female lamentation, so important in ancient and medieval cultures.[33] Hence male unease is compounded with, or expressed by, exasperation with this 'embarrassing' woman, whose subversive role has been analysed by Juliet Dusinberre:[34]

> KING PHILIP. O fair affliction, peace!
> CONSTANCE. No, no, I will not, having breath to cry.
> O that my tongue were in the thunder's mouth!
> Then with a passion would I shake the world,
> And rouse from sleep that fell anatomy
> Which cannot hear a lady's feeble voice,
> Which scorns a modern invocation.
>
> (III.iv.36–42)

Philip's impatience – 'You are as fond of grief as of your child' (III.iv.92) – and Pandolf's 'You hold too heinous a respect for grief' (III.iv.90) bring to mind Ulysses:

> UL[YSSES]. Now breake of al thy mothers tears I may no more-tyme spende.
> The grievous sorrowes of thy heart wil never make an end.
>
> (*Troas*, fol. 113r)

Constance's reply might be addressed to Ulysses as well as Philip and Pandolf:

> Grief fills the room up of my absent child,
> Lies in his bed, walks up and down with me,

> Puts on his pretty looks, repeats his words,
> Remembers me of all his gracious parts,
> Stuffs out his vacant garments with his form;
> Then, have I reason to be fond of grief?
>
> (III.iv.93–8)

Sister to Andromache and daughter to Hecuba in her refusal to be silenced, she has the final say. This tragic eloquence and its unassailable truth follow almost immediately her cry 'Never, never / Must I behold my pretty Arthur more' (88–9). Constance's anxiety and grieving encircle Arthur, distressing him in much the same way as Astyanax responds to Andromache's frenzied pleading with the only two, heart-breaking words he speaks in *Troades*:

> ARTHUR. Good my mother, peace.
>
> I would that I were low laid in my grave.
> I am not worth this coil that's made for me.
>
> (II.i.163–5)
>
> ASTYANAX. Miserere, mater.
>
> (*Troades*, 792)
>
> AST[YANAX]. Help me, mother.
>
> (*Troas*, fo. 113r)

Arthur: brother to Astyanax

When Constance is finally separated from him, Arthur exclaims 'O, this will make my mother die with grief!' (III.iii.5) – an empathy Jasper Heywood also expresses in lines he added to Seneca's text: 'For sory hart the teares myne eyes do stayne / To thinke what sorrow shall her hart oppresse, / Her little child to leese remedilesse' (fo. 107v). Analogies offering equally contrasting levels of emotional engagement may be found in the *Aeneid*, where Virgil inserts Aeneas's homely vignette of Andromache and Astyanax going down a passage to Priam's palace (II, 455–7) and inscribes maternal grieving in an epic context (III, 294–355, 482–91) – just as, in the *Iliad*, the vignette of Astyanax frightened by his father's helmet, and Hector's tenderness for his child and wife (VI, 466–93), provide a brief respite that is retrospectively charged with pathos.

Unlike Andromache, Constance is not confronted with her child's corpse. But she anticipates this in an image – which she simultaneously rejects as 'madly' impossible – that reduces him to a lifeless, disarticulated doll, suggestive of Astyanax's broken body: 'If I were mad, I should forget my son, / Or madly think a babe of clouts were he' (III.iv.57–8). Arthur's final words close on a powerful 'stones' / 'bones' rhyming couplet that echoes a similar rhyme in Jasper Heywood's account of Astyanax's fall (the emphasis is mine):

> NU[NCIUS]. What limmes from such a headlong fall could in a child remayne,
> His bodies payse throwne downe to ground hath batted at his *bones*.
> His face, his noble fathers markes are spoyld agaynst the *stones*.
> His necke unjoynted is: his head so daint with flint stone stroake,
> That scattered is the brayne about, the soul is all to broake.
> Thus lieth he now dismembered corps, deformd and all to rent.
> (*Troas*, fol. 117v)
>
> ARTHUR. O me! My uncle's spirit is in these *stones*.
> Heaven take my soul, and England keep my *bones*!
> (IV.iii.9–10)

What Constance understands is that she will never see her son again, that she must henceforth live (or die) with his absence. This refocusing of her mourning reinforces the pathos of the bond between mother and child, as Erasmus perceived:

> Aliter autem Andromache apud Euripidem filium vitae oculum vocat: ... Erat relictus gnatus hic mihi unicus / Vitae oculus, / propterea quod unicum esset in vita oblectamentum. Nam oculo nihil charius. Unde, quos adamamus, oculos vocamus.
>
> Andromache, in Euripides ... calls her son the eye of her life: 'This one son was left to me, / The eye of life', because he was the unique delight of her life, for nothing is dearer than the eye. Hence we call those we love, our eyes.
> (Erasmus, *Adages*, Adage 102, I.ii.2)[35]

Erasmus is quoting Euripides's *Andromache*, 406. A comparison of different translations into Latin shows that all use the phrase 'vitae oculus' or 'oculus vitae', with the line beginning with 'Unus' or 'Unicus'[36] – which Erasmus juxtaposes in his own translation of the line with 'vitae oculus', thereby reinforcing the sense of focus; hence his own phrase, 'unicum ... in vita oblectamentum' – 'unique delight of her life' – designating Andromache's tight bonding with Astyanax. This phrase is taken up as 'onely joy' by Jasper Heywood in *Troas*, where he associates it with Astyanax on three occasions, rhyming 'joy' with 'boy' and 'Troy':

> And Hectors sonne, Astyanax (alas)
> Pore seely foole his Mothers onely joy,

> Is judged to die by sentence of Calchas,
> Alas the whyle, to death is led the boy,
> And tumbled downe from Turrets tops in Troy.
>
> (fo. 97v)
>
> O childe, O noble fathers broode and Trojans only joy
> O worthy seede of thauncient bloud, and beaten house of Troy.
>
> (fo. 108v)
>
> O deere, O sweet, thy mothers pledge, farewel my onely joy,
> Farewel the flowre of honor left of beaten howse of Troy.
>
> (fo. 113r)

Constance's lines:

> O Lord, my boy, my Arthur, my fair son!
> My life, my joy, my food, my all the world!
> My widow-comfort, and my sorrows' cure!
>
> (III.iv.103–5)

seem to echo Erasmus's and Jasper Heywood's phrases, even while recollections of the child's father and his potential destiny linger on in the 'joy' / 'Troy' rhymes, as in Constance's final line. Erasmus's identification of maternal love with the eyes acquires a powerful resonance: Constance is unaware that Arthur narrowly escapes having his eyes put out.

Constance's despair extends beyond death ('never, never / Must I behold my pretty Arthur more') (III.iv.88–9). Her speech to the Cardinal carries Senecan resonances in its rejection of ultimate salvation,[37] as when the chorus in *Troades* addresses the issue of life, or its absence, after death: 'post mortem nihil est ipsaque mors nihil' (371–408, 397), 'Nothing taryeth after dying day' (*Troas*, fo. 107r). This occurs just after Calchas has announced that Astyanax must be killed and just before Andromache enters with the child. Similarly, while she is unaware of Arthur's exact fate, Constance's fears are borne out by the following scene, where he is confronted with Hubert and the executioners. His escape, however, is momentary:

> *Enter Arthur on the walls.*
> ARTHUR. The wall is high, and yet will I leap down.
> Good ground, be pitiful and hurt me not!
> ...
> I am afraid, and yet I'll venture it.
> ...
> As good to die and go, as die and stay.
>
> (IV.iii.0; 1–8)

History patterns itself on myth, not least so in the chronicles.[38] Holinshed leaves open the question whether Arthur jumped to his death or was secretly killed on John's orders.[39] The uncertainty surrounding the historical Arthur's fate parallels uncertainty about Astyanax's fate, which Homer left in the air.[40] Shakespeare sidesteps this with impressive stagecraft economy, in a single jump and ten lines, that contrasts with the suspense of the rhetorically elaborate 'torture-chamber' scene and compresses the opening, twenty-six-line scene of Part II of *The Troublesome Raigne of King John*, where the 'First Scene shows Arthurs death in infancie'.[41]

Shakespeare ensures that the audience is witness to the tragic fall. Directors have found creative ways of imprinting this moment on the audience's imagination and emotions. In Rourke's production, the

> staging of Arthur's fall was spectacular ... enacted with a live child falling at high velocity (or so it appeared) two floors onto the main Swan stage, making it the most believable death of Arthur I have seen ... The illusion created by the initial jump and the blackout immediately afterwards caused audiences to gasp in horror at the seeming reality of Arthur's death.[42]

In Avignon, Arthur stood front stage in a circle of light, arms out, before a pit strewn with bits of armour, balancing as though on the top of high walls. Then the stage plunged into darkness; at the same instant a line of white light zipped down the high upstage wall, thudding down to the ground in a luminous ball. Immediately, a pool of light revealed Arthur's twisted body front stage, among the fragments of armour, bringing to mind Constance's 'babe of clouts' and, perhaps, the scene in *Trojan Women* in which Hecuba appears, carrying Astyanax's broken body on his father's shield.

Arthur's words – 'As good to die and go, as die and stay', and wait to be killed – suggest a noble valour that he shares with Astyanax as redefined by Seneca. In Euripides, the enslaved Andromache is separated from Astyanax, before he is hurled from the top of the Trojan battlements by the Greeks. In Seneca's redramatisation, he jumps from what remains of Troy's battlements without waiting to be pushed:

> The neerer death more free from care he seemd and feare of hart.
> Amid his foes his stomacke swelles, and fierce he was to sight,
> Like Tygers whelpe, that threats in vayne with totles chap to bight.
> Alas, for pitty then each one, rew on his tender yeares,
> And al the route that present were, for him they shed their teares,
> Yea not Ulisses them restraynd, but trickling downe they fal,
> And onely he wept not (poore soole) whom they bewayled al.

But whyle on Gods Ulisses cald, and Calchas wordes expound,
In midst of Pryams land (alas) the child leapt downe to ground.
(fo. 117v)

In *King John*, the male courtiers express their horror at Arthur's death (IV. iii.35–56) in a chorus that recalls the women's lamentations in Seneca. In Avignon, they stood front stage, addressing the audience over Arthur's body.

Conflating a recurring pattern that may be traced through *Trojan Women*, *Metamorphoses*, *Aeneid* and *Troades*, the sight of Arthur's body on stage outside the walls brings to mind Astyanax's fall and Hector's corpse outside Troy, with analogous emotional impact on those who find the body ('murther's arms') (IV.iii.45–50).[43] The dramatic, trans-generational irony is all the more powerful when one remembers that it is Achilles who killed Hector and that Andromache is enslaved to his son Pyrrhus, who killed Priam.[44] Astyanax's fall is the ultimate personification of the fall of Troy.

Even as they interact with historical and other influences, Trojan shadows contribute to the complex, pervasive imagery of death and mourning in early modern culture.[45] *King John* is rich in allegories of death, and Arthur's fate resembles that of other children caught up in disputed, bloody successions (including the Bastard), sharing the tragic fate of the young princes in *Richard III*, while Constance joins Shakespeare's cohort of lamenting queens, in *Richard III*, *Henry VI* and *The Two Noble Kinsmen*. One of the most powerful representations of collective and individual destruction (alongside *the* Fall) was the story of the fall of Troy, to which the Elizabethans linked their own history, drawing from it motives of national pride and fears of disruption as well as inspiration for erotic poetry. These shadows of Troy belong to a Trojan aesthetics elaborated by a collective imagination in which mythological material and the associations it generates serve to elevate history to a tragic dimension as it engages with purported facts and characters participate in their transfer from chronicles to the stage. Myth provides a template that transcends events and those involved in them, mediating potentially conflictive material and contributing to further mythmaking. The effect amounts to a form of shadow play, whereby the dramatist retains an artistic distance and provides a multiplicity of voices that help to account for the play's ongoing appeal beyond the supposedly historical dimension it stages and beyond the context of its writing, initial performance and reception. At the same time, even while the rhetoric and imagery of Troy make their presence felt because of the sheer power of their deep collocation within contemporary representations, in the danger-laden context of Elizabeth's succession the non-naming of the Trojan material may have been a way of addressing the ambivalence of the figure of

King John. After his questionable behaviour and rhetoric throughout the first four acts of the play, he is redeemed so as to make way for his young successor, who describes himself as '[cygnet] to this pale faint swan' (V.vii.21). Cousin to Arthur, variously cast as another child (with the same actor doubling in both roles) or as an older look-alike, so as to emphasise the child Arthur's total isolation in the iron age of John's rule while hinting at some kind of genealogical redemption, Prince Henry reinstates the legitimacy of the Crown. He receives it from a 'batterer' of Troy-like walls and citizens, but also as a descendant of those selfsame Trojans whose shadowy presence continues to haunt early modern representations of the English monarchy's genealogy. Troy is, and is not, there, a mythological shadow in the consciousness of present-day performers and spectators, that continues to preserve, transform and redefine cultural memory.

Notes

I wish to thank Ruth Morse, Tanya Pollard and Boika Sokolova (as well as my fellow editors) for their stimulating comments, suggestions and friendship, and MUP's anonymous readers for their helpful feedback.

1 'In *Shakespeare: Leben, Umwelt, Kunst* (Wittenberg: Ziemsen, 1923 [1922]), p. 211, Alois Brandl records the suggestion that Constance's speeches in this scene are parallel with and might be derived from Andromache's speeches to Ulysses on behalf of Astyanax in Seneca's *Troades* 739ff., but the argument of influence is unconvincing.' A. R. Braunmuller (ed.), *King John*, The Oxford Shakespeare (Oxford: Oxford University Press, 1998 [1989]), p. 196, note to III.iv.23–36.
2 On Ate as a figure of vengeance, see Marguerite A. Tassi, *Women and Revenge in Shakespeare* (Selinsgrove: Susquehanna University Press, 2011), p. 35.
3 This is the case in Laurent Pelly's 1998 production for the Avignon Festival, which I shall be discussing. On the ambivalence of the Hercules motif, see Charlotte Coffin, 'Hercules' (2009), in Yves Peyré (ed.), *A Dictionary of Shakespeare's Classical Mythology* (2009–), www.shakmyth.org (accessed 24 April 2016): 'in *King John*, where the use of a lion's skin as a prop makes the Herculean reference stronger ... the Bastard does not live up to the mythological ideal. His speech suggests that Richard Lionheart was the true Hercules, and as an illegitimate son he is just a pale reflection of his two models'.
4 On the texturing of material derived from Roman history and mythology, see the discussion of *2 Henry VI* (IV.i) in the introduction to this volume.
5 See Chapter 11 (Ruth Morse).
6 Anne E. B. Coldiron, 'The mediated "medieval" and Shakespeare', in Ruth Morse, Helen Cooper and Peter Holland (eds), *Medieval Shakespeare: Pasts and Presents* (Cambridge: Cambridge University Press, 2013), pp. 55–77 (p. 57), and

pp. 63–8 on 'Shakespeare's Troys'. For a fuller discussion of 'Troys for England', see Anne E. B. Coldiron, *Printers without Borders: Translation and Textuality in the Renaissance* (Cambridge: Cambridge University Press, 2015), pp. 40–64.

7 Thomas Lodge, *The Wounds of Civil War*, ed. Joseph W. Houppert (London: Edward Arnold, 1970), IV.i.237–42.

8 On 'imagined pasts', see Ruth Morse, 'Shakespeare and the remains of Britain', in Morse, Cooper and Holland, *Medieval Shakespeare*, pp. 119–37 (p. 121). On scepticism in the face of these foundational myths, see Chapter 3 (Dominique Goy-Blanquet).

9 Historically, Constance died in 1201, Arthur in 1203, Eleanor in 1204.

10 Shakespeare, *King John*, ed. Braunmuller, p. 18.

11 See Geoffrey Bullough (ed.), *Narrative and Dramatic Sources of Shakespeare*, Vol. IV: *Later English History Plays: 'King John', 'Henry IV', 'Henry V', 'Henry VIII'* (London: Routledge and Kegan Paul, 1962), pp. 5–22.

12 *Ibid.*, p. 15.

13 References are to Thomas Heywood, *The First and Second Parts of 'King Edward IV'*, ed. Richard Rowland (Manchester: Manchester University Press, 2005).

14 '*France, before Angiers*' (II.i.0); 'Welcome before the gates of Angiers' (II.i.16); '*Enter [Hubert and other Citizens] upon the walls*' (II.i.199sd); '*Exeunt. [Hubert and Citizens remain above.] ... enter ... the Herald of France with Trumpets to the gates*' (II.i.298sd).

15 On the ways Pelly used the upstage wall and 'combined defocusing and refocusing techniques', see Florence March, 'Shakespeare at the Avignon Festival: Breaking down the walls', in Martin Procházka (ed.), *From Consumerism to Corpora: Uses of Shakespeare, Litteraria Pragensia: Studies in Literature and Culture*, 47:24 (July 2014), 72–83 (p. 76).

16 William Shakespeare, *King John*, ed. E. A. J. Honigmann, The Arden Shakespeare (London: Methuen, 1967 [1954]), p. lxiv.

17 'Dans la première partie qui bruit de combats et de débats internationaux, Laurent Pelly fait intervenir deux hautes passerelles qui se déplacent et s'affrontent comme deux chevaux de Troie' (In the first part, which is rife with battles and international debates, Laurent Pelly brings in two high platforms that move around the stage and confront each other like two Trojan horses). Gilles Costaz, 'Les cravates rouges', *Les Echos*, 27 July 1998.

18 In the *Aeneid*, see the description of Pyrrhus tearing down the gates of Troy and entering Priam's palace (II, 479–82, 491–4).

19 For information on Gregory Doran's production, see Robert Smallwood, 'Introduction', in Robert Smallwood (ed.), *Players of Shakespeare 6: Essays in the Performance of Shakespeare's History Plays* (Cambridge: Cambridge University Press, 2004), p. 12.

20 On the material conditions of transmission, bilingual editions and translations, and the impact of Greek drama on early modern theatre, see Tanya Pollard,

'Greek playbooks and dramatic forms in early modern England', in Allison K. Deutermann and András Kisery (eds), *Formal Matters: Reading the Materials of English Renaissance Literature* (Manchester: Manchester University Press, 2013), pp. 99–123. On the influence of Euripides and Seneca on the early modern reception and elaboration of the Astyanax story, see Susanna Phillippo, '"A future for Astyanax": Alternative and imagined futures for Hector's son in classical and European drama', *International Journal of the Classical Tradition*, 14:3–4 (2007), 317–68, esp. pp. 317–44.

21 Kelly Hunter, 'Constance in *King John*', in Smallwood, *Players of Shakespeare 6*, pp. 37–49 (p. 38). Mythological analogies inspired a psychologising vein, notably in the nineteenth century, which I do not pursue here. In *The Psychology of Shakespeare* (1859), John Charles Bucknill considered that 'The tenderness of love alone would have led [Constance] to shun contention and to withdraw her child from danger; as Andromache sought to withhold her husband from the field of honour with unalloyed womanly apprehension' (p. 169); in *Characteristics of Women, Moral, Poetical, and Historical* (1832), Anna Brownell Jameson compares Constance to Merope and Niobe (p. 77), while Charles Knight, in *The Pictorial Edition of the Works of Shakespeare* (1838–43), calls her 'The Niobe of a Gothic age, who vainly sought to shield her child' (p. 110). All page references are to Joseph Candido (ed.), *Shakespeare: The Critical Tradition. 'King John'* (London: Athlone Press, 1996). Thomas Davies, *Dramatic Miscellanies* (1783–84), considered Constance 'more moving than Clytemnestra, Hecuba, and the other great women of antiquity', to quote John W. Velz, who also records A. J. Carver's and C. J. Clay's juxtaposition of Constance and Hecuba (1844); John W. Velz, *Shakespeare and the Classical Tradition: A Critical Guide to Commentary 1660–1960* (Minneapolis: University of Minnesota Press, 1968), pp. 39, 42, 168.

22 The *editio princeps* of Seneca's plays was printed in 1484. Jasper Heywood's translation of *Troades* was first published in 1559 (London: Richard Tottyll), then in Thomas Newton's collective edition, *Seneca His Tenne Tragedies, Translated into English*, trans. John Studley, ed. Thomas Newton (London: Thomas Marsh, 1581). References are to this edition. Robert S. Miola only mentions *King John* in passing (pp. 95, 115) in *Shakespeare and Classical Tragedy: The Influence of Seneca* (Oxford: Clarendon Press, 1992).

23 Arthur and Henry are played by the same actor in Bernard Sobel's production (Gennevilliers, 1992), 'as if History were stuttering': Yves Peyré, 'notice' to *Le roi Jean*, in William Shakespeare, *Shakespeare, Œuvres complètes*, ed. Jean-Michel Déprats (Paris: Gallimard, 2008), Vol. III, pp. 1597–1616 (p. 1615).

24 Virgil, *The.xiii. Bookes of Aeneidos*, trans. Thomas Phaer and Thomas Twyne (London: William How, 1584), sig. E6r. The reference is to *Aeneid*, III, 482–91.

25 Jami Rogers, 'King John, directed by Josie Rourke for the RSC, The Swan, 11 September 2006', *Cahiers élisabéthains: The Royal Shakespeare Company Complete Works Festival*, 71:1 Suppl. (2007), 46–8 (p. 47).

26 'Constance's devastation at France's betrayal leads her to figure herself onstage as an emblem of grief, enthroned as its monarch'; Tassi, *Women and Revenge in Shakespeare*, p. 70.

27 Homer reads 'μαιναδι ιση', from 'μαινας' (woman transported with fury, maenad, fury), which is translated into Latin as 'furenti similis' by Lorenzo Valla (1537), Andrea Divo (Andreas Divus) (1538) and Jean de Sponde (1583); or 'similisque furentis' by Nicolao Valla (1510) and Eoban Hesse (1540); and which Chapman translates as 'furie-like' (George Chapman, *Chapman's Homer*, ed. Allardyce Nicoll (Princeton: Princeton University Press, 1998 [1956]), XXII, 401).

28 Thomas Fenne, *Fennes Frutes which Worke Is Devided in Three Severall Partes ... whereunto Is Added Hecubaes Mishaps, Discoursed by Way of Apparition* (London: T. Orwin for Richard Oliffe, 1590), sig. Bb3v.

29 Bridget Escolme, *Emotional Excess on the Shakespearean Stage: Passion's Slaves*, The Arden Shakespeare (London: Bloomsbury, 2014). See pp. 168–84 for a discussion of grief, melancholy and moderation (although she never mentions Constance). On immoderate demonstrations of grief, see also Chapter 6 (Katherine Heavey).

30 'Constance is one of the few voices of reason in a play peopled with irrational, unreasonable voices – Hubert and Arthur being the obvious two others'; 'there is *nothing* in the text to imply that Constance is mad; in fact she is able to talk at length, with great lucidity, of the difference between madness and grief ... The madness is in the eye of the beholder'; Hunter, 'Constance in *King John*', pp. 38, 47.

31 Geraldine Cousin, *King John*, Shakespeare in Performance (Manchester: Manchester University Press, 1994), p. 91. On Hecuba's powerful sense of rhetoric, see Claire Nancy, *Euripide et le parti des femmes* (Paris: Editions rue d'Ulm, 2016), p. 74–5.

32 See Katharine Goodland, *Female Mourning in Medieval and Renaissance English Drama: From the Raising of Lazarus to 'King Lear'* (Aldershot: Ashgate, 2005), p. 113. Also quoted in Tassi, *Women and Revenge in Shakespeare*, p. 71.

33 Tassi, *Women and Revenge in Shakespeare*, p. 71.

34 Juliet Dusinberre, '*King John* and embarrassing women', *Shakespeare Survey*, 42 (1990), 37–52. See also Jean E. Howard and Phyllis Rackin for a discussion of 'women in *King John* usurp[ing] masculine prerogatives', in *Engendering a Nation: A Feminist Account of Shakespeare's English Histories* (London: Routledge, 1997), pp. 120–4.

35 Erasmus, *Collected Works*, Vol. XXXI: *Adages Ii1 to Iv100*, trans. Margaret Mann Phillips, annot. R. A. B. Mynors (Toronto: University of Toronto Press, 1982), p. 147; Erasmus, 'Multae regum aures atque oculi', *Secundus tomus adagiorum ...* (Basel: Froben, 1540), pp. 60–1.

36 'Unicus filius hic erat mihi superstes, oculus vitae', in *Euripidis ... tragoedie XVIII*, trans. Dorotheus Camillus (Basel: Robert Winter, 1541), sig. Br; 'Unus iste filius

erat mihi reliquus, oculus vitae', in *Euripidis tragoediae*, trans. Philip Melanchthon (Frankfurt: Ludwig Luz [Ludovicus Lucius], 1562), p. 392; 'Unicus hic mihi erat filius, vitae oculus', in *Euripides ... in latinum sermonem conversus ...*, trans. Caspar Stiblin, annot. Jakob Moltzer and Jean Brodeau (Basel: J. Oporin, 1562), p. 254.

37 Jean-Christophe Mayer notes that 'through the desperate cries of the play's victims — often female, like Constance — we are gradually under the impression that *King John* is a story of broken faith'; 'Faith and doubt in Shakespeare's *Henry VI*, Parts 1 and 2, and *King John*', *Shakespeare Jahrbuch*, 149 (2013), 73–87 (p. 82). Goodland, *Female Mourning*, discusses Constance's passionate rhetoric from the perspective of Reformation prohibition of mourning rituals, pp. 119–33 (p. 133).

38 See Chapter 3 (Dominique Goy-Blanquet).

39 See Shakespeare, *King John*, ed. Honigmann, p. 109n; and Holinshed's account in the appendix, p. 154.

40 Homer's various options for Astyanax's future include Andromache's prediction that he will be hurled from the top of a tower. See Phillippo, 'A future for Astyanax', p. 319.

41 Bullough, *Narrative and Dramatic Sources of Shakespeare*, Vol. IV, p. 119.

42 Rogers, 'King John, directed by Josie Rourke', p. 47.

43 Ovid associates Astyanax's death and Hector's fatal defence of the city (*Metamorphoses*, XIII, 415–18), which Arthur Golding translates as follows: 'Astyanax downe was cast / From that same turret from the which his moother in tyme past / Had shewed him his father stand oft fighting too defend / Himself and that same famous realme of Troy, that did descend / From many noble aunceetors.' Ovid, *The .xv. Bookes of P. Ovidius Naso, Entytuled Metamorphosis ...*, trans. Arthur Golding, facsimile of the 1567 edition, ed. W. H. D. Rouse (London: Centaur Press, 1961), p. 261.

44 Peyré, in a note to this passage, suggests an analogy with Pyrrhus in *Hamlet*, II.ii.452–64; *Le roi Jean*, in Shakespeare, *Œuvres complètes*, Vol. III, p. 1625n11.

45 Constance's first speech (III.iv.23–36) – the scene in which Brandl saw analogies with Andromache – is dominated by imagery inherited from medieval representations of death that are similarly uppermost in Juliet's thoughts before she drinks Friar Laurence's potion: 'the necrophiliac allegory uncannily combines the emblematic tradition of the medieval Dance of Death with the oxymoron-based eroticism of Renaissance amatory poetry'; Luis Zenón Martínez, '"Needful woe": *King John* and the gods', *Cahiers élisabéthains*, 87 (2015), 21–41 (p. 32).

5

Venetian Jasons, parti-coloured lambs and a tainted wether: Ovine tropes and the Golden Fleece in *The Merchant of Venice*

Atsuhiko Hirota

THE *MERCHANT OF VENICE* abounds in allusions to the myth of the Golden Fleece, unlike the rest of the canon where key terms associated with the myth are rarely mentioned explicitly. The myth circulated widely in sixteenth-century Europe. Familiarity with its classical versions, known through Ovid's *Metamorphoses* and Seneca's *Medea*, in Latin and vernacular translation, was coloured by medieval traditions, chivalric and imperial (the Order of the Golden Fleece), amorous (Petrarchan comparisons of a mistress's hair to the Fleece) and spiritual (identification of the Fleece with the Holy Lamb).[1] All this informed reception in continental Europe as in England.[2] Jonathan Bate analyses the myth in *The Merchant of Venice* in the wider context of Shakespeare's Ovidianism, as an example of the 'capacity of Ovidian allusion to destabilize comedy's march towards harmony'; Elizabeth S. Sklar argues that Jason and Bassanio are morally ambiguous heroes of romance, 'Jason [being] a significantly apt prototype of Bassanio in both achievement and moral character'; and John Gillies explores the myth's significance in the context of the era's ambivalent cultural attitudes to Venice. More recently, Henry Weinfield has linked the allusions to the myth to Antonio's plot to strip ('to fleece') Shylock of his property.[3]

This article analyses the significance of the Golden Fleece myth as a sub-text of *The Merchant of Venice*. I contend that its contribution to the dramatic texture and spatial mapping of the play extends well beyond Ovidian and Senecan interactions: it also helps to shape the play's rich syncretic patterns of classical and biblical tropes. This intertextuality is enabled primarily by early modern variations on the myth, which include the use of metaphorical language to address economic issues, overseas trade and the importance of the wool industry: Mark Netzloff has analysed the myth in relation to early modern mercantilism and proto-capitalism as reflected in the play's economic language, and Roze Hentschell has shown the significance of sheep, particularly in the context that hit the cloth industry in the Jacobean period, after the debacle of the Cocayne project.[4] After considering the love/money complex represented mainly by the Jason-like Venetians, I shall focus on two ovine tropes – Shylock's mention of his profit as 'parti-coloured lambs' and Antonio's self-definition as a 'tainted wether of the flock'. I shall argue that the Golden Fleece myth and biblical parables are brought together in an intricate network of ovine images that radiates through the whole play, inviting audiences to revisit initial, male-induced representations of the play's three female figures, Portia, Nerissa and Jessica.

Venetian Jasons

The first reference to the Golden Fleece in *The Merchant of Venice* occurs in the opening scene. Although Bassanio is reluctant to reveal the name of the lady he is courting, after being persistently questioned by Antonio, he finally says:

> Her name is Portia, nothing undervalu'd
> To Cato's daughter, Brutus' Portia.
> Nor is the wide world ignorant of her worth,
> For the four winds blow in from every coast
> Renowned suitors, and her sunny locks
> Hang on her temples like a golden fleece,
> Which makes her seat of Belmont Colchis' strond,
> And many Jasons come in quest of her.
>
> (I.i.165–72)

The name Portia evokes brave perseverance and marital devotion through reference to her Roman namesake. Bassanio, however, does not linger on this model of exemplariness and goes on to compare Portia's hair to the Golden Fleece, Belmont becoming 'Colchis' strond', where the fleece was kept by King Aeëtes. Through the allusion to Portia as an embodiment of Roman virtues, Bassanio seeks to convince Antonio of his noble intentions; but he soon reveals his underlying motives, shifting from considerations of her moral value to her 'worth' as an object of (erotic and financial) desire, in a process of commodification whereby he stakes out the love/money, courting/trade, Golden Fleece/Medea tensions from the outset. In the myth as elaborated by Apollonius Rhodius in his *Argonautica* and successively handed down and reworked in a long and rich literary tradition that includes Ovid, Euripides, Seneca and Boccaccio, Jason wins the Golden Fleece with the help of Medea, the daughter of Aeëtes, who falls in love with the foreigner and betrays her father.[5] If Bassanio is to be a successful Jason in Belmont and win the Fleece, he will need a Medea: here, as we shall see, Portia doubles with the Golden Fleece, even though critics disagree on whether, or the extent to which, she actually helps Bassanio choose the right casket.[6] As if to confirm this connection, Bassanio returns to the colour of Portia's hair after finding her portrait in the right casket: 'Here, in her hairs, / The painter plays the spider and hath woven / A golden mesh t'entrap the hearts of men / Faster than gnats in cobwebs' (III.ii.120–3). Bassanio weaves his desire for gold with the spider's dangerous web: he is Jason-like in his quest for the golden-haired Portia; the poet is Arachne-like in the 'golden mesh' of associations he weaves, which entraps the characters while inviting spectators and readers to reinterpret the Petrarchan cliché.[7]

The primary significance, however, of the Golden Fleece trope for Bassanio, who has 'disabled' his estate (I.i.123), is with reference to Portia's property: 'In Belmont is a lady richly left, / And she is fair and, fairer than that word, / Of wondrous virtues' (I.i.161–3). The whole speech is constructed on a chiasmic pattern: Portia is 'richly left', fair (Golden Fleece), a pattern of virtue (true to her Roman namesake) and altogether desirable – the object of competing quests. Bassanio also compares her numerous suitors (including himself) to 'many Jasons', an additionally ominous comparison (for Portia), since Jason is not known for his fidelity: he deserted Hypsipyle, queen of Lemnos, before sailing for Colchis, then left Medea for Creusa (or Glauce), daughter of King Creon of Corinth.[8] The Golden Fleece is an apt metaphor for Portia's assets, which entice adventurers such as Bassanio, some of whom – like Jason and the Argonauts – have travelled from distant lands. Thus, from the outset, Bassanio's ambivalent use of the myth draws attention to motivations that are both financial and amorous, anticipating the bittersweet reconciliation in the final scene.[9]

Before this direct reference to the Golden Fleece and 'Jasons', Antonio is allusively compared to the classical hero too – there are indeed 'many Jasons' in this play. Soon after the opening of the play, Salerio tells Antonio, somewhat flatteringly:

> Your mind is tossing on the ocean,
> There where your argosies with portly sail
> Like signiors and rich burghers on the flood,
> Or as it were the pageants of the sea,

Do overpeer the petty traffickers
That cur'sy to them, do them reverence,
As they fly by them with their woven wings.

(I.i.8–14)

Although the term 'argosy' (a merchant-vessel of the largest size and burden) originates probably from the Italian word *ragusa*, it is inevitably resonant, especially in the context of this play, with the *Argo*, on which Jason and his companions sail to Colchis.[10] Just as Bassanio uses the Golden Fleece as a metaphor of Portia's property and, by metonymy, her golden hair, the association of Antonio and Jason signals that the merchant literally seeks his fortune by means of overseas trade: his argosies, also mentioned by Shylock (I.iii.16), are expected to bring him Golden Fleeces from various parts of the world. At the same time, the analogy is also suggestive of what Antonio is not: he does not sail in his *Argos* – he seeks the Golden Fleece at a distance, just as, one might argue, he seeks love by proxy, financing Bassanio's venture in Belmont. In that, he is no initiator of a new myth.[11]

Yet another reference to the Golden Fleece in *The Merchant of Venice* reveals further associations between the Venetians and the myth, pointing back to Bassanio's notion of the fleece and an amorous quest, which is developed into a collective mode. Gratiano, who has married Nerissa, Portia's confidante, greets Salerio in Belmont with 'How doth that royal merchant, good Antonio? / I know he will be glad of our success; / We are the Jasons; we have won the fleece' (III.ii.239–41). The colour of Nerissa's hair remains unknown. If, however, her name (possibly deriving from the Italian *nero*) suggests black hair, and considering the fact that Nerissa is no rich heiress, the reference to the Golden Fleece is further subverted when put in the mouth of Gratiano, who tends to devalue everything that relates to affect. Clearly, he is thinking in terms of sexual conquest – and seems to be unaware of the somewhat ominous prospect for their relationship, which may not have escaped some members of the audience: if Gratiano is a Jason, then perhaps Nerissa will prove a Medea.

Salerio's reply confirms that Antonio is indeed another Jason: 'I would you had won the fleece that he hath lost' (III.ii.242). Salerio is the bearer of a letter for Bassanio, informing him that Antonio has lost all his ships, the fleece referring to the goods that his 'argosies' should have brought back to Venice. Bassanio asks:

But is it true, Salerio?
Hath all his ventures fail'd? What, not one hit?
From Tripolis, from Mexico, and England,

From Lisbon, Barbary, and India,
And not one vessel scape the dreadful touch
Of merchant-marring rocks?

(III.ii.266–71)

The destinations of Antonio's ships confirm what Shylock had ascertained when evaluating the risks of Antonio's surety: 'He hath an argosy bound to Tripoli, another to the Indies; I understand moreover upon the Rialto, he hath a third at Mexico, a fourth for England, and other ventures he hath squandered abroad' (III.ii.16–20).[12]

In early modern England, Mexico evoked the image of precious metals, a commodity represented as the Golden Fleece. Mexico also brought to mind the piracy that their conveying encouraged – here suggested by the word 'fleece', which also meant 'a share of booty'[13] – and England's rivalry on the seas with Spain. In Christopher Marlowe's *Doctor Faustus*, Valdes, a German magician, lists what spirits conjured by magic can do:

From Venice shall they drag huge argosies,
And from America the golden fleece
That yearly stuffs old Philip's treasury,
If learnèd Faustus will be resolute.

(A-Text, I.i.132–5)[14]

Products brought to Europe from the New World under the Spanish rule were readily represented in terms of the Golden Fleece. Mythology, economics – both legal (merchant trade) and less so (piracy) – and politics mutually reinforce the ambivalence, not to say downright cynicism, of amorous, financial and diplomatic strategies. In Canto VII of *Troia Britanica* (1609), Thomas Heywood compares the Argonauts' journeying towards Colchis to 'our island voyages' – an expedition led by Robert Devereux, earl of Essex, to intercept a Spanish fleet bringing gold from America. Heywood describes 'Renowned Essex ... Who from Hesperia brought to Englands Greece / More gold then would have weigh'd down Jasons fleece' (stanzas 50–3). As Gaëlle Ginestet notes in her online edition of the canto, 'Essex failed in his mission, but Heywood rewrites history in his favour, fashioning a new myth as he elevates Essex to a status whereby he outdoes the mythological hero on whom he is modelled.'[15]

While *The Merchant of Venice* echoes Valdes's link between the Venetian merchants' international trading and the voyage of the *Argo*, Antonio's doomed trade with England is also relevant to the myth in the light of the identification between English wool and the legendary fleece. In the *Perambulation* of Kent (1570), William Lambarde compares the 'exceeding fineness of the fleece (which passeth all other Europe at this day)' with the 'auncient, delicate wooll of Tarentum, or the Golden Fleece of Colchos'.[16] The lost 'fleece' mentioned by Salerio might well have included – in the minds of Shakespeare's Elizabethan audiences – wool from England, since this was the country's main source of wealth in its overseas trade.

Thus in The Merchant of Venice the Venetians appear as 'Jasons' in quest of the Golden Fleece in its entwined amorous and economic associations. The identification is enabled by the appropriation of the myth in a culturally specific context. Bassanio's money/love ambivalence is based on the commodification of gold and interaction with the Petrarchan cliché, and evokes the subsequent tale of unfaithful Jason and violent Medea for audiences familiar with the myth in its classical and Renaissance variations. Antonio, on the other hand, emerges as another Jason in association with the economic significance of the myth as represented in Elizabethan texts and on the stage. The Venetian Jasons are the product of myth and its reconfigurations, which are interwoven historically and contemporaneously.

The Golden Fleece, Medea and Shylock's 'parti-color'd lambs'

To justify charging interest, Shylock tells Antonio and Bassanio the tale of Jacob's trick to ensure that Laban's ewes give birth to 'parti-color'd lambs' (I.iii.88). While Lars Engle observes an analogy between Shylock's position in the Venetian economy and Jacob's situation with Laban,[17] this narrative – based on Genesis 30:31–43 – is a source of puzzlement not only to Antonio but also to critics. In her analysis of the source for this allusion, Joan Ozark Holmer cites Mark Eccles's 'expression of perplexity', and writes 'In Shylock's defence of usury, drawn from the example of Jacob's conduct, there seems to be little appositeness or ingenuity; indeed, it is not easy to discover in what the parallelism of the two cases consists.'[18] While the Biblical parable signals Shylock's familiarity with the Old Testament, in keeping with his Jewish faith, sheep-breeding does not sound like a good analogy for the business of money-lending. When Antonio asks accusingly whether Jacob took interest, Shylock replies:

> No, not take interest, not as you would say
> Directly int'rest. Mark what Jacob did:
> When Laban and himself were compremis'd

> That all the eanlings which were streak'd and pied
> Should fall as Jacob's hire, the ewes being rank
> In end of autumn turned to the rams,
> And when the work of generation was
> Between these woolly breeders in the act,
> The skillful shepherd pill'd me certain wands,
> And in the doing of the deed of kind,
> He stuck them up before the fulsome ewes,
> Who then conceiving did in eaning time
> Fall parti-color'd lambs, and those were Jacob's.
>
> (I.iii.76–88)[19]

Antonio fails to see the connection between Jacob's manipulation and Shylock's charging interest: 'Was this inserted to make interest good? / Or is your gold and silver ewes and rams?' (I.iii.94–5). While the Geneva Bible glosses the description of Jacob's manipulation of rods, or 'wands', to justify his action, 'Jakob herein used no deceit: for it was Gods comma[n]dement ...' (Genesis 30:37), Shylock seems to hedge: 'I cannot tell, I make it breed as fast' (96).[20] From the perspective of Antonio and the Christians in the play, it is outrageous to compare sheep-breeding, a natural act, to the taking of interest. Antonio's question, however, leads to identifying sheep and precious metals. This identification in turn introduces an overlapping of the biblical parable and the classical myth, especially with reference to Antonio's Mexican trade. By agreeing to lend Bassanio money with Antonio's expected profit as surety, Shylock further interweaves the two ovine tales, since he is exchanging his biblical lambs for the Venetian's Golden Fleece.[21]

The twofold, biblical and mythological aspects of these ovine tropes further intermingle in Jessica and Lorenzo's elopement. The tale of Medea and Jason resurfaces in their dialogue in the final act of the play. At the opening of V.i, Lorenzo banteringly compares himself to Troilus, imagining how he thought of Cressida (1–6) in similarly bright moonlight. This comparison, however, inevitably invites a parallel between Jessica and Cressida, a complex, self-styled *figura* of unfaithful woman.[22] Jessica's choice of the tale of Pyramus and Thisbe in response (6–9) may suggest her conciliatory attempt to bring the dialogue back to instances of faithful (albeit tragic) love.[23] Lorenzo, however, is more interested in unfaithful lovers. He mentions Dido 'with a willow in her hand' waving as Aeneas departs (9–12). With this reference to Dido, Lorenzo might be implying that men as well as women are unfaithful. If so, the analogy here is between Jessica and the forsaken Dido, which makes him a 'false' Aeneas.[24] Jessica then refers to Medea: 'In such a night / Medea gathered the enchanted herbs / That did renew old Aeson' (12–14). Although Jessica focuses on Medea's witchcraft and her power of rejuvenation rather than on the winning of the Fleece and subsequent flight from Colchis, the comparison between Medea and herself naturally leads on to a symmetry between Lorenzo and Jason – another unfaithful lover – and invites the suggestion that Lorenzo is modelling himself both on the mythological figure and on his prototype in the play, Bassanio – all the more so since this bantering is taking place in the gardens of Belmont. Katherine Heavey suggests that 'Jessica's use of the inappropriate story in *The Merchant of Venice* exposes her own foolish innocence, while simultaneously hinting at a suppressed undercurrent of darkness and potential tragedy'.[25] Foolish as Jessica may be, and ignorant of mythology's complex layers of meaning, this mention of Medea is indeed ominous given the previous references to the Golden Fleece in the play. Lorenzo's next speech is more focused:

> In such a night
> Did Jessica steal from the wealthy Jew,
> And with an unthrift love did run from Venice,
> As far as Belmont.
>
> (14–17)

Although the verb 'to steal' applies here to Jessica's secret departure from her father's house in darkness and in disguise, it simultaneously evokes theft.[26] In the trial scene, Antonio calls Lorenzo 'the gentleman / That lately stole his daughter' (IV.i.384–5), also describing the elopement in terms of stealing. It is as if Lorenzo, another Jason of Venice, had organised his own flight from Colchis, running away with Jessica, a Medea-like daughter, and her father's wealth – his Golden Fleece. The economic dimension of the Fleece imagery once again interweaves with the love motif, with a new twist in the yarn. Bassanio hopes to increase his own wealth by winning Portia; Antonio's trade ventures are expected to generate more wealth while being exposed to various hazards. Lorenzo, in contrast, lacks his fellow Venetians' sense of mercantile strategies and Jacob's profit-seeking cunning, even though he shares their opportunism: his love gives signs of being 'unthrift', in that he seems to have linked his fate to someone who spends 'fourscore ducats' in one night in Genoa and buys a monkey in exchange for a turquoise ring that carries emotional and economic value (III.i.118–23).

Jessica is further like Medea. Earlier in the play, Lorenzo says 'She hath directed / How I shall take her from her father's house, / What gold and jewels she is furnish'd with …' (II.iv.29–31), and reveals the initiative

Jessica took when planning her elopement. She throws a casket from the window (II.vi.33–4) and says before she joins her lover 'I will make fast the doors, and gild myself / With some moe ducats' (49–50). The same sexual synecdoche (the casket) links Portia and Jessica: while the former may have subtly bent the rules concerning the three caskets left by her father, the latter casts herself actively in the dual Fleece/Medea role that Bassanio had assigned to Portia. Jessica 'gilds' herself, choosing to play the part in which Portia has been initially cast, a Golden Fleece, which she doubles with another part, that of the father-betraying Medea. According to Salanio, Shylock rages about in the streets of Venice listing the damage as follows:

> A sealed bag, two sealed bags of ducats,
> Of double ducats, stol'n from me by my daughter!
> And jewels, two stones, two rich and precious stones,
> Stol'n by my daughter! ...
> She hath the stones upon her, and the ducats.
>
> (II.viii.18–22)

Jessica's taking of the 'stones' has an obvious sexual connotation, making her reference to Medea's rejuvenation of Aeson particularly ironic. Jessica, in a sense, outdoes Medea: not only does she betray her father and elope with a foreigner, ill-gotten-treasure and all, but she also symbolically castrates him in much the same way that Medea, more indirectly if more horrifically, denies her father a lineage by killing her brother. It is as if the darkness, her disguise as a page and the excitement of elopement disinhibited her, revealing a (literally) darker side to her love. Her dissemination of Shylock's treasure, including his 'stones', is comparable to Medea's scattering of Apsyrtus's limbs – which Katherine Heavey discusses in the next chapter – and features Jessica all the more impressively as another Medea in the play.[27] The men who set out in quest of Golden Fleeces seem to overlook the rest of the story: successful Jasons are apt to get their Medeas too – with a vengeance.

Jessica shares this combination of castration and dismemberment with John Studley's Medea, in his translation of Seneca's play. Studley, who refused 'to feel bound by his original' and displayed a 'fondness for incongruous colloquialism and expansion', introduces the theme of castration, which does not appear in the Latin original.[28] On learning that Jason is deserting her, Studley's Medea lists the criminal deeds she has committed for him:

> My tender Brother eke, that with my Syer did me pursue,
> Whom with his secret parts cut of, I wicked Virgin slewe,

> Whose shreaded and dismembered corps, with sword in gobbits hewd,
> (A wofull Coarse to th' Fathers heart) on Pontus ground I strewed.[29]

The sexualised scattering of limbs reveals a feature of the Elizabethan reconfiguration of the Golden Fleece myth in which both Studley and Shakespeare participate: their rewriting of the myth lays emphasis on Medea as a threat to masculinity.

Shylock's 'parti-color'd lambs' are destined to become a Golden Fleece for both Antonio and Lorenzo. In the sentence meted out to Shylock, Portia says:

> It is enacted in the laws of Venice,
> If it be proved against an alien,
> That by direct, or indirect attempts
> He seek the life of any citizen,
> The party 'gainst the which he doth contrive
> Shall seize one-half his goods; the other half
> Comes to the privy coffer of the state ...
>
> (IV.i.348–54)

One half of Shylock's 'goods' becomes Antonio's property, presumably to help fund a new fleet of argosies in quest of yet more Golden Fleeces. The other half goes to the exchequer ('privy coffer') of the Venetian State. The details of the 'goods' mentioned here are not given, but Shylock's response, 'You take my life / When you do take the means whereby I live' (IV.i.376–7), suggests that they include the capital he needs for his money-lending business. Invited to show mercy, Antonio proposes an adjustment of this sentence. He says:

> So please my lord the Duke and all the court,
> To quit the fine for one-half of his goods,
> I am content; so he will let me have
> The other half in use, to render it
> Upon his death unto the gentleman
> That lately stole his daughter.
>
> (IV.i.380–5)

Although what Antonio means here is not altogether clear, it seems that he is asking the Duke to remit the half of Shylock's goods assigned to the State by Portia's sentence for Shylock's own use and that he will become the trustee of the other half (the portion given to him by Portia), which is to become Lorenzo's property on Shylock's death. After demanding that Shylock become a Christian immediately, he continues, 'The other, that he do record a gift, / Here in the court, of all he dies possess'd / Unto his son Lorenzo and his daughter' (388–90). What Shylock will possess at his death, namely the remnant of half his goods to be remitted thanks to Antonio's 'mercy', will also become the property of Lorenzo and Jessica. The trial thus decides that the whole of Shylock's 'goods' will end up becoming the property of his Jason-like son-in-law, Lorenzo, who has also won a Medea-like Jessica. Shylock's 'parti-color'd lambs' become finally identical with the Golden Fleece, syncretising the biblical and the classical strands of the play through the commodified sheep.

The revival of 'a tainted wether in the flock'

When Antonio asks Shylock to lend Bassanio 3,000 ducats, he offers as surety the profits that he expects his argosies to bring back. In his mind the Golden Fleece cargo of his argosies is exchangeable with Shylock's 'parti-color'd lambs', which help to finance Bassanio's own quest for a Golden Fleece at Belmont. This exchange is refused by Shylock, who does not take this prospect of gain as guaranteed. Shylock is too familiar with the risks of maritime trade. During their negotiation, Shylock introduces yet another ovine trope, when he proposes a bond of one pound of Antonio's flesh, which he compares with that of mutton and other ruminants, in place of the expected trade profit: 'A pound of man's flesh, taken from a man, / Is not so estimable, profitable neither, / As flesh of muttons, beeves or goats' (I.iii.165–7). Through this ovine reference, Antonio's flesh is redefined as a commodity, exchangeable with Shylock's money. Remarkably, merchants were sometimes compared with sheep in early modern England. John Stow writes in defence of commercial profits:

> And truely Marchants and Retaylors doe not altogether *intus canere*, and profit themselves only, for the prince and realme both are enriched by their riches: the realme wonneth treasure, if their trade be so moderated by authority, that it berake not proportion, & they besides beare a good fleece, which the prince may sheare when shee [he] seeth good.[30]

Thomas Moisan quotes this passage in his argument about the relevance of Antonio's mercantile activity to an English audience.[31] While Moisan does not particularly emphasise the ovine metaphor, this passage shows that the merchant–sheep association, particularly with its focus on fleece, was readily available for Shakespeare and his audience.

Antonio himself introduces another ovine image when his ventures fail. In the trial scene, he tells Bassanio:

> I pray you, think you question with the Jew:
> You may as well go stand upon the beach
> And bid the main flood bate his usual height;
> You may as well use question with the wolf
> Why he hath made the ewe bleat for the lamb ...
>
> (IV.i.69–73)

Insisting on the futility of all attempts to obtain Shylock's mercy, Antonio compares the Jew with a wolf and himself with a lamb.[32] Antonio, whose flesh has become exchangeable with Shylock's 'parti-color'd lambs', thus develops the metaphor of the lamb, which also links him to Jesus's sacrifice.[33] This, in turn, takes him into another, medieval network of images related to the Golden Fleece myth since, as we see in the *Ovide moralisé*, allegorical interpretations identified the Fleece with Christ:

> Jason prist la toison doree:
> Jhesu en la vierge honnoree
> Prist char et humaine nature.
> C'est la toison, c'est la courture
> Dont Dieux, douz moutons, fu couvert,
> Qui dou glaive ot le cors ouvert
> Pour home, et fu sacrefiez
> Et pendus et crucefiez.
>
> (VII, 799–806)

> Jason took the Golden Fleece:
> Jesus in the honoured Virgin
> Took on flesh and human nature.
> 'Tis the Fleece, 'tis the hide
> That covered God the gentle lamb
> Whose body was cut open by the spear
> For mankind; who was sacrificed
> And hanged and crucified.[34]

Antonio as a sacrificial lamb stands at an intersection of biblical and classical tropes, and the theme of sacrifice is further developed in biblical and classical associations with ovine references. In the trial scene, Bassanio encourages Antonio, saying somewhat irresponsibly and optimistically, 'Good cheer, Antonio! What, man, courage yet! / The Jew shall have my flesh, blood, bones and all, / Ere thou shalt lose for me one drop of blood' (IV.i.111–13).

Antonio replies, 'I am a tainted wether of the flock, / Meetest for death' (114–15). Editors of the play have noted the association between this 'tainted wether' and the ram Abraham sacrifices in place of his son Isaac (Genesis 22:13).[35] Sacrifices in the Old and New Testaments thus overlap in Antonio, showing a further interplay of the ovine images.

Furthermore, with this self-definition, Antonio emerges as an old ram who nonetheless still has some life in him, since Portia saves him from imminent death. In a sense, he is given a new lease of life, in much the same way as Aeson is rejuvenated by Medea in Ovid's *Metamorphoses*. Although the rejuvenation of Aeson, which Jessica refers to, is a rare example of Medea's benevolent use of her magic, Ovid's narrative is extremely bloody: she slits the old man's throat and lets his blood run out before filling his blood vessels with an enchanted potion (VII, 285–7). Also, she cuts the throat of a black sheep and drenches the ditches she has dug with its blood in sacrifice to Hecate and the god of youth (242–5). More horrifyingly, this episode is followed by another attempt at rejuvenation, which ends up with the murder of Pelias (Jason's uncle, who had sent him in quest of the Golden Fleece in order to get rid of him). This tale is also filled with blood, both of an old ram (312–17) and of Pelias himself, who is stabbed to death by his own daughters at the instigation of Medea (332–49). Bloodshed is a central issue in the trial scene. The references to blood that precede Antonio's self-definition as a 'tainted wether' reveal that Bassanio anticipates the inevitable bloodshed. Antonio, however, is rescued from a bloody death by Portia, one of the Medea-like women in the play, in the role of life-preserver. Far from being abandoned, the play's initial identification between Portia and Medea is thus reactivated, emphasising the play's shift in perspective, from a patriarchal, male-centred vision of Portia (her father's and Bassanio's) that casts her in the passive role of a desirable erotic and financial commodity, to the unease one senses in Antonio about owing his life to a disturbing, uncontrolled agent of change.[36] In the references and allusions to the Golden Fleece myth, Antonio is comparable to the sacrifices in the bloody Ovidian tale of Medea as well as those in the Bible, embodying the interweaving of the biblical and classical images using the ovine references pursued throughout the play.[37]

It is generally agreed that the plot of *The Merchant of Venice* comes mostly from the tale of Giannetto's courting of a lady of Belmonte in Giovanni Fiorentino's *Il pecorone*. This narrative, however, does not contain ovine tropes, whether biblical or classical. As in other plays, Shakespeare reinjects mythological material into his main source text, enriching the original plot with narrative strands lifted from the classics and his script with direct and indirect mythological allusions that incorporate successive rewritings and interpretations. In *The Merchant of Venice* Shakespeare interweaves the Golden Fleece myth with the Italian tale, and works in biblical elements. Bassanio and Gratiano compare themselves to Jasons, appropriating the interplay between the myth and Petrarchan tropes while hinting, perhaps unwittingly, at a comparison between their wives and Medea. Antonio's quest for profit through his fleet of argosies is comparable to Jason's expedition to Colchis. The economic associations of the myth also enable Bassanio to identify Portia with her property. Furthermore, Jessica's reference to Medea reveals the similarity between Shylock's daughter and the sorceress who betrays her father and helps her lover steal the Golden Fleece – with Lorenzo as another Venetian Jason in this play. The extensive references to the Golden Fleece myth in *The Merchant of Venice* thus provide role models for the play's characters. The myth's significance, however, is more extensive and essential to the play. Addressing central preoccupations (such as anxiety over profitable but risky overseas trade, money/love ambivalence in marriage, and misogynistic fear of female power), the Golden Fleece myth, both in its classical versions and its later rewritings, informs the framework and the poetic fabric of the play, and attaches contemporary relevance to its seemingly timeless world.

The myth also presents an example of Shakespeare's handling of plural subtexts. Shylock's narrative of Jacob and his parti-coloured lambs draws the audience's attention to sheep and introduces another interaction with the Golden Fleece trope. Like Aeëtes's Golden Fleece, Shylock's profit from money-lending is stolen, by the Medea-like Jessica and her Jason-like lover, Lorenzo. At the end of the play, all of Shylock's property is to fall into the hands of this couple: Shylock's Old Testament lambs end up as Lorenzo-Jason's Golden Fleece. Antonio's representations throughout the play also show how tightly interwoven the mythological and biblical tropes are and how they also interact in processes of reversal. Antonio, who first appears as one of the Venetian Jasons in quest of his own Golden Fleece, is also represented as a sacrificial lamb, comparable to Jesus, whose body the mythological Fleece allegorically represents. He is also analogous to the ram of Abraham's sacrifice through self-definition as a 'tainted wether'. This ovine image further reveals his likeness to the ram in the tale of Medea's rejuvenation when he is rescued and given a new lease of life by Portia. The mythological fleece is juxtaposed, transferred onto and interwoven with biblical sheep imagery. In *The Merchant of Venice*, sheep function as what Peyré calls a 'metapoetic intertextual marker',[38] revealing an instance of multiple layers of interaction among subtexts – classical and biblical, medieval and Renaissance. This intertextuality results in a network of meanings that give the play contemporary significance through cultural and material associations – especially misogynic and mercantile. Antonio's closing words – 'Sweet lady, you have given me life and living, / For here I read for certain that my ships / Are safely come to road' (V.i.286–8) – signify his revival as a Jason-like merchant, thus ending the play on a final reference to the myth. The emasculating power attached to Medea-like women in the play, however, has changed spectators' views of the Venetian Jasons and the Golden Fleeces they quest for, leaving room for uneasiness about the quality of this revival.

Notes

This chapter developed from papers I presented at the IRCL (Université Paul-Valéry Montpellier 3) in 2014 and at seminars hosted by the Shakespeare Society of Japan (in 2011 and 2013). I am grateful to Professors Jean-Christophe Mayer, Andrew Gurr, Mariko Ichikawa, Shoichiro Kawai and Manabu Tsuruta, the organisers of these occasions. My gratitude also extends to the editors of this volume, whose comments have been most valuable. Part of the research for this article has been enabled by the JSPS Grant-in-Aid for Scientific Research (no. 26370276).

1 See Yves Peyré, 'Marlowe's Argonauts', in Jean-Pierre Maquerlot and Michèle Willems (eds), *Travel and Drama in Shakespeare's Time* (Cambridge: Cambridge University Press, 1996), pp. 106–23. On the Order of the Golden Fleece, mentioned in *1 Henry VI* (IV.vii.68–9), see Chapter 3 (Dominique Goy-Blanquet).

2 I shall not be discussing Prospero's speech (*The Tempest*, V.i.33–50), which rewrites Medea's in *Metamorphoses*, VII, 197–206, already discussed by others: e.g. Stephen Orgel, 'Introduction to *The Tempest*' (Oxford: Oxford University Press, 1987), p. 19, and Jonathan Bate, *Shakespeare and Ovid* (Oxford: Clarendon Press, 1993), pp. 8, 250–5; nor Seneca's *Medea* and *Macbeth*, discussed by Inga-Stina Ewbank, 'The fiend-like queen: A note on *Macbeth* and Seneca's *Medea*', *Shakespeare Survey*, 19 (1966), 82–94, Robert S. Miola, *Shakespeare and Classical Tragedy: The Influence of Seneca* (Oxford: Clarendon Press, 1992), pp. 103–9, and Colin Burrow, *Shakespeare and Classical Antiquity* (Oxford: Oxford University Press, 2013), pp. 191–3.

3 Elizabeth S. Sklar, 'Bassanio's Golden Fleece', *Texas Studies of Literature and Language*, 18 (1976), 500–9 (p. 501); Bate, *Shakespeare and Ovid*, p. 151; John Gillies, *Shakespeare and the Geography of Difference* (Cambridge: Cambridge University Press, 1994), pp. 132–7; Henry Weinfeld, '"We are the Jasons, we have won the Fleece": Antonio's plot (and Shakespeare's) in *The Merchant of Venice* (what really happens in the play)', *The European Legacy*, 15 (2010), 149–58.

4   Mark Netzloff, 'The lead casket: Capital, mercantilism, and *The Merchant of Venice*', in Linda Woodbridge (ed.), *Money and the Age of Shakespeare: Essays in New Economic Criticism* (Basingstoke: Palgrave Macmillan, 2003), pp. 159–76 (pp. 166–7); Roze Hentschell, *The Culture of Cloth in Early Modern England: Textual Constructions of a National Identity* (Aldershot: Ashgate, 2008), pp. 22–4, 162–77.
5   Early modern readers knew the story mainly through Ovid's *Heroides*, XII, and *Metamorphoses*, VII; Seneca's *Medea*; and Boccaccio's *Famous Women*, XXXVIII, and *Genealogy of the Pagan Gods*, IV, xii.
6   See William Shakespeare, *The Merchant of Venice*, ed. John Drakakis (London: Bloomsbury, 2011), notes to III.ii.62 sd and 64; and Jay L. Halio's note to III.ii.63–72 in his edition of the play (Oxford: Oxford University Press, 1993). Michael Zuckert traces the Portia–Medea analogy in Bassanio's casket choice in 'The new Medea: On Portia's comic triumph in *The Merchant of Venice*', in Joseph Alulis and Vickie Sullivan (eds), *Shakespeare's Political Pageant: Essays in Literature and Politics* (Lanham: Rowman and Littlefield, 1996), pp. 3–36 (pp. 8–13).
7   See Yves Peyré, 'Iris's "rich scarf" and "Ariachne's broken woof": Shakespeare's mythology in the twentieth century', in Jonathan Bate, Jill L. Levenson and Dieter Mehl (eds), *Shakespeare and the Twentieth Century* (Newark: University of Delaware Press, 1998), pp. 280–93; and the introduction to this volume.
8   As Bate observes, 'He [Jason] has the dubious distinction of being the recipient of two letters from deserted lovers in the *Heroides* … Jason is *fallax Iason*, an archetype of male deceit and infidelity' (*Shakespeare and Ovid*, p. 153). Chaucer defines Jason as the 'rote of false lovers' in 'The legend of Hypsipyle and Medea' in *The Legend of Good Women* (IV, 1378). William Caxton's *The History of Jason* (1477), dedicated to Margaret, the Yorkist duchess of Burgundy, presents Jason in a more favourable light: see Katherine Heavey, *The Early Modern Medea: Medea in English Literature, 1558–1688* (Basingstoke: Palgrave Macmillan, 2015), p. 44; and Chapter 6 (Katherine Heavey) in this volume.
9   Bate writes: 'His stressing of wealth before beauty and virtue has the effect that his subsequent term "worth" comes to mean cash-value more than moral excellence' (*Shakespeare and Ovid*, p. 151). Alexander Leggatt considers that this comparison is 'not metaphorical enough to be romantic; his concern for the gold *as gold* is all too real'; *Shakespeare's Comedy of Love* (London: Methuen, 1974), p. 125. Peter Holland observes that Bassanio's description of the voyage to Belmont – a 'speculative enterprise' comparable to Antonio's mercantile ventures – as an 'epic quest' may be regarded as a 'kind of demeaning assessment of the meaning of his enterprise': '*The Merchant of Venice* and the value of money', *Cahiers élisabéthains*, 60 (2001), 13–31 (pp. 19–20). In *Shakespeare and the Economic Imperative: 'What's aught but as 'tis valued?'* (London: Routledge, 2008), pp. 93–5, Peter F. Grav compares Bassanio with Fenton and Petruchio.
10 See Sklar, 'Bassanio's Golden Fleece', pp. 508–9n14, for the argosy–*Argo* connection.

11 Barbara K. Lewalski reads the term 'venture' used by Salerio (I.i.15–17) as a running metaphor for Antonio's practice of Christian love, present in her view from the opening of the play, as inspired by Matthew 6:19–21, 31–3: 'Biblical allusion and allegory in *The Merchant of Venice*', *Shakespeare Quarterly*, 13:3 (1962), 327–43 (p. 329). The interweaving of the classical and biblical subtexts would thus be present from the outset.

12 On Shylock dismissing Antonio's ventures as 'squandering', see Holland, '*The Merchant of Venice* and the value of money', p. 19.

13 *Oxford English Dictionary*, s.v. 'fleece', 2b, obs.

14 Christopher Marlowe, *Doctor Faustus: A- and B-Texts (1604, 1616)*, ed. David Bevington and Eric Rasmussen (Manchester: Manchester University Press, 1993). See Netzloff, 'The lead casket', pp. 166–7, for representations of the 'precious metals of Americas' as the Golden Fleece. Another reference is to be found in Christopher Marlowe, *The Jew of Malta* (IV.ii.93–6), ed. N. W. Bawcutt (Manchester: Manchester University Press, 1990). Ithamore, Barabas's slave and accomplice, compares Bellamira, a courtesan, to the Golden Fleece as he plans to escape from Malta with the Jew's money – just as Lorenzo and Jessica elope, taking Shylock's money. See Peyré, 'Marlowe's Argonauts', pp. 116–17. Ithamore–Bellamira–Barabas and Lorenzo–Jessica–Shylock suggest the ways contemporary dramatists interweave mythological matter and style, emulating each other while inspired by the classics.

15 See Gaëlle Ginestet (ed.), *Troia Britanica canto VII* (2015), in Yves Peyré (gen. ed.), *Thomas Heywood: Troia Britanica (1609)*, an online edition, www.shakmyth.org (accessed 30 June 2016).

16 Quoted in Hentschell, *The Culture of Cloth*, p. 23. On the importance of the wool trade in sixteenth-century England, see pp. 3–9.

17 Lars Engle, '"Thrift is blessing": Exchange and explanation in *The Merchant of Venice*', *Shakespeare Quarterly*, 37:1 (1986), 20–37 (p. 31).

18 Joan Ozark Holmer, '"When Jacob graz'd his uncle Laban's sheep": A new source for *The Merchant of Venice*', *Shakespeare Quarterly*, 36:1 (1985), 64–5 (p. 64). Heather A. Hirschfeld points out that this scene functions 'as a touchstone for critical accounts of the way the play dramatizes the triumph, however complicated, of Christian over Hebraic biblical exegesis and of the new law over the old': '"We all expect a gentle answer, Jew": *The Merchant of Venice* and the psychotheology of conversion', *English Literary History*, 73:1 (2006), 61–81 (p. 61). See also Marc Shell, *Money, Language, and Thought* (Berkeley: University of California Press, 1982), pp. 48–55; and Julia Reinhard Lupton, *Citizen Saints: Shakespeare and Political Theology* (Chicago: University of Chicago Press, 2005), pp. 79–84. None of these critics has established a link between the classical and biblical sources in *The Merchant of Venice*.

19 The phrase 'parti-color'd lambs' suggests that Shylock is referring to the Geneva Bible (1560): 'the yong of party colour' (Genesis 30:39), '[t]he partie coloured'

(Genesis 31:8) and 'the she goates that are parti coloured, spotted with little & great spottes' (Genesis 31:12). The Bishop's Bible (1568) reads 'lambes ryngstreaked, spotted, and partie', 'the ringstraked' and 'the sheepe that are ringstraked, spotted, and partie'.

20   Another gloss in the Geneva Bible (Genesis 31:9) confirms Jacob's righteousness: 'This declareth that the thing which Iaakob did before was by Gods co[m]mandement, & not through deceite.' The gloss on Genesis 30:37 in the Bishop's Bible is more ambiguous, as if seeking to anticipate criticism: 'It is not lawfull by fraude to seke recompense of injurie: therefore Moyses sheweth afterward that God thus instructed Jacob.'
21   Gillies calls the Jason myth and the Old Testament story 'fleece' myths, both of which 'signif[y] a legendary origin of "profit" and "advantage"': *The Geography of Difference*, p. 134.
22   On *Troilus and Cressida*, see the introduction to this volume.
23   See *Metamorphoses*, IV, 55–166; and *A Midsummer Night's Dream*, III.i.1–106 and V.i.108–342.
24   On Dido and 'false' Aeneas, see Chapter 9 (Agnès Lafont) in the current volume.
25   Katherine Heavey, 'Medea' (2014), in Yves Peyré (ed.), *A Dictionary of Shakespeare's Classical Mythology* (2009–), www.shakmyth.org (accessed 30 June 2016). As she observes, Jessica's reference to Medea has been subject to critical disagreement. Bate writes: 'Shakespeare is contaminating a superficially lyrical interlude with a precursor text' (*Shakespeare and Ovid*, p. 155); Charles Martindale contends that Jessica's naive invocation does not suggest tragedy: 'Shakespeare's Ovid, Ovid's Shakespeare: A methodological Postscript', in A. B. Taylor and Charles Martindale (eds), *Shakespeare's Ovid* (Cambridge: Cambridge University Press, 2000), pp. 198–215 (pp. 202–3). I read this dialogue ironically, given the context for the reference and the couple's tainted characterisation, through their extravagant spending before coming to Belmont. This passage is discussed from a different perspective in Chapter 9 (Agnès Lafont).
26   For the ambiguity of this term in this speech, see Holland, '*The Merchant of Venice* and the value of money', pp. 21–2.
27   On Apsyrtus's murder, see Chapter 6 (Katherine Heavey); and Peyré, 'Absyrtus' (2014), in Peyré, *A Dictionary of Shakespeare's Classical Mythology*.
28   Heavey, *The Early Modern Medea*, p. 52.
29   Seneca, *Seneca His Tenne Tragedies, Translated into English*, trans. John Studley (1581), ed. Thomas Newton, Vol. II (London: Constable, 1927), p. 61.
30   John Stow, *A Survey of London: Printed from the Text of 1603*, ed. C. L. Kingsford, 2 vols (Oxford: Clarendon Press, 2000 [1908]), Vol. II, p. 211.
31   Thomas Moisan, '"Which is the merchant here? And which the Jew?": Subversion and recuperation in *The Merchant of Venice*', in Jean E. Howard and Marion F. O'Connor (eds), *Shakespeare Reproduced: The Text*

in *History and Ideology* (New York: Routledge, 1990 [1987]), pp. 188–206 (p. 191).

32 See *ibid.*, p. 193, for the wolf epithets applied to Shylock and present in early modern anti-usury tracts.

33 For Antonio's identification with Christ, see Lewalski, 'Biblical allusion and allegory', pp. 334, 339.

34 Quoted in Peyré, 'Marlowe's Argonauts', p. 118, with the English translation.

35 See Shakespeare, *The Merchant of Venice*, ed. Drakakis (p. 341), ed. Halio (pp. 49 and 193). As Janet Adelman notes in *Blood Relations: Christian and Jew in 'The Merchant of Venice'* (Chicago: University of Chicago Press, 2008), p. 183, in Play IV of the *Chester Mystery Cycle* the term 'wether' is used for the lamb that substitutes for Isaac. Abraham says 'Sacrifyce here mee sent ys, / and all, lorde, through thy grace. / An horned wether here I see'.

36 While Gillies considers that the play's initial identification between Portia and Medea is dropped (*The Geography of Difference*, p. 135), Zuckert notes the parallel between Portia's saving of Antonio and Medea's rejuvenation of Aeson ('The new Medea', p. 26).

37 The image of castration attached to the phrase 'tainted wether' blurs the distinction between Antonio and Shylock, whose stones were stolen by a Medea-like daughter. Portia/Balthazar's question draws attention to this: 'Which is the merchant here, and which the Jew?' (IV.i.174).

38 For this term, see Chapter 1 (Yves Peyré) in this volume, p. 32.

6

Fifty ways to kill your brother: Medea and the poetics of fratricide in early modern English literature

Katherine Heavey

IN THE POETIC COLLECTION *Hesperides* (1648), Robert Herrick includes the brief verse 'To his booke', in which he addresses his own literary creation, and reflects on its potentially unhappy afterlife in the hands of readers and critics:

> If hap it must, that I must see thee lye
> Absyrtus-like all torne confusedly:
> With solemne tears, and with much grief of heart,
> Ile recollect thee (weeping) part by part;
> And having washt thee, close thee in a chest
> With spice; that done, Ile leave thee to thy rest.[1]

This 'Absyrtus' (or Apsyrtus)[2] is the younger brother of the classical sorceress and infanticide Medea, and he meets his death at her hands, killed and torn to pieces so that Medea, along with her lover Jason and the rest of the Argonauts, might escape her pursuing father Aeëtes after their conquest of the Golden Fleece. Although he plays a relatively minor part in Medea's story, Apsyrtus is also foregrounded in one of Shakespeare's only direct references to Medea's myth, in *2 Henry VI*, when Young Clifford vows to avenge his father, killed by the duke of York during the Wars of the Roses:

> YOUNG CLIFFORD. ... Meet I an infant of the house of York
> Into as many gobbets will I cut it
> As wild Medea young Absyrtus did.
>
> (V.iii.57–9)

There is an obvious focus, in both the Stuart poem and the Elizabethan history play, on the rending and dismemberment of the boy: a bodily disintegration that seems somehow more important than his death. Beyond this, the two uses might seem to have little in common, not least because, while Young Clifford speaks from the point of view of Medea, Herrick evokes the *consequences* of her first crime against patriarchy and monarchy, imagining himself in the position of her grieving father Aeëtes. However, as I shall show, Herrick's choice of Apsyrtus, like Shakespeare's, is rooted in the knowledge of a combination of classical sources (particularly Ovid and Seneca) and in early modern translations of both classical authors. Moreover, both Herrick and Shakespeare use the figure of Apsyrtus, entirely innocent, but horribly and irrevocably divided from himself, to register anxieties about other kinds of division and destruction. Clifford hopes to emulate Medea in destroying not just a child, but the hopes of the Yorkist dynasty, and Shakespeare's audience are invited to consider the self-destructive and self-defeating effects of civil war. For Herrick, Apsyrtus is used to register fears about the future of his 'offspring' – his book – but simultaneously to express anxiety about the proper male reaction to the loss of a child, whether real or figurative: as I shall show, Herrick's imagining of himself as the father of an Apsyrtus-like child springs from a medieval and early modern tradition of probing Aeëtes's reaction to the death of his son. Apsyrtus's story becomes increasingly independent of the larger myth of Medea's career, and was often isolated or emphasised in order to give voice to anxieties about the proper behaviour of men (as kings and fathers) and women (as daughters and sisters) in prose, poetry and drama from the fifteenth century to the seventeenth.[3]

Sisters and brothers in the ancient and early modern world

In the essay 'Why did Medea kill her brother Apsyrtus?' Jan N. Bremmer surveys ancient versions of Medea's fratricide, showing how the tale gradually evolved from the third century BCE version of Apollonius Rhodius (the *Argonautica*) in which Jason kills an adult Apsyrtus in a temple, to the much more common classical story, referenced by Euripides, and subsequently by Ovid and Seneca.[4] This sees Medea killing her infant brother and scattering his limbs, in order to distract her father Aeëtes, as Jason and Medea flee. As Bremmer shows, successive ancient authors adopt but also adapt the models of their predecessors, layering earlier versions with their own additions.[5] For example, Seneca's *Medea* contains many more mentions of the fratricide than Euripides's play, and this exaggeration of emphasis may have been prompted by Seneca's desire to blacken Medea's name, but also by his knowledge of the intervening works of Ovid (particularly the *Tristia* and *Heroides*) that mention the crime. Bremmer argues that this fratricide was regarded with particular horror by classical authors, and is representative of Medea's absolute rejection of blood ties: 'Through Apsyrtus's murder, she simultaneously declared her independence from her family and forfeited her right to any protection from it.'[6] It has been suggested that it does not matter that it is a male sibling Medea chooses to kill,[7] but Bremmer points out that 'brother–sister conflicts are very rare in Greek myth'.[8] Moreover, he shows that the ancient world often stresses the closeness of the brother–sister relationship, and that 'The motif of the sister who privileges her brother's life over those of her husband and children' features in the literature of ancient Persia and India, as well as Greece.[9] What Medea undermines so horrifyingly, through the brutal killing of her brother (rather than of her rarely mentioned sister Chalciope), is the traditional intimacy of the brother–sister relationship.[10] She also challenges the *gendered* hierarchy of the classical family, and her place at the bottom of this hierarchy: Bremmer points out that the closeness of brothers and sisters in the classical world 'arose in part from the fact that the brother was responsible for the sister, and she was dependent upon him'.[11] In killing Apsyrtus to flee with Jason, Medea rejects this traditional reliance on her brother's protection, and refuses to respect the actual patriarchal control of her father, or the hypothetical control that her younger brother would have come to wield over her life and her romantic choices.

For medieval and early modern English writers, Medea's murder of Apsyrtus was no less troubling than it had been to classical authors, although it is a relatively minor episode in a career marked by murder and sorcery. Unsurprisingly, the fratricide directly contravened early modern as well as classical thinking about women's obedience and, particularly, about the 'ideal' relationship between brothers and sisters. Naomi J. Miller and Naomi Yavneh explain that in early modern thinking, a sister ought to be nurturing and quasi-maternal, but also a kind of possession, subservient to her brother's more important desires:

> Sisters ... were often constructed as their brothers' 'treasures', both because they could be married off and because they looked out for their brothers' interests, monetarily, socially or even emotionally ... Brothers, in turn, often assumed authority over their sisters, whether to protect them or to control any threats to the family's honor.[12]

Ovid may describe her in the *Metamorphoses* as 'spolia altera' (*Metamorphoses*, VII, 157) – 'another spoil' – as Jason leaves Colchis in triumph,[13] but in the end, Medea is nobody's treasure. Here, she places her own desire to marry

Jason far above the life of her brother, the happiness of her father or the continued security of the kingdom she leaves behind, just as she will eventually privilege her own desire for revenge over Jason's happiness, and even over the lives of her own children. Moreover, if a brother would usually bear responsibility for his sister, in both classical and early modern thought, equally important is this idea that sisters 'looked out for' their brothers, in a quasi-maternal fashion. Therefore, Medea's murder of Apsyrtus, already shocking, is made more horrifying by his youth. Bremmer notes that in some of the earliest classical versions (such as the lost work of Pherecydes) Apsyrtus is 'a (very) young child'.[14] This idea of youth was retained in later classical works: in the *Metamorphoses* Medea refers to him as a child (VII, 54), while Seneca's Medea describes him as her 'parvus comes' ('little companion') (131). Medieval and early modern literary tradition followed Seneca and Ovid in emphasising Apsyrtus's affecting youth, just as these classical authors had followed Greek forebears. In the fourteenth-century compendium *De claris mulieribus*, Giovanni Boccaccio specifically describes Apsyrtus as 'a small child', while in John Lydgate's fifteenth-century poem *The Fall of Princes*, Aeëtes is confronted by the grisly sight of 'His child dismembrid'.[15] Shakespeare's Clifford hopes to kill an Apsyrtus-like 'infant' (*2 Henry VI*, V.ii.57), and Thomas Heywood describes him as 'yong Absyrtus' in his mythological play *The Brazen Age* (*c*. 1613), which recounts Medea's betrayal of her father, and her flight from Colchis.[16] The taboo of a sister killing a much younger brother meant that the story of Apsyrtus packed an emotional punch absent from other tales of classical dismemberment (for example that of Orpheus by the maenads). This emphasis on Apsyrtus's youth exaggerates the wickedness of Medea's fratricide, and her total deviation from 'ideal' sisterly, quasi-maternal behaviour.[17] His youth also emphasises how her killing of her brother foreshadows her later murders of her own children, which are worse in every way: two children, rather than one; her sons, rather than a brother; needlessly cruel rather than necessary as a means of escape (since in the Senecan and Euripidean tragedies Medea is able to flee Corinth with divine assistance).[18] Ovid's Hypsipyle, the woman Jason abandons for Medea, certainly perceives the way in which Medea's various feminine roles are fatally linked: in *Heroides*, VI, her letter to Jason, she exclaims of Medea 'quam fratri germana fuit miseroque parenti / filia, tam natis, tam sit acerba viro!' ('A bitter sister to her brother, a bitter daughter to her wretched sire, may she be as bitter to her children, and as bitter to her husband!') (159–60). In a study of sibling relationships in medieval Germany, Jonathan R. Lyon points to the importance that medieval thinking placed on brotherhood and sisterhood, but also argues that 'brotherhood and sisterhood are ... performative, and a person must behave like a sibling to be recognized as one'.[19] In her self-serving murder of her brother, Medea 'performs' as the worst sister and daughter imaginable, and an authorial mention of this early crime hints that she is well on her way to also becoming the worst of mothers and wives, even long before her infanticide.

English authors were fascinated by Medea's deliberate mockery of the sister's caring and submissive role, and they draw specific attention to her shocking deviation from the expected norms of the brother–sister relationship. For example, in *The Fall of Princes*, Lydgate adds to his French source, Laurent de Premierfait, emphasising the filial relationship that Medea disregards, and urging his readers to search their memories for a comparable example of disloyalty: 'For who sauh ever or radde off such a-nothir, / To save a straunger list to slen hir brothir?' (lines 2232–3). Almost 150 years later, Richard Robinson's Medea, one of the speakers in his moralistic dream-vision poem *The Rewarde of Wickednesse* (1574), emphasises her rejection of expected womanly and sisterly behaviour, and recalls how she '"gainst nature and womanhood [her] Brother slewe'.[20] In *The Brazen Age*, Heywood elects to give a voice to the usually silent Apsyrtus, and, moreover, a voice that demonstrates first an apparent closeness between the siblings (Apsyrtus jokes with his sister as she schemes to meet Jason) and then, poignantly, the protective and maternal role that a more ideal older sister would assume. Medea invites Apsyrtus (who addresses her repeatedly as 'sister' through the play) to follow her offstage, and the boy promises that he will go 'Anywhere with you sister' (sig. G4r). If Heywood's audience were unaware of her brother's imminent demise, and her role in this fate, Medea makes it perfectly clear to them. When he makes his final appearance, she puns grimly on the meaning of 'late', greeting him with 'O happy met, though it be late Absyrtus / You must along with me' (sig. G4r)[21] before explaining in an aside:

> This lad betweene me and all harme shall stand;
> And if the King pursue us with his Fleet,
> His mangled limbes shall (scattered in the way)
> Worke our escape, and the Kings speed delay.
>
> (sig. G4r)

Of course, dysfunctional brother–sister relationships are to be found throughout early modern English literature, for example in *The Duchess of Malfi*'s portrayal of a sister who defies her brothers' wishes and marries a man of her own choosing. However, Medea's calculated and self-serving violence against her much younger brother is a grotesque exaggeration of a sister's potential for wilfulness, and Heywood's play makes the murder doubly disturbing, as it is so clearly and callously premeditated. In this dramatic depiction of the events leading up to the fratricide, Heywood layers Ovid's *Metamorphoses*, VII (which depicts Jason's wooing of Medea) with the *Tristia* (which emphasises the killing) and with Seneca's *Medea*. He also seems to have made use of one of the most extensive medieval accounts of Medea's career: William Caxton's *History of Jason*, a translation of the French of Raoul Lefèvre. In this prose work (discussed in more detail below), Heywood would have found the unnerving sense of premeditation that he dramatises in his play: Caxton's Medea does not kill her brother herself, but she arranges that he be slaughtered and dismembered in advance, whereas in the *Tristia* the crime seems more of a desperate reaction to her father's pursuit. Heywood takes the most memorable elements of the brother–sister relationship he found in his classical and medieval sources, and fits these to the frame of a Jacobean tragedy: *The Brazen Age* sees Jason callously exploit Medea, and she in turn double-cross her father and manipulate her brother to help him. In Heywood's dramatic blending of his medieval and classical sources, Medea stands in stark contrast to more exemplary early modern sisters such as Shakespeare's Innogen (or Imogen), who cooks and keeps house for her exiled brothers Arviragus and Guiderius before she even realises who they are (*Cymbeline*, IV.ii). Medea's cruelty towards Apsyrtus, and her refusal to accept a subservient and nurturing sisterly role in relation to her brother, thus become the focus of early modern anxieties about wayward and wilful women, particularly those who reject their expected role as daughters and sisters.

The fratricide in Ovid and Seneca

As Bremmer has shown, classical authors portrayed the fratricide with a variety of emphases: for example, in the third century BCE Apollonius Rhodius attributes the killing of the adult Apsyrtus to Jason (though Medea colludes with her lover by luring Apsyrtus to his death). In the first century CE, Valerius Flaccus's *Argonautica*, a Latin redaction of Apollonius, describes Medea's brother as 'primis ... in annis' (*Argonautica*, V, 457) – 'stripling' – but his death is not described, although this Apsyrtus is more of a threat to his sister, and takes up arms to champion Styrus, her father's choice of suitor.[22] Before Apollonius, Euripides's Medea refers briefly to her regret and sense of shame at the fratricide, but it was Seneca and particularly Ovid who influenced English versions of the story in the Middle Ages and early modern period. In Ovid's *Heroides*, XII, Medea merely touches upon the killing of

Apsyrtus as an example of the sacrifices she made for Jason, before declaring herself unable to describe it in more detail.[23] However, the fratricide is recounted far more fully in the *Tristia*. In Book III, elegy 9, Ovid describes Medea catching sight of the pursuing Colchians, as she and Jason flee her father's kingdom with the Golden Fleece:

> dum quid agat quaerit, dum versat in omnia vultus,
> ad fratrem casu lumina flexa tulit.
> cuius ut oblata est praesentia, 'vicimus' inquit:
> 'hic mihi morte sua causa salutis erit'.
> protinus ignari nec quicquam tale timentis
> innocuum rigido perforat ense latus,
> atque ita divellit divulsaque membra per agros
> dissipat in multis invenienda locis.
> neu pater ignoret, scopulo proponit in alto
> pallentesque manus sanguineumque caput
> ut genitor luctuque novo tardetur et, artus
> dum legit extinctos, triste moretur iter.
>
> (lines 21–32)

As she was seeking what to do, turning her countenance on all things, she chanced to bend her gaze upon her brother. When aware of his presence she exclaimed 'The victory is mine! His death shall save me!' Forthwith while he in his ignorance feared no such attack she pierced his innocent side with the hard sword. Then she tore him limb from limb, scattering the fragments of his body throughout the fields so that they must be sought in many places. And to apprise her father she placed upon a lofty rock the pale hands and gory head. Thus was the sire delayed by his fresh grief, lingering, while he gathered those lifeless limbs, on a journey of sorrow.

In the *Heroides*, Medea expresses her own guilt and regret as she berates Jason, while in the *Tristia*, it is not Medea who tells the story, and the emphasis shifts to the brutality of the impulsive killing, and the distress of her father Aeëtes. In Seneca's *Medea*, Medea refuses to bear responsibility for this first crime, telling Creon that it is Jason's sin as much as hers. Later, she acknowledges the personal consequences of her violent act, sarcastically asking Jason if she should agree to his new marriage to Creusa, and return to 'patriumque regnum quaeque fraternus cruor / perfudit arva?' ('my father's kingdom, and the fields soaked in my brother's blood?') (452–3). Here, Medea emphasises the extent to which she has, as Bremmer suggests, irreversibly cut ties with her former life and her family: the comparable scene in Euripides's *Medea* makes no mention of Apsyrtus, who is far more prominent in Seneca's tragedy. As the play progresses, Medea increasingly rejects the hinted regret of her Euripidean and Ovidian forebears, exclaiming 'iuvat, iuvat rapuisse fraternum caput, / artus iuvat secuisse' ('I am glad, yes glad, to have torn away my brother's head, glad to have cut up his limbs') (911–12). Finally, having resolved to kill her children, Medea convinces herself that in this way she will balance out the betrayals of her father and brother, and recover all that she has lost through her fatal association with Jason: 'iam iam recepi sceptra germanum patrem ... rediere regna, rapta virginitas redit' ('Now in this moment I have recovered my sceptre, brother, father ... My realm is restored, my stolen maidenhead restored') (982–4). In a realisation of the Ovidian Hypsipyle's wish (*Heroides*, VI, 159–60), her debt to her brother can be 'settled' only in that the memory of the killing can drive Medea to an even worse crime, and it is seemingly seeing the shade of Apsyrtus, at the end of the Senecan tragedy, that spurs Medea to her final and most notorious murders.[24]

The early modern English translations of Ovid and Seneca include their sources' mentions of the fratricide: George Turberville, Elizabethan translator of the *Heroides* (1567), has Medea describe how her letter 'ginnes to faint', such is her reluctance to acknowledge or remember this crime.[25] In Seneca's play, Medea refers to herself, peculiarly, in the third person, urging herself to remember 'nefandae virginis parvus comes / divisus ense, funus ingestum patri / sparsumque ponto corpus' ('the criminal girl's little companion cut apart with the sword, his death thrust in his father's face, his body scattered on the sea') (131–3). John Studley's translation (1566) has Medea drop the third person, with its distancing effect, and instead grotesquely exaggerate the bloodthirsty details of the crime, remembering 'my tender brother', 'Whose shreaded and dismembered corpse ... on Pontus ground I strewd'.[26] If Seneca multiplied the references to the fratricide he had found in Euripides, Studley gleefully expands on the bloodthirstiness of these mentions. His Medea reminds Creon of her 'brothers blody flesh that mang- / led was with carvynge knyfe' (lines 978–9). She urges Jason to think of the 'gorye swetyng feldes, that wyth / my brothers blood do reeke' (1374–5), tells him she took only her brother's 'slaughtred flesh' (1476) away from Colchis, and rejoices in the memory of how she 'smot of my brothers hed / And slasht his members of' (2565–7). For Studley, Apsyrtus's youth is not of paramount importance (though Medea's brother is certainly young). Rather, it is the episode's potential for violence that he relishes, and the image of the horribly and irredeemably sundered male body that is of greatest interest: he would return to this idea of the sundered body, its reduction to 'gobbets', in his translation of Seneca's *Hippolytus* (1567), where the eponymous hero is reduced to 'gobbets sparst and broken lumps of flesh' as a result of his stepmother's machinations.[27]

Like Studley, Thomas Churchyard, translator of the *Tristia* (1572), augments both the terrible nature of the crime and the grief of Aeëtes, calling Medea a 'wicked wight', and describing her 'cancred cruell spight' as she attacks Apsyrtus, before dwelling on the king's 'wayling new' and 'sobbing sore'.[28] The influence of such Elizabethan translations quickly became apparent in Medea's literary incarnations. One of the period's most extensive and inventive treatments of Medea, Robinson's *Rewarde of Wickednesse*, takes its cue from both Studley's *Medea* and Churchyard's *Tristia* in its emphasis on the grisly circumstances of Apsyrtus's death, and in its focus on paternal grief: Medea describes the chopped pieces of her brother's body, and how her father weeps and rends his cheeks at the terrible sight. Simultaneously, though, the sorrow is also Medea's, and she is made (too late) a grieving sister and a penitent sinner, as she recounts her crime from the afterlife. This transformation renders Medea comforting for the early modern reader in more ways than one, for she is both a criminal acknowledging and regretting her transgression, and a sister mourning for her brother, exhibiting the 'sisterly ties' that Miller and Yavneh argue are demonstrated by women's acts of grieving for and memorialising siblings in the early modern period.[29] Robinson reshapes the fratricide as he had found it in early modern translations (which had already exaggerated their source material), increasing the brutality and the emotional impact of Medea's crime, in ways that demonstrate the importance that early modern authors attached to the brother–sister relationship, and their horror at its being so thoroughly corrupted.

The spectacle of grief

However, if Medea's rejection of her sisterly role is fascinating to these authors, they were equally interested (and far more so than their classical sources) in the reaction of her father Aeëtes, using his response to meditate on what it means to grieve, as a man, a father and a king. The anonymous author of the fourteenth-century French poem the *Ovide moralisé*, a long allegorical work loosely based on the *Metamorphoses*, incorporates material from the *Tristia*, describing the killing and dismemberment of Apsyrtus and, crucially, the devastation of Aeëtes, and interweaving its classical sources to emphasise this interest.[30] The overwhelming grief of the father for his son is also mentioned in Lydgate's *Fall of Princes*, in which Aeëtes is described as '[f]ull pale off cheer' (line 2222) and 'disconsolat' (2228), having witnessed the slaughter. His reaction is described more extensively in the most detailed English account of Medea's career in the Middle Ages: William Caxton's *History of Jason* (1477). This long prose work, a close translation of the French *Histoire de Jason* of Raoul Lefèvre (c. 1464), vilifies Medea at every opportunity, for its convoluted aim is to make Medea appear worse, and Jason better.[31] In Lefèvre and Caxton, Medea's fratricide is premeditated, although she does not commit the act herself: she plots with her nursemaid and, before she flees Colchis with Jason, finds her brother (whose age is given as sixteen months) and orders the old woman 'to cutte his throte pryvely for certayn causes which shall here after be declared'.[32] Here, Lefèvre (and, following him, Caxton) makes explicit the terrible fact only hinted at by Ovid (that Medea takes Apsyrtus with her when she leaves Colchis in case he is needed as a distraction). This already shocking act is made particularly remarkable by Medea's justification. As she and Jason flee, she sees her father and 'toke the hede & lifte it an hyghe wherof Hercules Jason & other seyng this had grete horrour of this cruelte & were sore abasshed'.[33] She then explains that it was a kindness to kill her brother and display his corpse so publicly – an act she performed to prevent her father from becoming involved in a battle with the Argonauts that he could not hope to win. Aeëtes, unsurprisingly, sees things very differently from his daughter. Much space is given to his initial discovery that his son is missing and to his horrified realisation that Medea has the child, and his reaction to the murder is also stressed. In a typically close translation of Lefèvre, Caxton notes the angry Colchian response to Medea's audacious display of her brother's head:

> the kyng Oeetes and his peple heering and seeing the grete inhumanyte & cruelte began to escrie right pietously & dolourously And were so sore vexed & trobled of this mervaillous aventure that they wist not what to do. som ther were that began to wepe tenderly the other smote them self on the brestes & som began to araye hem to goo to bataille & escried to deth the knightes of Grece shoting on them arowes & other trait by grete corage for tavenge them.[34]

The king's grief is described, and his distress is then displaced onto his subjects, whose reactions to the murder and dismemberment range from confusion to physical violence. Very quickly, though, Aeëtes assumes control of the situation, subsuming his grief to his public role, and telling his subjects 'Certes fayr sires I praye you to travayle you nomore for to recouvre Medea she hath murdrid her propre broder Absirthius whiche was my sone and he that in time to come shulde have ben youre naturell lord.'[35] Aeëtes thus makes the irreparable damage that Medea has done to the body politic of Colchis, in killing its future 'naturell lord', very obvious, and goes on to tell his men that if he could, he would kill her himself, despite his previous love for her.

In the sixteenth and seventeenth centuries, literary depictions of Aeëtes's grief at this moment become almost unbearably emotive, and increasingly fixated on the physical and literal damage done to the king (and, by extension, the kingdom). In Robinson's poem *The Rewarde of Wickednesse*, it is Medea herself who must recall, and recount, the effects of her crime on her father, and his grief is described in far more detail than the fratricide itself:

> Then downe his Aged face, doeth tumble teares apace
> and up in armes the Martyred head doeth gette:
> Oh Sonne most deare, alas (quod hée) for grace,
> and many a kisse on deadlye mouth doth sette.
> And then with nayles, his face he rentes and teares,
> that downe the purple streames of blood doe flée:
> And readye death within his face appeares,
> but styll he cryed (alas) deare sonne for thée.
>
> (sig. F4r)

The physical manifestations of Aeëtes's grief – the descriptions of him weeping, tearing at his face; the 'purple streames' of his blood; his desperate kissing of his dead son's head – are deeply disturbing, because they are described by the daughter responsible for this grief (as they were in Seneca's *Medea*) but also because they are suggestive of an emasculating lack of control over his own bodily reactions, and a womanly response to grief that is particularly troubling when it is manifested in public, and by a king.[36] In fact, unlike Caxton's Medea, who argued that in killing Apsyrtus she was saving her father from harm, Robinson's Medea acknowledges that her fratricide would have driven her father to suicide, were it not for the intervention of his men:

> For verye woe hée pulleth out a blade,
> to slea him selfe for sorrowe of his sonne.
> But yet his men and servauntes chaunste to come,
> my carefull Father there they did prevent:
> Or else no doubte more mischiefe had béene done
> and all through mée, accurst and disobedient.
>
> (sig. F4r)

In her work on early modern mourning, Andrea Brady argues that '[v]iolent grief had long been associated with women, whose restriction to the domestic sphere was validated by characterising them as irrational and emotive'.[37] Thus, Aeëtes's excessive and stereotypically female grieving responses (weeping, rending the hair and cheeks) would provoke anxiety in the early modern reader. Moreover, the public expression of grief by important men was also a source of concern, because of the risk that it might be, as Brady puts it, somehow 'catching'.[38] Caxton's *History of Jason* had shown how, if a father is also a king, his grief for a son who is also a prince can be dangerously public, infecting his subjects and resulting in a widespread loss of control, and in her recollection of her father's near breakdown in the presence of his men, and his alarmingly feminised physical reactions, Robinson's early modern Medea hints that the damage she has done to Colchis goes beyond the killing of its prince.

Aeëtes's exaggerated and troubling grief for his son is used with similar pathetic effect decades later, in the closet tragedy *Mirza* (c. 1647/55), by Robert Baron.[39] Jennifer Vaught has suggested that as the sixteenth century became the seventeenth, early modern society began to exhibit 'a greater compassion for those who grieve',[40] and in Baron's play, Aeëtes's grief-stricken reaction and viewpoint are privileged, in a reflection of the growing interest in the affective (rather than horrific) elements of the story. However, Baron's play, like Robinson's poem, also emphasises the danger that public grief might pose, particularly to masculine and kingly identity. Only the fratricide is described, a decision that signposts authorial interest in Aeëtes's reaction, and the murder's growing importance as a stand-alone crime, dissociated from the rest of Medea's story, and her affair with Jason. Bremmer notes that the fratricide was very rarely depicted in ancient art,[41] but in this play, the young Persian princess Fatima looks at a painting of Medea's flight from Colchis, and demands of her nurse 'Why do's this woman look so angry here?'.[42] Aeëtes is clearly also meant to be depicted, for her older brother Soffia asks 'What ailes that old man so to weep? I can't / Indure to see a man weep it showes cowardly' (sig. Cr). Her nurse describes the murder of Medea's brother, and how Aeëtes

> stopt his vaine pursuit ot's cruell Daughter,
> To gather up by peace meal his torn son,
> And seems to bath each piece with teares, as if
> He thought them Cement strong enough to set
> The tatter'd joynts and flesh again together.
>
> (sig. Cr)

Once again, Aeëtes's distress is foregrounded, this time with a poignant emphasis on his vain hope that he might be able to reassemble the fragments of his son.⁴³ Soffia's reaction to the king's grief, though – his statement that he 'can't / Indure to see a man weep' – suggests a male anxiety (manifested as distaste) at such an immoderate display: as Gail Kern Paster points out, in early modern thinking 'it was woman's normative condition to leak', while tears reduce the weeper to 'a passive and feminized state'.⁴⁴ Again, too, it is the public nature of the display of grief that is particularly alarming for the early modern reader or interpreter. Patricia Phillippy quotes Samuel Clarke's description of Martin Luther mourning his daughter Magdalen's death, from Clarke's biographical work *The Marrow of Ecclesiastical History* (1650, revised and reprinted 1654). Clarke writes that in private, Luther 'wept plentifully' for his daughter and for the German nation, but in public 'he so restrained his affection that he shed not a tear'.⁴⁵ Thus, Phillippy notes, while the anecdote 'clearly posits paternal affection as a Christian virtue', it also 'asserts the decorum governing public mourning', a decorum that both men and women were expected to observe.⁴⁶ Clarke's approval of Luther's decorous grieving, appropriately heartfelt, but altered in tone depending on whether it is public or private, again suggests excessive public grief as a source of anxiety in the middle of the seventeenth century, and for Soffia, to see a man weep publicly is particularly distasteful. Vaught has argued that extravagant male grief (and particularly weeping) is not always emasculating, and in fact may be a positive affirmation of male identity, when displayed by characters such as Richard II.⁴⁷ However, in works such as Robinson's, Aeëtes is almost obliterated by his distress, physically attacking himself in front of his subjects, and then disappearing almost immediately from his own story. When his public and debilitating grief is considered as fundamentally destabilising to the early modern sense of male, royal self, and thus by extension as damaging to the kingdom as the death of his heir, Soffia's disgust at his reaction becomes more understandable.

In his account of Luther's grieving, Clarke also records that Luther wept simultaneously for his daughter and for the German nation: Phillippy notes that Clarke's description 'interjects into the moment of private child-loss the memory of civic government ... Luther's mourning for his lost daughter is painfully conflated with his sorrow for the nation.'⁴⁸ As we have seen, the medieval and early modern Aeëtes also grieves for his child and his kingdom. Caxton, for example, has Aeëtes remind his men that the boy would have been their future king, a fact that compounds the wickedness of Medea's crime, which becomes an act against State as well as family. This dual focus does not make Aeëtes's grief any less heartfelt or affecting: Lynne Dickson Bruckner has shown that '[paternal] affection and the desire for a secure hereditary line should not be considered mutually exclusive categories'.⁴⁹

Soffia's blunt condemnation of his excessive reaction demonstrates discomfort not so much with Aeëtes's emotion, but with his mode of expression: the extravagant and public nature of his mourning is clearly at odds with early modern thinking on how men (particularly men in positions of power) ought to behave. These repeated authorial returns to Aeëtes's grief (which is hugely exaggerated from the classical sources) thus show how classical allusions might be reshaped to reflect contemporary anxieties. The image of kingly grief, and particularly the idea that a body (or a body politic) cannot be easily reassembled once it has been violently sundered, would have resonated with Herrick, who dedicated *Hesperides* to the future Charles II in 1648, and would also have been particularly poignant for Baron's royalist readers, especially if, as Birchwood argues, the printed version of the play should be dated to 1655, after the execution of Charles I.[50]

If Soffia's reaction suggests there is an appropriately male, public way to grieve (one that Aeëtes does not observe), Fatima's reaction suggests how women ought to respond to such a tragedy. Unlike her brother, Fatima is greatly affected by both the painting and the nurse's explanation of Medea's crime, and by the old king's distress.[51] She exclaims to her brother 'Was she a sister? O I could not do / So by you SOFFIA for all the world', and remarks:

> I hate all cruelty so perfectly:
> Yet could I bear a part with that old man,
> And weep as fast as he; so infectious
> Is a just sorrow, chiefly in old persons.
>
> (sig. Cr)

Unlike her brother, she sees Aeëtes's grief as not only understandable, but somehow enjoyably 'infectious'. Though she protests that she could not bear to see the story acted, she relishes its sentimentality in painted form, telling her mother and nursemaid

> This piece shall be
> My m[e]lancholly study, and sad Tutor.
> When I have either cause or will to weep,
> Ile take up this, and sit, and think, I see
> The tender boy stretcht out his hands unto me
> For help, and sigh, because I cannot rescue him.
> Then think again, the old man calls out to me
> To help him gather up his sons limbs; and weep
> Because I cannot.
>
> (sig. Cv)

Her enthusiastic participation in the grieving process (albeit at a remove) casts Fatima as surrogate and idealised sister and daughter to Apsyrtus and Aeëtes respectively – like Robinson's Medea, who mourns for her brother and empathises with her father from the afterlife, Fatima exhibits the 'correct' female mourning response, in her distress at the death of the innocent child. She is also, though, a surrogate for Apsyrtus, and for Medea's own children, in that she is an innocent who will eventually be killed, by her father Mirza. In this way, a mention of Apsyrtus's death reflects male anxieties about propriety and the gendered control of the emotions, which have been in evidence since Caxton's *History of Jason*, but it also functions in the same way as many brief references to the Medea myth in early modern tragedy, in that it foreshadows further murder and, specifically, child-killing.

The body in pieces

In works such as Baron's *Mirza* the fratricide is described with an emphasis that seems to set Apsyrtus apart from his better-known sister, and privilege his role as victim, rather than her role as a ruthless murderer. Indeed, as Herrick's use of Apsyrtus in the *Hesperides* suggests, in the seventeenth century authors are often more fascinated with the metaphorical possibilities of Apsyrtus's grisly end than with recounting the episode (or the rest of her story) in its entirety. In such cases, it is not just the emotive death of a young, royal child, at the hands of his sister, which authors find so compelling. Equally important is the irreversible act of dismemberment and scattering: in her work on English Civil War atrocities, Diane Purkiss notes that 'Mutilation is ... loss of self, loss of image and propriety, and loss of ownership and control over appearance and the body.'[52] This deep-seated fear of a loss of identity and control, though apparent as early as Caxton, becomes particularly acute by the middle of the seventeenth century, with the image of Apsyrtus's dismembered corpse being used in sermons and polemic to plead for unity, both national and religious.[53] This anxiety about the sundering of a body that was at once both private and political, a brother and son and a royal heir, clearly informs Herrick's use of Apsyrtus to represent *Hesperides*, a work composed in private that the author is making public, and thus vulnerable to critique or even destruction. Stephen B. Dobranski argues that the poet's choice of this myth (instead of that of Orpheus) 'conveys the treachery that Herrick attributes to his ungenerous readers and the hardship that he hopes such readers will, like Jason and Medea, eventually suffer'.[54] Here, Dobranski sees Herrick positioning himself as the father figure, grieving for his son and creation, while the disrespectful reader who might rend his pages is aligned with Medea. The emotive potential of the comparison may have prompted Herrick to ignore Orpheus (and his more obvious connection to artistic composition) in favour of Apsyrtus, the ill-fated boy who should have been his father's legacy. However, early modern writers have also betrayed a clear anxiety about the spectacle of Aeëtes's fatherly grief, even as they have dwelt on it. That Herrick is not entirely serious when he imagines his own 'solemne tears' at the dismembering and burial of his book is suggested by earlier poems in the collection, which imagine deliberately exaggerated destruction being wrought on the book by the ungrateful reader (for example, they may use its leaves as toilet paper). Moreover, the idea of the dispersed pages of the book being treated as holy relics, washed and placed reverently in a perfumed box, is undercut as the preceding poem in the 1648 edition, 'Upon Ralph', describes how its repellent subject 'pares his nayles, his warts, his cornes' (sig. Aa2r), and preserves them in boxes with a similar care. In 'To his booke', Herrick adopts what Purkiss calls 'the old familiar book-as-son trope',[55] and the exaggerated paternal grief that Baron's Fatima found so affecting, and Soffia so distasteful, is employed to condemn the destructive tendencies (whether literal or figurative) of the unappreciative and Medea-like reader. By his use of Apsyrtus, Herrick thus exaggerates the quasi-parental concern that authors typically expressed at the idea of their books making their own way in the world: his literary infant, he suggests, risks a particularly savage end. At the same time, though, the comparison of a torn book to a brutally dismembered child is deliberately hyperbolic, and when it is considered alongside Ralph's similar memorialising of his bodily leavings, a more subversive reading becomes possible, through which the precious and overly emotional author is mocked, as much as the ungrateful reader is criticised. Such a use is particularly sophisticated, as it demands knowledge of the classical story of Apsyrtus's death, and of its usual, affective use in English literature, by authors such as Caxton, Lydgate, Robinson and Baron. Simultaneously, Herrick's tongue-in-cheek use also recalls recent iconoclastic uses of the story by authors such as James Shirley, who makes blackly comic and irreverent references to the fratricide in *The Schoole of Complement* (1625) and in his masque *The Triumph of Beautie* (printed in 1646).[56]

Herrick was not the first to compare the fruits of authorial labour to the dispersed limbs of Medea's brother: Thomas Gataker does so in 1626, dedicating a printed sermon to Thomas Chapman, and explaining that it had previously existed 'in scatterd notes only (like Absyrtus his limmes)', in which 'I had the summe and heads of it, which I have againe here recollected, & cast (as neare I could) into that mould and frame that it was delivered in at first.'[57] In the preface to a 1650 edition of the work of Launcelot Andrewes, bishop of Winchester, the printer Roger Norton describes an earlier, inferior edition of the work, whose 'stately structures' were 'so mangled and defaced, so scattered and dismembred, like *Medeas Absyrtus*, that they appear scarce shadows of themselves'.[58] For Gataker and Norton, the dismemberment (being only figurative) is something that can be reversed, and via printing or reissuing the works in question can be reconstituted, and even perfected. Herrick takes, on the face of it, a more traditional view of the dismemberment, emphasising that it is irreversible, and can only be mourned, rather than remedied: and as I have argued, his choice of a specifically royal myth of division seems particularly timely.[59] Also apparent, though, is a lightness of touch, a desire to reshape, rather than simply repeat, the image of paternal mourning that earlier authors had found so affecting and troubling, to make it speak simultaneously to his own fears for the country, and (rather less seriously) to his anxiety about his own work.

Apsyrtus is dismembered again and again, from the fifteenth century to the seventeenth, but never in quite the same way twice, and the episode and its transformations are a testament to English literature's inventive relationship with the classical past, its insistence on reshaping classical material in ways that were carefully attuned to the historical and cultural moment of literary production. The classical Medea kills her brother to escape Colchis, to sever ties with her blood family and to prove the strength of her devotion to Jason. That she keeps killing him in the English literature of the fifteenth, sixteenth and seventeenth centuries is reflective of the cultural and creative resonance that later authors perceived in this brief and terrible episode. A taboo from its earliest classical incarnations, the story of Medea's callous murder of her brother retained its power to shock into the early modern period, while increasingly taking on a life of its own. Seneca's Medea, who repeatedly makes reference to the fratricide throughout the play, describes it suggestively as 'scelere in uno non semel factum scelus' ('a single crime involving many acts of crime') (474). The Elizabethan translator John Studley rendered this as Medea's 'gylt that wrought so many gyltes' (line 1442), and it is this sense of multiplicity that made this myth so appealing to early modern authors. Such authors augmented classical and medieval sources, layering them with new details (such as Studley's focus on violence, or Robinson's and Baron's emphasis on Aeëtes's grief) that reflected their own authorial and societal preoccupations. Though it is clearly a herald of her future crimes against family and kingdom, through this process of layering, Medea's killing of Apsyrtus retained its emotive and horrifying impact, but could also be made to reflect a whole host of contemporary concerns: misogynist horror of the bad sister and daughter; masculine anxiety about the proper control of the emotions; fear about the stability and continuity of monarchical rule; or authorial fear about the integrity and future survival of one's own body of writing.

Notes

1. Robert Herrick, *Hesperides; or, The Works Both Humane & Divine of Robert Herrick, Esquire* (London: John Williams, 1648), sig. Aa2r.
2. Variations on Medea's brother's name can be found in classical and English literature. This chapter refers to him throughout as Apsyrtus, but when quoting it retains each author's original choice.
3. Shakespeare's Apsyrtus will not be the focus of this essay. On this, see Yves Peyré, 'Absyrtus' (2014), in Yves Peyré (ed.), *A Dictionary of Shakespeare's Classical Mythology* (2009–), www.shakmyth.org (accessed 30 June 2015); Katherine Heavey, *The Early Modern Medea: Medea in English Literature, 1558–1688* (Basingstoke: Palgrave Macmillan, 2015), pp. 171–4; Katherine Heavey, 'An infant of the house of York: Medea and Absyrtus in Shakespeare's first tetralogy', *Comparative Drama*, 50:2 (2016), 233–48.
4. Jan N. Bremmer, 'Why did Medea kill her brother Apsyrtus?', in James J. Clauss and Sarah Iles Johnston (eds), *Medea: Essays on Medea in Myth, Literature, Philosophy and Art* (Princeton: University of Princeton Press, 1997), pp. 83–100. See Apollonius Rhodius, *Argonautica*, IV, 451–78; Euripides, *Medea*, lines 166–7 and 1333–5; Ovid, *Heroides*, VI, 159–60 and XII, 113–15; Ovid, *Tristia*, III, ix, 19–32; Seneca, *Medea*, lines 131–3, 278, 452–3, 473, 488.
5. Bremmer, 'Apsyrtus', pp. 85–6. On the ways in which classical authors echoed and altered earlier versions, see Alain Moreau, *Le mythe de Jason et Médée: le va-nu-pied et la sorcière* (Paris: Belles Lettres, 1994), pp. 71–72n66.
6. Bremmer, 'Apsyrtus', p. 100.
7. Jennifer R. March, 'Medeas', review of *Medea: Essays on Medea*, *The Classical Review*, 49:2 (1999), 362–3 (p. 363).
8. Bremmer, 'Apsyrtus', p. 96.
9. *Ibid.*, pp. 93–9 (p. 97).
10. *Ibid.*, p. 100, notes that Sophocles and Apollonius somewhat alleviate the taboo of fratricide, by making Medea and Apsyrtus only half-brother and -sister. Apollonius attributes the crime to Jason, who is of course no relation.
11. *Ibid.*
12. Naomi J. Miller and Naomi Yavneh, 'Introduction: Thicker than water. Evaluating sibling relations in the early modern period', in Naomi J. Miller and Naomi Yavneh (eds), *Sibling Relations and Gender in the Early Modern World* (Aldershot: Ashgate, 2006), pp. 1–14 (p. 12).

13 Ovid, *Metamorphoses*, VII, 157.
14 Bremmer, 'Apsyrtus', p. 86n 11. See also Moreau, *Jason et Médée*, pp. 71–72n 66.
15 Giovanni Boccaccio, *On Famous Women*, ed. and trans. Guido A. Guarino, 2nd edn (New York: Italica Press, 2011 [1963]), p. 35. John Lydgate, *The Fall of Princes*, ed. Henry Bergen, Vol. I (Washington: Carnegie Institute of Washington, 1923), line 2226.
16 Thomas Heywood, *The Brazen Age* (London: Nicolas Okes, 1613), sigs F2r and G4v.
17 Similarly Shakespeare emphasises Arthur's youth in *King John*. See Chapter 4 (Janice Valls-Russell).
18 The Euripidean Medea kills her sons rather than leave them to be punished by the citizens of Corinth. However, she also acknowledges that the murders are the most effective way to hurt Jason (line 817).
19 Jonathan R. Lyon, *Princely Brothers and Sisters: The Sibling Bond in German Politics, 1100–1250* (Ithaca, NY: Cornell University Press, 2013), pp. 3, 6.
20 Richard Robinson, *The Rewarde of Wickednesse* (London: William Williamson, 1574), sig. F4v.
21 See *Oxford English Dictionary*, s.v. 'late', adj. 1.
22 Valerius Flaccus, *Argonautica*, V, 457, trans. J. H. Mozley (London: Heinemann, 1934). The poem is unfinished, and Apsyrtus is last seen mourning Styrus's death, but is described as 'quem[que] insontem meliora manerent' ('one whose innocence deserved a fairer future') (V, 458).
23 Ovid, *Heroides*, XII, 114–15. Medea exclaims 'deficit hoc uno littera nostra loco. / quod facere ausa mea est, non audet scribere dextra' ('In this one place my pen fails. Of the deed my right hand was bold enough to do, it is not bold enough to write').
24 Bremmer, 'Apsyrtus', p. 84, notes that in post-archaic Greece, the dismemberment of an unjustly murdered victim was supposed to prevent the return of a vengeful ghost – Seneca inverts this idea by having Medea apparently see the shade of her brother.
25 Ovid, *The Heroycall Epistles of the Learned Poet Publius Ouidius Naso*, trans. George Turberville (London: Henry Denham, 1567), p. 72.
26 Seneca, *Studley's Translations of Seneca's 'Agamemnon' and 'Medea', Edited from the Octavos of 1566*, trans. John Studley, ed. E. M. Spearing (Louvain: Uystpruyst, 1913), lines 491–8. For Shakespeare's adaptation of this in *2 Henry VI*, see Heavey, 'An infant of the house of York'.
27 Seneca, *Hippolytus*, trans. John Studley, ed. Thomas Newton, *Seneca His Tenne Tragedies, Translated into English* (London: Thomas Marsh, 1581), sig. L2r. This is the earliest extant printing of the play.
28 Ovid, *The Three First Bookes of Ovid de Tristibus Translated into English*, trans. Thomas Churchyard (London: Thomas Marsh, 1580 [1572]), pp. 23–4.
29 Miller and Yavneh, 'Introduction', pp. 2–3.

30 For the text and translation see Peyré, 'Absyrtus'.
31 On the background and context of Lefèvre's *Histoire*, see Ruth Morse, 'Problems of early fiction: Raoul Lefèvre's *Histoire de Jason*', *Modern Language Review*, 78:1 (1983), 34–45.
32 Raoul Lefèvre, *L'Histoire de Jason*, trans. William Caxton, ed. John Munro (London: Early English Text Society, 1913), p. 144. Boccaccio's *Famous Women* also absolves Medea of actually carrying out the crime (though she is still condemned fiercely): the reader is told that Medea 'had her brother dismembered' (p. 35).
33 Lefèvre, *L'Histoire de Jason*, trans. Caxton, p. 147.
34 *Ibid.*, p. 149. For the French, see Raoul Lefèvre, *L'Histoire de Jason*, ed. Gert Pinkernell (Frankfurt: Athenäum Verlag, 1971), XVI.v.2–7, p. 214.
35 Lefèvre, *L'Histoire de Jason*, trans. Caxton, p. 150.
36 On physical expressions of 'feminine' grief, see Jennifer C. Vaught, *Masculinity and Emotion in Early Modern English Literature* (Aldershot: Ashgate, 2008), pp. 1–3, 178; and Gail Kern Paster, *The Body Embarrassed: Drama and the Disciplines of Shame in Early Modern England* (Ithaca, NY: Cornell University Press, 1993), p. 60. That both Apsyrtus and Aeëtes bleed uncontrollably as a result of Medea's actions is also alarming: for bleeding as associated with women, see Paster, *The Body Embarrassed*, pp. 66, 92, 94, 97–9, 104.
37 Andrea Brady, *English Funerary Elegy in the Seventeenth Century: Laws in Mourning* (Basingstoke: Palgrave Macmillan, 2006), p. 8.
38 *Ibid.*, p. 36.
39 The play is traditionally dated to *c.* 1647, but Matthew Birchwood, *Staging Islam in England: Drama and Culture 1640–85* (Cambridge: D. S. Brewer, 2007), argues that though preparation on the work could have begun long before, the printed version of *Mirza* should be dated to 1655 (pp. 77–8).
40 Jennifer C. Vaught, 'Introduction', in Jennifer C. Vaught with Lynne Dickson Bruckner (eds), *Grief and Gender, 700–1700* (Basingstoke: Palgrave Macmillan, 2003), pp. 1–14 (p. 5).
41 Bremmer, 'Apsyrtus', p. 100.
42 Robert Baron, *Mirza a Tragedie* (London: Humphrey Moseley, 1647?), sig. Cr.
43 One effect of the emphasis on Aeëtes's reaction is to stress that he *witnesses* the terrible death of his son, as other fathers, such as Seneca's Theseus, do not.
44 Paster, *The Body Embarrassed*, pp. 9, 105.
45 Samuel Clarke, *The Marrow of Ecclesiastical History* (London: Robert White for William Roybould, 1654), quoted in Patricia Phillippy, *Women, Death and Literature in Post-Reformation England* (Cambridge: Cambridge University Press, 2002), p. 157.
46 Phillippy, *Women, Death and Literature*, p. 157.
47 Vaught, *Masculinity and Emotion*, pp. 1–2 and *passim*.
48 Phillippy, *Women, Death and Literature*, p. 157.

49 Lynne Dickson Bruckner, 'Ben Jonson's branded thumb and the imprint of textual paternity', in Douglas A. Brooks (ed.), *Printing and Parenting in Early Modern England* (Aldershot: Ashgate, 2005), pp. 109–30 (p. 110).
50 See n39, above.
51 Compare Lucrece's empathising with Hecuba, on seeing a painting depicting the fall of Troy, in Shakespeare's *The Rape of Lucrece*, lines 1443–98.
52 Diane Purkiss, 'Dismembering and remembering: The English Civil War and male identity', in Claude J. Summers and Ted-Larry Pebworth (eds), *The English Civil Wars in the Literary Imagination* (Columbia: University of Missouri Press, 1999), pp. 220–41 (p. 223).
53 For example, see John Thornborough, *A Discourse Shewing the Great Happiness that Hath and May Still Accrue to His Majesties Kingdomes of England and Scotland by Re-Uniting Them into One Great Britain* (London: R. H., 1641), p. 158; and Edmund Calamy, *An Indictment against England because of Her Selfe-Murdering Divisions* (London: I. L., 1645), sig. C4r.
54 Stephen B. Dobranski, *Readers and Authorship in Early Modern England* (Cambridge: Cambridge University Press, 2005), p. 169.
55 Purkiss, 'Dismembering', p. 228. On this trope in a wide range of early modern writing, see Brooks, *Printing and Parenting*.
56 See Heavey, *The Early Modern Medea*, pp. 142–8.
57 Thomas Gataker, *An Anniversarie Memoriall of Englands Delivery from the Spanish Invasion Delivered in a Sermon on Psalm 48. 7, 8* (London: John Haviland, 1626), sig. A2v.
58 Launcelot Andrewes, *The Pattern of Catechistical Doctrine at Large* (London: Roger Norton, 1650), sig. **3r.
59 Colin Burrow also sees a connection among the mutilated body of Seneca's Hippolytus, the futile attempts of Theseus to reconstruct the body's pieces and the authorial desire (perhaps equally hopeless) to reconstruct 'a classical tradition' of literature: *Shakespeare and Classical Antiquity* (Oxford: Oxford University Press, 2013), p. 171. Like Orpheus, Hippolytus is an adult: as I have suggested here, Apsyrtus's frequently emphasised youth and innocence make his grisly end more affecting, while the idea of the father losing a young or infant son speaks even more clearly to authors' anxiety about the fate of their newly born literary creations. See also Purkiss, 'Dismembering', pp. 227–8, on the comparison between a printed work and an infant son.

7

'She, whom Jove transported into Crete': Europa, between consent and rape

Gaëlle Ginestet

AMONG THE NUMEROUS MAIDENS (and young men) who were kidnapped by Jupiter, Europa is sometimes remembered as the maid who consented to be taken away from her family and her land – 'la pucelle amiable', as she is described in *La Métamorphose d'Ovide figurée* (1557).[1] It is this transitory moment of departure, with the homeland still in sight, that the visual arts mostly chose to fix in the Renaissance, and Bernard Salomon's *pictura* for 'Europe ravie' in *La Métamorphose d'Ovide figurée* (Figure 1) seems to recapture the equilibrium depicted in Roman mosaics such as the one in the Musée départemental Arles antique (dated 250–200 BCE): Salomon's Europa is seated on the bull's back, holding one of his horns – a symbol of virility – whilst looking back towards the shore at her companions (Figure 2). This inspired Virgil Solis's woodcut in reverse, which circulated widely in print and became a template for embroideries and other forms of decorative arts.[2] Renaissance artists such as Veronese or Hendrick van Balen painted Europa being seated on the white bull by her attendants, who deck her as though for her wedding, while Cupid hangs flowers over the horns. In these engravings and paintings Europa is represented in the foreground as unresisting, showing rather more wonderment than fear, but in the background of Veronese's painting of the rape of Europa in the Doge's Palace in Venice (Figure 3), we glimpse her waving, or reaching out, to her companions as the bull plunges into the waves – and that is the moment Titian chooses to show in his painting (*c.* 1560–62), with Europa precariously lying on the bull's back, half-naked and in disarray (Figure 4).[3] Unsurprisingly, the myth appealed to Renaissance poets; Elizabethan authors of love poetry, more especially sonneteers, used it to idealise courting, since

Figure 1 'Europe ravie', from anon., *La Métamorphose d'Ovide figurée* (Lyon: Jean de Tournes, 1557), p. 34.

Figure 2 The Rape of Europa (mosaic).

such a seemingly idyllic scene suited a rhetoric of persuasion, to the point of becoming commonplace. Sir Philip Sidney mocked the frequent use of the myths of Europa, Leda and Danae by his fellow poets: 'Some one his song in Jove, and Jove's strange tales attires, / Broadred with buls and swans, powdred with golden raine.'[4] In contrast, George Sandys, commenting on the myth in 1632, condemned the way in which 'our Jupiter becomes a beast to obtaine his bestiall desires'.[5]

Similar dissensions divide twentieth-century (male) scholars. One of France's leading specialists of classical mythology in European literature, Pierre Brunel, considers that he cannot find any hint of violence in the myth of Europa, while Jonathan Bate, in his discussion of Jupiter's 'divine rapes', argues that 'Ovid is the *locus classicus* for the motif of dissembling in sexual pursuit'.[6]

The myth of Europa is often referred to as 'the rape of Europa'. Etymologically, it should be more accurately 'the rapes of Europa', implying

Figure 3 Veronese (Paolo Caliari) (1528–88), *The Rape of Europa* (oil on canvas).

both 'abduction' and/or 'forced sexual intercourse'. The ambivalence of the vocabulary chosen by poets when considering this myth mirrors the troubling links between the rhetoric of persuasion and male fantasies of sexual coercion, between mythology and horror; the spectres of violence and rape loom over this abduction, as over most of Jupiter's conquests, breaking through the brief, initial illusion of consent. This chapter contends that the reception of the Europa myth is more complex than either side may argue, then as now, and that the two poles of reception, cultural and scholarly, owe much to the subtleties of Moschus, Horace and Ovid's source texts, as well as to the ways in which they journeyed down the centuries and inspired a variety of traditions to produce a rich texture of visual and literary art forms. Shifts in significance also depend on the context in which a given myth, or version of a myth, is received, in relation to other myths or to other texts and illustrations. I shall show how Elizabethan sonneteers and Shakespeare drew on these multiple levels of interaction, the ways they both played on different interpretations of the myth itself and interwove it with other myths.

'She, whom Jove transported into Crete'

Figure 4 Titian (Tiziano Vecellio) (*c*. 1488–1576), *Europa*, 1559–62 (oil on canvas).

A two-strand tradition of reception

The most complete ancient account of the myth is to be found in Moschus's Greek epyllion 'Europa' (Idyll II, *c*. 150 BCE). Moschus tells the story as follows. The night before the abduction, Agenor's daughter Europa 'δοιὰς περὶ εἷο μάχεσθαι, / Ἀσίδα τ᾽ ἀντιπέρην τε φυὴν δ᾽ ἔχον οἷα γυναῖκες' ('thought she saw two continents contend for her, Asia and the land opposite; and they had the form of women') (8–9). In spite of this dream, her encounter with Jupiter as a bull is initially cheerful, even though the reader is given to understand what is going to happen: 'Οὐ μὲν δηρὸν ἔμελλεν ἐπ᾽ ἄνθεσι θυμὸν ἰαίνειν, / οὐδ᾽ ἄρα παρθενίην μίτρην ἄχραντον ἔρυσθαι' ('not for long was she to please her heart with the flowers or keep her virgin girdle undefiled') (72–3). Like her playfellows, the maiden is attracted by this fascinating beast: 'τοῦ δή τοι τὸ μὲν ἄλλο δέμας ξανθόχροον ἔσκε, / κύκλος δ᾽ ἀργύφεος μέσσῳ μάρμαιρε μετώπῳ, / ὄσσε δ᾽ ὑπογλαύσσεσκε καὶ ἵμερον ἀστράπτεσκεν' ('his body was golden colored; but a silvery circle gleamed in the middle of his forehead, and his eyes shone brightly from underneath and shot forth desire like lightning') (84–6). He licked her neck. Unabashed by this display of male courtship, Europa 'καὶ ἠρέμα χείρεσιν ἀφρόν / πολλὸν ἀπὸ στομάτων ἀπομόργνυτο καὶ κύσε ταῦρον' ('calmly with her hands wiped away the mass of foam from his mouth, and she kissed the bull') (95–6); then she climbed onto the animal's back. Up to that moment, the poem shows Europa as curious and trusting (or yielding to the bull's persuasiveness), but when he leapt up and dived into the sea, 'ἡ δὲ μεταστρεφθεῖσα φίλας καλέεσκεν ἑταίρας χεῖρας ὀρεγνυμένη, ταὶ δ' οὐκ ἐδύναντο κιχάνειν' ('She turned round and kept calling her dear companions, stretching out her hands; but they could not reach her') (111). Moschus develops the flight, over the ocean, with dolphins and other sea-beasts frolicking and Tritons sounding marriage music; he then goes on to give a voice to the frightened maid, who asks the bull what he wants of her. He merely answers that she has nothing to fear, since he is Jove and she will become his wife. This time, Moschus does not specify what she said or thought of this, but simply observes that 'Ζεὺς δὲ πάλιν σφετέρην ἀνελάζετο μορφήν / λῦσε δέ οἱ μίτρην ... / ἡ δὲ πάρος κούρη Ζηνὸς γένετ' αὐτίκα νύμφη' ('Zeus took on his own shape again, and loosened her girdle ... And she that was formerly a girl at once became the bride of Zeus') (163–5).

Horace's Ode III, 27 carries echoes of Moschus's Idyll 2. The story of Europa takes up thirteen of the nineteen stanzas, which the speaker addresses to Galatea as she sets forth on a journey. Horace begins with her abduction, which he presents as voluntary: 'Europa niveum doloso / credidit tauro latus' ('she yields her snow-white body to the deceitful bull') (lines 26–7). The tone is darker than in Moschus. The sea is full of monsters and traps. Europa voices regrets and her lamentations to her father extend to thoughts of suicide, which include the idea of hanging herself, ironically enough, with her girdle (lines 58–60). Horace's ode ends with Venus revealing Jupiter's identity, promising Europa marriage and predicting that her name will be given to a major part of the earth.

Ovid's accounts are less detailed than those of Moschus and Horace, but were more widely influential, given the immense popularity of *Metamorphoses* throughout Renaissance Europe. Ovid tells the story twice in *Metamorphoses* (II, 836–75, overflowing into III, 1–25; and VI, 103–7), and again in *Fasti* (V, 605–16). Following Horace, he does away with Europa's ominous dream, but he ironically transposes the virginity of her 'snow-white body' onto the bull, whose massive gleaming flanks make him readily identifiable in the major paintings of the Renaissance. Ovid's Europa is more cautious than

Moschus's: 'quamvis mitem metuit contingere primo' ('although he seemed so gentle, she was afraid at first to touch him') (II, 860). Ovid expands the bull's treacherous nature – 'falsa pedum' ('borrowed hoofs') (II, 871) – and is more explicit about the anxiety in Europa's backward glance at her homeland: 'pavet haec litusque ablata relictum / respicit' ('she trembles with fear and looks back at the receding shore') (II, 873–4): this attitude, fixed by Salomon, became a marker of the myth in the Renaissance. Book II of *Metamorphoses* ends on the image of the maiden carried away over the sea: 'tremulae sinuantur flamine vestes' ('her fluttering garments stream behind her in the wind') (II, 875) – suppressing Moschus's seascape and veiling the ensuing rape. The maiden girdle disappears and we next find Jupiter 'posita fallicis imagine tauri / se confessus erat' ('the god having put off disguise, owned himself for what he was') (III, 1–2).[7]

In Book VI of *Metamorphoses* Arachne weaves the story of Europa into her tapestry:

> Maeonis elusam designat imagine tauri
> Europam: verum taurum, freta vera putares;
> ipsa videbatur terras spectare relictas
> et comites clamare suas tactumque vereri
> adsilientis aquae timidasque reducere plantas.
>
> (VI, 103–7)

> Arachne pictures Europa cheated by the disguise of the bull: a real bull and real waves you would think them. The maid seems to be looking back upon the land she has left, calling on her companions, and, fearful of the touch of the leaping waves, to be drawing back her timid feet.

This brief ekphrasis emphasises Europa's fear with the hypallage 'timid feet'. The insertion of this and other stories in the tapestry is a *mise en abyme* of Ovid's own poetics, an acknowledgement of the embedded influences that structure *Metamorphoses*: Arachne draws on the stories of the gods (which include those told in the poem) in the same way that Ovid draws on a variety of influences, interweaving sources into his own mythological programme.

From these different versions of the myth, two loose traditions emerge that in turn shift in focus and reorganise themselves in later rewritings – one that centres on the flight, the other on the rape – with varying degrees of emphasis on the links between the two aspects of the story. Furthermore, the links among the Moschus/Horace/Ovid source texts illustrate the importance of considering Ovid in the context and continuity of both Latin and Greek authors, to whom Renaissance artists and authors in turn also had access.⁸ Moschus was one of the first Greek authors to be printed in the fifteenth century and his *Idylls* were published in anthologies of poetry in Greek as well as in Latin translation.⁹ Sixteenth- and early-seventeenth-century readers had access to several editions of Horace's *Odes* in Latin before selections of his poetry were printed in translation from 1621 onwards, the first complete edition appearing in 1638.¹⁰ Ovid, of course, was immensely popular, and his *Metamorphoses* were available in Latin and in translation.

Salomon's engraving catches the moment of the flight over the sea, Europa's garment billowing as in Moschus and Ovid, but the sense of equilibrium that the illustration suggests takes on a different significance when replaced in the printed context:

> Le haut tonant voulant jouir d'Europe
> Fille de Roy, en beauté admirable,
> Qui lors aus champs jouoit avec sa trope,
> D'un blanc taureau print forme decevable.
> Ainsi mué, la pucelle amiable,
> Le trouvant beau, l'aproche & le manie,
> Monte sur lui, tant il se rend traitable:
> Mais las! Deçue, en fin se vid ravie.¹¹

> (The high thunderer, wishing to enjoy Europa,
> A king's daughter of admirable beauty,
> Who was then playing in the fields with her companions,
> Of a white bull took the deceiving shape.
> Hence changed, the kind maiden,
> Finding him beautiful, comes closer and strokes him,
> Climbs on his back, since he was so amiable,
> But alas! Deceived, in the end, she was ravished.)

The epigram below the illustration tells how Europa, 'la pucelle amiable', approached the bull and sat on its back, and concludes: 'Mais las! deçue, en fin se vid ravie' (But alas! Deceived, in the end, she was ravished).¹² The combination of the engraving and the commentary reveals the ambivalence at the heart of the story: reception varies according to emphasis and context. In his translation of *Metamorphoses*, Arthur Golding heightens the sense of Europa's terror by adding the detail of her shaking limbs: 'The Lady, quaking all for fear, with rueful count'nance cast' (II, 1093).¹³ He retains Ovid's hypallage: 'The Lady seemèd looking back to landward and to cry / Upon her women and to fear the water sprinkling high / And shrinking up her fearful feet' (VI, 130–2). This is unsurprising on the part of Golding, whose 'Preface to the Reader' strongly condemns the lust of the pagan gods: 'Who, seeing Jove ... / In shape of eagle, bull or swan to win his foul desire ... would take him for a god?' (33–42). Anticipating Sandys, he follows Boccaccio who, in his *Genealogia deorum gentilium*, emphasises the sexual violence, through the verb 'rapuisset' – 'cum rapuisset Iuppiter Europam' (II, 63)[14] (when he carried her away by force) – which one also finds in a 1579 Latin translation of Moschus: 'eam quam volebat rapuisset'[15] (she whom he wished to carry away by force). Furthermore, Boccaccio uses the verb *opprimere* twice: 'natans in Cretam transtulit. ubi in veram redactus formam, eam oppressit, & oppressu praegnantem fecit' (swimming, he crossed to Crete where, resuming his true shape, he forced himself upon her, and through that ravishment, made her pregnant). The meaning is clear, and would certainly have been so to Elizabethan authors. Thomas Cooper translates *opprimere* as 'to oppresse: to grieve: to thrust hard: to keepe or shut in: to take sodeinly: to ravish a woman'.[16]

Boccaccio and Golding link up with the medieval moralists, who invited readings of Ovid through the prism of Christian allegorisation. Focusing on the rape, they strongly condemned Jupiter's actions – or at least seemed to do so. In the early fourteenth century, the anonymous author of the *Ovide moralisé* writes that Europa hesitated before touching the beast, owing to 'paours et coardie' (fear and cowardice); when Jupiter took away 'sa proie' (his prey), the maiden became frightened and discouraged; once in Crete, the god took her virginity, '[d]ont molt fu liez et esjoïs' (of which he was very happy and joyous).[17] A century or so later, the equally anonymous author of the *Ovide moralisé en prose* offers a similar narrative: the god 'ravit subtillement' (slyly ravished) Europa, who 'doubtait le peril de sa personne' (feared for her person), and 'fist son plaisir d'icelle Europe' (made his pleasure with said Europa).[18] As with the example of the engraving, however, no reading is unidirectional, and some of these narratives of rape are backed up by allegorical interpretations that undermine first-level condemnations: Jupiter may be a sexual predator, but he also represents Christ coming down to earth, debasing himself by assuming the shape of an animal to save the human soul and take it with him to heaven. In the *Ovide moralisé en prose*, Europa embodies the Virgin Mary impregnated by God. Europa's experience, brought on by forces she cannot control, thus becomes a transformative, spiritual journey – reminding us that the words 'rape' and 'rapture' share the same Latin etymology.

Whether expanding Europa's fears or relating them more or less explicitly to Jupiter's sexual violence, these reappropriations suggest growing empathy for the maid and condemnation of the god. Attempts to elevate the abduction to a spiritual dimension lose ground or take on new forms as, perhaps, in Titian's painting, with its multiple reading of physical fear, sensual disarray and submission to uncontrollable forces: Europa seems to be in danger of falling into the dark waters, where a Cupid rides a dolphin and a monster-like fish rears its head (recalling the descriptions of the sea in both Moschus's and Horace's poems), even while she gazes up at two Cupids in the sky.[19] Simultaneously, depictions of the rape that lack Moschus's elliptic subtlety survive in moral readings that coexist with rediscoveries and translations of the source texts. Early modern writers draw on the two strands of this tradition, interweaving them or swinging from one to the other, achieving effects of shifting perspectives. Close readings show effects of cross-fertilisation, with myths leading into each other, and horizontal, intervernacular exchanges.

Europa in Elizabethan sonnets: male-centred fantasies and 'dolefull dreames'

The discourse of love sonnet sequences aims to seduce a lady, and to persuade her to requite the (male) *persona*'s love that he is at pains to present as sincere and chaste. For that reason, the love rhetoric tends to obliterate allusions to rape, or tone them down to oblique conceits, even though they sometimes resurface. Owing to Ovid's greater influence, Moschus's references to the unloosening of Europa's maiden girdle tend to disappear – even though we shall see how this topos of classical literature, which extended into medieval, courtly literature, possibly resurfaces in a poem by Barnabe Barnes in his sonnet sequence *Parthenophil and Parthenophe* – which includes his own version of Moschus's Idyll I, 'The first eidillion of Moschus describing love'.

As in Arachne's tapestry, Europa appears alongside other mythological figures, generally in clusters of myths that bring together Jupiter's conquests. In his *Hekatompathia*, a collection of poems published in 1582 that he calls 'passions', Thomas Watson emphasises his lady's beauty:

> Not she, whom Jove transported into Crete;
> Nor Semele, to whom he vowd in hast;
> Nor she, whose flanckes he fild with fayned heate;
> Nor whome with Ægles winges he oft embrast;
> Nor Danaë, beguyl'd by golden rape;
> Nor she, for whome he tooke Dianaes shape;
> Nor faire Antiopa, whose fruitefull love
> He gayned Satyr like; nor she, whose Sonne
> To wanton Hebe was conioyn'd above;

> Nor sweete Mnemosyne, whose love he wunne
> In shepheardes weede; no such are like the Saint,
> Whose eyes enforce my feeble heart to faint.[20]

Watson lists the women Arachne depicts in her tapestry (Europa, Leda, Asteria, Danae, Callisto, Antiopa, Alcmene, Mnemosyne) and he adds Semele, whose fate Ovid describes in *Metamorphoses* (III, 253–315). Watson's catalogue of seduced women ends on a paradox and an admission of defeat: unlike them, his lady is a 'Saint' on whom his Jove-like desires – or fantasies – have no hold. She, therefore, remains outside the picture.

While no condemnation of Jupiter's behaviour is discernible in Watson's poem, which rather expresses a sense of frustration, Thomas Lodge's Sonnet 34, in his collection to Phillis, revolves on the verb 'surprise', mid-way through the poem.

> I would in rich and golden-coloured rain,
> With tempting showers in pleasant sort descend
> Into fair Phillis' lap, my lovely friend,
> When sleep her sense with slumber doth restrain.
> I would be changèd to a milk-white bull,
> When midst the gladsome field she should appear,
> By pleasant fineness to surprise my dear,
> Whilst from their stalks, she pleasant flowers did pull.
> I were content to weary out my pain,
> To be Narcissus so she were a spring,
> To drown in her those woes my heart do ring,
> And more; I wish transformèd to remain,
> That whilst I thus in pleasure's lap did lie,
> I might refresh desire, which else would die.[21]

Lodge's poem is actually a faithful translation of one of Ronsard's sonnets to Cassandre, in *Le premier livre des amours*, which he published in 1552:

> Je voudroy bien richement jaunissant
> En pluye d'or goute à goute descendre
> Dans le giron de ma belle Cassandre,
> Lors qu'en ses yeux le somne va glissant.
> Puis je voudroy en toreau blanchissant
> Me transformer pour sur mon dos la prendre,
> Quand en Avril par l'herbe la plus tendre
> Elle va fleur mille fleurs ravissant.
> Je voudroy bien pour alléger ma peine,
> Estre un Narcisse et elle une fontaine,

Pour m'y plonger une nuict à sejour;
Et si voudroy que ceste nuict encore
Fust eternelle, et que jamais l'Aurore
Pour m'esveiller ne rallumast le jour.[22]

Both Ronsard's and Lodge's sonnets have a powerful erotic charge: the imagination is the only locus where the persona of the poet can hope to come into physical contact with the lady. As Guy Demerson writes in his study of the French Pléiade poets: '[L]a métamorphose permet à l'esprit que déçoit le réel de s'échapper dans le monde imaginaire de la création poétique'[23] (metamorphosis allows the spirit, when disappointed with reality, to escape into the imaginary world of poetic creation). Both poems explore three myths, the first two being Jupiter's metamorphoses. Ronsard and Lodge identify themselves with Jupiter as a golden shower raining into Danae's lap then changing himself into a bull to ravish Europa. John E. Jackson perceives a 'spring idyll' in the second quatrain by Ronsard, but this does not take into account all the meanings of 'ravissant', which the verb 'prendre' (take), two lines earlier, anticipates.[24] The verb *ravir*, like 'to ravish' in English, both signifies 'to delight' and 'to abduct'. It has the same Latin root, *rapiere*, as the English verb 'to rape' and recalls 'rapuisset' in Boccaccio and in the Latin translation of Moschus. Thus, the last line of Ronsard's second quatrain can mean that Cassandre delights the flowers with her beauty, a flower among a thousand flowers, 'fleur mille fleurs ravissant' (as on a millefleurs tapestry), or that she 'abducts' (picks) flowers. Remarkably, Lodge reproduces this ambiguity of perception in a single verb, 'surprise', just as Ronsard did. The lexical field of joy abounds in Lodge's second quatrain: 'gladsome', 'pleasant' (twice), 'fineness'. Nevertheless, like *ravir*, 'to surprise' also meant '[t]o capture, seize; to take possession of by force'.[25] This polysemy of 'surprise' invites contrasted, simultaneously suggested interpretations: Phillis-Europa being carried away by force, or consenting to be abducted. Lodge shifts away from Ronsard's vision of Phillis as a flower among flowers: his description of her pulling pleasant flowers from their stalks suggests a violence, in which the male speaker may find some licence for his own violence. Both poems then move on to depict the lover as Narcissus with, once again, images of liquid and penetration – 'Drown in her', 'm'y plonger' – that the opening lines had associated with Jupiter's rape of Danae. The wish for an eternal night of love, more explicit in Ronsard's poem, recalls yet another of Jupiter's metamorphoses, when he conquered Alcmene in the guise of her husband Amphitryon and tripled the length of the night. In Lodge's version, the poem reverts in its final couplet to Danae, reworking the image of her (and Phillis's) lap to widen out into the fantasy of a nameless 'pleasure's lap'. Simultaneously, though, the poet is 'transformèd' by the power of his own art, from a would-be Jupiter to Narcissus. The transformation results not from Jupiter's multiple metamorphoses but from the association of different images of rain and liquidity, and the process illustrates both the mutability of the mythological material and the creative processes that result from a reorganisation of motifs associated with individual myths. After imagining himself as the rain that would 'descend' ('descendre') into Danae's/Phillis's lap, the speaker projects himself in a more passive (post-coital) role, no longer as Jupiter surprising Europa, but as Narcissus drowning in the fountain of love. The myth of Narcissus, however, suggests the ultimate failure of the attempts at metamorphosis, since it is about auto-eroticism, an idea emphasised in Lodge's sonnet by the rhyme 'lie/die' of the final couplet.

In Barnabe Barnes's *Parthenophil and Parthenophe* (1593), the male character Parthenophil also indulges in fantasies of metamorphosis:

> Jove for Europaes love tooke shape of Bull;
> And for Calisto playde Dianaes parte
> And in a golden shower, he filled full
> The lappe of Danae with coelestiall arte,
> Would I were chang'd but to my mistresse gloves,
> That those white lovely fingers I might hide,
> That I might kisse those hands, which mine hart loves
> Or else that cheane of pearle, her neckes vain pride,
> Made proude with her neckes vaines, that I might folde
> About that lovely necke, and her pappes tickle,
> Or her to compasse like a belt of golde,
> Or that sweet wine, which downe her throate doth trickle,
> To kisse her lippes, and lye next at her hart,
> Runne through her vaynes, and passe by pleasures part.[26]

Barnes starts with three of Jupiter's spectacular disguises, two of them involving once again Europa and Danae, the third being his transformation into Diana to rape Callisto. As in Lodge and Ronsard, his narrator tries to close the tantalising distance between him and his beloved. He considers objects that belong to Parthenophe, and come into contact with her skin: gloves, a necklace and a belt – transforming the unloosening of the girdle in Moschus's poem into an image of encirclement. Parthenophil transmutes Jupiter's 'golden shower' into a 'belt of golde' and into 'sweet wine', picturing himself both as constraining and penetrating 'pleasures part', in a form of total possession that reduces the beloved to a passive receptacle. The impression the poetic voice strives to give is that there is no trace of overt violence in this sonnet, rather forms of deception ('arte') and transformation that enable the lover to take possession of the anatomised lover's body: violence, here, is insidious, as in Moschus, yet this sense of male domination proves just as ruthless as Jupiter's treatment of Europa, Callisto and Danae in Ovid's *Metamorphoses*. Once again, meanings shift or acquire a different emphasis when the perspective or context changes: the sonnet's combination of the three mythological episodes and the final, twofold metamorphosis into a belt and wine take yet another, still darker colouring when considered against the last poem in the *Parthenophil and Parthenophe* sequence. The collection, which also contains sestinas, songs, madrigals, odes and elegies, ends in a very unusual way for an Elizabethan love sonnet sequence, with a long poem (111 lines) that describes what amounts to a rape:

> Oh dye, live, ioye: what? last continuall night,
> Sleepe Phoebus still with Thetis: rule still night.
> I melt in love, loves marrow-flame is kindled:
> Here will I be consum'd in loves sweet furies.
> I melt, I melt, watche Cupid my love-teares:
> If these be furies, oh let me be woode!
> If all the fierie element I bare
> 'Tis now acquitted: cease your former teares,
> For as she once with rage my bodie kindled,
> So in hers am I buried this night.
>
> (Sestina 5, lines 102–11)

After calling on Hecate and the Furies and resorting to the black arts, Parthenophil succeeds in persuading the weeping Parthenophe to undress and, once she is 'naked and bare' (line 72), to 'embrace' him. At the end of this triple sestina, the Petrarchan topos of icy fire ('I melt in love, loves marrow-flame is kindled') is given a hyperbolic dimension: the usual courtly compliment is replaced by an account of sexual consummation. Here, the mythological figures are more often associated with obscure forces of destruction and black magic than with love: 'the transgressive nature of magic functions as a complex metaphor for unrestrained lust'.[27] The idea of an endless night encountered in Ronsard's sonnet and its translation by Lodge recurs, suggesting that the whole scene of sexual consummation is nothing but a dream that overturns the codes of Petrarchan poetry – or pushes them to their most extreme logic.

Another suggestion of rape is to be found in Alexander Craig's *Amorose Songes, Sonets, and Elegies*, which were published in 1606, towards the end of the vogue for love sonnet sequences and after the death of Elizabeth I. The image of the ideal lady is seriously undermined in this collection, which is addressed to no fewer than eight women, only one of whom – Erantina – represents the Petrarchan ideal, which the sequence sets in perspective, 'as one among many valid attitudes to love'.[28] One of the last women he addresses is Lais, who is named after a Greek courtesan, appropriately enough, since the aim is to establish that her chastity is far from perfect. She resembles the Dark Lady of Shakespeare's *Sonnets*, which Craig echoes, and she is the addressee of the following poem about 'dole-full dreames':

> Brave Troilus the Trojan stout and true,
> As more at length in Chauser wee may find,
> Dreamd that a faire white bull, as did insue,
> Had spoyld his love, and left him hurt behind.[29]

'Spoil' is here used to mean 'ravish or violate (a woman)'. To express his jealousy and anger, the persona establishes a parallel with Troilus's dream in Book V of Chaucer's *Troilus and Criseyde*. What is remarkable is that he seems to superimpose this passage from Chaucer's work onto the myth of Europa. In Chaucer's text, Troilus dreams that Criseyde is lying beside 'a boar with tuskes grete' (V, 1238) and kissing the animal. Whether deliberate or not, the conflation makes poetic sense. The two beasts bear horns or tusks and are symbols of strength, fury and virility – the bull 'is a fierce and lustful animal', Natale Conti writes in his chapter on Europa.[30] In Chaucer's work, Criseyde is portrayed as betraying Troilus, since *she* is kissing the boar, just as Europa kisses the bull in Moschus. In his first poem to Lais, Craig terms her 'a facill Dame' (sig. C6r); by the end of the sequence, she has become a whore: 'thou art thrise as great a whoore as shee' (sig. I4v), 'The world shall say, thou art a shameles whore' (sig. I8r). Here he lightens his criticism by reversing the situation and assimilating her to the trusting Europa: in referring to 'a faire white bull' that 'Had spoyld his love', he seems to lay the blame on the metamorphosed god, not the woman. Simultaneously, though, the association between Lais and Criseyde invites another reading: in both cases, their names have come to be associated with faithlessness. The abduction of Europa serves as a bridge in Craig's male-centred vision: it is not the lady (Criseyde, Europa, Lais) who is 'hurt' by the rape, but the lover (Troilus, the male speaker).

Beatrice and Perdita: reclaiming agency for Europa

Shakespeare's plays, like Elizabethan love sonnets, offer different ways of suggesting sexual coercion through the myth of Europa, transferring the poetic subject of Jupiter's loves to the stage.

First, sexual violence can purely and simply be denied. One way of not acknowledging the rape is to adopt a male-centred viewpoint and pretend that it is all in fact a game. That is what Claudio does in *Much Ado about Nothing*, as Benedick is about to be married:

> CLAUDIO. Tush, fear not, man, we'll tip thy horns with gold,
> And all Europa shall rejoice at thee,
> As once Europa did at lusty Jove,
> When he would play the noble beast in love.
>
> (V.iv.44–7)

Here, Jove's bull is the symbol of the cuckold, as it is also in *The Merry Wives of Windsor* ('Remember, Jove, thou wast a bull for thy Europa, love set on thy horns') (V.v.3–4) and *Troilus and Cressida* ('the goodly transformation of Jupiter there, his [brother] the bull, the primitive statue and oblique memorial of cuckolds') (V.i.53–5). Claudio is not using the language of love poetry, indulging instead in the bawdy vein that suits male bantering on the eve of Benedick's marriage. The myth is distorted so as to suit the masculine context and, more broadly, the comedic genre that assumes that sexual relationships within the context of marriage should be pleasurable since all's well that is supposed to end well.

In *The Taming of the Shrew*, Shakespeare veils the rape by choosing not to mention how the story ends and showing Jupiter in a favourable light. Like Watson in *Hekatompathia*, 75, Lucentio's purpose in *The Taming of the Shrew* is above all to insist on Bianca's nonpareil beauty:

> LUCENTIO. O, yes, I saw sweet beauty in her face,
> Such as the daughter of Agenor had,
> That made great Jove to humble him to her hand
> When with his knees he kiss'd the Cretan strond.
>
> (I.i.167–70).

Lucentio's courtship of Bianca stands in contrast to Petruchio's wooing of Katharina. In I.i, Lucentio uses the Petrarchan language of love poetry ('I saw her coral lips ...') (I.i.174), with its mythological similes. Wayne A. Rebhorn observes that *The Taming of the Shrew* contains a tissue of allusions to various sorts of rapes and analogous notions of (usually) male domination, ranging from the offer to show Christopher Sly erotic pictures of Adonis, Io, and Daphne (induction, 2.47 ff.), through Lucentio's reference to the rape of Europa (I.i.164–7), down to Petruchio's praise for Kate as 'a second Grissel, / And Roman Lucrece' (II.i.295–6).[31]

Lucentio refers to the myth of Europa, but chooses to imagine a scene of courtship and consent, in which a humble god wooed and won the maiden. Lucentio's toned-down rewriting of the myth seems to push references to a potential rape elsewhere in the play: they are in a sense expurged from the main plot and transferred to the Induction in other references to the gods' victims: Adonis, Io and Daphne (50–1, 54–6, 57–60). Yet there is a twist in his tale, since the scene of courtship he describes does not occur in Europa's homeland, at the beginning of the story, as it were, but after the abduction, in Crete, moments before the rape – or, if one chooses to heed Venus in Horace's ode, marriage.

Bate establishes a parallel between male rhetoric in Ovid's works and in Elizabethan poetry: '[w]omen in both Ovidian and Elizabethan poetry usually have to be seduced and hence to some degree coerced – the dividing-line between the verbal coercion of rhetoric and the physical rape is thin, as Shakespeare shows in *The Rape of Lucrece*'.[32] In *The Winter's Tale*, Florizel seems to be aware of that when he tries to convince Perdita that their love is not impossible.

> FLORIZEL. Apprehend
> Nothing but jollity. The gods themselves,
> (Humbling their deities to love), have taken
> The shapes of beasts upon them. Jupiter
> Became a bull, and bellow'd; the green Neptune
> A ram, and bleated; and the fire-rob'd god,
> Golden Apollo, a poor humble swain,
> As I seem now.
>
> (IV.iv.24–31)

This passage is inspired by Robert Greene's *Pandosto*, in which Dorastus tells himself: 'shame not at thy shepherd's weed. The heavenly gods have sometime earthly thoughts. Neptune became a ram, Jupiter a bull, Apollo a shepherd: they gods, and yet in love; and thou a man appointed to love.'[33] In their attempt to reassure Perdita that a difference in social status need not be an impediment to love, Dorastus and Florizel turn to Arachne's tapestry for their mythological exempla – appropriately enough for princes with a training in the classics but not perhaps conducive to reassuring the loved one, Florizel realises, unless the reference is inflected:

> Their transformations
> Were never for a piece of beauty rarer,
> Nor in a way so chaste, since my desires
> Run not before mine honor, nor my lusts
> Burn hotter than my faith.
>
> (IV.iv. 31–5)

Like Europa, Theophane was snatched away from her land and made pregnant. She is mentioned only in reference to Neptune, whom Ovid addresses directly: 'aries Bisaltida fallis' ('as a ram deceivedst Bisaltis') (VI, 117). Actually, Ovid meant Bisaltis's daughter, Theophane, as corrected by Golding ('in the shape of ram / Begetting one Theophane, Bisalty's imp, with lamb') (VI, 144–5), who may have got the right information from Hyginus, and who tells how Neptune abducted her, changed her into a ewe and fathered upon her the Golden-Fleeced Ram (Aries Chrysomallus) that launched the Argonauts' quest in Colchis.[34] Of Apollo, Ovid writes: 'ut pastor Macareida luserit Issen' ('as a shepherd he tricked Macareus' daughter, Isse') (VI, 124). Golding doubles the idea of trickery: 'how he [Apollo] in a shepherd's shape was practising a wile / The daughter of one Macary, Dame Issa, to beguile' (VI, 154–5).[35] While comparing Florizel with Apollo is appropriate in the sense that they are both in shepherd's disguise, it is also disquieting for Perdita since the god's intentions, as the audience well knew, were not chaste – and this is confirmed by Florizel's use of the word 'lusts'. Shakespeare seems to be staging here the genesis of a love poem, as he did with Orlando composing verse for Rosalind alluding to the myth of Diana and Acteon (*As You Like It*, III.ii. 1–10). We witness Florizel struggling with classical rhetoric to try and produce an adequate discourse of love, like the poets' personae in the sonnets studied earlier.

This passage about Europa is located at the beginning of a scene that opens with Florizel comparing Perdita to Flora (IV.iv.2). Like Flora, like Moschus's and Ovid's Europa before Jupiter carries her away, Perdita is bedecked with flowers, but she herself chooses to invoke Proserpina:

> Now, my fair'st friend,
> I would I had some flow'rs o' th' spring, that might
> Become your time of day – and yours, and yours,
> That wear upon your virgin branches yet
> Your maidenheads growing. O Proserpina,

For the flow'rs now, that, frighted, thou let'st fall
From Dis's waggon!
(IV.iv.112–18)

Ovid tells the story of Proserpina in *Metamorphoses* (V, 385–571) and *Fasti* (IV, 417–620). Like Europa, she is abducted when picking flowers, an activity that, as Charles and Michelle Martindale note, 'prepares for the loss of her virginity'.[36] The flower-picking also links the two figures to Flora. Shakespeare interweaves the references to Proserpina, Flora and Europa into a single scene that centres on Perdita's chastity and desirability. The dialogue between Florizel and Perdita intimates potential exposure to abduction and male lust, but the context of pastoral and romance contains the dangers that this mythological material suggests and channels passions into the rhetoric of courtship and convention of future marriage.

This prospect of 'abduction' follows upon Perdita's earlier experience of displacement. Banished as an infant, rejected by her own father and borne over the sea, she now faces the danger of being taken away once again, this time by a lover: what she cannot yet know is that their journey over the sea will in fact bring her back to her homeland and complete the cycle, reinstating her in the role she was originally cast for, that of an eligible princess. But whereas she had no agency as a child, here she is torn between fear and consent, hesitation and expectation in a floral, verdant context of promise, like Europa in the paintings referred to earlier. And she too knows her classics. She is unconvinced that gods or princes might 'humbl[e] their deities to love': as rephrased by Golding, Ovid warns that 'Betweene the state of Majestie and love is set such oddes, / As that they can not dwell in one' (II, 1057–8). And if Perdita has read Golding, she knows that Europa, once in Crete, is reduced to the status of 'pretie trull' (III, 2), one of those 'simple country trulles' with whom George Whetstone has 'mightie Jove' dally.[37] In fact, Perdita is on the threshold of her new life; no longer a child, she is a maiden about to step into marriage. The role models that are held up by the male speakers of the poems – and Florizel – are ambivalent: 'trull' (maiden) or 'trull' (prostitute)? The pastoral setting attenuates the darker shadows of the picture, and provides a benevolent frame not unlike Horace's solicitous words to Galatea at the beginning of Ode III, 27, which seek to transform Europa's journey into a 'metaphorical journey into maturity', as Jenny Strauss Clay suggests:

> The fantastical adventure and destiny of Europa, as Horace tells it, are in a sense the adventure and destiny of every young girl on the brink of womanhood. Galatea's metaphorical journey into maturity has its literal counterpart

in Europa's strange journey from her childhood home over a frightening sea to a strange and terrifying destination, leading finally to a glorious and undreamt of fate.[38]

The dialogue between Perdita and Florizel not only re-establishes a dialogue that was broken between Leontes and Hermione, it also enables Perdita to respond to Florizel's evocation of the gods. She is no simple addressee, as in the sonnets. And on Shakespeare's stage, the Europa story is no longer confined to crude exchanges between men, outside the presence of women: unlike Europa, but like a more mature, confident Perdita, Beatrice has a say in her destiny. She is given agency and will not be coerced into matrimony. While male desire underwrites mythological references, the story of Europa also anticipates pleasure and hopes of *discordia concors* in marriage for Beatrice and Benedick. The references in *The Taming of the Shrew* and Florizel's clumsy eagerness in *The Winter's Tale* suggest that it is difficult altogether to ignore the grey areas of the myth; but Beatrice stands in the wings, a potential model for Perdita.

Beyond Europa: refashioning borrowings and influences

In their reception of the myth of Europa, the works of Elizabethan and Jacobean authors are as varied as the paintings by Veronese or Hendrick van Balen on the one hand, and Titian on the other. Like Titian's canvas, showing a truly frightened Europa and a bull with eyes widened by desire, authors such as Alexander Craig heighten the phallocentric nature of the myth, which other writers such as Lodge, Ronsard or Watson choose to address less explicitly. If Europa indeed climbs willingly onto the bull's back, consent stops at the moment when Jove carries her away over the sea. As this article has attempted to demonstrate, mythological writing inspires a creative process that radiates from, and within, a selection of motifs that travel down the centuries, from country to country and from one genre to another. In the case of Europa, the first part of the myth is the only one that fits the rhetoric of persuasion in love sonnet sequences and in Shakespeare's plays. A modest veil is cast on the other two sections of the myth, the perilous sea voyage and the sexual consummation. As Lynn Enterline notes:

> When we first consider how far Ovid's narrator participates in the various masculinistic fantasies with which he dramatizes his own rhetoric of animation – the stories of Apollo, Pan, Orpheus and Pygmalion – we discover several disquieting emotions: a desire to rape, a desire to escape from female

form altogether, or profound indifference to what the 'beloved' woman might say or want.[39]

Although she does not mention Jupiter, her observation is relevant to the myth of Europa. Jupiter's metamorphoses have in common deceit, selfishness, sexual drive and more often than not violence. Ancient mythological tales of abduction were generally male-oriented, yet not entirely exempt from disenchanted self-perception: male confidence is occasionally undermined, as in Watson's poem where the accumulation of Jupiter's conquests only serves to emphasise his own helplessness in the presence of his saint-like lady. As in Sonnet 53 of Fulke Greville's *Cœlica*, the myth of Europa can also illustrate the speaker's jealousy and distress when the beloved chooses to leave him: 'Ladies, shew you how Juno did complaine, / Of Jupiter unto Europa going ... / And who intreats, you know intreats in vaine, / That Love be constant, or come backe againe.'[40] For once, roles are reversed: the man is unwillingly playing Juno's role and the woman that of the inconstant Jupiter.

Close readings of the Europa story cast light on the writing processes of Elizabethan love poets, whether in sonnets or for the stage: it catches them in the process of playing on, and with, courtly conventions of seduction, some of which amount to forms of emotional abduction, while pulling the myth in the more explicit direction of sexual desire. Borrowings and influences do not travel merely in a vertical transmission: exchanges are also horizontal, intervernacular and transgeneric; one myth leads into another, through analogy or contrast – or folds back upon itself.

Notes

1 Anon., *La Métamorphose d'Ovide figurée* (Lyon: Jean de Tournes, 1557), fo. 34. The woodcuts are by Bernard Salomon, and the octets are by Barthélemy Aneau, Charles Fontaine and Jean Vauzelle. http://gallica.bnf.fr/ark:/12148/bpt6k71516d/ (accessed 31 May 2016).
2 A long cushion, 'The rape of Europa', mentioned in the 1601 inventory of Hardwick Hall, reproduces Solis's reversed woodcut. Santina M. Levey, *The Embroideries at Hardwick Hall: A Catalogue* (Glasgow: National Trust, 2007), pp. 318–19.
3 In Veronese's other painting of Europa at the National Gallery, which may be an earlier version in reverse, the bull is merely suggested, far out at sea, and Europa is no longer visible. On the iconography of Europa, see Christian de Bartillat and Alain Roba, *Métamorphoses d'Europe: trente siècles d'iconographie* (Turin: Bartillat, 2000).

4 Philip Sidney, *Astrophil and Stella; the Poems*, ed. W. A. Ringler, Jr (Oxford: Clarendon Press, 1962), Sonnet 6.
5 George Sandys, *Ovid's Metamorphosis Englished, Mythologiz'd and Represented in Figures* (1632), ed. Karl K. Hulley and Stanley T. Vandersall (Lincoln: University of Nebraska Press, 1970): 'Upon the second booke of Ovid's Metamorphosis', p. 124.
6 Pierre Brunel, 'Europe ou le consentement', in *Dix mythes au féminin* (Paris: Librairie Jean Villeneuve, 1999), pp. 41–2; Jonathan Bate, *Shakespeare and Ovid* (Oxford: Clarendon Press, 1993), p. 35.
7 Erotic Alexandrian literature, Roman mosaics and other works of art may also have influenced Ovid. See Odile Wattel-de Croizant, 'Ovide et l'enlèvement d'Europe: aspects littéraires et mosaïques du Ier siècle', in Raymond Chevallier (ed.), *Colloque présence d'Ovide* (Paris: Les Belles Lettres, 1982), pp. 79–100.
8 See also Chapter 1 (Yves Peyré).
9 James Hutton, 'The first Idyl of Moschus in imitations to the year 1800', *The American Journal of Philology*, 49:2 (1928), 105–36 (p. 109). Idyll 2 was included in bilingual anthologies: Moschus, *Idyll II*, in *Theocriti aliorumque poetarum idyllia* ... (Paris: Henri Estienne, 1579); *Callimachi Cyrenaei hymni, epigrammata et fragmenta, quae extant. Et separatim, Moschi Syracusii et Bionis Smyrnaei idyllia* ... (Antwerp: Plantin, 1584); *Theocriti, Moschi, Bionis, Simmii quae extant* ... (Geneva?: Commelinianus, 1604).
10 Several editions of Horace's poems in Latin were published in London, starting with *Q. Horatii Flacci Venusini, poetae lyrici, poëmata omnia doctossimis scholiis illustrate* (London: [J. Kingston], 1574). The first complete, printed translation was by Henry Rider, *All the Odes and Epodes of Horace* (London: John Haviland, 1638).
11 Anon., *La métamorphose d'Ovide figurée*, fo. 34.
12 On the iconography of Europa in emblem books, see Gerlinde Huber-Rebenich, 'L'iconographie de l'enlèvement d'Europe, d'après les éditions des *Métamorphoses* d'Ovide parues jusqu'en 1800', in Rémy Poignault and Odile Wattel-de Croizant (eds), *D'Europe à l'Europe. I: Le mythe d'Europe dans l'art et la culture de l'antiquité au XVIIIe siècle* (Tours: Centre de Recherches A. Piganiol, 1998), pp. 163–72.
13 I quote from *Ovid's Metamorphoses*, trans. Arthur Golding, ed. Madeleine Forey (London: Penguin, 2002).
14 Giovanni Boccaccio, *[Genealogia deorum gentilium] Joannis Boccatii ... deorum libri quindecim cum annotationibus Jacobi Micylli* (Basel: Johann Herwagen, 1532), II, lxii (p. 50); II, lxiii (p. 51), for the quotation in the next sentence.
15 *Theocriti aliorumque poetarum idyllia*, p. 275.
16 Thomas Cooper, *Thesaurus linguae Romanae et Britannicae* ... (London: Berthelet, 1565), sig. QQqq5v.
17 *Ovide moralisé*, II, 5033, 5057, 5073. References are to anon., *Ovide moralisé: poème du commencement du quatorzième siècle*, ed. Cornelis de Boer, 5 vols (Amsterdam: Johannes Müller, 1915–36), Vol. I, pp. 278–9.

18 References are to anon., *Ovide moralisé en prose: texte du quinzième siècle*, ed. Cornelis de Boer (Amsterdam: North Holland, 1954), XLI, p. 110.
19 Stephen J. Campbell, 'Europa', in Alan Chong, Richard Lingner and Carl Zahn (eds), *Eye of the Beholder: Masterpieces from the Isabella Stewart Gardner Museum* (Boston: ISGM and Beacon Press, 2003), pp. 103–7. See also www.gardnermuseum.org/collection/artwork/3rd_floor/titian_room/europa (accessed 6 June 2016).
20 Thomas Watson, Passion 75, in *The Hekatompathia or Passionate Centurie of Love* [1582], in *English and Scottish Sonnet Sequences of the Renaissance*, ed. Holger M. Klein, 2 vols (Hildesheim: Georg Olms, 1984), Vol. I. See Chapter 2 of the current volume (Tania Demetriou) for a discussion of Watson's pastoral vein and his translation of Colluthus's *Abduction of Helen*.
21 Thomas Lodge, Sonnet 34, in *Phillis, Honoured with Pastorall Sonnets, Elegies and Amorous Delights* (London: J. Busbie, 1593). The edition used here is Thomas Lodge, *Phillis, Honoured with Pastorall Sonnets, Elegies and Amorous Delights*, in *Elizabethan Sonnets*, ed. Sidney Lee, 2 vols (Westminster: Constable, 1904), Vol. II, pp. 1–22 (p. 18).
22 Pierre de Ronsard, Sonnet 20, in *Le premier livre des amours*, in *Œuvres complètes*, ed. Jean Céard, Daniel Ménager and Michel Simonin, 2 vols (Paris: Gallimard, 1993), Vol. I, p. 34. 'How I wish I could turn a rich yellow and rain down in a shower of gold drop by drop into the lap of my lovely Cassandre, as sleep is stealing into her eyes. Then I wish I could change into a white bull to take her on my back, when in April she walks through a meadow of tenderest grass, a flower herself, ravishing a thousand flowers. How I wish, in order to ease my pain, that I might be a Narcissus and she a fountain, so that I could plunge into it a whole night through at my pleasure; and furthermore I wish that this night would last for ever, and that Aurora would never light up the day again and wake me up.' Pierre de Ronsard, *Selected Poems*, trans. Malcolm Quainton and Elizabeth Vinestock (London: Penguin, 2002), p. 4.
23 Guy Demerson, *La mythologie classique dans l'œuvre lyrique de la 'Pléiade'* (Geneva: Droz, 1972), p. 209.
24 '[I]dylle printanière', in John E. Jackson, *Le corps amoureux: essai sur la représentation poétique de l'éros de Chénier à Mallarmé* (Neuchâtel: Baconnière, 1986), p. 21.
25 *Oxford English Dictionary*, s.v. 'surprise', v. 2b.
26 Barnabe Barnes, Sonnet 63, in *Parthenophil and Parthenophe: Sonnettes, Madrigals, Elegies and Odes* (London: John Wolfe, 1593). I follow Victor A. Doyno's edition (Carbondale: Southern Illinois University Press, 1971), p. 39.
27 Jeffrey N. Nelson, 'Lust and black magic in Barnabe Barnes's *Parthenophil and Parthenophe*', *Sixteenth-Century Journal*, 25:3 (1994), 595–608 (p. 601).
28 Ronald D. S. Jack, 'The poetry of Alexander Craig: A study in imitation and originality', *Forum for Modern Language Studies*, 5:4 (1969), 377–84 (p. 378). See also Gaëlle Ginestet, 'Les huit Dames d'Alexander Craig (*The Amorose Songes, Sonets and Elegies*, 1606)', in Armel Dubois-Nayt, Pascal Caillet and Jean-Claude

Mailhol (eds), *L'Écriture et les femmes en Grande-Bretagne (1540–1640): le mythe et la plume* (Valenciennes: Presses Universitaires de Valenciennes, 2007), pp. 249–60.

29 Alexander Craig, 'To Lais', in *The Amorose Songes, Sonets, and Elegies* (London: William White, 1606), sig. G8v. On Craig and Shakespeare, see Jack, 'The poetry of Alexander Craig', p. 380.

30 Natale Conti, *Mythologia*, trans. John Mulryan and Steven Brown, 2 vols (Tempe: Arizona Center for Medieval and Renaissance Studies, 2006), Vol. II, p. 797.

31 Wayne A. Rebhorn, 'Petruchio's "rope tricks": *The Taming of the Shrew* and the Renaissance discourse of rhetoric', *Modern Philology*, 92:3 (1995), 294–327 (p. 306).

32 Bate, *Shakespeare and Ovid*, p. 63.

33 Robert Greene, *Pandosto* (London: Thomas Cadman, 1588). I quote from William Shakespeare, *The Winter's Tale*, ed. J. H. P. Pafford (London: Methuen, 1963), p. 210. For another perspective on this passage, see Chapter 8 in the current volume (Nathalie Rivère de Carles).

34 Hyginus, myth CLXXXVIII, in *The Myths of Hyginus*, trans. Mary Grant (Lawrence: University of Kansas Press, 1960). On the sheep motif in *The Merchant of Venice* and the Golden Fleece, see Chapter 5 (Atsuhiko Hirota).

35 'Issa the daughter of Machareus with hir shepheard' is mentioned, along with Danae, Alcmene, Antiopa and Asteria, in Francesco Colonna, *Hypnerotomachia: The Strife of Love in a Dreame* (London: Simon Waterson, 1592), p. 90v.

36 Charles Martindale and Michelle Martindale, *Shakespeare and the Uses of Antiquity* (London: Routledge, 1994 [1990]), p. 88.

37 George Whetstone, *An Heptameron of Civill Discourses* (London: Richard Jones, 1582), sig. Q2r.

38 Jenny Strauss Clay, '*Providus auspex*: Horace's Ode 3.27', *The Classical Journal*, 88:2 (1993), 167–77 (p. 177).

39 Lynn Enterline, *The Rhetoric of the Body from Ovid to Shakespeare* (Cambridge: Cambridge University Press, 2000), p. 74.

40 Fulke Greville, *Cælica*, in *Poems and Dramas of Fulke Greville, First Lord Brooke*, ed. Geoffrey Bullough, 2 vols (London: Oliver and Boyd, 1939?), Vol. I, p. 105. While Greville's sonnets were published in 1633, '[t]here is evidence that the first 76 poems were written before Sidney's death in 1586 but Greville may have gone on revising and composing until the end of his life': Fulke Greville, *Selected Writings of Fulke Greville*, ed. Joan Rees (London: The Athlone Press of the University of London, 1973), p. 17.

8

Subtle weavers, mythological interweavings and feminine political agency: Penelope and Arachne in early modern drama

Nathalie Rivère de Carles

THE MYTHS OF PENELOPE and Arachne connect the three 'lives' Aristotle defines as the components of the human quest for happiness: sensual enjoyment, political achievement and intellectual contemplation.[1] Arachne's sensuous tapestry and Penelope's erotic delaying and performance of uxorial love are essential components of their mythical lives. However, the myths do not solely relate to sexual virtue. Their woven works merge the physical and the intellectual, and reveal an agency transcending their often limited gendered representations. They are the instruments of a bold discussion ranging from the preservation to the reform of political and civic virtue. Glenda McLeod notes that the epideictic rhetoric used to portray the *mulier clara* in mythographies 'had long been associated with civic virtue [and] anticipates future links between the good woman and the good state'.[2] The weaver's political character favours the reassessment of the moralised tales of feminine virtue. This chapter intends to show how Penelope and Arachne resisted a limiting mythographical moralisation through a successful association of gender, political agency and intellectual observation on the stage. It focuses on the re-emergence of the weavers' political function and work in Jacobean drama.

The Homeric Penelope and the Ovidian Arachne are a *mise en abyme* of the creation and the creator. They are both the subject of the text and the text itself, and their creative agency is located *sub tela*, under the cloth. Their identity, their deeds and purposes are subtle in essence, yet do not partake of a negative δόλος (craftiness). *Metis*, the art of subtlety, is Penelope's characteristic. Beneath Laertes's shroud lies her political purpose. As for Arachne, her tapestry bears 'vetus in tela argumentum', 'an old story traced on the loom' (*Metamorphoses*, VI, 69). Similarly, beneath her woven tales lies a political motivation. Both weavers challenge the other characters' and the reader's vision, and in his commentary on John Lyly's *Euphues*, Yves Peyré suggests that this visual challenge should be the analytical prism for the myths: 'it is Arachne who weaves the rainbow, and if any colours seem to be missing, one should imagine that they are on the other side of the cloth'.[3] The Ovidian Arachne is sentenced to the monochrome of the spider's web, while the Homeric Penelope weaves an arras that is too bright to be fully described. Although both tapestries seem to have chromatically disappeared, their colours and contents are situated behind their apparent ellipsis. Penelope's arras is not blank, any more than the spider's web is an instance of Arachne's art being wiped out: the shroud and the web are material metonymies for an ellipsis, that of the dialogue between a hidden feminine political *metis* and excessive rulers.

This *sub tela* approach to the weavers requires a heuristic view of the mythical figures and an analysis of the way this subtlety both weaves together past and present representations of the figures and interweaves the histories of the two figures. Early modern drama weaves a new classical myth in two ways: internal interweaving of the components of one single myth and external interweaving of several myths. In *Euphues*, Arachne's rainbow is a combination of the Lydian's web and of Penelope's colourful arras. Jonathan Bate distinguishes 'between heuristic and dialectical imitation', and explains that 'the difference is essentially tonal in that heuristic imitation seeks to hold together past and present, whereas dialectical imitation is a more aggressive attempt to reject the past'.[4] The study of Penelope and Arachne necessitates avoiding the trap of seeing early modern imitation as a purely dialectical destruction of antique exempla. Early modern critique is directed at the moralisation of the myths and not at the myths themselves. Hence, this chapter offers a heuristic approach, looking beneath the mythographical cloth of a silent exemplarity so as to retrieve the political 'voice of the shuttle'.[5]

To analyse the part played by the mythological weavers in early modern drama is to measure what Tania Demetriou calls their 'balancing act'.[6] This chapter shows how theatre enables the mythical weavers to retrieve their agency thanks to female characterisation. It projects the concept of a 'balancing act' out of the strictly domestic sphere by confronting Penelope with her 'bolder face', Arachne, and thereby demonstrates how Arachne's bold questioning and Penelope's balancing effort merge in a reformative dynamics that aims to reach a political *mean*.[7] In *Nicomachean Ethics*, Aristotle posits the theory of the μεσότης (the mean), or 'middling disposition' and explains that it is not an arithmetical absolute 'between too much and too little, or between greater and lesser intensity, but rather what is moderate in the sense of correct'.[8] The mean is not what is, but what should be: its applicability relies on a rhetoric of measure that includes balancing actions. In literature, it is conveyed by mediating characters whose virtue lies between excess and deficiency and by the playwrights' balancing approach to genres. Nonetheless, the characters representing the mean on the early modern stage present an altered vision of the Aristotelian theory. The Penelopean and Arachnean doctrine of the mean implies reinjecting excess and deficiency into the equation of the mean in order to solve it.

According to Aristotle, the mean 'is grasped by perception'.[9] This chapter thus starts with the sixteenth-century perceptions of Boccaccio's moralised Penelope and Arachne, revealing the weavers' virtuous *sub tela* political agency. This alternative mythographical reading of Penelope and Arachne provides the background to the subsequent study of the weavers' re-emergence in early modern drama as civic and political commentators and agents. Thus, analysing the internal interweavings of the Penelopean myth in John Fletcher, Nathan Field and Philip Massinger's *The Honest Man's Fortune* and William Shakespeare's *Coriolanus*, I will stress how the weaver questions domestic hierarchy. Furthering this critique of male hubris, I will show that early modern plays offer a second, even more political, form of interweaving of the weavers' myths: the external interweaving of the Penelope and Arachne myths in *The Winter's Tale*. This last play exemplifies how the weaver moves from reflector to political agent and shapes a new operational feminine character.

The mythographical tradition and the re-emergence of the weavers' political virtue

In *Metamorphoses*, Ovid uses the ekphrasis of Arachne's tapestry and its destruction as a subtle political critique.[10] Arachne is the mortal mirror of Minerva: both are motherless figures, and Minerva's disproportionate reaction matches Arachne's arrogance. The Lydian weaver is a double political instrument dealing with necessary disobedience and excessive authority. However, during the medieval and the Renaissance eras, Ovid's tale of textile resistance was subsumed by the condemnation of disobedience. Arachne's moral arraignment by Vatican Mythographer I (*c.* 875–1075) became the normative template: his Arachne 'boasted more insolently than befits a mortal woman' who had forgotten that 'she had received [her skill] from Minerva', and was then 'reproachfully driven away by Minerva'.[11] Intemperance, blasphemy and self-forgetting were the focus of mythographical commentaries on Arachne. Boccaccio pursued the moral indictment in *De mulieribus claris* (1361), translated by Lord Morley as *Of the Ryghte Renoumyde Ladies* (1547).[12] Morley's text is an artefact of Tudor politics: it was dedicated to King Henry VIII and presented to him as a gift on New Year's Day 1543.[13]

Morley's translation reprises his predecessors' unquestioning moralisation of Arachne, but the Ovidian political undertones of the myth also resurface in both Boccaccio's Latin version and Morley's social portrait of the weaver: 'Aragnes Asiatica atque plebeia feminina', Boccaccio writes, which Morley translates as 'Aragne of Asia, a woman of the country, that is to meane, of noo greate stocke borne' (fo. 9b11–12). The word *plebeia* means 'non-patrician', 'common people', 'from the people', and Arachne primarily represents lower degrees taking on higher degrees. Morley's translation is more cautious and tries to put Arachne at a distance from divine or political authority through an expansive translation of the word 'plebeia'. Her example seems to require that she be kept at a temporal and spatial distance. Arachne stands for the problematic political voice of the lower degrees and of the creative woman. Thus she is confined to a silent part where her textual voice is never heard but always commented upon. Françoise Frontisi-Ducroux explains that the weaver's silent language reveals the secrets kept by the female community. Thus the 'voice of the shuttle' evokes a knowledge that generates male anxiety.[14] In medieval and Renaissance culture it comes to represent the feminine voice and provides a template for the *Distaff Gospels* (c. 1570), an anonymous medieval compilation of feminine wisdom, which primarily reinforces the cliché of female gossip, but also represents the transmission of knowledge through the feminine.[15] Arachne's tapestry counterbalances her own hubristic voice. It actually encompasses a socially and sexually relevant topic under Henrician rule: a political 'distaff gospel' containing the feminine experience and knowledge of abusive authority.

The dialectical articulation of silence and speech, humility and authority, rebellion and obedience is the hallmark of another disciple of Athena/Minerva: Penelope. While Athena is challenged by Arachne's *metis* as a weaver, the goddess acts as protector of Ulysses and Penelope. Yet Penelope triggers similar sexual and political anxieties in mythographers. The Homeric Penelope had been appropriated in a dialectical manner since Roman antiquity. Like Arachne, she was both the object and the subject of a literary and moral interpretative issue, opposing chastity and lasciviousness.[16] Seneca dismissed the rhetoricians limiting Penelope to a unique behavioural and ethical category.[17] Yet this confinement to 'an entirely un-Homeric fixed resolution'[18] of chastity permeated St Jerome's, Boccaccio's and subsequent mythographical texts.[19]

Morley's translation reiterates the exclusive focus on uxorial constancy: 'Penelope was the doughter of Ycarus and wife unto the right hardy knyghte Ulixes, of chastity and undefylede wyfely honeste a moste holy example, for ever to remayne' (fo. 37a6–8). The Henrician importance of male authority in the definition of female identity, the substance of which is limited to continent conjugal sexuality, is the prism of a second appropriation of the Homeric Penelope. Boccaccio weaves Penelope anew and Morley interweaves the medieval appropriation with the Henrician obsession with a faithful wife producing a legitimate heir. The limited moral programme is stated in the dedicatory epistle:

> And albeit, as Bocas wrytethe in hys proheme, he menglyssheth sum not verey chaste emongste the goode, yet hys honeste excuse declarethe that he dyd it to a goode entent, that all ladyes and gentlewomen, seynge the glorye of the goode, may be steryde to folowe theym, and seynge the vyce of sum, to flee theym.
>
> (fo. 2a13–18)

McLeod recalls that the word *claris* meant 'famous' in the sense of 'notorious' more than 'illustrious'.[20] Thus Morley's justification of the confusing indiscrimination characterising Boccaccio's gallery of women contributes to the creation of a dubious feminine virtue: 'Nor I wyllnot that the reder shall thynke it congruente that I do compare Medea and Sempronia with Lucres and Sulpicia. All thoughe I have mynglede theym with thies moste chastyste wyfes, my mynde is nothynge that ways' (fo. 3b6–10). Morley tries to create a more significant contrast between feminine vice and virtue by restoring a balanced number of exempla on both sides. While Boccaccio added Penelope to his list of virtuous models (line 23), Morley omits her: he may have been cautious not to mingle the ideal wife (Penelope) with figures of feminine literary authority (Sulpicia) and resistance to male tyranny (Lucrece) in a book given to Henry VIII in 1543, the year he married his last wife, Katherine Parr.

Penelope's intelligence and patience are virtues solely aimed at the preservation of her uxorial chastity. Such a monolithic vision of the mythical figure triggered an excessive exemplarity, open to ironic counter-interpretations.[21] The crux of the moralisation of Arachne and Penelope was to deal with the problematic issue of feminine rule. Both weavers were then subjected to the same rhetorical strategy of control: distancing. Arachne was distanced socially and geographically while the noble Penelope was turned into a *rara avis* – a rare bird – a woman of exception who is elided from the narrative. The weaver became an allegory of exemplarity, a semiotic object rather than an agent.

However, the sixteenth century marks a heuristic turning-point in the perception of the weavers, allowing their political essence to re-emerge. Penelope's remoteness makes her *metis* virtuous in new mythographical interpretations. Christine de Pizan and Ludovico Ariosto use Penelope and Arachne to promote feminine rule. Christine's *The Book of the City of Ladies* (c. 1405) calls Penelope 'sensible' and carefully separates the moral from the intellectual.[22] The same portrayal applies in Brian Anslay's English translation (1521): 'And she was wyse and prudent and devoute to her goddes and of fayre and good behavynge'.[23] This reassessment of Penelope's political intelligence is echoed in Ariosto's portrait of Isabella d'Este in *Orlando furioso* (1516): 'solo perche casta visse / Penelope non fu minor d'Ulisse' (13.60) and later in John Harington's 1591 translation, 'Penelope in spending chast her dayes, / As worthie as Ulysses was of praise' (XIII, 423–4).[24] Both versions rely on the comparative of equality, on isocolons and similar syntactical inversions. They equate male and female valour, but above all suggest that feminine political agency is neither unruly nor dangerous. The Penelopean political stance is an oblique one referring the reader back to the Homeric ὁμοφροσύνη (like-mindedness) of the Odyssean couple. This like-mindedness lies in a mean state of power: Penelope and Ulysses are 'an unusual model for gender relations' as 'they alternate between subordinating and dominating each other. Hence … they provide an internal model for the kind of agonistic communication effected by Homer's song'.[25] The Homeric motif of the 'heroic couple' as the embodiment of the mean is used as a defence of feminine rule or regency.

Christine de Pizan openly questioned the sanitised moralisation of Penelope and Arachne by focusing on feminine action more than on feminine ontology.[26] Thus she portrays the weaver as an 'extraordinary resourceful and clever' inventor and as a figure of progress: 'In my view, this woman did no small service to humanity, which has since derived great pleasure and profit from her inventions.' The weaver's power is no longer a symptom of selfish hubris, but a beneficial political action spreading from Arachne's loom into the *polis*. Christine answers Boccaccio's reductive view of Arachne by redefining weaving through a positive materialism: 'because things in themselves [are] good and invaluable when used correctly and wisely'.[27] She focuses on the virtue of practical wisdom – that of a Renaissance prince – a virtue she also grants Penelope. Christine shows that the mythical figures are primarily agents whose pragmatic use of intelligence testifies to a fertile political subjectivity and heralds the re-emergence of her political agency on the stage.

Internal interweavings: the new Penelopean route to political virtue

The weavers' political *metis* re-entered early modern culture through the dramatisation of the more benignly domestic figure of Penelope. Demetriou shows that Odyssean translations in the 1590s depict Penelope as a balancing figure.[28] Unsurprisingly in the Elizabethan context, Penelope symbolised a feminine political mean, and even John Rainolds's anxious response to the performance of Gager's *Ulisses redux* insists on feminine virtue:

> on speech concerning wemen; Quas ne quis unquam spernere dehinc audeat, Hippolytus ecce horribile documentum dedit; Impunè temnat nemo terrestres Deas. And what if all, who were present, not the young men only, did admire the constancie of Penelope? Could no evill affection bee therefore stirred in anie by seeing a boy play so chast a part? ... Hee [Quintilian] would not have his youth to counterfeit a womans voice: you procure Minerva, Penelope, Euryclea, Antonoë, Eurynome, Hippodamia, Melantho, Phædra, the Nurse, the Nymph, besides I know not whom in the unprinted Comedie, to bee played by yours.[29]

Yet, in this excerpt from *Th'overthrow of Stage-Playes* (1599), Rainolds rejects the equation between the male acting body and female virtue. The transfer onto the male performing body did not make the mythical figure's power more acceptable. However, the appropriation of the feminine myth on the male-dominated stage thanks to a tragicomedy gave a new dimension to the issue of feminine *metis* at the service of a political mean. Drama cancels out the traditional rhetoric of distancing applied to the weavers. To puritanical critics such as Rainolds, Penelope was all the more dangerous in so far as she was embodied and physically close to the audience; and the cross-dressed performance could protect her feminine virtue from criticism (some would consider a female ruler acceptable as long as her body is that of a man) as well as invite its condemnation. Besides, tragicomedy, with its inherent quest for structural and substantial balance, seemed to be the best-fitted genre for a return of the Homeric Penelope and her balancing *metis*.

Both the Elizabethan and the Jacobean eras testify to a return of a subtly political Penelope.[30] Yet the Jacobean period is the age of a reasserted *patria potestas* and of the tragicomic quest for measure, a particularly interesting context for the weavers' political impact. *The Honest Man's Fortune* (1613) stages a complex love triangle involving the duke of Orleans; his wife; and the man to whom she had previously been betrothed, Montaigne, who was thought dead.[31] Montaigne's return challenges Lady Orleans's virtue and forces a reassessment of her marriage to the cruelly scheming duke. At first sight, Montaigne is an Odyssean avatar, while the duke stands for one of Penelope's suitors. Yet, soon the Odyssean template is given a new unexpected twist as Ulysses and the suitor keep swapping roles. In this play, Fletcher, Field and Massinger appropriate the myth of Penelope and use it as the warp they weave with the weft of their plot. Applying the tragicomic combination of opposites, the playwrights play on the myth and its interpretations, which they blend in order to create their plot. Penelope's chaste waiting is combined with the moral quality of her chastity, but also with her tactical and sexual deceptiveness. In an exercise of *mythofiction*, the playwrights posit a new predicament: what if Penelope had married a suitor but remained faithful to Ulysses? Their Penelope shows the rise of an unexpected feminine form of political virtue underpinned by a sacrificial obliqueness and predicated on a paradoxical form of balance. This mean is not an absolute, it is relative to the audience and to a situation:[32] it requires a particular sense of timeliness relying on synchrony rather than diachrony. The initial chronology of the myth is thus disrupted in favour of focusing on its balancing outcome, which now guides its use in the construction of the dramatic plot. The internal interweaving of components of the same myth reveals Penelope as a virtuous middling figure who saves Ulysses (Montaigne) by mediating physically with the suitors and guaranteeing political and matrimonial harmony. Lady Orleans represents a literary reassessment of the mean based on the structural malleability of the Homeric myth.

In I.ii, the duke and Lady Orleans quarrel about matrimonial chastity and friendship between the sexes. Having dishonestly convinced her to marry him, Orleans sets out to test his wife's constancy, as Ulysses did when he came back to Ithaca in disguise. Orleans acts as a suspicious Ulysses when he alludes to his wife's close bond with her friend Montaigne – 'Your friend sweet Madam / ... / Your Montaigne, Madam' (2–4) – and harbours an Odyssean jealousy when commenting on the destruction of his rival: 'when his wants / And miseries have perish'd his good face, / And taken off the sweetnesse that has made / Him pleasing in a womans understanding' (17–20). Yet, contrasting with the Odyssean myth, his anger is matched by his wife's surprising reverence for an unwanted suitor:

> ORLEANS. This may be truly spoken, but in thee
> It is not honest.
> LADY ORLEANS. Yes, so honest, that
> I care not if the chast Penelope
> Were now alive to hear me.
>
> (I.ii.46–50)

Lady Orleans refuses to be the Penelope to Orleans's Ulysses. Indeed, in the play she is faithful to the man who should have been her husband – that is, Montaigne. Orleans explains his wife's Penelopean attachment later in the scene: 'This Lady who by promise of her own / Affection to him, should ha bin his wife; / I had her, and withheld her like a pawne' (I.ii.73–5). Orleans's admission of his forfeit changes the perspective of the mythological intertext. Instead of the initial bawdy dismissal of Penelope's chastity, the playwrights keep the trope of Penelope's faithful attachment to her lost husband and alter the figure of Ulysses. Orleans is a usurping Ulysses while Montaigne appears to have been heavily wronged. The play offers a version of the myth where a suitor seems to have unfairly won his way into Penelope's bed. Ulysses loses his heroic power but Penelope retains her loving faithfulness since Lady Orleans remains true to her first and only love, Montaigne. The ironical superimposition of the adulteress and the chaste wife creates a surprising effect. The real husband is not the one the audience expects, while the sinful wife proves to be an obliquely virtuous Penelope. As for Orleans, his usurping the part of Ulysses makes him into a symbolic tyrant *absque titulo*.[33]

Orleans is a suitor in the trappings of Ulysses; Lady Orleans is a Penelope who is both a chaste wife to Orleans and faithful to Montaigne, the actual Ulysses. Lamira, the lady who helps Lady Orleans when she is cast away by Orleans, joins in this dramatic retake on the Odyssean myth. She is a helper but she is also pursued by some suitors: Laverdure, Mallicorne and La-Poope ('I would we might woe her twenty years like Penelopes suitors') (III.iii.193–4). Lamira is, then, both Eurychma and another Penelope. Yet, in tragicomedy, both characters resist the suitors' lecherous transformation.

In Act III, the satirical internal interweaving of the Penelopean myth extends to staging the suitors hidden behind a hanging in the hope of confounding Montaigne, Lady Orleans and Lamira. The play thereby invites the audience to look *sub tela*, or rather from behind the hanging, and paves the way for a different interpretation of Penelopean virtue. The ending diverges from the myth as Montaigne eventually marries Lamira. However, its internal interweaving of Odyssean characters obliquely reasserts the Homeric Penelopean virtue. Lady Orleans's constancy is indeed preserved by the play's happy ending taking the form of Lamira's marriage to Montaigne. By weaving the Homeric myth anew, the playwrights turn the tradition of mythographical scepticism regarding Penelope into a critique of matrimonial policies and gender relations.[34] Downgrading the potential Ulysses of the play to the level of a devious suitor is a way to question masculine authority in the domestic context of matrimony.

Similarly, Shakespeare had appropriated the structure of the Homeric myth in *Coriolanus* in order to discuss excessive male authority on the political stage. Shakespeare wove the myth anew in a dual manner: he separated the various threads belonging to each character and rewove the ensemble tapestry on the loom of his plot's contingencies. In addition, he interwove the initial myth and its commentaries and the expectations the latter generated. This process is akin to a complex internal interweaving of the myth, which paradoxically enables a heuristic dialogue with the tenets of the original myth. In the case of the weavers, it allows a *sub tela* return of the Homeric Penelope as agent of the political mean.[35]

Besides, this dramatic form of internal interweaving provides a new mythographical commentary on Penelope. *Coriolanus* seems to give a dialectical interpretation of the Homeric Penelope, changing her temperance into sterility.[36] Yet the play requires a more heuristic reading. In Act I, Virgilia is accused of being 'another Penelope', whose strategy of preservation of the kingdom is criticised: 'You would be another Penelope: yet they say, all the yarn she spun in Ulysses' absence did but fill [Ithaca] full of moths' (I.iii.82–4). However, if political stasis is condemned, political hubris is obliquely indicted in this scene.

Homer's Penelope explains to the Stranger – Ulysses in disguise – the *metis* of Laertes's shroud: its unravelling, her obligation to weave and to marry, her parents' pressure to find a husband and Telemachus's anger at the suitors' devouring his patrimony (*Odyssey*, XIX, 158–61). In *Coriolanus*, this state of the art is not performed by the Penelopean character (Virgilia) but by a Melantho-like third party (Valeria) backed by the family-character (Volumnia). Shakespeare's scene is an appropriation of Book XIX of the *Odyssey*, which is revisited through the mythographical portrayal of Penelope as devious and lustful.[37] Virgilia's temperance is superseded by the accusation of social sterility, and credit is given to problematic characters. In the absence of actual suitors, Virgilia is seen as too monolithic, as there seems to be no need for a tactical delay. The accusation is not only laid against Penelope, Shakespeare also dismisses the mythographical celebration of Penelopean exceptionality as sterile isolation. However, the criticism of Virgilia is provided by Valeria, who acts as both the treacherous Melantho and the suitors, and Volumnia, who combines Penelope's parents' pressuring her to remarry and the suitors. Interweaving various Homeric figures in each character has ironic consequences: Valeria and Volumnia become the 'moths' of their own prophecy. Their excessive nagging is not only a condemnation of Penelope's delay, which is perceived as bringing on social sterility – it also represents the temptation of political excess. Shakespeare combines the internal reconfiguration of the characters of the myth and the criticism of moral mythography in order to show the rise of a Penelopean political mean. The Penelopean episode could appear solely as an indictment of the government of women in that period of regime change, but *Coriolanus* is also a reflection on the ills of political male hubris. The negative female characters are matched by the tyrannical excess and the stubbornness of their masculine counterparts. Virgilia's Penelopean temperance verges on sedition as she deliberately goes against the martial frenzy of the patricians, here represented by Valeria and Volumnia. This Penelope becomes Arachnean in her way of rebelling against the hierarchical authority represented by Volumnia.

This subtle junction between Penelope's temperance and Arachne's dissent permeates Stuart drama and is clearly stated in *The Lady-Errant* (1628–38). This play by William Cartwright mocks the moralised versions of Penelope and reintroduces her Homeric political sense through actively rebellious female characters.[38] The political agency of the Homeric Penelope is retrieved through their attempt to seize power and the redefinition of the woven work into an 'entangled net' (III.ii.147). Reprising the Erasmian superimposition of Penelope's and Arachne's webs in *A Young Man and an Echo* (1526) and Shakespeare's interweaving of both figures in *The Winter's Tale* (1611), Cartwright redefines the Penelopean character through an Arachnean prism and stages a controversial feminine political agency.

The process of mythological interweaving favours a significant dialogue between the past and present of the myth and enables the playwright to adapt it to current debates. Yet interweaving is not confined to a heuristic dialogue of one myth with itself and its interpretations. It can also involve several myths and their commentaries: this is external interweaving. The mythical figure engages in a metamorphic dialogue with another figure and this outward-looking dynamic is the starting point of the newly created figure's agency. Out of the interweaving of Penelope with Arachne emerges a rare figure on the early modern stage, the woman-council. Henceforth, the weaver is not solely a reflector of political imbalance but an agent of the political mean.

External interweavings and resistance to tyranny

Yves Peyré's sense of the radiating effects of myth is at work in cases of external interweavings.[39] The underground network of mythological language operates in the background of the spoken speech and takes its full political dimension when one considers the general economy of a play. It is particularly effective when the interweaving process relies on two distinct myths as the warp and the weft of Shakespeare's dramatic tapestry. In *The Winter's Tale*, Shakespeare gives a different vision of the Penelopean stance by combining it with the other mythical weaver: Arachne. This tragicomedy compels the audience to look *sub tela* both figuratively and literally so as to perceive the political effect of interweaving the figures of Penelope and Arachne. It departs from Erasmus's view of the combination of Arachne and Penelope as epistemological sterility and reasserts the weavers' agency.[40] In IV.iii.14, Autolycus claims to have worn 'three-pile', a velvet made of the weaving of three types of thread. This pattern actually mirrors the play's triple mythological interweaving and its subsequent reassessment of the weavers' work. While Erasmus paired Penelope and Arachne with Echo, Shakespeare chooses Pygmalion as his mythological template. Leontes is this Pygmalion-like creator who gets so entangled in the creative power of his imagination that the erotic tyranny it provokes leads to the destruction of his symbolic and literal creations. Paulina acts as a virtuous counter-Pygmalion in search of a fertile conclusion. However, Pygmalion is only the play's warp, and its weft thread is itself an interweaving of Penelope and Arachne.

The Penelopean trail actually starts with Autolycus, the three-piled thief who unveils the structuring role of the Odyssean myth in the play. In Book VII of Ovid's *Metamorphoses*, Autolycus is the grandfather of Ulysses, the weaver of words.[41] This mythological background is coherent with the literal and symbolic view of fabrics in Shakespeare's tragicomedy. The play is structurally made of various generic threads, but its very narrative core relies on the combination of different mythical weavers. The plot combines an Odyssean pattern (a tale of exile and waiting) and an Arachnean conflict (hubris, divine authority and punishment) with the myth of Pygmalion (obsession, delusion and artistic creation). Shakespeare interweaves Penelopean patient *metis* using the curtain in the last scene as a way of creating a temporal stasis enabling Ulysses's return, Arachne's bold resistance to tyranny and Pygmalion's hubristic love for his creation. Aristotle already notes that 'it is the nature of cures to be effected by contraries',[42] but Shakespeare's complex interweaving of myths takes this a step further and unveils the mechanisms of a renovated doctrine of the mean that integrates Erasmus's rhetoric of *copia*. The formal excess of cumulated interwoven myths is compensated by the fact that each myth contains a different type of mean (Penelopean patience and Arachnean indignation).[43] Excess thus proves a virtuous instrument to implement a political mean.

Lyly already associates Arachne and Pygmalion in *Alexander and Campaspe* (V.iv.15–17).[44] Yet the actual association of the three myths is first found in Pliny's and Philostratus's references to a painting by Zeuxis as noted by Franciscus Junius in *The Painting of the Ancients* (1638).[45] The link between Penelope and Pygmalion is made through Zeuxis's capacity to paint deceiving images that seem to come to life:

> The ancient Artificers ... had they by continuall observation a more excellent gift of conceiving the lively images of all manner of passions and affections ... Zeuxis painted Penelope, expressing in her picture the much commended modestie of her chaste behaviour, Plinie xxxv, 9. (p. 236)

The link between Penelope and Arachne is enacted through the inclusion of the spider and her web in the portrait:

> The picture of Penelope likewise doth not only take them with the sight of that famous web, but they fall also upon a little spider which sheweth itselfe hard by; *to represent the spider so delicatly after the life,* say they, *and to paint her laborious net, is the worke of a good Artificer, and of such a one as is well acquainted with the truth of things &c.* see *Philostratus Iconum lib.* II, *in Telis.* (p. 330)

Penelope and Arachne are cast as weavers with a power of *enargeia* (vividness),[46] while Arachne and Pygmalion are part of mythological catalogues of delusional creators whose tyrannical, obsessive love for their art proves deadly. Such is the canvas of Shakespeare's own tale of tyranny. Pygmalion is not the main mythological structural network of *The Winter's Tale* but only a part of it. Although the play features a statue, the latter is not the trigger of Leontes-Pygmalion's obsession but its paradoxical solution. What, then, is the object of our new Pygmalion's hubris? Hermione and her web of words.

In I.ii, Shakespeare carefully interlaces Penelopean and Arachnean features in Hermione's linguistic web. Leontes compels his wife to play a game of rhetorical seduction with Polixenes and she wittily obliges him by turning herself into a scold: 'We'll thwack him hence with distaffs' (I.ii.37). This first metamorphosis into a spinning woman is the initial material hub that will permit the weaving of the myths of Penelope and Arachne. The distaff brings together several visual and textual mythographical comments of classical and biblical figures. In antiquity, the distaff was Athena's emblem[47] and during the medieval era it was also associated with Eve.[48] Hermione already links herself with the hubristic goddess, through the use of the royal 'we' and the threatening gesture, which is reminiscent of the angry divinity chastising Arachne for her disobedience. Polixenes is momentarily seen as an unruly element opposing Hermione's authority in the divided line: 'HERMIONE. Nay, but you will? POLIXENES. I may not, verily' (I.ii.45). The distaff is the material locus of an interweaving of the Arachnean myth and Eve's medieval representation confirmed by Polixenes's self-comparison with an Arachnean Eve: '... we should have answer'd heaven / Boldly, "Not Guilty"; the imposition clear'd / Hereditary ours' (I.ii.73–5).

The material link is reinforced by Leontes's vision of Polixenes and Hermione at the end of the scene. Having convinced their guest to stay, Hermione, Leontes's obedient wife, is left with Polixenes. Leontes observes them and tries to interpret the chirology of their 'paddling palms and pinching fingers' (I.ii.115). Besides erotic arousal and penetration, the metadramatic lexicon relates to weaving: paddling the wool and pinching the threads are part of a weaver's gestures. Not only does it confirm the link of Hermione with the figure of the weaver, but it adds another possible source to her metamorphosis into a weaver. Leontes provides a comment in an aside, as in disguise, on a scene he interprets as a suitor's threat to his wife's chastity. The scene seems to echo the trial of Ulysses's jealousy in Book VIII of the *Odyssey*, while Hermione is cast as the unruly Penelope of some mythographies. Moreover, the figure of Penelope is woven with that of a disobedient Arachnean Eve whose intemperance is first transferred onto a male character, Polixenes, and then absorbed by Hermione, who inadvertently portrays herself as lustful: 'If you first sinn'd with us, and that with us / You did continue fault, and that you slipp'd not / With any but with us' (I.ii.84–6).

However, far from being a mere indictment of problematic femininity, the plural motif of the weaver is an ironic conceit that discloses Leontes's nefarious hubris. When he uses the spider metaphor, his speech evokes Athena turning the bold Arachne into a spider: 'I have drunk and seen the spider' (II.i.45). His delusional discovery of the spider puts him in the position of Athena trying the disobedient. Yet the myth's timeline is warped as Leontes performs the retributive metamorphosis before the trial. Passion replaces his conscience and perception, and impacts the monarch's views of individual development and social bonds. Once jealousy has replaced reason and sits in Leontes's heart, it is bound to contaminate the entire body natural and the body politic of the sovereign.

Thus Pygmalion is re-envisaged through the prism of Athena's hubristic authority. Leontes has fashioned his weaving chaste wife into a lecherous Eve and into a disobedient Arachne, the spider. This interweaving of Pygmalion, Penelope and Arachne is a way to enhance Leontes's excess as well as his political tyranny. The latter is, in the words of Plato, 'the power of doing whatever seems good to you in a state, killing, banishing, doing all things as you like'; it is the government for desire and by desire.[49] The Arachnean motif supersedes the two others in Act IV when Leontes's unbridled passion verges on incestuous tyranny. The latter is proleptically evoked in Florizel's 'metamorphic catalogue' featuring the rapes of the gods:[50]

> ... The gods themselves
> (Humbling their deities to love) have taken
> The shapes of beasts upon them. Jupiter
> Became a bull and bellow'd; the green Neptune
> A ram and bleated; and the fire-rob'd god,
> Golden Apollo, a poor humble swain,
> As I seem now.
>
> (IV.iv.25–31)

This catalogue of celestial crimes is described in Ovid's ekphrasis of Arachne's tapestry and is also used in Book III of Spenser's *The Fairie Queene* as décor to the castle of Busyrane, the sexual tyrant. Florizel unwittingly enacts the metamorphosis of Perdita into one of the figures in the Arachnean arras.[51] Shakespeare uses this 'metamorphic catalogue' as a way to foreshadow the next stage of Leontes's sexual hubris: the incestuous wooing of his lost daughter. The Arachnean myth loops back to Perdita's exile as well as to the obstacles to a full comic resolution of the plot. The Homeric Penelope's patient preservation of the kingdom and the Ovidian Arachne's anti-tyrannical boldness redefine thoroughly the Pygmalion intertext and tame masculine excess. Philip Hardie goes as far as to compare Hermione in the final scene to the ageing Penelope Ulysses has preferred to Circe and Calypso.[52]

By the end of the play, Leontes-Pygmalion is cured of his hubris by the intervention of another bold speaker associated with a piece of fabric: Paulina. Her dissimulation of the Penelopean Hermione behind a curtain reinforces the hypothesis of the topoi of weaving and of the mythical weavers as cohesive elements. The onstage epistemology of the fabric exemplifies the final throes of Leontes's redress and the exemplarity of the good government of women. Like Penelope and Arachne, Paulina is the creator of a scheme that includes the manipulation of fabric. Like Arachne, she is characterised by her untangled speech (III.ii.215–16). Paulina is a Pygmalion who underwent an Arachnean metamorphosis in the Ovidian sense. She represents not unruly speech but the alternative to the masculine tyranny she was indicting in II.ii.115. Here she stands for the quest of the Aristotelian mean: 'he who stands his ground against things that are terrible and delights in this or at least is not pained is brave' (*Nichomachean Ethics*, II.3, 1104b7–9). Inviting the faulty Pygmalion to look *sub tela*, the new Arachne has rescued Galatea from her stupor and Penelope from the misinterpretation of her *metis*. *The Winter's Tale* offers a complex interweaving of different myths through the material elements of the mythographical tales of Penelope and Arachne. This interweaving overturns the mythographical condemnation of feminine moral excess and offers instead a Penelopean and Arachnean agency as an instrument of political mean. The latter favours a restoration of stable government of the self and of the state.

Paulina's Pygmalion combines the Homeric Penelope's *sophrosynê* (moderation) and the Ovidian Arachne's virtuous *parrhesia* (free speech). She offers a renovated doctrine of the mean that relies on a controlled use of excess, and she follows Aristotle's methodology.[53] She makes Leontes good by forming new habits in him: patience, justice, endurance.[54] However disappointing the play's ending may be from a feminine point of view, *The Winter's Tale* still stages a tutor in political mean in the shape of a woman and initiates a subtle renovation of feminine characterisation.

Secularising the mythical weaver

The various appropriations and interweavings lead to an oblique rehabilitation of Penelope and Arachne after centuries of active moralising confinement, but the literal transfer from mythological figure to dramatic character is rare (if we except Gager's *Ulisses redux*, a play in Latin featuring a rare occurrence of a speaking Penelope). Sentenced to eternal suspension and spinning, Arachne is limited to textual referentiality, and the anti-tyrannical stance is often erased in favour of selfish hubristic creativity. The feminine *parrhesia* she represents is used negatively as a symbol of folly and vanity. Besides, mythological interweavings can also be affected by the cultural transformation of objects and subjects acting as structural elements of the myth. The figure of the weaver in early modern England was the locus of a sexual and social debate. In her study of the gender repartition in the early modern weaving trade, Natasha Korda stresses the sexual *agon* caused by the arrival of Dutch women in the cloth industry: 'A significant number of alien women worked as silk-weavers, an occupation considered to be the province of men by the London Weavers' Company.'[55] She also points at the fact that the dramatic world made a point of not staging the historical weaver as a woman, but as a man. Onstage female weavers were sexualised and rephrased as promiscuous, like *Troilus and Cressida*'s composite Ariachne (V.ii.152), and they were only presented as honest crafts*men*.[56] They were played by women only in civic pageants.[57] The onstage cross-gendering reflects the ongoing social strife between migrant and local weavers, but also a cultural defiance regarding female weavers. Turning them into honest crafts*men* appears to be a way of airbrushing their political and sexual agency. Similarly, Penelope is confined to the textual voice of the mythological shuttle used to weave early modern dramatic plots. Apart from Shakespeare's Bianca speaking the epistle of Penelope to Ulysses from Ovid's *Heroides* in *The Taming of the Shrew* (III.i.28–9), Penelope is more spoken of than speaking. This chapter could then conclude on the following question: have the mythological figures of the weavers been silenced or have they become subtle political voices interwoven in dramatic works so as to fuel the *querelle des femmes*?

The presence of a female character named Penelope in two of James Shirley's plays, *The Witty Fair One* (1628) and *The Gamester* (1633), could hint at the latter rather than the former in the above question. James Shirley was a member of the Cavalier circle, which included also Edward Sherburne, whose brother John translated Ovid's *Heroides* and more particularly "The Epistle of Penelope to Ulysses". Edward wrote a commendatory poem to John's *Heroides*. Sherburne's translations are listed in the *Calendar State Papers Domestic* of the reign of Charles I, suggesting that Penelope may have constituted a rhizomatic political exemplum during the Caroline era.[58] In Shirley's plays, Penelope has been apparently demythologised and secularised. Her presence is limited to the name of dramatic characters. *The Witty Fair One* is a city comedy staging the strategies of Violetta and Penelope to impose their emotional subjectivity. Still portrayed as obedient daughters, they conspire against Violetta's suitor, Sir Nicholas Treedle, whom her father has imposed on her. Penelope is herself pursued by a lecherous suitor, Fowler. Violetta stages a bed-trick involving her chambermaid to avoid marrying Treedle, while Penelope humiliates Fowler by having him feign his own death and forcing him to listen to his friends' misgivings about him. The bed-trick, a recurring dramatic convention, may also act as a dramatic rewriting of Penelope's bed-plot, while the episode of Fowler in disguise and his friends is reminiscent of Ulysses in disguise (*Odyssey*,

VIII). Although the city comedy is about domestic and moral virtue, it shows two female characters boldly and cunningly gaining a degree of autonomy, and critiques the social and political conflicts of Caroline society.[59] Of course, this assertiveness is contained within the moral limits of the seventeenth century. Yet it displays the mythical weavers' *metis* as an instance not of vice but of intellectual and political virtue. The mythological interweavings of Penelope and Arachne in early modern English drama and their articulation with the political and social culture of the time repair the destructive moralisation of the previous centuries and announce a change in feminine characterisation. They signal the *sub tela* rise of a different portrait of feminine virtue as 'a state of character concerned with choice'.[60]

Notes

1. Aristotle, *Nicomachean Ethics*, ed. Anthony Kenny (Oxford: Oxford University Press, 2011), I, v.
2. Glenda McLeod, *Virtue and Venom: Catalogs of Women from Antiquity to the Renaissance* (Ann Arbor: University of Michigan Press, 1991), pp. 6–7.
3. Yves Peyré, 'Iris's "rich scarf" and "Ariachne's broken woof"': Shakespeare's mythology in the twentieth century', in Jonathan Bate, Jill L. Levenson and Dieter Mehl (eds), *Shakespeare and the Twentieth Century* (Newark: University of Delaware Press, 1998), pp. 280–93.
4. Jonathan Bate, *Shakespeare and Ovid* (Oxford: Clarendon Press, 1993), p. 46.
5. Aristotle quotes this phrase from Sophocles's now lost play on Tereus and Philomela in *Poetics*, XVI, 4.
6. Tania Demetriou, '*Periphrōn* Penelope and her early modern translations', in Tania Demetriou and Rowan Tomlinson (eds), *The Culture of Translation in Early Modern England and France, 1500–1660* (Basingstoke: Palgrave Macmillan, 2015), pp. 86–111 (p. 89).
7. Nancy Miller, *Subject to Change: Reading Feminist Writing* (New York: Columbia University Press, 1988), p. 81; Liz Oakley-Brown, *Ovid and the Cultural Politics of Translation in Early Modern England* (Aldershot: Ashgate, 2006), p. 126.
8. Ursula Wolf, 'The sense of Aristotle's doctrine of the mean', in Aristotle, *Aristotle's 'Nicomachean Ethics'*, ed. Otfried Höffe, trans. David Fernbach (Leiden: Brill, 2010), pp. 69–88 (p. 74). See Aristotle, *Nicomachean Ethics*, II, vi, 1106b20–3.
9. Aristotle, *Nicomachean Ethics*, II, ix, 1109a20.
10. Françoise Frontisi-Ducroux, *Ouvrages de dames: Ariane, Hélène, Pénélope* ... (Paris: Seuil, 2009), pp. 162–3. On the Augustan moral emphasis on female weaving, see Suetonius, *De vita Caesarum*, II, 64, 73 (Cambridge, MA: Harvard University Press, 1989), pp. 220–1, 238–9.

11 Ronald E. Pepin, *The Vatican Mythographers* (Fordham: Fordham University Press, 2008), p. 49.
12 Giovanni Boccaccio, *Forty-Six Lives Translated from Boccaccio's 'De claris mulieribus'* by Henry Parker, Lord Morley, ed. Herbert G. Wright, Early English Text Society, OS 214 (Oxford: Oxford University Press, 1970 [1943]).
13 James P. Carley, 'The writings of Henry Parker, Lord Morley: A bibliographical survey', in Marie Axton and James P. Carley (eds), *'Triumphs of English': Henry Parker, Lord Morley, Translator to the Tudor Court. New Essays in Interpretation* (London: British Library, 2000), pp. 27–68.
14 Françoise Frontisi-Ducroux, 'Procné et Arachné, les malheurs de la tisserande', in *L'homme-cerf et la femme-araignée* (Paris: Gallimard, 2003), pp. 220–72 (p. 239).
15 See Madeleine Jeay and Kathleen Garay (trans. and eds), *The Distaff Gospels: A First Modern English Edition of 'Les évangiles des Quenouilles'* (Calgary: Broadview Press, 2006).
16 For a critical historiography of the Homeric Penelope, see Marilyn Katz, *Penelope's Renown: Meaning and Indeterminacy in the 'Odyssey'* (Princeton: Princeton University Press, 1991), pp. 9–15; Nancy Felson Rubin, *Regarding Penelope from Character to Poetics* (Princeton: Princeton University Press, 1991), pp. 2–20; Frontisi-Ducroux, *Ouvrages de dames*, pp. 91–115.
17 Seneca, *Epistulae morales ad Lucilium*, LXXXVIII, 8.
18 Demetriou, '*Periphrōn* Penelope', p. 89.
19 See Erasmus's comment on Jerome's statement that 'Penelopis pudicitia Homeri carmen est' (Penelope's chastity is Homer's song), in *Opera omnia: Tomus secundus*, in J. P. Migne (ed.), *Patrologiae cursus completus*, series latina (PL), 23 (1883), quoted in Hilmar M. Pabel, 'Reading Jerome in the Renaissance: Erasmus' reception of the *Adversus Jovinianum*', *Renaissance Quarterly*, 55 (2002), 470–97 (p. 481).
20 McLeod, *Virtue and Venom*, p. 7.
21 See Nathalie Rivère de Carles, '"The chaste Penelope": questionnement d'un modèle mythique', in Armel Dubois-Nayt, Pascal Caillet and Jean-Claude Mailhol (eds), *L'écriture et les femmes en Grande-Bretagne (1540–1640): le mythe et la plume* (Valenciennes: Presses Universitaires de Valenciennes, 2007), pp. 131–42.
22 Christine de Pizan, *The Book of the City of Ladies*, trans. Rosalind Brown-Grant (London: Penguin, 1999), II, 41 (pp. 292–3). Brown-Grant translates directly from Christine.
23 Christine de Pizan, *The Boke of the Cyte of Ladyes by Christine de Pizan Translated by Brian Anslay*, trans. Brian Anslay, ed. Hope Johnston (Tempe: Arizona Center for Medieval and Renaissance Studies, 2014). Anslay was an administrator working for Henry VII and Henry VIII. Brown-Grant's translation of Christine reads as follows: 'She was not only extremely wise and prudent, but also very moral and pious' (Christine de Pizan, *The Book*, p. 293).

24 Ludovico Ariosto, *Ludovico Ariosto's 'Orlando furioso': Translated into English Heroical Verse by Sir John Harington*, trans. John Harington, ed. Robert McNulty (Oxford: Oxford University Press, 2012 [1972]).
25 Felson Rubin, *Regarding Penelope*, p. 12.
26 Joelte A. Wisman, 'Christine de Pizan and Arachne's metamorphoses', *Fifteenth-Century Studies*, 23 (1997), 138–51. For the diffusion of Christine's work in Tudor England, see Christine de Pizan, *Christine de Pizan in English Print, 1478–1549*, ed. Anne E. B. Coldiron, MHRA Tudor and Stuart Translations, 6 (London: MHRA, 2015).
27 Christine de Pizan, *The Book*, I, 39, pp. 176–7. Similarly, Anslay's translation, *The Boke of the Cyte of Ladyes* (London: Pepwell, 1521), stresses Arachne's collective impact, thus breaking with Boccaccio's reduction of Arachne to selfish artistic hubris: 'So me semeth that this woman made no lytell service to ye worlde by the whiche syth men have founde grete profyte'; sig. N.n3r (N.n2v–3v for his presentation of Arachne).
28 Demetriou, '*Periphrōn* Penelope', pp. 102–5.
29 John Rainolds and William Gager, *Th'Overthrow of Stage-Playes* (Middleburgh: R. Schilders, 1599). The interpolated Latin quotation is from Gager's *Hippolytus* (1592), Epilogue, 387–8: That nobody would ever dare spurn them, here is Hippolytus, who gave a dreadful example; let nobody disdain these earthly goddesses with impunity.
30 See for instance III.iii of John Lyly's *Mydas* (1589).
31 Francis Beaumont and John Fletcher, *The Dramatic Works in the Beaumont and Fletcher Canon*, ed. Fredson Bowers, 10 vols (Cambridge: Cambridge University Press, 2008), Vol. X.
32 Aristotle, *Nicomachean Ethics*, II, vi, 1106a31.
33 There are two sorts of tyrants: the tyrant *ab exercitio* (the legitimate ruler who goes astray), and the tyrant *absque titulo* (the usurper). Aristotle, *Politics*, V, 8–12.
34 For the political nature of exemplary narratives in Fletcher's drama, see Gordon McMullan, *The Politics of Unease in the Plays of John Fletcher* (Amherst: University of Massachusetts Press, 1994), pp. 164–96.
35 Anny Crunelle Vanrigh, '"Seeking (the) mean(s)": Aristotle's *Ethics* and Shakespeare's *Coriolanus*,' *Cahiers élisabéthains*, 86:1 (2014), 23–44.
36 See Rivère de Carles, 'The chaste Penelope'.
37 *Ibid.*, p. 137.
38 For the use of Penelope by female characters in *The Lady-Errant*, see Nathalie Rivère de Carles, 'Entre texte et scénographie: théâtralité de la toile à la Renaissance' (Ph.D. dissertation, Université Paul Valéry Montpellier, 2005), pp. 301–5.
39 Yves Peyré, 'Niobe and the Nemean lion: Reading *Hamlet* in the light of Ovid's *Metamorphoses*', in A. B. Taylor (ed.), *Shakespeare's Ovid: The 'Metamorphoses' in the Plays and Poems* (Cambridge: Cambridge University Press, 2000), pp. 126–34.

40 For the weavers as sterile thinkers and Echo as their mythographer, see Erasmus, *The Collected Works of Erasmus*, ed. Craig R. Thompson (Toronto: University of Toronto Press, 1978), Vol. XXXIX, p. 798.
41 Odysseus is paralleled with Hephaistos, who weaves, literally and symbolically, a net to catch Ares and Aphrodite. In the *Odyssey*, the verb ὕφαινεν (to weave; IX, 422) is metaphorically applied to Odysseus as he weaves tricks and μῆτις to deceive the Cyclops. See Frontisi-Ducroux, *Ouvrages de dames*, p. 89.
42 Aristotle, *Nicomachean Ethics*, II, iii, 1104b17–18.
43 Indignation is the mean between envy and spite in *Ibid.*, II, viii, 1108b1–6.
44 John Lyly, *Campaspe and Sappho and Phao: John Lyly*, ed. George K. Hunter and David Bevington (Manchester: Manchester University Press, 1991).
45 See Franciscus Junius, *The Painting of the Ancients, in Three Bookes* ... (London: Richard Hodgkinsonne, 1638), p. 304. Franciscus Junius, also known as Francis Du Jon (1591–1677), was the earl of Arundel's librarian.
46 See the description of the moon-like brightness of Penelope's tapestry in Homer's *Odyssey*, XXIV, and the ekphrastic value of Arachne's tapestry in Ovid's *Metamorphoses*, VI.
47 Mary Harlow and Marie-Louise Nosch (eds), *Greek and Roman Textiles and Dress: An Interdisciplinary Anthology* (Oxford: Oxbow Books, 2014), p. 198.
48 See the illumination in *The Hunterian Psalter* (c. 1170) showing Eve with a distaff and spindle on fo. 8r (expulsion from Eden: Adam delving and Eve spinning), Glasgow University Library, MS Hunter 229 (U.3.2). Similarly, a rhyme, 'When Adam delved and Eve span, who was then the gentleman?', taken from John Ball's speech (1381), shows that this material definition of Eve had entered popular culture.
49 Plato, *Dialogues of Plato: Translated into English, with Analyses and Introduction*, trans. Benjamin Jowett, 4 vols (Cambridge: Cambridge University Press, 2010), Vol. III, p. 60.
50 Bate, *Shakespeare and Ovid*, pp. 34–5. Bate retraces the genealogy of Arachne's catalogue of celestial crimes from Lyly's *Euphues* to Greene's *Pandosto* and finally to *The Winter's Tale*. On Jupiter's rape of Europa, see Chapter 7 in the current volume (Gaëlle Ginestet).
51 For another discussion of this passage, see Chapter 7 (Gaëlle Ginestet).
52 Philip Hardie, *Ovid's Poetics of Illusion* (Cambridge: Cambridge University Press, 2002), p. 195n57.
53 Aristotle, *Nicomachean Ethics*, II, iv, 1105a30–34.
54 *Ibid.*, II, ii, 1104a33–1104b3.
55 Natasha Korda, 'Staging alien women's work in civic pageants', in Michelle M. Dowd and Natasha Korda (eds), *Working Subjects in Early Modern English Drama* (Farnham: Ashgate, 2011), pp. 53–68 (p. 56).
56 On this composite figure, see the introduction to this volume.
57 Korda, 'Staging alien women's work', p. 58.

58　William Douglas Hamilton and Sophie Crawford Lomas (eds), *Calendar of State Papers Domestic: Charles I, 1625–1649 Addenda* (London: Her Majesty's Stationery Office, 1897), pp. 767–78.
59　David Scott Kastan (ed.), *The Oxford Encyclopedia of British Literature* (Oxford: Oxford University Press, 2006), p. 7.
60　Aristotle, *Nicomachean Ethics*, II, vi, 1106b36.

9

Multi-layered conversations in Marlowe's *Dido, Queen of Carthage*

Agnès Lafont

GREEK AUTHORS CELEBRATE DIDO under the name of Elissa as the virtuous founder of Carthage.[1] When Virgil retells her story, in *Aeneid*, I and IV, she becomes a fallible woman, unfaithful to the memory of her husband Sychaeus; but Ovid enables her to voice her own rehabilitation in her letter to Aeneas in *Heroides*, VII, and in the *Ars Amatoria* (III, 33–40) he aligns her with other abandoned women, such as Medea, Ariadne, Phyllis. From text to text, down the centuries, authors have used these competing versions of Dido's life to interpret her behaviour *in bono* or *in malo*, according to their purpose; this tension was fruitfully exploited from the Middle Ages onwards in the European literary controversy over the status and role of women, the *querelle des femmes*.[2] Respectively drawing on Ovid or Virgil, pro- and anti-women authors have defended and attacked Dido in turn. Viewed in this context, Christopher Marlowe's *The Tragedy of Dido, Queen of Carthage*, which was first performed around 1585 and published in 1594, plays out the debate on the stage, in a generic shift that is marked by a mock-serious engagement with this staple of Latin culture.[3]

An early work initially intended for performance by boy actors on a private stage and for an educated audience, the play testifies to Marlowe's interest in humanist culture: as is well known, he studied the classics at the University of Cambridge; translated Ovid's *Amores* and the first part of Lucan's *Pharsalia*; and wrote a mythological epyllion in the manner of Ovid and late Greek epic narratives, *Hero and Leander*, which Tania Demetriou discusses in Chapter 2.[4] His knowledge of the *Aeneid* is extensive, first-hand and personal.[5] His aesthetic project combines Latin quotations and translations, and includes a number of comic additions, several of them Ovidian in source and spirit, and probably written with a young cast in mind, such as the opening scene, with Jupiter (maybe an older, taller boy, as in Perry Mills's 2013 all-boys production for the Edward's Boys?) infatuated with a young Ganymede, and the scenes with the old nurse, Barce, and young Cupid.[6] Iarbas and Dido are already lovers when Aeneas arrives on the Carthaginian shores; Marlowe also invents Anna's secret love for Iarbas, and the play culminates in their suicide. This original *dispositio* plays upon the expectations of a well-read audience while offering a jocular reorganisation of the Virgilian heritage. The hero is no longer Virgil's *pius* Aeneas and Marlowe clearly plays down the national dimension, so prominent in many readings of the *Aeneid*.[7] He adapts the Virgilian material to his own dramatic purpose by drawing on other versions of Dido's story. Ovid's centrality in his perception of an abandoned Dido lies at the core of his imitative translation, and the playwright engages the two classical models in dialogue, using Ovid's version of Dido's story to question the incriminating Virgilian scenario.[8]

Building on Oliver Lyne's notion of 'further voices' in the *Aeneid*, that contaminate the Augustan reading from within,[9] a number of scholars have invited new readings of Virgil and challenged the *Aeneid*'s epic interpretation of the Troy legend, to which the Tudors turned to anchor and legitimate the myth of their origins.[10] Emma Buckley considers that in refashioning *pius* Aeneas as 'false Aeneas' Marlowe 'is not so much rewriting literary tradition as uncovering an alternate one already to be found in the *Aeneid*': her detailed analysis shows how Marlowe the classicist critiques Virgil's text, with which he is so familiar, by 'embedding a Lydgatean Aeneas into his "translation" of the text'.[11] I wish to suggest here that Marlowe's Dido is similarly a composite figure, who owes her onstage dramatic consistency to the interactions of Virgil and Ovid as well as to the way he adds to the complexity of this first level of intertextuality – which follows standard humanist practice – by bringing in 'voices' from without, that the Virgil–Ovid tension generated. Challenging his own play's potential indictment of Dido, Marlowe enriches the Virgil–Ovid interaction by weaving in arguments from the *querelle* and pulling in Petrarchan topoi.[12] The result is a staged version of Dido's plight that is open to diverse interpretations, subverting the text that was received as an 'Augustan' epic from different perspectives. Marlowe thus does not merely exploit tensions within his avowed source, he also 'ventriloquises' all these different voices and simultaneously engages them in conversation, playing on unison, dissonance and complementarity to dramatic effect.[13] I hope to show that the play thus offers a locus for dialogue among competing versions, with Dido's story offering, in Yves Peyré's terminology, the 'intertextual marker' around which these exchanges take place, constructing a multi-layered rhetorical and visual aesthetic for the stage.[14]

First, I shall consider the medieval tradition of Dido that Marlowe was also heir to. I wish to demonstrate that *Dido* gains from being read against that tradition, which Tudor translators and printers ushered into early modern culture, so that it coexisted with readers' direct engagement with the classics through editions of the source texts and new vernacular translations. This coloured Marlowe's reading of the classics and contributes to the play's rich fabric of irony and pathos. Second, with this background in mind, I shall show how, although the choice of a proto-feminist stance in *Dido* is Ovidian in spirit, Marlowe's *inventio* simultaneously lies in a clever *dispositio* of Virgilian material. This implies that Dido's seeming inconsistencies on stage result from deeply embedded aesthetic choices. When Marlowe engages in playful intertextual games by giving voice to these direct and indirect traditions, he reflects on his own activity as a reader, a translator and a dramatist while sharing with his audience a common historical, literary and imaginary backdrop. Ovidian material irreverently influences the dramatic structure of the play; the love relationship between Jupiter and Ganymede – humorously performed by boy actors – induces intertextual games between the main plot and subplot while the threefold Iarbas–Aeneas–Dido exchanges on hunting and courting, imported from Petrarchan love poetry, further replicate the debates *in utramque partem* in pro- and anti-women treatises. As metaphors and as theatrical gestures, the motifs of the love-shaft, the suicide and the kiss offer playful variations on the famous episode of the cave: the multi-textually composed voice of the Ovidian *praeceptor amoris* slyly converses with the Petrarchan legacy. Conflicting and parallel traditions are woven into the play to stage a mythological discourse.

Arguing over Dido

Overall, Marlowe does not side with the misogynistic faction of the *querelle des femmes* – even though, as we shall see, he weaves some elements of the anti-women discourse into his characterisation of Dido. In the French *Roman d'Eneas* (c. 1160), untrustworthy Dido is an adulterous, sensuous and guilty widow, driven to suicide by her burning passion.[15] Similarly, in the anonymous *Ovide moralisé* (c. 1316–28), she is allegorised as embodying the temptations of the flesh.[16] Of course, these readings *in malo* originate with Mercury's indictment of Dido in Virgil, 'varium et mutabile semper / femina' ('a fickle and changeful thing is woman ever') (*Aeneid*, IV, 569–70), which Marlowe chooses to omit: contrary to Virgil's misogynistic condemnation, in Marlowe only the gods are to blame for Dido's infatuation – as is clearly shown in the

Edward's Boys production, which ends with the gods on stage, clearing up after the suicides to make room for further tragedy.[17]

Blaming 'false' Aeneas for his treacherous behaviour, Marlowe endows his play with female subjectivity through his combined use of Ovidian and derived sympathetic readings of Dido's plight that circulated widely in the sixteenth century. His sympathies align him rather with the pro-Dido faction led by Boccaccio, whose *De mulieribus claris* (1361–62) was translated into English by Lord Henry Parker around 1543,[18] and influenced Christine de Pizan's *Livre de la Cité des dames* (1404/05), a defence of women that Brian Anslay translated into English in 1521.[19] Supplementing Virgil with *Heroides*, VII while also familiar with Boccaccio, Chaucer defends Dido, presenting her as betrayed and forsaken while pregnant:

> Glorye and honour, Virgil Mantoan,
> Be to thy name! And I shal, as I can,
> Folwe thy lantern, as thow gost byforn,
> How Eneas to Dido was forsworn.
> In thyn Eneyde and Naso wol I take
> The tenor, and the grete effects make.
>
> (*The Legend of Good Women*, 924–9)

Chaucer even translates part of *Heroides* to voice Dido's complaint.[20] Similarly, in the *Canterbury Tales*, the Man of Law recalls how the sufferings of classical heroines are successfully rewritten by Chaucer, who 'Mo than Ovide made of mencioun / In his Episteles, that been ful olde' (Prologue, 54–5):

> Whoso that wole his large volume seke,
> Cleped the Seintes Legende of Cupide,
> Ther may he seen the large woundes wyde
> Of Lucresse, and of Babilan Tesbee;
> The swerd of Dido for the false Enee
>
> ('The Man of Law's Tale', 60–4)

Again, in *The House of Fame*, Dido is perceived as a victim of love: 'Rede Virgile in Eneydos / Or the Epistle of Ovyde / what that she wrot or that she dyd' (I, 378–80). So Aeneas is to blame, not Dido, according to the classics as reinterpreted by Chaucer. Moreover, what Chaucer's explicit intertextuality frames is the admixed reception of Dido, which paves the way for a more compassionate (and globally more Ovidian) reading of her plight in the Tudor period. If Chaucer irons out contradictions between Virgil and Ovid's versions, his work is in turn actively reshaped within the Tudor debate about the status of women that, activated by editors and printers, mediates and adapts the continental *querelle* for English readers. For instance, when John Stow published Chaucer's works in 1561, he bound them with pseudo-Chaucerian material, perhaps to inflect the reader's point of view on Chaucer's feminism.[21] This provides a stimulating literary and polemic context for Marlowe, his contemporaries and his audience, who could read and reassess the classical tradition in the light of late medieval texts, which were printed and bound so as to invite further connections even as the public reread them in the light of the classics.

William Caxton's paraphrase of Virgil's epic, *Eneydos*, which he printed in 1490, is also telling.[22] Although he acknowledges the pro-women stance, he does not fully endorse it. This never-reprinted narrative, a form of *hapax*, may be one of the last English editorial attempts at providing English readers with a late (French) medieval paraphrase of Virgil, probably itself loosely based on Boccaccio.[23] The anonymous French author clearly intervenes to express how these conflicting accounts surprise him – and Caxton replicates this questioning in his translation:

> the whiche in redynge, I was abasshed and had grete merveylle how bochace whiche is an auctour so gretly renommed, hath transposed, or atte leste dyuersifyed, the falle and caas otherwyse than vyrgyle hath in his fourth booke of Eneydos In whiche he hath not rendred the reason or made ony decysion to approve better the his than that other. And yf ony wolde excuse hym and saye that he hadde doon hit for better to kepe thonour of wymmen.
>
> (*Eneydos*, Chapter 6, sig. B7v)

Dido is both 'the fortitude virile of wymmen, or loos and pryce of chastyte femynyne, digne and worthi of honour' (Chapter 9, sig. C6r) and the woman in love. The narrator confronts two versions of the same story, Virgil's and Boccaccio's: 'And firste to shewe the dyfference of John bochace and of vyrgyle, to putte in bryef the falle of the sayd dydo recounted by bochace and after by the sayd virgyle' (Chapter 5, sig. B7r), before finally condemning Dido for her promiscuous behaviour. He nonetheless presents a chapter in her defence, 'A Comendacyon to dydo' (Chapter 9, sig. C6r). This juxtaposition, in the mythographic tradition, allows apparent inconsistencies to coexist and participates in an argument *in utramque partem* that is in line both with a medieval pro-women approach and with a 'clerical' reading.

Pamphlet-like poems also address the story of Dido in a similarly binary manner. Surprisingly, in what is generally described as misogynistic literature, some texts refute Dido's fickleness, showing her in a more favourable light than Criseyde; Thomas Feylde, in *Contraversye betwene a Lover and a Jaye* (c. 1527), writes that Dido is 'dolorous ... all for true love' (sig. F4r).[24] William Walter's *The Spectacle of Lovers* (1533) presents a dispute over good and bad women in which she is an unfortunate lover, alongside other forsaken heroines, 'That men ought ... to prayse and magnify' (sig. C2v).[25] Opposing Consulator, the moralising counsellor, Amator, a brokenhearted lover, presents Dido as the exemplum of wifely faithfulness, in the company of Artemisia, Thisbe and biblical widows:

> Elyssa
> After the dethe of her husbande Dydo
> For sorrow ranne
> unto the funeral fyre
> Her body with her lords
> to brenne was her desire.
>
> (sig. C2r)

Printed by Wynkyn de Worde, Feylde's and Walter's poems were anthologised together in at least one Tudor book, the Farmer *Sammelband*, which suggests that booksellers were eager to promote this proto-feminist literary genre, maybe for a growing female public.[26] In *The Defence of Women*, which was published in 1560, Edward More's narrator uses Dido to exemplify how widows, like virgins, may be misled by treacherous men ('as Vyrgyll doth it tell') (sig. B4r).[27] More's response to Edward Gosynhyll's anti-women *Schole House of Women* – which does not include any mention of Dido – praises Virgil in the prologue as a 'Champyan bold' of women.[28] These examples illustrate a wider literary trend that shows benevolence towards Dido, typifying her as an exemplary model, whether from an Ovidian, or even from a Virgilian, perspective.

A syncretic transmission collates Ovidian and Virgilian sources within literary texts; this also occurs in a number of editions. In 1552, Joachim Du Bellay published his translations of *Aeneid*, IV and *Heroides*, VII, bound in the same volume.[29] A multi-layering of versions of Dido's story also occurs within the transmission of Ovidian texts themselves. While Ovid's Latin text in *Metamorphoses* briefly and periphrastically recalls 'the Sidonian Queen's' predicament in four lines (*Metamorphoses*, XIV, 75–81), the anonymous medieval *Ovide moralisé* (XIV, 302–524) supplements this with a loose verse translation of *Heroides*, VII, which the author embeds in the narrative flow as a complaint rather than a letter.[30] Similarly, Richard Pynson's Tudor edition of Chaucer's *The Boke of Fame* (1526?) supplements Chaucer's texts about Dido with a 'copy' of her letter, which seems to be a text adapted from Octavien de Saint-Gelais's fifteenth-century translation into French of *Heroides*.[31] Thus 'The Letter of Dydo to Eneas' becomes a part both of the vernacular pseudo-Chaucerian canon and of the more directly Ovidian corpus, further enriching the compound Ovidian transmission of Dido's story.

Over the centuries, authors, translators and printers thus bring together Virgil's and Ovid's Didos. This reflects a sustained European engagement with the reception of a defamed Virgilian Dido alongside a compound, more sympathetic Ovidian Dido. In this context, when Marlowe translates Virgil with Ovid in mind, he is in resonance with a long tradition of reception and dramatises a sustained intertextual debate between voices that dissent while coexisting.

Shakespeare's later treatment of Dido in V.i of *The Merchant of Venice*, which comes after Marlowe's *Dido*, of course, provides a complementary angle to this discussion: in the dialogue between Jessica and Lorenzo in the gardens of Belmont, Shakespeare superimposes different textual voices in a multi-layered palimpsest, while pursuing a horizontal, hermeneutic conversation with the audience. A critical discussion has crystallised on the reference to Dido: is it Virgilian, Ovidian and/or Chaucerian? The circulation and transmission of the type of admixed source material described earlier anticipates and shapes Shakespeare's mention of Dido when Lorenzo says:

> In such a night
> Stood Dido with a willow in her hand
> Upon the wild sea-banks, and waft her love
> To come again to Carthage.
>
> (V.i.9–12)[32]

Colin Burrow notes that Shakespeare's references to Virgilian characters 'are often shadowed by allusions to the often less than simply heroical versions of them in Ovid: so Ovid's version in the *Heroides* of the departure of Aeneas as a betrayer and Dido as a heroine'.[33] What Shakespeare does in *The Merchant of Venice* is what Ovid did with Virgil in his time, casting 'sidelong glances at other classical authors' doings':[34] here, Shakespeare is thinking about Dido in *Heroides*, VII as well as about Ariadne waving to Theseus from Naxos, where he left her in *Heroides*, X ('And upon a long tree branch I fixed my shining veil') (X, 41). From these sources and inspirations, several readings, not mutually exclusive, are possible. Are these allusions 'shot through with irony'?[35] Or does the 'voice' of Virgil in *The Merchant of Venice* provide a contextual *imitatio*, activated via selected mythological vignettes culled from Ovid's amatory poetry?[36] Or should this mythological reference, in the context of the other mythological allusions in the dialogue between Jessica and Lorenzo (also) be heard as an echo of a Chaucerian source? In that case, it may not necessarily be fraught with dramatic irony but rather act as a knowledgeable game with the more educated members of the audience. Or, again, does this allusion refer back to texts such as Boccaccio's *De claris mulieribus* and the pro-women tradition? Dido offers a pointer to trace these multiple interpretations, which Shakespeare weaves into his dramatic text and invites the audience to nuance, since the words are spoken by Lorenzo, who is less than heroical. The combination of these fragmentary allusions from multiple channels of transmission with what Shakespeare conveys about the characters who speak them creates polyphonic 'conversations' that coexist in the spectators' minds with their own knowledge of the Dido story. Shakespeare plays on *aemulatio* and ironical distance, since, like members of his audience, he was no less conversant with the Tudor Didos than with their classical predecessors, and, quite possibly, Marlowe's.

Coexisting voices in *Dido, Queen of Carthage*

Marlowe's suffused Ovidianism in *Dido* follows a similar kind of multi-level conversational practice. He sets love at the core of the tragedy, centring the dramatic structure of his play on Books I, II and IV of the *Aeneid*. He is interested in the origins of love, the torments it causes, the complexity of its course. As in Ovid's *Heroides*, a form of rhetorical *ethopoeia*, which gives a voice to a mythological (or historical) character at a tragic moment of his/her life, Marlowe rewrites Virgil's script when, in their final dialogue, Dido pleads with Aeneas and reminds him of his pledge:

> O, thy lips have sworn
> To stay with Dido! Canst thou take her hand?
> Thy hand and mine have plighted mutual faith!
>
> (V.i.120–2).

Aeneid, IV reads:

> Nec te noster amor nec te data dextra quondam
> Nec moritura tenet crudeli funere Dido?
>
> Does neither our love restrain you, nor the pledge once given, nor the doom of a cruel death for Dido?
>
> (307–8)

Marlowe adapts and powerfully condenses:

> And woeful Dido, by these blubber'd cheeks
> By this right hand, and by our mutual rites
> Desires Aeneas to remain with her
>
> (V.i.133–5).

Virgil had:

> Mene fugis? per ego has lacrimas dextramque tuam te
> (Quando alius mihi iam miserae nihil ipsa reliqui),
> Per conubia nostra, per inceptos hymenaeos.
>
> Is it from me you are fleeing? By these tears and your right hand, I pray you – since nothing else, alas, have I left myself – by the marriage that is ours, by the nuptial rites begun.
>
> (*Aeneid*, IV, 314–16)

Marlowe transforms this into a third-person narrative that incorporates a first-person voice while following Virgil's text very closely, paring away and condensing Dido's speech to focus on the synecdoche of the hand and the ternary rhythm. This complex, dramatically intense rhetoric emphasises how she objectifies herself while pleading her own cause, aligning herself with other tragic heroines and depicting herself in a more domestic mode that may also have been intended to produce a comical dimension for an all-boys performance ('by these blubber'd cheeks'). Without transition, she goes on to quote directly Virgil's poignant lines in Latin, thus reverting to a first-person narrative. This rhetorical strategy, whereby the character strives to recall her royal, legendary status, also points to the young player behind the part and enhances his schoolboy declamatory training in the classics:

> 'Si bene quid de te merui, fuit aut tibi quidquam
> Dulce meum, miserere domus labentis: & istam
> Oro, si quis adhuc precibus locus, exue mentem.'
>
> (*Dido*, V.i.136–8)

> If ever I deserved well from you or if anything of mine has been sweet in your sight, pity a falling house, and if yet there be any room for prayers, put away, I pray, this purpose.
>
> (*Aeneid*, IV, 317–19)

This reorganisation of material from *Aeneid*, I and IV around the character of Dido points to the Ovidian influence behind the Virgilian storyline. The material for the adaptation comes faithfully from Virgil, but Ovid's voice is telling Virgil's story.

Ovidian voices from *Metamorphoses*, ironically commenting on a well-known story, are also audible elsewhere in the play. Marlowe's learned and oblique additions are not merely nods in the direction of the young cast's schooling. They unveil dramatic tensions written into the structure of the play. The staged duplication of mythological patterns introduces ironies and metamorphoses that are reminiscent of Ovidian aesthetics. Marlowe's first important addition is the burlesque prologue, staging Jupiter and a sullen Ganymede, which he elaborates from *Metamorphoses*:[37]

> Nec mora, percusso mendacibus aere pennis
> Abripit Iliaden; qui nunc quoque pocula miscet
> Invitaque Iovi nectar Iunone ministrat.
>
> Without delay he [Jove] cleft the air on his lying wings and stole away the Trojan boy, who even now, though against the will of Juno, mingles the nectar and attends the cups of Jove.
>
> (*Metamorphoses*, X, 157–61)

Juno's proverbial jealousy, also recorded in *Aeneid*, underlies Marlowe's portrayal of her:

> ... manet alta mente repostum
> Iudicium Paridis spretaeque iniuria formae,
> Et genus invisum et rapti Ganymedis honores.
>
> ... deep in her [Juno's] heart remain the judgement of Paris and the outrage to her slighted beauty, her hatred of the race and the honours paid to ravished Ganymede.
>
> (*Aeneid*, I, 25–8)[38]

These elements find a direct echo in the play when Juno confesses to tormenting Aeneas because Ganymede was favoured over her daughter by Jupiter: 'When for the hate of Trojan Ganymede, / That was advanced by my Hebe's shame' (*Dido*, III.ii.42–3). Marlowe picks on this jealousy to stage a mythological interlude, which opens up the possibility of multiple reverberations between Ganymede and Cupid. This pairing of two beautiful boys in *Dido* is far from incidental in the early modern period; Cupid is the archetype of beauty and desire for men and women, depicted either as an adolescent (in the Ovidian literary tradition) or as a little boy (in Anacreontic poetry for instance), thereby weaving more threads between the birth of love and the nature of homo- and heterosexual desire.[39] The association between the two boys illustrates the power of Love over gods and humans alike – and plays along with the actors' young age.

Like a visual emblem, the scene opens with 'Jupiter dandling Ganymede upon his knee': adults fondling young boys offer a recurring scenic image of subjection through love, as in the scene where Dido fusses over Cupid dressed as Ascanius (III.i.30–2), and when Barce, the nurse, pampers Cupid, who is here again disguised as Ascanius (IV.v.36–7) – simultaneously this is questioned and put at a distance by the fact that all the parts were played by children. Helen Osborne noted the effectiveness of this staging strategy in the Edward's Boys production: 'The scene in which he [Cupid as Ascanius] teased the lascivious Nurse ... and encouraged her lustful attentions was both startling and extremely funny.'[40] Dido also explicitly compares Aeneas to Jupiter, taking the Ovidian allusion further:

> Now looks Aeneas like immortal Jove:
> O where is Ganymede, to hold his cup,
> And Mercury to fly for what he calls?
> Ten thousand Cupids hover in the air
> And fan it in Aeneas' lovely face!
>
> (IV.iv.45–9).

As Yves Peyré has analysed elsewhere, this scene, in which the beloved is now subjected to Dido's desire, recalls the initial moment when Jupiter is subjected to his desire for Ganymede, while the grotesque scene when old Barce falls in love with young Ascanius/Cupid blends the comic and the amorous genres.[41] As Lois Potter records, Tim Carroll's 2003 production of *Dido* for the Globe also played on this discrepancy between the age of the actors (adult actors holding baby dolls) and the role of the gods, all the more so as the season ran *Dido* back to back with Timothy Walker's *Edward II*, emphasising that 'power is in the hands of cruel and greedy children'.[42]

The maternal gesture, 'dandle', is foreshadowed by the initial dramatic emblem; when Hermes explains Venus's substitution of the boys, Aeneas exclaims: 'No marvel Dido, that thou be in love, / That daily dandlest Cupid in thy arms!' (V.i.44–5). Dido holds Ascanius in her arms (or so she thinks) because he looks like his father, who is Venus's son and therefore brother to Cupid: the staging thus explicitly redefines *pius* Aeneas as both son and brother to Love, once again undermining the heroic reading of Virgilian epic. Both characters are also addressed in the same manner by Jupiter, who names Ganymede 'sweet wag' (I.i.23), 'my little love' (I.i.42); Dido echoes these names when she speaks to Cupid as Ascanius: 'boy' and 'wag' (III.i.24, 35).[43] The love Dido bears Cupid/Ascanius therefore may sound quasi-incestuous: in the play, he repeatedly calls her 'mother', insisting on the connection between Dido and Venus. This, in turn, throws an oblique light on Jupiter's love for young Ganymede – all this being heightened further by the choice of young actors. Staged mythological rewriting uses the process of dramatic reduplication to throw into relief how the Ovidian precedent is repeatedly made to converse with Virgilian material to give it erotic and parodic overtones. The Ovidian and metamorphic voice cleverly informs Virgilian matter, offering dissenting points of view on a tragic love story early modern audiences were familiar with.

'I will spend my time in thy bright armes' (I.i.22): Timothy Crowley traces a self-conscious echo in Ganymede's promise to Jupiter in this opening scene, with 'armes' punning on the first line of Ovid's *Amores*, I, 'Arma gravi numero violentaque bella parabam edere' ('Arms, and the violent deeds of war, I was making ready to sound forth'), which itself recalls the famous beginning of the *Aeneid*: 'Arma virumque cano' ('I sing of arms and the man'), thereby establishing a literary and humorous link between love-making and warfare.[44] Another visual and textual pun illustrates how Marlowe layers several sources and reorganises the Virgilian episodes to endow them with this type of self-conscious Ovidian coherence: the metaphor of the amatory wound. Marlowe follows Virgil when he uses Cupid as the agent of love, but he alters the way this love is inflicted upon Dido; in *Aeneid*, Venus tells Cupid '[when] Dido takes you to her bosom, embraces you and imprints sweet kisses ['oscula dulcia'], you may breathe into her a hidden fire and beguile her with your poison ['inspires ignem fallasque veneno']' (I, 683–8); in the play, Cupid must 'then touch her white breast with this arrow head, / That she may dote upon Aeneas' love' (II.i.326–7). This alteration does not seem to derive from a dramatic tradition (it is not in Gager's 1583 *Dido*), but Jane Kingsley-Smith suggests that it bears some affinity to a well-known iconographic tradition, used by Michelangelo in his *Venus and Cupid*, which was extensively copied and circulated in the sixteenth century: Venus, absent-mindedly caressing her child, is threatened by his arrow. Intertextuality and iconography fuse on stage to animate and parody an emblematic vignette when Dido, in III.i, comically wavers between her desire for the seemingly helpless young boy and her love for Iarbas – Marlowe's addition to the story, which makes the character of Dido more complex by drawing on the anti-women stance and portraying her as an inconstant widow:

> IARBAS. Come, Dido, leave Ascanius, let us walk.
> DIDO. Go thou away; Ascanius shall stay.
> IARBAS. Ungentle queen, is this thy love to me?
> DIDO. O stay Iarbas and I'll go with thee.
> CUPID. And if my mother go, I'll follow her.
> DIDO (TO IARBAS). Why stay'st thou here? Thou art no love of mine.
>
> (III.i.34–9)

Like Venus trying to lay aside Cupid's arrow, Dido unsuccessfully waves away Ascanius and is finally wounded by Love on stage. Her disoriented reactions reduce her to a puppet in the hands of the (little) almighty god of love, while reminding readers and spectators who might have been familiar with that contemporary iconography that Venus too can be the victim of love. This suggests another possible layer in the staged conversation between Marlowe, Virgil and Ovid, and in the play's engagement with the audience: a form of mythological *feuilletage* that uses Ovid to correct the Virgilian text by dint of the early modern iconography of the kiss and a stage property, the love-shaft.

Ovid's Dido already compared the amatory wound and suicide by the sword:

> Over my cheeks the tears roll, and fall upon the drawn steel – which soon shall be stained with blood instead of tears. How fitting is your gift in my hour of fate! You furnish forth my death at a cost but slight. Nor does my heart now for the first time feel a weapon's thrust; it already bears the wound of cruel love.
>
> (*Heroides*, VII, 183–90)

This image (also to be found in *Ars amatoria*, I, 167–71) and its later emblematic reading may justify Marlowe's alteration of the Virgilian source: he stages the wound of love to comic effect. Moreover, he alters the classical tradition of Dido's highly symbolical suicide at the point of Aeneas's sword. In the play, she throws the sword into the fire before throwing herself alive onto the pyre. This is reminiscent of Elissa's death, purified by fire, as in Boccaccio's *De claris mulieribus* or Christine de Pizan's *Cyte of Ladyes*: 'She cast herselfe in a grete fyre that she let make and so she brente herselfe. And others say that she slewe herselfe with the swerde of Eneas.'[45]

This is also recalled by later poets, such as William Walter in *The Spectacle of Lovers* (sig. C2r). Marlowe's invented gesture is highly dramatic: it merges the widow's loyalty and the lover's despair as if to emphasise the superiority of her sacrifice in comparison with Aeneas's betrayal. These powerful conflations constantly hinge on the tension between the two facets of Dido.

Cupid's love-shaft is thus a handy property to evoke love and death on the stage, since, from a metaphorical point of view, it plays on the medieval topos of the love hunt and, from a dramatic point of view, offers a powerful visual emblem. It also deeply affects Dido's staged characterisation: wounded by Ascanius/Cupid, she is no longer Diana but metamorphosed into another Venus. In the play, Dido wavers between chaste Elissa and an amorous woman, prone to change, moving from her first husband Sychaeus to Iarbas to Aeneas, to whom she eventually offers Sychaeus's sceptre: 'Sichaeus, not Aeneas, be thou call'd; / The King of Carthage, not Anchises' son' (III.iv.57–8).

In line here with the anti-women tradition, Marlowe reinforces her inconstant attitude, inventing a new past for her and making Iarbas her lover (III.i.8–10). She even boasts about having refused numerous suitors (III.ii.139–66) to underline her desirability. At the same time, Marlowe once again subverts this tradition by using Ovidian aesthetics, in that she resorts to erotic strategies reminiscent of *Ars amatoria*.[46] He achieves similar ambiguity in the way he adapts to the stage Virgil's scenario of the hunt. Hoping to seduce the Trojan warrior during a hunting party, Dido plays on the erotic image of a Venus–Diana: 'We two will go a-hunting in the woods' (III.ii.173).

In III.iii, Marlowe makes a number of alterations. Dido appears on stage, drawing attention to the fact that she is dressed as Diana:

> Aeneas, think not but I honour thee,
> That thus in person go with thee to hunt.
> My princely robes, thou see'st, are laid aside,
> Whose glittering pomp Diana's shrouds supplies;
> All fellows now, dispos'd alike to sport;
> The woods are wide, and we have store of game.
> Fair Trojan, hold my golden bow a while,
> Until I gird my quiver to my side.
>
> (III.iii.3–8)

This recalls the earlier comparison in *Aeneid*, I, when Aeneas first sees Dido:

> Haec dum Dardanio Aeneae Miranda videntur,
> Dum stupet obtutuque haeret defixus in uno,
> Regina ad templum, forma pulcherrima Dido,
> Incessit, magna iuvenum stipante caterva.

> qualis ... exercet Diana choros ...; illa pharetram
> fert ...
> Talis erat Dido.
>
> While these wondrous sights are seen by Dardan Aeneas, while in amazement he hangs rapt in one fixed gaze, the queen, Dido, moved towards the temple, of surpassing beauty, with a vast company of youth ... Even as ... Diana guides her dancing bands ... She bears a quiver on her shoulder ... Such was Dido.
>
> (*Aeneid*, I, 494–500, 503)

Armed like the goddess of chastity, she appears unassailable. In III.iii, however, Marlowe substitutes this portrayal for the pomp of *Aeneid*, IV, which the more educated in his audience were familiar with – and which Dido herself refers back to when she tells Aeneas that she has laid aside her 'princely robes':

> Tandem progreditur magna stipante caterva,
> Sidoniam picto chlamydem circumdata limbo.
> Cui pharetra ex auro, crines nodantur in aurum,
> Aurea purpuream subnectit fibula vestem.
>
> At last she cometh forth, attended by a mighty throng, and clad in a Sidonian robe with embroidered border; her quiver is of gold, her tresses are knotted into gold, a buckle of gold clasps her purple cloak.
>
> (*Aeneid*, IV, 136–9)

By displacing the reference to Diana to this scene, Marlowe draws a parallel between Venus dressed as one of Diana's nymphs, come to advise her son without his recognising her (I.i.182–94), and Dido, who, having chosen to dress as a hunting Diana, will, Venus-like, nonetheless seduce, and yield to, Aeneas in the cave. Whereas in *Aeneid*, I, Dido is still Elissa, faithful to Sychaeus, Marlowe's Dido follows Ovid's advice in *Ars amatoria* and uses Diana's costume to seduce Aeneas. In drawing attention to her outfit, she echoes the self-conscious comment of the boy actor playing Venus: 'Now is the time for me to play my part' (I.i.182). Impersonating Diana all the better to seduce Aeneas, she is as devious as Venus, who wears a similar costume in Act I to approach her son. Hence the locating of both scenes in the same place, as Achates notes:

> As I remember, here you shot the deer
> ... and here we met fair Venus, virgin-like,
> Bearing her bow and quiver at her back.
>
> (III.iii.51, 54–5)

Marlowe creates this original topography – which also had practical implications, with one set serving for two scenes.[47] The hunting ground becomes a *locus amoenus* for a love hunt, a topos inherited from the medieval tradition that attenuates the Virgilian thunderstorm visited by Juno on the lovers.[48] Marlowe does not translate the famous simile that compares Dido to a wounded doe (*Aeneid*, IV, 68–72) but he transposes it metaphorically and theatrically through the fusion of the two hunts, *amor* and *venatio* – which reaches back to Ovid's *Ars amatoria*. Where Virgil specified that Aeneas killed seven deer in that spot, Marlowe regenders the kill – Dido becomes a doe stricken by the hunter – while keeping the term 'deer', which typically puns with 'dear'. Thus this Virgilian scene is staged as an Ovidian recreation of the love hunt in a dramatic context, combining all the Renaissance connotations of an amorous Diana. The translation of Virgil's storyline of Dido's plight and the Petrarchan topos of the love *venatio* intersect with the defence of a faithful Dido. These commenting and dissenting voices, according to the principle of *in utramquem partem*, dramatise the tensions between emblematic exemplarity and rhetorical flexibility. Moving well beyond a binary vision, Marlowe creates a polyphonic portrait on the Elizabethan stage.

Just as Ovid rewrote and reimagined Virgil in his *Heroides*, VII; *Amores*; *Ars amatoria*; and *Metamorphoses*, Marlowe draws on material from medieval and early modern sources to reimagine and dramatise the Virgilian epic. The inherited Ovidian mythological material (with its numerous related images, its expanded glosses and even its alternative retellings) shows how borrowings from several sources animate the Virgilian rewriting of Dido on the Marlovian stage. Mythological allusions, or creations, taken from a corpus of sources derived from Ovid, undermine the main epic model, traditionally centred on *pius* Aeneas, resulting in the polyphonic portrait of an inconsistent, playful, erotic Dido, whose case invites glossing and contributes more widely to the play's comedic internal tensions. The use of diverging voices, while highlighting the role of a dialogic transmission in the sixteenth century, also adds complexity. Neither a defence, nor a defamation, the play seems to engage voluptuously and humorously with the two sides of Dido's literary fame. This taste for variety is at the heart of Marlowe's literary creation, as reader, translator and dramatist. The early modern play shows through and animates superimposed and contradictory versions of the *fabula* of Dido without erasing any of them. When Marlowe engages with and revises his primary source, he calls attention to the mechanics of (re)writing, and his *Dido*, made up of compounded, multi-layered textual and visual sources, suggests an intriguing and fecund *feuilletage* and a conversational perception of antiquity.

Notes

This chapter expands work presented in seminars at Montpellier and Stratford-upon-Avon, part of which appeared in French as 'Virgile au prisme d'Ovide: la *Didon* (entre 1585–1588) de Christopher Marlowe', in Evelyne Berriot-Salvadore (ed.), *Les figures de Didon: de l'épopée antique au théâtre de la Renaissance* (2014), www.ircl.cnrs.fr (accessed 30 June 2016).

1. See Timaeus's text (356?–260? BCE), in Deborah L. Gera, *Warrior Women: The Anonymous 'Tractatus de mulieribus'* (Leiden: Brill, 1997), pp. 7–8; Karen Haegemans, 'Elissa, the first queen of Carthage, through Timaeus' eyes', *Ancient Society*, 30 (2000), 277–91; and Marcus Junianus Justinus, *Epitoma historiarum Philippicarum Pompei Trogi (Abrégé des Histoires Philippiques de Trogue-Pompée)*, ed. and trans. Marie-Pierre Arnaud-Lindet (Forum Romanum Online, 2003), XVIII, 4, 3–6, 12.
2. Armel Dubois-Nayt, Nicole Dufournaud and Anne Paupert (eds), *Revisiter la querelle des femmes: discours sur l'égalité/inégalité des femmes et des hommes, de 1400 à 1600* (Saint Etienne: Publications de l'Université de Saint-Etienne, 2013).
3. All references to *Dido* are from Christopher Marlowe, *Dido Queen of Carthage and The Massacre at Paris*, ed. H. J. Oliver (London: Methuen, 1968). At least three other *Dido* tragedies were staged between the 1520s and 1598, all in Latin (by John Rightwise or, perhaps, his wife Dionysia, in 1522–32; by Edward Halliwell in 1564; by William Gager in 1583). See Alfred Harbage, *Annals of English Drama 975–1700*, 3rd edn, rev. S. Schoenbaum and Sylvia Stoler Wagonheim (London: Routledge, 1989 [1964]); Richard Beadle, 'Rightwise, John (c. 1490–1533)', in *Oxford Dictionary of National Biography* (Oxford University Press, 2004) online edn (2008), www.oxforddnb.com/view/article/23649 (accessed 9 July 2016).
4. On the date of the play, see Roma Gill, *The Complete Plays of Christopher Marlowe, Vol. I: Translations* (Oxford: Clarendon Press, 1987), pp. 115–23. The 1594 title page indicates that it was performed by 'the Children of her Majesties chappell'. The play has enjoyed a revival of interest in the UK since the 2000s.
5. On English translations and commentaries, see David Scott Wilson-Okamura, *Virgil in the Renaissance* (Cambridge: Cambridge University Press, 2010), pp. 27–30.
6. On parallels with Ovid's *Amores* in the added prologue, see Fred B. Tromly, *Playing with Desire: Christopher Marlowe and the Art of Tantalization* (Toronto: University Press of Toronto, 1998), pp. 46–65.
7. Aeneas calls himself 'pius Aeneas' twice (*Aeneid*, I, 378 and X, 836); 'pius' is associated fifteen times with his name in the narrative and eight times by other characters: Nicholas Moseley, 'Pius Aeneas', *The Classical Journal*, 20:7 (1925), 387–400 (p. 387).
8. See Patrick Cheney, *Marlowe's Counterfeit Profession: Ovid, Spenser, Counter-Nationhood* (Toronto: University of Toronto Press, 1997), pp. 99–114; Sara Munson Deats, 'Marlowe's interrogative drama: *Dido, Tamburlaine, Faustus,*

and *Edward II*', in Sara Munson Deats and Robert A. Logan (eds), *Marlowe's Empery: Expanding His Cultural Contexts* (Newark: University of Delaware Press, 2002), pp. 107–30 (pp. 110–13); Michael L. Stapleton, *Marlowe's Ovid: The Elegies in the Marlowe Canon* (Farnham: Ashgate, 2014).

9   R. O. A. M. Lyne, *Further Voices in Vergil's 'Aeneid'* (Oxford: Oxford University Press, 2001 [1987]), pp. 1–3.

10 On Troy as a myth of origins, see Chapter 3 (Dominique Goy-Blanquet). Critics have read *Dido* as a play about Queen Elizabeth's chastity and her ageing environment: see Deanne Williams, 'Dido Queen of England', *English Literary History*, 73:1 (2006), 31–59 (p. 43). Conversely, Timothy D. Crowley, in 'Arms and the boy: Marlowe's Aeneas and the parody of imitation in *Dido, Queen of Carthage*', *English Literary Renaissance*, 38:3 (2008), 408–38, discusses Ovid's poetic strategies, along with Lucan's *Pharsalia*, to assess the polarisation between Eros and militarism in the play's compound *imitatio*, which he reads as 'fuel[ling] a critique of contemporary investment in the *Aeneid*'s imperial theme' (p. 438).

11 Emma Buckley, '"Live false Aeneas!" Marlowe's *Dido, Queen of Carthage* and the limits of translation', *Classical Receptions Journal*, 3:2 (2011), 129–47 (p. 144). She shows how Lydgate's *Troy Book* provides 'another layer of duplicity to Marlowe's Aeneas' (p. 138), as Marlowe undercuts 'the authority of his own ostensibly orthodox translation by slyly embedding this medieval traitor into his text' (p. 138). I am grateful to Margaret Tudeau-Clayton for bringing this article to my attention. See also Lucy Potter, 'Marlowe's Dido: Virgilian or Ovidian?', *Notes and Queries*, 56:4 (2009), 540–4, who contends that *Dido, Queen of Carthage* is less an Ovidian rewriting and more a reappraisal of how Virgil was read in the Renaissance through a dramatic capital essentially borrowed from the medieval reading of the *Aeneid*.

12 See Deats, 'Marlowe's interrogative drama', p. 110: 'the play does not offer an ethical synthesis as the drama argues *in utramque partem questionis*'.

13 Elizabeth D. Harvey, *Ventriloquized Voices: Feminist Theory and English Renaissance Texts* (London: Routledge, 1992), p. 10: '[a]n intertextual allusion opens a text to other voices and echoes of other texts, just as ventriloquism multiplies authorial voices, interrogating the idea that a single authorial presence speaks or controls an utterance'.

14 See Chapter 1 (Yves Peyré).

15 Anon., *Roman d'Eneas*, ed. Aimé Petit (Paris: Livre de Poche, 1997).

16 Anon., *Ovide moralisé*, ed. Cornelis de Boer (Amsterdam: Verhandelingen der Koninklijke Akademie van Wetenschappen, 1938), XIV, 527–30; Kathryn L. McKinley, *Reading the Ovidian Heroine: 'Metamorphoses' Commentaries 1100–1618* (Leiden: Brill, 2001), pp. xx–xxii.

17 See Helen Osborne's review, '*Dido Queene of Carthage*, Edward's Boys', *Marlowe Society of America Newsletter*, 33:2 (2014), 7, http://users.ipfw.edu/stapletm/msa/docs/332Sp14.pdf (accessed 9 July 2016).

18 Henry Parker, *Forty-Six Lives Translated from Boccaccio's 'De claris mulieribus'* by *Henry Parker, Lord Morley*, ed. Herbert G. Wright, Early English Text Society, OS 214 (Oxford: Oxford University Press, 1970 [1943]). This is the second English translation, after one in Middle English (c. 1440–60). See Guyda Armstrong, *The English Boccaccio: A History in Books* (Toronto: University of Toronto Press, 2013), pp. 139–54.

19 Christine de Pizan, *Livre de la Cité des dames* (1404/05), trans. Brian Anslay: *The Boke of the Cyte of Ladyes* (London: Pepwell, 1521), Chapter 45: 'this Dydo was fyrst named Elyxa the connynge of her prudence shewed well' (sig. O3r).

20 'But who wol al this letter have in mynde, / Rede Ovyde, and in hym he shal it fynde' (*The Legend of Good Women*, 1366–67). On Chaucer's unmediated familiarity with Ovid, see Kathryn L. McKinley, 'Gower and Chaucer: Readings of Ovid in late medieval England', in James G. Clark, Franck T. Coulson, Kathryn L. McKinley (eds), *Ovid in the Middle Ages* (Cambridge: Cambridge University Press, 2011), pp. 197–230. On Chaucer's 'subversion' of Virgil's literary authority, see Helen Cooper, 'Chaucer and Ovid: A question of authority', in Charles Martindale (ed.), *Ovid Renewed: Ovidian Influences on Literature and Art from the Middle Ages to the Twentieth Century* (Cambridge: Cambridge University Press, 1988), pp. 71–82, esp. p. 80.

21 See Lindsay Ann Reid, *Ovidian Bibliofictions and the Tudor Book: Metamorphosing Classical Heroines in Late Medieval and Renaissance England* (Burlington: Ashgate, 2014), pp. 65–6.

22 William Caxton, *Eneydos, compyled by Vyrgyle, which Hathe be Translated Oute of Latyne in to Frenshe, and Oute of Frenshe Reduced in to Englysshe by me Wyll[ia]m Caxton* (London: William Caxton, 1490); William Caxton, *Caxton's 'Eneydos' (1490): Englished from the French 'Livre des Eneydes' (1483)*, ed. W. T. Culley and F. J. Furnivall (London: Oxford University Press, 1962 [1890]).

23 Anon., *Le livre des Eneydes compilé par Virgille, lequel a esté translaté de latin en françois* (Paris: Guillaume Le Roy, 1483). On the material from Virgil and Boccaccio, see Culley and Furnivall in Caxton, *Caxton's 'Eneydos'*, pp. vi–xi.

24 Thomas Feylde, *Contraversye bytwene a Lover and a Jaye* (London: Wynkyn de Worde, 1527).

25 William Walter, *The Spectacle of Lovers* (London: Wynkyn de Worde, 1533?).

26 Alexandra Gillespie analyses this *Sammelband* in 'Poets, printers, and early English *Sammelbände*', *Huntington Library Quarterly*, 67:2 (2004), 189–214, esp. pp. 211–13. Also Julia Boffey, 'Wynkyn de Worde or misogyny in print', in Geoffrey Lester (ed.), *Chaucer in Perspective: Middle English Essays in Honour of Norman Blake* (Sheffield: Sheffield Academic Press, 1999), pp. 236–51.

27 Edward More, *A Lytle and Bryefe Treatyse, Called the Defence of Women ... Made agaynst the Schole Howse of Women* (London: John Kynge, 1560).

28 In his treatise, sig. A2r, More states that he is responding to Edward Gosynhyll's *Lytle Boke Named the Schole House of Women ...* (London: Thomas Petyt, 1541).

29 Ovid and Virgil, *Le quatriesme livre de l'Eneide de vergile, traduict en vers Francoys: la complaincte de Didon à Enée, prinse d'Ovide*, trans. Joachim Du Bellay (Paris: Vincent Certenas, 1552).

30 This is signalled by Paule Demats in *Fabula: trois études de mythographie antique et médiévale* (Geneva: Droz, 1973), pp. 103–4; and further studied in Marilynn Desmond, 'French translations of Ovid's amatory works', in Clark, Coulson and McKinley, *Ovid in the Middle Ages*, pp. 108–22 (p. 111).

31 See Julia Boffey, 'Richard Pynson's *Boke of Fame* and *the Letter of Dido*', *Viator*, 19 (1988), 339–54; and Reid, *Ovidian Bibliofictions*, pp. 125–8.

32 William Shakespeare, *The Merchant of Venice*, ed. John Russell Brown, The Arden Shakespeare (London: Routledge, 1991 [1955]). See Chapter 5 (Hirota Atsuhiko) for a discussion of this passage from a different perspective.

33 Colin Burrow, *Shakespeare and Classical Antiquity* (Oxford: Oxford University Press, 2013), p. 98. In *A Midsummer Night's Dream* (I.i.173–6), Shakespeare invites empathy with Dido as a paragon of the woebegone deserted woman.

34 Burrow, *Shakespeare and Classical Antiquity*, p. 98. Yves Peyré explores this in detail in the current volume (Chapter 1).

35 Jonathan Bate, *Shakespeare and Ovid* (Oxford: Clarendon Press, 1993), pp. 155–7 (p. 155).

36 See Charles Martindale's perspective, which differs from Bate's, in 'Shakespeare's Ovid, Ovid's Shakespeare: A methodological postscript', in A. B. Taylor (ed.), *Shakespeare's Ovid: The 'Metamorphoses' in the Plays and the Poems* (Cambridge: Cambridge University Press, 2000), pp. 198–215, esp. pp. 203, 207–8.

37 On the burlesque, travesty and humour in Marlowe, see Tromly, *Playing with Desire*, pp. 54–6.

38 There are two allusions to this episode in *Aeneid*. See also *Aeneid*, V, 253–6.

39 See James Saslow, *Ganymede in the Renaissance: Homosexuality in Art and Society* (New Haven: Yale University Press, 1986), pp. 125–37.

40 Osborne, '*Dido Queene of Carthage*, Edward's Boys'.

41 See Yves Peyré, *La voix des mythes dans la tragédie élisabéthaine* (Paris: CNRS Editions, 1996), pp. 53–70, and more particularly pp. 60–1. In his review of the 2015 performance by The Globe's Young Players, '*Dido Queen of Carthage* feels as youthful as ever', *Londonist* (12 April 2015), Sam Smith notes the antithetic shifts in tone: 'Jasmine Jones as Dido … captures the humorous moments, such as when she keeps changing her position after being pierced by Cupid's arrow, with great discretion'; http://londonist.com/2015/04/dido-queen-of-carthage-feels-as-youthful-as-ever (accessed 9 July 2016).

42 See Lois Potter, 'Marlowe in theatre and film', in Patrick Cheney (ed.), *The Cambridge Companion to Christopher Marlowe* (Cambridge: Cambridge University Press, 2004), pp. 262–81 (p. 279).

43 On intimations of incest in *Dido*, see Jane Kingsley-Smith, *Cupid in Early Modern Literature and Culture* (Cambridge: Cambridge University Press, 2010), p. 143.
44 Crowley, 'Arms and the boy', pp. 415–16.
45 Christine de Pizan, *The Boke of the Cyte of Ladyes*, Chapter 54, sig. N3r.
46 Stapleton suggests that Marlowe may be 'infusing Dido with Ovid's erotic mentality' when she is disingenuous in her relationship to Iarbas (*Marlowe's Ovid*, p. 93).
47 Oliver, in Marlowe, *Dido*, ed. Oliver, note to III.iii.50–3 (p. 53).
48 See Marcelle Thiébaux, *The Stag of Love: The Chase in Medieval Literature* (Ithaca, NY: Cornell University Press, 1974).

10

Burlesque or neoplatonic? Popular or elite? The shifting value of classical mythology in *Love's Mistress*

Charlotte Coffin

THOMAS HEYWOOD's *Love's Mistress* tells the story of Cupid and Psyche, adapted from Apuleius's *The Golden Ass* (second century CE). In 1634, Heywood was reaching the end of a long career as a playwright, during which he had experimented with many genres and trends[1] – including mythological drama, with the *Ages* cycle in the early 1610s.[2] *Love's Mistress* has a remarkable staging history. While we associate Heywood with the Red Bull Theatre and its (supposedly) low-brow audience,[3] he wrote this play for Queen Henrietta's Men, who performed it both at the Cockpit/Phoenix Theatre – a venue then 'almost equal in social standing' to the Blackfriars[4] – and at court, at the queen's request, in Denmark House for Charles I's birthday on 19 November 1634. It gave such satisfaction that a second performance took place within a few days.[5] For some, this was 'the apex of Heywood's career'.[6] *Love's Mistress* is also the only Heywood play repeatedly staged during and after the Restoration.[7] Samuel Pepys saw it no fewer than five times in the 1660s.[8] Therefore, this chapter will be concerned not with mythological metaphors or allusions, but with the representation of classical characters and episodes on stage. Through an analysis of *Love's Mistress*, I shall seek to address how cultural tastes and approaches to classical learning evolved in the first half of the seventeenth century, and to highlight the influence of French fashions.

The play's three-tier structure complicates its significance for anyone interested in the circulation of classical mythology in early modern England. The main plot closely follows Apuleius as it unfolds the story of Psyche, from Apollo's oracle and Cupid's amorous abduction, through the betrayal of her lover (on her treacherous sisters' advice) and her persecution by Venus, to final redemption. Heywood adds a subplot based on a Clown character, which includes Cupid's comic revenge on the Clown's provocations and a singing contest between Pan and Apollo (borrowed from Ovid's *Metamorphoses*, XI) which the Clown wins on behalf of Pan. Both plot and subplot are framed by the regular interventions of a two-character chorus: Apuleius, the initial presenter, is led by Midas's criticisms to alter the performance by inserting extra shows and to explain the plot's allegorical meaning. Thus the play involves three specific mythological subtexts (Cupid and Psyche from Apuleius; Pan and Apollo plus Midas from Ovid) as well as the representation of Olympians at their usual tasks (Apollo's oracle, Venus's emotions, Mercury's messages, Vulcan's forge).[9] The three structural levels exemplify different approaches: mythological story, low comedy, interpretative debate. However, the points of interaction among plot, subplot and chorus suggest that things are not separate but interwoven. Midas is a member of the chorus and a character in the subplot, where he arbitrates the competition between Pan and Apollo; Cupid is a protagonist in the main plot, and also a liminal figure who delivers the prologue and epilogue and settles the controversy between Apuleius and Midas; the Clown comes into contact with Psyche when he steals Proserpina's box of beauty.

With its complex structure, *Love's Mistress* has given rise to contradictory readings. Most critics take the Apuleius character seriously: Jackson Cope offers an allegorical interpretation of the play;[10] Jane Kingsley-Smith elaborates on its neoplatonic dimension – though she recognises the ambiguities affecting Cupid;[11] Arthur Clark believes Apuleius is Heywood's spokesman and wonders whom Midas might represent in this 'topical allegory'.[12] By contrast, Richard Rowland demonstrates how unreliable Apuleius is, and argues, through detailed analysis of historical context and topical allusions, that Heywood stands with Midas and Pan on the side of popular culture. He sees the play as Heywood's 'most incisive critique of Caroline court culture' – specifically, of Charles I's Apollonian politics and Henrietta Maria's neoplatonism.[13]

Rowland's brilliant study, however, raises new questions. His analysis counters previous supporters of the Apuleius character – but it perpetuates the critical polarisation induced by the double chorus, as if one ought to choose one's camp.[14] By seeing the characters as representatives of court culture or popular culture, he, like the others, emulates Apuleius's allegorical method, reading mythology *as* something else. More importantly: if the play is deeply subversive, why did it please the royal couple and their courtiers so much? The play's success becomes puzzling and paradoxical, and could not have happened 'unless they closed their eyes and their ears'.[15]

In the pages that follow, I shall consider why *Love's Mistress* was so successful with its elite public, despite or perhaps because of its sturdy, potentially subversive comedy. My analysis is based on poetics rather than politics, and it seeks to move beyond the polarities embedded in previous discussions of the play. I shall first question the elite/popular divide through a comparison with the vogue for burlesque in seventeenth-century France — the native country of Queen Henrietta Maria. Second, I shall argue that taking sides in the play's several controversies matters less than appreciating the situations of arbitration that Heywood consistently emphasises, making this a play not just about mythology, but about the critical apprehension of mythology and drama. Finally I shall address the generic complexity of *Love's Mistress*, including its relationship to Heywood's earlier *Ages*, contemporary pageants, and masques. Comparison with James Shirley's *Triumph of Peace*, which was performed in February 1634, suggests that Heywood may have drawn inspiration from his rival's innovations. Through these arguments, my purpose is to displace the problem of courtly versus popular culture — or art versus ignorance as Apuleius sees it[16] — and look at the complex ways in which classical mythology could be received *within* a cultured audience in the 1630s. This in turn reflects back on Heywood, who right up to the end of his dramatic career proves quite up to date on poetical and theatrical trends.[17]

Love's Mistress and French burlesque

The Cupid-and-Psyche plot was well suited to the queen's tastes. Her iconographic representations and her commissions reveal a personal interest in the myth.[18] Coming from an author well versed in Platonism, the story could be allegorised as the marriage between Love and the Soul, emphasising the correspondence between Beauty and Virtue, and reflecting the neoplatonic fashion Henrietta Maria encouraged at court. Together with her taste for pastoral literature, this neoplatonic culture has been associated with the queen's French origins, and in particular with seventeenth-century *salons* where women moved to the foreground of literary debates and developed a new culture of *préciosité*.[19] No-one, to my knowledge, has contemplated an equivalent possibility for the parodic parts of the play: I would like to explore the potential association with another French trend — burlesque.[20]

In *L'Antiquité travestie et la vogue du burlesque en France* (2014 [2007]), Jean Leclerc redefines burlesque poetics and qualifies Gérard Genette's famous definition based on the contrast between high subject and low style.[21] Moving away from strict binarism, Leclerc's analysis rests on the notions of *discordance* (discrepancy) and *bigarrure* (motley), and investigates the stylistic features of mythological *travestissements*.[22] While *Love's Mistress* is not burlesque throughout, many passages qualify for that particular style or mode, and they are not limited to the comic subplot.

The clearest example is the Clown's retelling of the Trojan War as a quarrel in 'a village of some twenty houses' between the 'bousing lads' of Priam and 'Menelaus, a farmer, who had a light wench to his wife called Helen'. In this version Agamemnon is 'high Constable of the Hundred', Ulysses a 'town clerk' and Ajax 'a butcher',

> who upon a holiday brings a pair of cudgels, and lays them down in the midst, where the two Hundreds were then met, which Hector, a baker, another bold lad of the other side, seeing, steps forth, and takes them up; these two had a bout or two for a broken pate, and here was all the circumstance of the Trojan wars.
>
> (II.iii.50–5)[23]

This parodic purple patch pleased Samuel Pepys, who records it as a 'good jeere' in 1661 – indicating that educated spectators enjoyed such 'low' transpositions.[24] In the play it illustrates what the Clown thinks of this 'company of pitiful fellows called Poets' and prolongs another virtuoso piece, which uses accumulation and alliteration to deride Cupid:

> Then hearken, oh you hoydes, and listen, oh you illiterates, whilst I give you his style in folio: he is King of cares, cogitations and coxcombs; Viceroy of vows and vanities; Prince of passions, prate-apaces, and pickled lovers; Duke of disasters, dissemblers, and drowned eyes; Marquis of melancholy and mad folks; Grand Signor of griefs and groans; Lord of lamentations; Hero of heigh-hos; Admiral of ay-mes and Monsieur of mutton-laced.
>
> (II.iii.20–7)

The competition between Pan and Apollo is also a case in point, with the Clown having to sub for a hoarse Pan. His song rests on a culinary pun: Apollo's sunbeams cannot compare to the powers of Dripping/Frying/Pudding Pan. As the second stanza puts it,

> They call thee son of bright Latona,
> But girt thee in thy torrid zona,
> Sweat, baste and broil, as best thou can,
> Thou art not like our Dripping Pan.
>
> (III.ii.72–5)[25]

The jarring rhyme of 'Latona' and 'zona', the obscene pun on 'zona',[26] the accumulation of trivial verbs all contribute to the comic subversion.

In the main plot, an overworked Vulcan in his forge complains about his fellow gods' unreasonable demands:

> Here's the devil and all!
> What would they have me do? I toil and moil
> Worse than a mill-horse, scarce have slept a minute
> This fortnight and odd days. I have not time
> To sit and eat.
>
> (IV.i.27–31)

As Cupid comes to beg for help, they address each other as 'young whoremaster' and 'sweet honey sugar-candy dad' (IV.i.54, 72). References to 'horns' in Vulcan's presence participate in the parodic depiction of Venus's cuckold husband.[27] Venus appears as a shrew, exasperated at first when her son and fellow goddesses make her wait ('Anon, forsooth' is a comic leitmotiv in I.ii), then raving when she mistreats Psyche (e.g. III.ii.236–84). Mercury's solemn message reaches an abrupt conclusion when hearers point to Psyche: 'If any can bring Psyche unto Venus – ... Then here ends Mercury's commission. / Psyche, in Venus' name, I do arrest thee' (III.ii.227–30).

These quotations illustrate such characteristics of burlesque as modern-day transposition, trivialisation, double entendre, the use of low vocabulary and comically accumulative language, and the constant play on discrepancies in both tone and situation. It is in keeping with this aesthetic that gods should be portrayed in various modes: sometimes full of authority, as when Apollo delivers his oracle (I.ii.10–48) or Cupid descends to reprimand Psyche's father (III.ii.188–210), and sometimes comically childish, as when Apollo is disgruntled at Pan's victory (III.ii.116–32) or Cupid asks his father for help (IV.i). Finally, the chorus scenes emblematise the dynamics of burlesque writing in so far as they rely on the recurrent deflation of Apuleius's ambitions through Midas's blunt remarks: when Apuleius asks him the way to 'the Muses' hill', Midas answers 'Follow thy nose ... The Muses? Hang the Muses ... I care for no such toys' (I.i.22–3, 26, 38).

Taken together, these passages reveal not just a recurrent use of comedy, but the more specific choice of burlesque as a poetic mode applied to mythology – at every level of the plot, subplot and chorus. However, burlesque does not exist ahistorically, and the point I wish to make concerns the conditions of its development in seventeenth-century France.

While it is tempting to distinguish serious and burlesque rewritings of myths along the lines of high and low culture, Leclerc's investigation into the history of the burlesque craze reveals that the genre was actually born in aristocratic circles. Like *préciosité*, it is associated with the *mondanisation* of poets and literature. As they sought to make their way into fashionable, elite circles, seventeenth-century French poets distanced themselves from academic pedants and looked for ways to entertain noble patrons with their learning without boring them. The witty elegance of *préciosité* is one way; the *enjoué* (playful) parody of burlesque is another. Thus Leclerc places the origins of burlesque in *salon* culture, and he especially links it to a feminine cultured public.[28] His findings corroborate Claudine Nédélec's in *Les États et empires du burlesque* (2004).[29] They confirm and expand Dominique Bertrand's statement that 'Les parodies de l'épopée, qui en appelaient à un plaisir éminemment savant et littéraire de connivence et de reconnaissance culturelle, ne pouvaient que séduire l'élite cultivée'[30] (parodies of epic texts, which brought about an eminently learned and literary form of pleasure based on complicity and cultural recognition, could not but seduce the cultivated elite), as well as Bernard Beugnot's caveat that 'la parodie burlesque n'est pas un genre populaire, mais le divertissement d'une élite qui joue sur la connivence d'une culture partagée'[31] (burlesque parody is not a lower-class genre, but an elite form of entertainment relying on complicity around a shared culture).

Admittedly, 1634 may seem an early date to speak of burlesque both in France and England. Leclerc situates the genesis of mythological burlesque between 1643 and 1648 – that is, between Scarron's *Recueil de quelques vers burlesques* and the first volume of his *Virgile travesty*, which triggered the burlesque craze and a race for publication.[32] Nédélec traces the first use of the word in French to the printer's preface in *Satyre Ménippée de la vertu du Catholicon d'Espagne et de la tenue des Estats de Paris* (1594), but deems it a hapax: the word reappears in 1638 and is considered new in the early 1640s.[33] My own lexicographic analysis, using the *Lexicons of Early Modern English* (*LEME*) database, shows that 'burlesque' appears as early as 1611 in England, in Randle Cotgrave's *A Dictionary of the French and English Tongues* (which defines it as 'Jeasting, or in jeast, not serious; also, mocking, flouting')[34] – but then disappears to resurface in Thomas Blount's *Glossographia or a Dictionary* (1656). Entries in dictionaries from 1668 to 1702 progressively emphasise the literary quality of burlesque, mentioning the 'Mocking imitation of Poem'[35] or referring to verse,[36] and finally stating: 'Travested or disguised; as the Poems of Virgil, or Ovid travested, i.e. turn'd into burlesque verse'.[37]

Lexical currency, however, does not cover the origins of burlesque, the period when the mode was inchoate, unnamed yet progressively emerging. Leclerc mentions Italian influences such as Bracciolini's *Scherno degli Dei* (1618), Tassoni's *Secchia rapita* (1614), and Lalli's *Eneide travestita* (1633). He also quotes French harbingers such as Charles Sorel's *Berger extravagant* (1627) and Saint-Amant's 1631 volume.[38] Interestingly, *préciosité* raises a similar problem: though Erica Veevers uses the term in association with Queen Henrietta Maria, Karen Britland deems it anachronistic.[39] Myriam Dufour-Maître considers that *préciosité* developed in the 1650s, not around Honoré d'Urfé's *L'Astrée* (1607–27) but around Madeleine de Scudéry's *La Clélie* (1654–60); other critics favour a wider periodisation.[40] Again, it depends on whether one is looking for word occurrence, or a more general cultural atmosphere.

My main point lies in the fact that French *salons* accommodated the two fashions (*préciosité* and burlesque), both of which developed in cultivated circles, and were particularly directed at a female audience. In the French elite circles that Henrietta Maria came from, the contrasting tones of *Love's Mistress* were equally acceptable, and equally pleasing. They were sometimes practised by the same persons, such as the poet Vincent Voiture (1597–1648), who produced elegant amatory verse and burlesque poems. He was one of the early representatives of the genre, and the posthumous publication of his works (with a section entitled 'Vers burlesques') contributes to the chronological difficulties faced by critics. Voiture was part of the entourage of Henrietta Maria's brother, Gaston d'Orléans, and he was sent on an embassy to England's queen in the autumn of 1633, one year before *Love's Mistress*. While Britland underlines the political negotiations Voiture probably carried out in aristocratic circles, I am curious about the literary discussions he may have had.[41]

As sociological enquiries invite us to consider burlesque an elite genre, broader cultural implications emerge.[42] Burlesque is not just about 'low' presentation: it requires familiarity with the source text that is being degraded. It is the awareness of the discrepancy that produces pleasure. The retelling of the Trojan War in *Love's Mistress*, for instance, is more entertaining for whoever knows Homer's *Iliad* (made more widely available by the publication of Chapman's translation between 1598 and 1611). Subtle pleasure comes from recognising that burlesque poems often picked up on incongruities in the source texts – Rowland underlines Apuleius's original playfulness.[43] Sensitivity to intertextual games also increases the appreciation of burlesque: the Clown's caricature of Trojan and Greek heroes resonates with

Ovid's less dignified version and Shakespeare's *Troilus and Cressida*; repeated mentions of Venus's grief over Adonis's death both reinforce the contrast with her shrewish character and echo Shakespeare's *Venus and Adonis*, which combines tragic and comic elements, including a goddess prone to uncontrollable gestures.

Beyond a knowledge of sources, the burlesque rewriting of myths raises the broader issue of the authors and their public's relationship with humanist culture – which becomes both the condition and the target of the rewriting. To some extent, burlesque suggests adults seeking revenge on the texts they were subjected to as children. The Clown's parodic Latin lesson is a case in point:

> I'll show thee the contrary by her own name: *Amor* is love, *illis* is ill – is ill, cannot be good; *ergo*, 'Amorillis' is stark naught. Let one or two examples serve for more: there's one of our fairest nymphs called Susanna – what is Susanna but *Sus* and *anna*, which is in plain Arcadian, 'Nan is a sow'.
> …
> What's *titule tu patule* but 'titles and pages'; what's *propria que maribus*, but 'a proper man loves marrow-bones'; or *feminno generi tribiuntur*, but 'the feminine gender is troublesome'; what's Ovid, but quasi a 'void'.
>
> (II.iii.66–79)

The virtuoso demonstration moves from playful pseudo-etymology to deconstruction of textbook phrases to iconoclastic anagram,[44] as the Clown engages with Latin and pedagogy, posing as a teacher to the 'swains'. From another angle, burlesque transposition is also a way of asserting one's mastery of and playful distance from the humanist legacy – in a period when classical culture is still very much present in elite education, but people increasingly feel a need to move on to other things. As Leclerc underlines, the triangular relationship between modern author, classical author and audience is key in establishing both a system of exchanges and a protected space where laughter is acceptable, however harsh the attacks. He stresses the importance of narrator interventions and prefatory texts, which set up a crucial 'frame' for the parodic revision. The same is true of the chorus scenes in *Love's Mistress*, where the debates between Apuleius and the ever-blunt Midas frame authorise, and to some extent neutralise, the subversive passages. Like the narrators in French texts, Apuleius repeatedly addresses or gestures to the audience, drawing them in as they watch the play.[45] Similarly, the layout of the printed text emphasises protective paratext: the 1636 and 1640 quartos print a dedication, a letter to the reader, three different prologues and the epilogue before the main text. The dedication is to the earl of Dorset – the queen's Lord Chamberlain in other words – the official whose responsibility it was to determine the acceptability of a play. Those accumulated texts flaunt the courtly reception of *Love's Mistress* as a form of advertisement, but they also legitimise the play, making whatever disruptive allusions it may contain acceptable.

Considering burlesque in its various dimensions – historical, sociological, cultural, structural – helps us understand why *Love's Mistress*, with all its subversive potential, pleased its elite audience in 1634. As I continue to challenge polarised interpretations of the play (Midas/Apuleius, popular/elite, parodic/serious), I shall now turn to the representation of judgement in *Love's Mistress*.

Judges, arbiters, critics

Heywood's additions to the myth repeatedly introduce situations of arbitration. The opening chorus frames the entire play as an object for trial, asking the audience to arbitrate between Apuleius and Midas:

> We two contend – Art here, there Ignorance.
> Be you the judges; we invite you all
> Unto this banquet academicall.
>
> (I.i.82–4)

And while the spectators cannot deliver their verdict, Cupid acts as their delegate at the close of the play:

> I by the favour of these gentlemen
> Will arbitrate this strife. One seeks to advance
> His Art, the other stands for Ignorance.
> Both hope, and both shall have their merits full:
> Here's meed for either, both the apt and dull.
> Pleased or displeased, this censure I allow:
> Keep thou the ass's ears, the laurel thou.
> [*To the audience.*] If you, judicious, this my doom commend,
> Psyche by you shall doubly crowned ascend.
>
> (V.iii.135–43)

The terms of the debate are clearly recalled and the language of arbitration is insistent – and yet the printed text does not explicitly state who 'keep[s]' the ass's ears, who the laurel. As Rowland remarks, there is no indication that Apuleius has discarded the ass's ears he was carrying in the opening scene, having been recently restored to his human shape.[46] I would add that there is no clear mention either of Midas wearing ass's ears at any point.[47] While the ambiguity has to be resolved on stage, readers are left with a sense of indeterminacy: this resonates with the point I wish to make, namely, that the situation of arbitration and call for judgement matter more than the eventual verdict. (In the same vein, I would stress how the polarity between Apuleius and Midas is recurrently blurred. Though Midas finds the play tedious and requests dancing shows to keep him awake, the insertion of a pageant of asses fulfils Apuleius's initial plan 'To expose to them the shapes of all those asses / With whom my lost soul wandered in a mist' (I.i.70–1). Midas criticises the plot yet keeps asking Apuleius for allegorical explanations. Each declares himself satisfied with the other's endeavours, whether farcical or neoplatonic.)[48]

The play contains three similar situations, all Heywood's additions to Apuleius's tale. The first is the Apollo–Pan contest, with Midas playing the judge between the gods' substitutes. The second is the elaborate staging of 'Hell's court' (IV.iii.52), whereas in *The Golden Ass* (VI, 20) Psyche moves quickly in and out of the underworld. In Act V, Minos, Aeacus and Rhadamantus are solemnly waiting for Psyche. Together with Pluto and Proserpina, the three judges have to decide whether they will grant Venus's request to keep Psyche prisoner, or Psyche's own prayer for deliverance. The third instance is the trial of Psyche's sisters. In *The Golden Ass* (V, 26–7) Psyche takes her own bloody revenge. In the play, the sisters witness her rehabilitation and Mercury announces:

> Now, Psyche, you must see your sisters judged,
> Unstai[d] Petrea, and unkind Astioche.
> Admetus, you must be their sentencer.
>
> (V.iii.76–8)[49]

Psyche pleads their cause and they become her handmaids: Raymond Shady considers this display of clemency necessary to the play's final harmony[50] – but the scene also contributes to the insistence on judgement.

The emergence of arbitration as a recurrent pattern in *Love's Mistress* may be related to contemporary developments in the spheres of literature and theatre. Andrew Gurr argues that under the influence of Charles I the 1630s witnessed 'a rise in the status of plays to the level of "poetic" works'.[51] This circumstance fostered the development of a critical awareness among theatre audiences. Prologues from the 1630s, for instance, indicate that 'a new currency of judicious criticism was being minted'.[52] Commenting on 'the settled sense which audiences now had of themselves as judges', Gurr states that

> The self-conscious function of gentle audiences at the hall playhouses was to 'censure'. For the first time plays had become respectable matter for serious discussion. The king himself made critical notes in the margins of his playbooks and more than once interceded on a matter of critical judgement with the Master of the Revels. It became a mode of the town.[53]

As the quote suggests, this new sense of critical power emerged particularly in the 'hall playhouses', such as Blackfriars and the Cockpit/Phoenix.

Tiffany Stern makes a related point about first performances, especially in the 1630s. As she demonstrates, first performances were crucial for playwrights. Though '[e]ntrance charges were highly inflated for a play's opening', people struggled to get in and the public was different from later performances – that is, had more wealth and time on their hands.[54] As a consequence, the audience on the first day felt particularly entitled to pass judgement on the show:

> This was because, in a highly ritualised theatrical moment, the spectators' 'judgement', solicited at the end of the first performance, would shape what was to be altered or cut from the play – and, more than that, would determine whether or not the play would 'survive' to be performed again.[55]

Stern makes much of prologues, which were often written for such opening performances (the first prologue of *Love's Mistress* indicates the play 'is both fresh and new') (line 17) and articulated the writer's anxiety at the same time as they invited the audience's arbitration.[56] I suggest that Heywood integrated this rising phenomenon into *Love's Mistress*, especially as he endows Midas, the primary spectator of Apuleius's play, with the power to alter the performance. To please him, and to prevent him from either leaving or falling asleep,[57] Apuleius successively inserts a pageant of asses (I.vi.9–45), a dance of '*Pan, Clown, Swains, and Country wenches*' (II.v.9sd), another dance of 'Love's Contrarieties' (III.iii.19) and one of '*Vulcan and his Cyclops*' (IV.iii.10sd).

My proposition is therefore that *Love's Mistress* is not so much about art versus ignorance or popular culture versus court culture, as it is about judgement. The situation of arbitration matters more than the actual verdict. In this the play may tie in both with the growing critical awareness of theatrical audiences (especially elite ones at court and indoor playhouses), and with the equally growing detachment from classical models mentioned above. Heywood offers a full retelling of a widely known mythological tale, but he offers it in such a way as constantly to create critical distance. As we shift from serious to burlesque moments, and from mythological narration to debate in the chorus, we are repeatedly forced to adjust our focus, so to speak, and look at the story through different lenses. The play invites emotional participation in Psyche's ordeals, intellectual games of (pseudo-)neoplatonic interpretation and parodic deconstruction. It simultaneously sets up a mythological tale and a theatrical illusion, and deconstructs them – as when the first encounter between Cupid and Psyche gives way to Midas's comment:

> thou brings't here on the stage
> A young green-sickness baggage to run after
> A little ape-faced boy thou term'st a god!
> Is not this most absurd?
>
> (I.vi.52–5)

His indignation exposes both the constraints of early modern theatrical practice and the incongruity inherent in the mythological material.[58] The end result is neither neoplatonic celebration nor unequivocal subversion, but the pleasure that critical distance per se adds to the retelling of mythology. Unlike scholars who have favoured either the serious or the parodic side of the controversy, I believe the play is designed to emphasise the critical debate itself. In this respect it interweaves mythology together with the latest theatrical fashions – which contributes to explaining why it pleased its elite public.

Generic interweavings

The critical appreciation of myth depends largely on the insistent metatheatricality of *Love's Mistress*, with the two chorus characters not just introducing the various acts, but disparaging or praising the show, and discussing its interpretation. As I move on to a discussion of the play's generic complexity, metatheatricality will prove a key factor. My underlying question is whether Heywood was imitating well-established forms, or innovating for his select 1634 audience. A brief survey of Heywood's *Ages* (performed c. 1610–13), his pageants from the 1630s and contemporary masques will help contextualise *Love's Mistress* by focusing on two features: the alternation of 'low' and 'high' modes, and the role of the presenter.

Beyond the transposition of mythological material, Heywood's *Ages*, like *Love's Mistress*, rely on the juxtaposition of serious and comic moments, make use of a chorus at the beginning of every act, and give pride of place to spectacular displays such as gods' descents and ascents.[59] However, the contrasting modes are more compartmentalised in the *Ages*, as in *The Golden Age*, where the stories of Callisto (Act II) and Danae (Act IV) are inserted in between epic conflicts. Their comic treatment, based on Jupiter's undignified disguises and the Clown's sexual puns, anticipates the 1634 play without conveying the variety and complexity of burlesque, nor the impression of critical distance from mythology.[60] This is also due to the different use of the chorus. In three of the five *Ages*, Homer presents the plot: he fills in temporal gaps, accelerates the action through dumb shows, explains what has happened to other characters. Occasionally he offers allegorisations of mythological figures (especially in *The Brazen Age*) or general moral statements. But he does not provide a critical appreciation of the plays, nor is he challenged by anyone.[61] While Apuleius's entrance at the opening of *Love's Mistress* recalls this precedent – and Apuleius is much more the source of the play than Homer ever was – Midas's reluctance and dissatisfaction force him into a different role. Unlike Homer, Apuleius interprets and argues. In *Love's Mistress*, Heywood complicated the older model of the first three *Ages* by interlacing the comic and serious moments more intricately and making the chorus a site of dispute. The two parts of *The Iron Age*, however, are different: both are more critical of their mythological material, and devoid of the Homeric chorus (even though they actually draw from the *Iliad*). Thersites makes disparaging comments on the action, and develops his parodic counter-discourse in the second part through dialogue with another 'episceptic', Synon.[62] I have argued elsewhere that when *1 Iron Age* was performed in c. 1613, Heywood was responding to Chapman's translation of Homer as well as Shakespeare's *Troilus and Cressida*.[63] It is also possible that the plays were revised before their publication, which was not until 1632. Either way, Heywood devoted some attention to those texts and their critical characters (who do not, however, engage in interpretative conflict or stand as a proper chorus) not long before he wrote *Love's Mistress*. In this last mythological play, it is as if he mixed features from the *Ages* in a creative way, blending the traditional qualities of the Homer chorus of the first three plays with the provocative outlook of the sceptical characters of the last two, so as to transform the chorus into a locus of metatheatrical and mythological debate.

In the 1630s Heywood wrote several pageants for the annual Lord Mayor's Show. They recurrently feature mythological characters, who alternate with allegorical and Christian figures. Pageants use a variant of the theatrical chorus as they usually include one 'speaker' for each show – Heywood's pageants comprise five or six separate tableaux or 'shows' placed along the mayor's route, the first always 'upon the water' and the others 'by land'. The speaker delivers a speech, usually directed to the 'great Magistrate',[64] which both identifies the mute figures standing in complex arrangement and allegorises them in such a way as to flatter and advise the newly appointed official. The presenter's role is not completely univocal, in that there is room for political nuance, but the contrast is strong between the official presentation delivered by an authorised figure and the conflicting interaction of the liminal characters in *Love's Mistress*. Heywood's pageants involve no such metatheatrical debate, yet they resonate with Apuleius's efforts at allegory – including his most far-fetched flights of fancy.

In the printed texts of four of his pageants, Heywood mentions yet refuses to describe the third 'show by land', pointing out that 'This is more Mimicall then Materiall',[65] and that it 'meerly consisteth of Anticke gesticulations, dances, and other Mimicke postures, devised onely for the vulgar'.[66] He did not need to include a speaker, he writes, for this

> is a Modell devised for sport to humour the throng, who come rather to see then to heare: And without some such intruded Anti-maske, many who carry their eares in their eyes, will not sticke to say, I will not give a pinne for the Show.[67]

Heywood is concerned with the cultural status of his pageant texts, and constructs the printed accounts quite separately from the performances. While David M. Bergeron underlines Heywood's unique emphasis on such visual shows, I believe he marginalised them to promote his texts.[68] It seems Heywood invented pageant 'Anti-maske[s]'.[69] By calling them thus he gives them cultural prestige and contributes to what some critics see as the guilds' competing with court entertainments,[70] yet in the same paragraph he dismisses them as low-brow productions. Similar ambivalence is perceptible in *Love's Mistress*, which proudly subtitles itself *The Queen's Masque*, yet has Apuleius echo Heywood's disparagement of 'the Vulgar, who rather love to feast their eyes, then to banquet their eares':[71]

> Then by the leave of these spectators here,
> I'll suit me to thy low capacity.
> Of Vulcan's cyclops I'll so much entreat,
> That thou shalt see them on their anvil beat.
> 'Tis music fitting thee, for who but knows,
> *The vulgar are best pleased with noise and shows.*
>
> (IV.iii.5–10, my emphasis)

The dance that follows seems typical antimasque: that is, a form of entertainment that has been part of court shows for twenty-five years, and clearly does not delight the 'Vulgar' only.[72]

Love's Mistress thus uses mythological material and liminal presenters, which are conventional ingredients of Heywood's pageants, as are allegorical interpretations and alternating high and low shows. The play differs from civic ceremonies in terms of performance context and critical content. At a deeper level, however, one notices a similar ambivalence as to what type of show is elite or popular, with the same contradictions being played out in a court play and in the printed versions of mass entertainments.

Masque is the genre closest to *Love's Mistress*, and the one it claims contiguity with from the 19 November court performance onwards, 'bearing (from that time) the title of *The Queen's Masque*' as the second prologue indicates (p. 6), and flaunting it as a subtitle on the title pages of the 1636 and 1640 editions. Performed at Denmark House before the king and queen, *Love's Mistress* fits the label in several respects: the mythological figures and allegorical discourse, the comic dances (or antimasques) inserted at regular intervals, the importance given to music, and the changing sceneries designed by Inigo Jones. Rowland notes that it transgresses the structure of the masque, in that the antimasque characters are not evacuated, their unruly energies not contained.[73] The gods all dance together in the final scene: Apollo with burlesque Pan, and Vulcan and Venus are still there with Apollo. Midas stays till the end and never fulfils Apuleius's prophecy that 'I'll make thee then ingenuously confess / Thy treason 'gainst the Muses' majesty' (I.i.75–6) – instead, his last words are a final challenge, 'And even in that thou fool'st thyself' (V.iii.134).

We risk oversimplification if we take the masque/antimasque structure as the rationale for *Love's Mistress*. Masques involving similar figures, such as Ben Jonson's *Pan's Anniversary* (performed for King James's birthday in 1621), *Love's Triumph through Callipolis* and *Chloridia* (with Cupid and Venus; the two masques form a pair celebrating Charles I and Henrietta Maria in February 1631), differ greatly from the play in their lack of interaction and metatheatricality.[74] *Pan's Anniversary* is closest to *Love's Mistress* because of its two presenters, the shepherd and the Fencer, promoting contrasting forms of expression.[75] The polarised framework may be a precedent for the Apuleius/Midas chorus; however there is no debate between the two, no metatheatrical comment beyond the Fencer's 'How like you this, shepherd? Was not this gear gotten on a holiday?' (lines 129–30). The Fencer intrudes, presents his own competing show, and leaves (twice); he does not talk the shepherd into altering his ceremony – and it is a ceremony, not a theatrical entertainment like Apuleius's.

The 1631 entertainments feature antimasques that may echo *Love's Mistress*, such as a dance of twelve distracted lovers (comparable to the procession of asses and the dance of 'Love's contrarieties') in *Love's Triumph through Callipolis*, and one of hellish characters in *Chloridia*, which also includes storm effects. However, in the very short text of *Love's Triumph* Euphemus seems to introduce both the parodic and the allegorical parts, and does so as if they were events rather than shows: there is no critical distance. Neither is there any debate in *Chloridia*, though it includes two presenters, Zephyrus and Spring: these are at one in their efforts to explain the situation, and do not create any distance between the story and the audience. The Jonsonian masques, then, relate to *Love's Mistress* in terms of their presenters and antimasques, but they do not offer the same kind of metatheatrical critique.

One masque, however, plays on metatheatricality in a similar way to *Love's Mistress*, and it was performed just nine months earlier: James Shirley's *Triumph of Peace*, 'A Masque, presented by the Foure Honourable Houses, or Innes of Court. Before the King and Queenes Majesties, in the Banqueting house at White Hall, February the third, 1633' (actually 1634).[76] Like *Love's Mistress*, it was remarkably successful: first the king asked to see again the opening grotesque procession, then a repeat performance was given on 13 February.[77] While its subject is not mythological, it bears striking analogies with Heywood's play. It starts with Opinion, Novelty and Confidence welcoming Fancy and his companions, Jollity and Laughter:

> FANCY. I come to do you honour with my friends here,
> And help the masque.
> OPINION. You'll do a special favour.
> FANCY. How many antimasques ha[ve] they? of what nature?
> For these are fancies that take most; your dull
> And phlegmatic inventions are exploded;
> Give me a nimble antimasque.
> OPINION. They have none, sir.
> LAUGHTER. No antimasque! I'd laugh at that, i'faith.
> JOLLITY. What make we here? No jollity!
> FANCY. No antimasque!
> Bid'em down with the scene, and sell the timber,
> Send Jupiter to grass, and bid Apollo
> Keep cows again; take all their gods and goddesses,
> For these must farce up this night's entertainment,
> And pray the court have some mercy on 'em,
> They will be jeer'd to death else for their ignorance.

> The soul of wit moves here; yet there be some,
> If my intelligence fail not, mean to shew
> Themselves jeer majors; some tall critics have
> Planted artillery and wit murderers.
> No antimasque! let'em look to 't.
>
> (pp. 265–6)

The characters clearly designate the masque as such, creating metatheatrical distance from the start. Fancy not only expresses his own disappointment, but underlines that antimasques are absolutely necessary to please 'the court'. He stresses the courtiers' critical appreciation of the show, as well as the masque's vulnerability to such 'jeer majors' and 'tall critics'.

Like Apuleius and Midas, Opinion and Fancy become a two-character chorus that introduces and remarks on the various parts of the entertainment. They too hold contradictory views, Fancy favouring dances and comic shows, and Opinion preferring serious allegories. The situation is reversed compared to *Love's Mistress*: Fancy becomes the prime presenter and serious-minded Opinion is the dissatisfied spectator always asking for something different.[78] In both cases the final production results from the interaction and debate between the liminal figures, and unlike in other masques it seems to be created as they talk: like Midas, Opinion forces Fancy to 'improvise' new shows. The entire masque is explicitly a play within the play, a thoroughly metatheatrical device. This is further emphasised by the noisy intrusion of 'a Carpenter, a Painter, one of the Black Guard, a Tailor, the Tailor's Wife, an Embroiderer's Wife, a Feather maker's Wife, and a Property man's Wife' (p. 280), claiming their right to view the show they helped stage! The subversive plan falls through when the Tailor, intimidated by the audience's laughter and the masquers' stillness, suggests ''tis our best course to dance a figary ourselves, and then they'll think it a piece of the plot, and we may go off again with the more credit' (p. 281). After the dance he concludes 'Now, let us go off cleanly, and somebody will think this was meant for an antimasque' (p. 281). As the characters accept their own aesthetic and political containment, the antimasque code is respected and exposed in a single movement. It seems to me that *The Triumph of Peace* renews the genre by introducing metatheatricality and critical debate. I suggest that Heywood, when writing his own pseudo-masque, found inspiration in this atypical masque.[79] The metatheatrical distance perhaps comes from their both being professional playwrights, approaching the masque as outsiders all the more conscious of its rules. But in its playful handling of the codes the performance is bound to please an educated audience: as with mythological burlesque, this kind of pleasure is based on a shared cultural ground.

I have tried to move beyond polarised critiques of *Love's Mistress*, which side with either allegory-minded Apuleius or iconoclastic Midas. While I appreciate Rowland's argument that the play promotes popular culture versus court culture, I have sought to provide explanation for the play's success within elite circles. This question opens perspectives on how the reception and reappropriation of classical mythology evolved in the 1630s. I have thus connected *Love's Mistress* with two contemporary cultural phenomena: the emergence of burlesque and the development of critical judgement among theatre audiences; and explored its relationship with three dramatic genres, including Heywood's own mythological plays, his civic pageants and courtly masques. This survey reveals a network of potential interactions. The adaptation of mythology in *Love's Mistress* is interwoven with cultural, literary and generic concerns that go far beyond the reception of Apuleius. The incorporation of critical appreciation into mythological transposition seems to me a key element that reflects a 'late early modern' engagement with classical culture. My hypotheses may also contribute to shifting the perception of Heywood, as we see him picking up on new trends right up to the end of his dramatic career. The comparison with *The Triumph of Peace* in particular suggests that Heywood did not so much rehearse familiar forms in *Love's Mistress* as emulate one of the 'leading new writers' of the time, his young rival James Shirley.[80]

Notes

1. *Love's Mistress* is his last play, though he continued writing pageants and miscellanies. Heywood died in 1641.
2. Performed c. 1610–13, *The Golden Age, The Silver Age, The Brazen Age* and Parts I and II of *The Iron Age* recount classical myths from Saturn's reign to the fall of Troy and the Atreids' mutual destruction.
3. The traditional contemptuous view of the Red Bull, epitomised in Gerald E. Bentley's *The Jacobean and Caroline Stage*, 7 vols (Oxford: Clarendon Press, 1941–68), Vol. VI (1968), pp. 238–47, has been challenged since the 2000s. See the dedicated issue of *Early Theatre*, 9:2 (2006); and Eva Griffith, *A Jacobean Company and Its Playhouse: The Queen's Servants at the Red Bull Theatre (c. 1605–1619)* (Cambridge: Cambridge University Press, 2013).
4. Andrew Gurr, *Playgoing in Shakespeare's London*, 3rd edn (Cambridge: Cambridge University Press, 2004), p. 210; see also Andrew Gurr, *The Shakespearian Playing Companies* (Oxford: Clarendon Press, 1996), pp. 416–23.

5   See Arthur M. Clark, *Thomas Heywood: Playwright and Miscellanist* (Oxford: Basil Blackwell, 1931), pp. 130–1; and Thomas Heywood, *Love's Mistress; or, The Queen's Masque*, ed. Raymond Shady (Salzburg: Institut für Englische Sprache und Literatur, 1977), pp. xxvii–xxviii. The title page and the three prologues in the first quarto (London: Robert Raworth, 1636) refer to these circumstances.
6   Clark, *Thomas Heywood*, p. 131.
7   See Ben Ross Schneider, Jr (ed.), *Index to the London Stage 1660–1800* (Carbondale: Southern Illinois University Press, 1979). Only six plays by Heywood seem to have been revived, with two performances for *The Fair Maid of the West* and only one for *Queen Elizabeth's Troubles, The Rape of Lucrece, The Royal King and the Loyal Subject* and *The Wise Woman of Hogsdon*. By contrast, *Love's Mistress* was performed twenty-six times between 1661 and 1704.
8   See Richard Rowland, *Thomas Heywood's Theatre, 1599–1639: Locations, Translations, and Conflict* (Farnham: Ashgate, 2010), p. 233.
9   There are also occasional references, such as the one to Marsyas (from Ovid's *Metamorphoses*, VI), which Rowland investigates in *Thomas Heywood's Theatre*, pp. 257–67.
10 Jackson Cope, *The Theater and the Dream: From Metaphor to Form in the Renaissance* (Baltimore: Johns Hopkins University Press, 1973), pp. 173–96.
11 Jane Kingsley-Smith, *Cupid in Early Modern Literature and Culture* (Cambridge: Cambridge University Press, 2010), pp. 170–7.
12 Clark, *Thomas Heywood*, pp. 113–43 (p. 133).
13 Rowland, *Thomas Heywood's Theatre*, pp. 233–97 (p. 234).
14 Paule Desmoulière is an exception, as she does not promote one perspective over the other but argues that Heywood strove to reconcile opposite modes through a poetics of hybridity. See Paule Desmoulière, 'Psyché sur la scène anglaise: *Love's Mistress* de Thomas Heywood', *Silène* (2006), www.revue-silene.com (accessed 17 June 2016).
15 Rowland, *Thomas Heywood's Theatre*, p. 297.
16 'We two contend – Art here, there Ignorance' (I.i.82). For convenience's sake all quotations refer to Shady's edition (see n5), though I take into account Rowland's warning that 'its accuracy cannot be relied upon' (*Thomas Heywood's Theatre*, p. 234).
17 Because Rowland has already analysed the combination of sources and Heywood's attitude to Apuleius, I shall not dwell on the origins of the plot; the interweavings I focus on are the relationships between the mythological material and seventeenth-century fashions and genres.
18 See Rowland, *Thomas Heywood's Theatre*, pp. 288–9; Kingsley-Smith, *Cupid in Early Modern Literature and Culture*, p. 173.
19 See Erica Veevers, *Images of Love and Religion: Queen Henrietta Maria and Court Entertainments* (Cambridge: Cambridge University Press, 1989); Karen Britland, *Drama at the Courts of Henrietta Maria* (Cambridge: Cambridge University Press,

2006), who rejects the term *préciosité* but expatiates on *salons* and neoplatonism; Myriam Dufour-Maître, *Les Précieuses: naissance des femmes de lettres en France au XVII*ᵉ *siècle*, 2nd edn (Paris: Honoré Champion, 2008).

20 Though Desmoulière mentions burlesque she does not develop a contextual analysis of that style. See 'Psyché sur la scène anglaise', p. 8.
21 Gérard Genette, *Palimpsestes: la littérature au second degré* (Paris: Seuil, 1982).
22 Jean Leclerc, *L'Antiquité travestie et la vogue du burlesque en France (1643–1661)* (Paris: Hermann, 2014 [2007]). Claudine Nédélec, *Les États et empires du burlesque* (Paris: Honoré Champion, 2004), has a similar perspective.
23 For the entire passage see II.iii.35–55.
24 See Rowland, *Thomas Heywood's Theatre*, p. 233.
25 For the complete song see III.ii.68–95.
26 '[W]hilst the "torrid zone" was a clearly defined region in which the sun god was believed to operate … "zona", as Heywood the accomplished classicist well knew, was Latin for belt or girdle'. Rowland, *Thomas Heywood's Theatre*, p. 276.
27 See for instance IV.i.140–53.
28 See Leclerc, *L'Antiquité travestie*, pp. 31–125.
29 Nédélec, *Les États et empires du burlesque*, pp. 64–70, also dwells on *mondanisation* and *salons*. She stresses how burlesque mockery is an elite prerogative, the apparent disrespect coming from a place of confident cultural legitimacy.
30 Dominique Bertrand, *Dire le rire à l'âge classique: représenter pour mieux contrôler* (Aix-en-Provence: Publications de l'Université de Provence, 1995), p. 90 (also quoted in Leclerc, *L'Antiquité travestie*, p. 163).
31 Bernard Beugnot, 'L'invention parodique', in *La Mémoire du texte: essai de poétique classique* (Paris: Champion, 1994), p. 340 (also quoted in Leclerc, *L'Antiquité travestie*, p. 163).
32 Leclerc, *L'Antiquité travestie*, pp. 31–84.
33 Nédélec, *Les États et empires du burlesque*, pp. 25–70.
34 Dictionary quotations are from *Lexicons of Early Modern English*, http://leme.library.utoronto.ca (accessed 6 June 2016). Nédélec mentions Cotgrave and believes he picked up the word from *Satyre Ménippée* (*Les états et empires du burlesque*, p. 43).
35 John Wilkins's *An Essay towards a Real Character and a Philosophical Language* (1668).
36 See Guy Miège's *A New Dictionary French and English, with Another English and French* (1677); B. E.'s *A New Dictionary of the Terms Ancient and Modern of the Canting Crew* (1699).
37 John Kersey the Younger, *A New English Dictionary* (1702).
38 Leclerc, *L'Antiquité travestie*, pp. 42–5.
39 See Veevers, *Images of Love and Religion*; and Britland, *Drama at the Courts of Henrietta Maria*, pp. 12–13.
40 See Dufour-Maître, *Les Précieuses*, pp. 11–20, esp. pp. 14–15.

41 Britland, *Drama at the Courts of Henrietta Maria*, pp. 133–4.
42 The next two paragraphs touch on issues discussed at length by Leclerc, *L'Antiquité travestie*, pp. 122–227.
43 Rowland, *Thomas Heywood's Theatre*, esp. pp. 241–5.
44 Rowland points out that 'Q1 reads "avoide", but Shady's emendation … is surely right' (*Ibid.*, p. 253).
45 See I.i.19–20, 67–8, 82–4; I.vi.93–5; II.v.52–3; III.iii.54; IV.iii.5–6, 50–3; V.iii.127–33.
46 Rowland, *Thomas Heywood's Theatre*, p. 285.
47 Apuleius mentions his 'silver hairs' (I.i.40); Midas describes himself as 'king of beasts' but associates the title with the 'wool crown' he made for himself (I.i.61); Apollo prophesies 'may thy ears longer grow, / As shorter still thy judgement' (III.ii.120–1), yet the comparative structure is no sure clue to the use of a stage prop before or after this statement.
48 E.g. Midas: 'Thou prompt'st my understanding pretty well' (I.vi.69); Apuleius: 'I am well pleased with your pastoral mirth' (II.v.12).
49 'Unstain' is an obvious misprint in Shady's edition, which has 'Unstaid' in the notes (*Love's Mistress*, p. 155).
50 *Ibid.*, pp. liii–liv.
51 Andrew Gurr, *The Shakespearean Stage 1574–1642*, 3rd edn (Cambridge: Cambridge University Press, 1992), p. 20.
52 Gurr, *Playgoing in Shakespeare's London*, p. 210.
53 *Ibid.*, p. 211.
54 Tiffany Stern, *Documents of Performance in Early Modern England* (Cambridge: Cambridge University Press, 2009), p. 85.
55 *Ibid.*, p. 86.
56 See *Ibid.*, pp. 81–119.
57 See Midas's complaints in II.v.3–7 and III.iii.10–13, and Apuleius's fraught conclusion to Act III: 'And for thy part, Midas, / Laugh, sleep, or flout, nay snarl, and cavil too, / [*Gestures to the audience.*] Which none of these here met I hope will do' (III.iii.52–4).
58 Pepys thought 'it was strange to see so little a boy as that was to act Cupid, which is one of the greatest parts in it' (*Love's Mistress*, ed. Shady, p. xxxv).
59 The staging of hell in *The Silver Age* foreshadows 'Hell's court' in *Love's Mistress*, though the latter emphasises music at Denmark House, and the former has 'fireworkes all ouer the house' in the open-air Red Bull Theatre. Thomas Heywood, *The Silver Age*, in *The Dramatic Works of Thomas Heywood*, Vol. III (New York: Russell and Russell, 1964), pp. 159–61 (p. 159).
60 Agnès Lafont, however, writes about the burlesque dimension of *The Golden Age*: see 'Métamorphoses burlesques de la *fabula* classique dans le théâtre anglais de la fin de la Renaissance', *Revue de la société d'études anglo-américaines des XVIIe et XVIIIe siècles*, 60 (2005), 25–30.

61 I discuss the *Ages* at greater length in a forthcoming online edition of *The Golden Age* in the CNRS-sponsored Early English Mythological Texts series (gen. ed. Yves Peyré) at www.shakmyth.org.
62 See *1 & 2 The Iron Age*, in Heywood, *The Dramatic Works*, Vol. III.
63 Charlotte Coffin, 'Heywood's *Ages* and Chapman's Homer: Nothing in common?', in Tania Demetriou and Tanya Pollard (eds), *Homer and Greek Tragedy in England's Early Modern Theatres*, *Classical Receptions Journal*, 9 (2017) (special issue), 55–78.
64 Thomas Heywood, *Londons jus honorarium* (London: Nicholas Okes, 1631), sig. B1r.
65 Thomas Heywood, *Londini artium & scientiarum scaturigo* (London: Nicholas Okes, 1632), sig. B4r.
66 Thomas Heywood, *Londini speculum* (London: J. Okes, 1637), sig. C2r.
67 Thomas Heywood, *Londini emporia* (London: Nicholas Okes, 1633), sigs B3v–4r.
68 See David M. Bergeron, 'Stuart civic pageants and textual performance', *Renaissance Quarterly*, 51:1 (1998), 163–83; and Charlotte Coffin, 'From pageant to text: The silent discourse of Heywood's omissions', in L. Coussement-Boillot and C. Sukic (eds), *'Silent Rhetoric', 'Dumb Eloquence': The Rhetoric of Silence in Early Modern English Literature* (Paris: Université Paris VII-Denis Diderot, 2007), pp. 71–96.
69 See David M. Bergeron, *English Civic Pageantry 1558–1642*, 2nd edn (Tempe: Arizona State University Press, 2003 [1971]), pp. 214–35.
70 Ibid., p. 5.
71 Heywood, *Londini artium & scientiarum scaturigo*, sig. B4r.
72 Britland traces the origin of the bipartite structure of English court masques to Ben Jonson's *Masque of Queens* (1609). Interestingly, she advocates a reconsideration of the connections between pageants and masques. See Karen Britland, 'Masques, courtly and provincial', in Julie Sanders (ed.), *Ben Jonson in Context* (Cambridge: Cambridge University Press, 2010), pp. 153–61, esp. pp. 154–5 and 158.
73 Although the Clown disappears at the end of V.vii, he is as confident as ever and supremely unaware of Cupid's revenge. See Rowland, *Thomas Heywood's Theatre*, p. 295.
74 See Ben Jonson, *The Complete Masques*, ed. Stephen Orgel (New Haven: Yale University Press, 1969). The reference below is to this edition.
75 Although *Pan's Anniversary* was performed thirteen years earlier and was not published when Heywood wrote *Love's Mistress*, Rowland suggests Heywood may have had access to a manuscript version through his collaboration with Richard Brome, Jonson's former 'man' (see *Thomas Heywood's Theatre*, pp. 277–8).
76 See James Shirley, *The Triumph of Peace*, in *The Dramatic Works and Poems of James Shirley*, ed, W. Gifford and A. Dyce, Vol. VI (New York: Russell & Russell, 1966), pp. 253–85. Parenthetical references below are to this edition.

77 See the chronological table in Veevers, *Images of Love and Religion*; and Kevin Sharpe, *Criticism and Compliment: The Politics of Literature in the England of Charles I* (Cambridge: Cambridge University Press, 1990 [1987]), pp. 212–19. Like Rowland with *Love's Mistress*, Sharpe stresses the subversive quality of Shirley's masque and its criticism of the court. I would underline that both productions come from professional playwrights.

78 See for instance p. 267: 'FANCY. How like you this device? / OPINION. 'Tis handsome, but – / LAUGHTER. Opinion will like nothing ... / OPINION. I could wish something, sir, of other nature, / To satisfy the present expectation.'

79 Shirley's masque was entered to the Stationers' Register on 24 January and went through four print runs in 1634, by John Norton for William Cooke; *STC* adds Nicholas Okes, Heywood's long-time printer, in the first record. Most importantly Shirley was the leading dramatist of Queen Henrietta's Men – 'the writer-in-residence at the Cockpit' (Gurr, *The Shakespearian Playing Companies*, p. 152).

80 Gurr, *The Shakespearian Playing Companies*, p. 419; see also pp. 148–54.

11

Pygmalion, once and future myth: Instead of a conclusion

Ruth Morse

From Shakespeare's odd use of one figure in one myth (taken apparently out of context), this final chapter will consider some metamorphoses of Shakespeare and of Ovid; it has general points to reiterate about imaginative association, influence, historically diachronic descent study, as evidenced in that kind of critical work that finds in a keyword an attractive pretext for the projection of an author's particular interest or, more worryingly, of a critic's. *Measure for Measure*'s Lucio's multiply insulting reference to Pygmalion invites us to linger over questions of allusion and interpretation in Shakespeare and his contemporaries: what was it that continued to make Pygmalion so useful to Shakespeare, and to Shakespearean reinterpretations in the late twentieth and early twenty-first centuries? If it proposes more questions than it answers, that must offer the sense of an ending intended as continuing the mythological studies to which Yves Peyré has dedicated so many years. Here it is, typical of Lucio's pretentious attempts at wit:

> What is there none of Pigmalions Images newly made woman to bee had now, for putting the hand in the pocket, and extracting clutch'd?[1]

Lucio's dramatic context is his standing to watch the bawd, Pompey, led across the stage to gaol. As Pompey passes Lucio he is foolish enough to address him in public and ask for bail, as from a friend. Lucio's ten-second reference alludes to a figure otherwise unnamed in (but perhaps not absent from) Shakespeare's plays. Like influence, allusion is a tricky business that requires knowledge of historically varied associations, and attentive contextual reading (beyond electronic keyword searches) to support assertions of recognition and interpretation. 'Attentive' in this instance implies the circumstances of the play at the moment of utterance, the speaker, interlocutor and onstage audience. Where Shakespeare is concerned, as is often remarked, the speaker may be a vehicle for more than a speech, as the play enlarges its thematic content all unbeknownst to the character speaking. I ask not only the actor's question, 'Why does my character say this?', but also 'What does this contribute to the textures of the play?'.

Usually critics assume that the recognition of Pygmalion is another memory of Ovid's *Metamorphoses*. 'Pygmalion' is one more of Ovid's myths of change, where 'myth' means a story involving interaction between gods and men, when it contains archetypal emotion and experience. And one familiar kind of study traces a line of descent, a diachronic history of the myth's occurrences, also often without much reference to synchronic context. 'Myth' is the common identifier for Ovid's contents, and has transferred through different periods, arts and literatures, in different languages; so that 'the myth of Pygmalion' has also come to embrace 'myths of Galatea' – or of statues, clockwork, robots, androids and so forth, adored by their makers or metamorphosed into life.[2] But that cannot be right for Lucio, however right it is for the educated in the audience or the study. In Ovid the story does begin with disgust at local female promiscuity, but that is a pretext for a more sentimental tale of a lonely sculptor enchanted by means of his own art. The sentimental ending erases all previous disapprobation. In psychopathology, Pygmalion's obsession offered Richard von Krafft-Ebing the study of agalmatophilia (compulsive attachment to statues) and subsequent mental health categories of fetishism, including life-size rubber dolls. Historiographically, as well, perhaps, as historically, the 'female' object is delighted to live and to serve her maker. A contemporary example is the urban legend of men becoming obsessed with their imagined woman behind the soothing female voice on global positioning systems, who apparently ousted the Speaking Clock in sad fantasies. Both examples turn on the widespread belief that 'she' has a name.[3]

The first part of this chapter explores how the unpleasant crack in the mouth of the chancer, Lucio, came to be there; how it might be understood; and what it implies for the circumstances of this play, but also for interpretation more generally. 'Allusion' will raise many of the difficulties familiar from studies of 'influence': here, too, one must beware of mistaking a resemblance for an apparent line of direct descent. So I begin by looking at a slightly less short extract, enlarging its scope, then moving to the interpretative difficulty of noticing both apparent presences and real absences; of expectations disappointed and fulfilled; of bringing together what might be habits of linguistic association, but might be coincidence; of attending to the implicit variations in structural and thematic resemblances and, most delicate of all,

Pygmalion, once and future myth

knowing what to do with what's not there. For example, whatever Lucio's pretences to be one of the gentles may be, he is unlikely to have read the high medieval commentary tradition of allegorised Ovid.

Measure for Measure, III.ii

Pompey, having fallen foul of Vienna's new rigour, and into the hands of the law, is led off to gaol by Elbow, who threatens hanging presently, while the observing 'Friar' threatens perdition afterwards. This public shaming is part of the punishment, not a 'perp walk' in today's slang; it is obviously also part of the play's thematic 'punishment'. Lucio's mockery rebuffs Pompey with play on Pompey's name, and perhaps also Elbow's unheroic demeanour, in a stream of self-regarding invective,

> How now, noble Pompey? What, at the wheels of Caesar? Art thou led in triumph? What, is there none of Pygmalion's images newly made woman to be had now, for putting the hand in the pocket, and extracting [it] clutch'd? What reply? Ha?
>
> (III.ii.43–7)

The non sequiturs then move into what appeals to an idea of a sad tune, depending, perhaps, upon the exact moment of Lucio's entrance.[4] In accusing Pompey of faking virgins for sale, Lucio's other nastinesses here include the accusation that Pygmalion himself set a precedent, or manufactured, 'images' of virgins – thus fakes (as that exceptional reader George T. Wright has pointed out).[5] Wright's alertness reminds us to ask about the audience, both in the theatre and in the study. Who recognised Lucio's travesty of the sculptor and his metamorphosed beloved? Was anyone led to meditate upon the sculptor – for surely no-one meditated upon the statue, at the outset, as here, nameless?[6] It is part of Shakespeare's habit of associative structures that, beyond the play's condemnation of Lucio's casual cruelty, Lucio contributes to that other theme of love for sale, part of the play's texture of recalcitrant unclarities and contradictions about legitimate sex, intercourse and marriage. In the tight economy of Shakespeare's comic justice, that reference to Pygmalion is part of a pattern of misprision, indiscipline and mistaking, from the minor characters up to the Duke himself. In Act II Escalus's interrogation of Elbow and Pompey may look like a distraction, but as Elbow's comic accusations warn, Pompey's prunes and promiscuity suggest that his punishment, and Lucio's own, is coming. What no audience could have predicted is how it fits the crime: Lucio reveals the false friar as the real

Duke, who readily condemns him to real marriage with his – also nameless – pregnant punk, one of Lucio's Pompey's Pygmalion's fakes. The parallels to Angelo and Isabella, Isabella and the Duke, Claudio and Juliet, will be clear to readers familiar with Shakespeare's permutations and combinations, but, on the face of it, no audience will have an 'aha' moment about Pompey and Mistress Overdone, Lucio and his whore, or Pygmalion. It is not even clear that anyone will remember this, when Lucio sees the Duke's retributive sentence as worse than judicial punishment. Marriage was a life sentence. The prison list underlines this: Vienna's prison contains not only Claudio, but also Barnardine and the already-dead notorious pirate; Juliet is confined awaiting her mean but sufficient confinement, her baby a poor but innocent prisoner; Mariana imprisons herself in her moated grange; and Isabella, evidently, belongs in this roll call, with her desire for self-imprisonment among the nuns.

Lucio is unexceptional in his sexual nastiness, as in his flip-side adoration of Isabella as 'a thing enskied and sainted' (I.iv.34). As clichés go, 'saints or whores' is common enough. In the erotic verse of the epyllion, Shakespeare's contemporary John Marston offered another crude cliché, that any woman will be warmed up, changed, by the 'ardent affection' of her lover – and for Marston's satire, this TNT view of female sexuality is taken for granted; when Ovid's Pygmalion wonders, as he caresses his statue, if she is not becoming flesh, it is by contrast *his* fantasy.[7] Renaissance Ovids came in many kinds, and so did versions of the *Roman de la rose*, in which Pygmalion's shoddy role may commence. Varieties of editions of the *Metamorphoses* offered Shakespeare books that contained varieties of commentaries, including 'moralisations', sometimes multiple *in bono/malo* allegories of goodness and of vice. As Yves Peyré discusses in Chapter 1 of this volume, ideas and phrases often persisted through an afterlife of reference and citation. Twentieth-century critics are happy to choose a Pygmalion as the kind of fool who sees and judges from the outside; here is Peyré on the place of Marlowe in Shakespeare's canon of memorial reference:

> Faustus, sot Pygmalion, s'énamoure d'une piètre morceau de bois par lui sculpté parce qu'à ses yeux l'art n'est qu'une forme. Il n'imite que de façon extérieure et superficielle l'artiste, dont la fonction est de retrouver dans la forme et la matière les énergies naturelles, afin que son œuvre devienne lieu de synthèse et de communion, c'est-à-dire qu'elle prenne vie comme sous les doigts d'un authentique et admirable Pygmalion.[8]
>
> (Faustus, a foolish Pygmalion, falls for a paltry piece of wood he sculpted himself, because in his eyes art is just a form. Only in a superficial and external

fashion does he mimic the artist's function, which is to recover in form and matter such natural energies that his work becomes a place of synthesis and communion. That is, the work catches life as it does in the hands of an authentic and admirable Pygmalion.)

It is this striking use of a name as familiar shorthand that marks a change in the understanding of Ovid's story: Faustus is a fool ready to fall for the imitation of the shell of art, and falls short of the obligation of humane recognition. In *Measure for Measure*, Mariana has this gift, as does Juliet. Perhaps the Duke learns it; but perhaps not, and perhaps the same is true of Isabella. I will argue below that this is an ethical imperative, not only for Shakespeare, and that this intimate structure, calling what one has only imagined into life, informs centuries of subsequent reuses of this plot.

Reading's histories

It would be a mistake to attribute responsibility for this travesty to Lucio, and ridiculous to invent a life for him in which he was influenced by his reading of moralised Ovids, as might an actor preparing to bring him to another kind of life; but some cultural memory of condemnation lingered, or Lucio's author could not have used it. Lucio sullies what he touches, like a cheap Iago. In context, Lucio runs apparently unrelated classical names together; and this is not the only example of a reference beyond the reach of other characters on stage. To show this technique at work, a brief digression will be useful, as it illuminates a series of imaginative associations and offers a more familiar example of Shakespeare's deep imaginative collocations. These collocations are textual and literary rather than images from nature belonging to the author. Shakespeare's technique here is to invite attention to a present absence.

'Pygmalion', though not a common name, was borne by a historical king of Tyre (late ninth, early eighth centuries BCE), associated with the founding of Carthage. When this Pygmalion killed his brother-in-law, Dido's husband, for his gold, she fled to found the new city where she fell in love with the Trojan refugee Aeneas. That passion arose because Venus intervened on Aeneas's behalf, her meddling part of her support of the Trojans: Dido was collateral damage (thus far from Pygmalion's situation). 'Widow Dido' had more than one name, and is sometimes referred to as 'Elissa', though not in Shakespeare. My epithet is part of a familiar Shakespearian example, by which I can illustrate the tenor of my argument about complex association.

In *The Tempest*, this widowed sister of King Pygmalion illustrates recognisable habits of polite, literate interpretations – here Gonzalo's habits, which, even in a true gentleman, were susceptible to mockery. We already know that this well-read book appreciator supplied Prospero's leaky boat with the books he loved.

> GONZALO. Methinks our garments are now as fresh as when we put them on first in Afric, at the marriage of the King's fair daughter Claribel to the King of Tunis.
> SEBASTIAN. 'Twas a sweet marriage, and we prosper well in our return.
> ADRIAN. Tunis was never grac'd before with such a paragon to their queen.
> GONZALO. Not since widow Dido's time.
> ANTONIO. Widow! a pox o' that! How came that widow in? Widow Dido!
> SEBASTIAN. What if he had said 'widower Aeneas' too? Good Lord, how you take it!
> ADRIAN. 'Widow Dido', said you? You make me study of that: she was of Carthage, not of Tunis.
> GONZALO. This Tunis, sir, was Carthage.
>
> (II.i.69–84)

In the absence of context, the courtiers' confusion is understandable, and Adrian politely hesitates before offering a correction. Gonzalo seems to be making a witty, if abstruse, historical point geographically appropriate to Tunis, formerly Carthage, but the courtiers only hear names, and miss the point. Pedants are always in season when the less bookish are in search of a butt; Shakespeare uses this kind of passing association to thicken the texture of a play in which Prospero's books play such a role. It is true that Prospero was not the most practical applier of his reading, which was supposed to instruct princes, not encourage them to withdraw from governing. Gonzalo is about to offer a fantasy of good government, long recognised (at least by readers) as from Florio's Montaigne. That Gonzalo twice demonstrates his own mockable habit of reference similarly calls attention to Shakespeare's habit of repeating important things; this time it's a point about books, reading, interpretation – and in the theatre both these tiny incidents appear to be exasperation in the service of comedy. After-theatre conversation in the bar is unlikely to include 'Did you catch the courtiers' reference to Virgil?'. Yet such shell references contribute to the play's themes of love, legitimacy and good government. Reference to recognisable names (Dido, Carthage) can be multi-potential shifters that both contextualise and decontextualise themselves; they distract by association with Argiers. Today, when critical best practice insists on taking into account the context of what is quoted, whatever the text, it is easy to forget the long and still current history of extracting, decontextualising and misinterpreting quotations, common when 'Shakespeare' or 'the Bible' are called upon as authorities for saying what they could never have meant: in the dramatist's case, what not 'Shakespeare', but a character, said to another character, in a place and time in the unfolding of the action.

King Pygmalion came to be conflated or confused with, or, indeed, erased by, the more familiar Pygmalion, an ivory carver in Cyprus. The most important source of Pygmalion's fame is the series of mainly tragic tales in Ovid's *Metamorphoses*, X (Pygmalion is X, 243–97), in which he becomes a celibate misogynist in reaction to the Propoetides, a promiscuous group of women. Venus punished them for denying her and her worship, first condemned to lives as painted whores available to all comers, then inexorably reduced to stone statues by their counterfeit love and hardheartedness. But Pygmalion the sculptor in ivory, restricting himself to his own creations, fell in love:

> by wondrous Art an image he did grave
> Of such proportion, shape, and grace as nature never gave
> Nor can to any woman give. In this his worke he tooke
> A certaine love. The looke of it was ryght a Maydens looke,
> And such a one as that yee would beleeve had lyfe, and that
> Would moved bee, if womanhod and reverence letted not:
> So *artificial* was the work. He woondreth at his Art [*technical achievement*]
> And of *his counterfetted* [*its imitated*] corse conceyveth love in hart.
>
> (265–72)[9]

By contrast to the Cypriot Venus-deniers who have preceded this part of Book X, Pygmalion worshipped Venus, and on her feast day he prayed that one day his wife might be a woman as beautiful and as chaste as his ivory: and, as we know, Venus granted his wish beyond his wildest dreams, making the statue itself his beloved, his artist's gentle hands wooing its ivory into soft bodiliness, filling his heart with thanks to the goddess for this chaste body that blushed when 'at the length he put his mouth to hers who was as then become a perfect mayd' (317–18). Nine months later the couple's son, Paphus, was born (whose name attached itself to the island, Paphos).

So Dido immolated herself on her husband's pyre, the free-thinking Cypriot women were turned to stone and Pygmalion was rewarded with his heart's desire – all through the power of Venus, playing on human desire, including acquisitive greed. Stone and ivory play a part, too, in an association of statues, simulacra and automata. Into this heady imaginative and associative mix we could add hints of Vulcan, the greatest of smiths, and the greatest of mortal inventors, Daedalus. This is not the place to explore the larger context of Book X, but Ovid expanded his ideas in techniques that Shakespeare found sympathetic: repetition and variation, juxtaposition of difference to create similarity, and interpretation that changes in the experience of accretion. Among Ovid's less happy metamorphoses in Book X is that in which Pygmalion's great-granddaughter falls in love with her father, Pygmalion's grandson.

Playing with Ovid

The functions and meanings of narrative memes, characters and situations have been analysed using more narratological methods to break down the evolution of myth- (or, indeed, legend-) content, from the work of Vladimir Propp in identifying narrative structures and the collection known as the Stith Thompson Motif-Index, which collated and cross-referenced structure, character and other kinds of enduring story-telling motifs.[10] As Helen Cooper, among others, has emphasised in her work on both Chaucer and on romance, content retains both a remarkable continuity and an equally remarkable malleability as stories are recycled to respond to quite different interpretations in the written romances of Western Europe.[11] The interpretative metamorphosis that interests me here is not the advent of idolatry as an error in worship, but the constant ambivalence of the narrators' projections of lust onto an object that remains, however touched, itself untouched. In that sense the reinterpretations of the Pygmalion story are fictions rather than myths. To quote Frank Kermode:

> Myth operates within the diagrams of ritual, which presupposes total and adequate explanations of things as they are and were ... Fictions are for finding things out, and they change as the needs of sense-making change. Myths are the agents of stability, fictions the agents of change. Myths call for absolute, fictions for conditional assent. Myths make sense in terms of a lost order of time ... fictions, if successful, make sense of the here and now.[12]

It is to the metamorphoses of Pygmalion in critical thought that I now turn.

Scholarship as fantasy

Some interpretations are delighted by the exploration of the psyche. Kenneth Gross catches the strange sexuality of the Pygmalion story: it

> suggests how much the divagations of erotic fantasy haunt their more refined, aesthetic sublimations, but perhaps also how much anything we want to call sexuality or eros is bound to the domain of fantasy itself, to its literalisations and ambivalences, and how much the meaning even of intimate physical contact is conditioned by a fantasy of a body.[13]

Arthur Golding's was the translation Shakespeare used to supplement his Latin – and perhaps add to his pleasure. George Sandys, in the second important translation into English, adds glosses to Ovid's text, including two commentaries on the sudden blushing that indicates the statue's awakening (and its contrast to the shameless Propoetides). One can hardly overstate the force of the male gaze and its power over the statue, whatever her size – and her size, in much medieval illumination, is that of a tiny statue, not the full-sized erotic fantasy of later painting. Much of the modern scholarship on Pygmalion, statues that come to life, androids that may or may not be alive, is unselfconsciously the study of male desire. That does not mean that the artistic recyclings or adaptations are without perceptions that offer a different point of view, whoever the author.

But some interpretations were not, or affected not to be, about the psyche's desire at all. The interlude in historical interpretation of the kind to which Lucio alludes dates largely from thirteenth-century changes in reading and commentary that came with medieval Christian expectations of allegorical reading. Readers came to late antique and medieval editions of commented classical texts armed with their versions of Revelation, which demoted worshippers and gods alike as necessarily benighted, deprived of salvation because born too soon, and idolaters not of gods, but of devils taking false forms in order to deceive worshippers of idols – so counterfeits not as 'imitations', but as seriously deceiving fakes. For some readers, Pygmalion came ill out of this prejudice. His idolatry is not even for a divinity, but for a statue from his own hand, like Faustus's in the quotation from Peyré above. This is not the place to invoke the large bibliography of commentary on this commentary tradition: the moralised Ovids have been well documented and explored not in Ovid alone, but also in Jean de Meun's thirteenth-century vernacular French continuation of *Le Roman de la rose*.

Jean's serio-comic Pygmalion demonstrates serious symptoms of Barbie-fixation, or in medieval terms, seduction by an ivory succubus, like Ovid's Latin sculptor, dressing and undressing the statue, kissing and caressing, and sleeping next to it; he, too, is convinced that it is turning into flesh, but Jean makes it his own flesh he touches. This flirtation with sin (or sins, since a variety are suggested), with male fantasies, dissolves at the moment of waking, when the statue itself denies the obvious temptation to see it as a devil, and modestly calls itself Pygmalion's *amie*.[14] Among other influential texts, two stand out: independent fourteenth-century texts of 'Ovid' made safe: Pierre Bersuire's Latin *Ovidius moralizatus*, and its anonymous contemporary in 70,000 lines of French octosyllabic couplets, *Ovide moralisé*. They christianised and allegorised the *Metamorphoses* practically out of recognition (moralised here means 'turned into allegories', recognising the hidden depiction of either – or both – good or evil). But there were many readers who resisted this metamorphosis of the *Metamorphoses*, and continued to read Ovid's stories as stories, and with non-religious pleasure. Fourteenth-century vernacular writers, including Petrarch in Italy and Chaucer and Gower in England, shared a strong interest in Ovid, first in his poetry, and then in his narrative; they were well aware of the French poem and its allegorising, but not much affected by it.[15] Nonetheless, as Peyré shows in Chapter 1 of the present volume, material in the commentaries had lives of its own, adding details here and there to subsequent uses of Ovid that did not appear in the originals the commentators were illuminating.[16] It is, however, where Lucio got his ideas of a counterfeiter of virgins.

Pygmalions

One generalises about Shakespeare at one's peril, but throughout his plays, characters whom audiences, readers and other characters recognise as good consistently condemn characters who use people instrumentally, or as less than persons – that is, as things rather than as ends in themselves. He allows for redemption, for characters who start insensitively, egotistically, who mature ethically, who come to recognise the error of their previous ways, including ways of seeing the world's inhabitants: Posthumus and Leontes, but not Bertram or Othello. There are many styles of treating women as things, and Shakespeare knew what *thing* most enraged. 'Thing' is a word with a complicated history.[17] In Elizabethan English 'thing' could still be used as a euphemism for sexual parts, male *or* female, but like many euphemisms it was wearing out, and had derogated into a negative, typically used, in

Shakespeare's plays, by a man insulting a woman, as it continued to do in Restoration comedy. A man can treat a woman as a 'thing', but is constantly reminded that she is not *his* thing, since she is not a thing at all. Since a woman notoriously has desires of her own, he has no control over *her* thing, and may find himself frustratedly wondering if she does either. The 'accused queens' motif depends upon this dilemma being true everywhere, with nobility of birth no bar to the fundamental misogynistic belief about all women's potential warmed-up whoredom.

Young men in the happy comedies of the 1590s get their come-uppances from young women (despite accusations of whoredom in *Much Ado about Nothing*); the abused queens and falsely accused wives of the tragedies and romances regularly show up the calumniators and the louts who believe any man who fabricates a lie rather than the woman they know and ought to believe. In Shakespeare's permutations and variations of power, injury and virtuous victimhood, something about Pygmalion plays a part. That part includes recognition.

So let us consider Shakespeare's transformative economy through male characters whose errors resemble but do not imitate Pygmalion's instrumentalism. Several may be 'sot Pygmalions' – there are so many – but behind them lies the least stupid of artists, constructing his underlying themes by permutation and combination, by juxtaposition and by silence.[18] Pygmalion helps us think about Shakespeare's metamorphoses: love's transforming power includes the ass head and the male lovers of *A Midsummer Night's Dream*, where the comedy defuses any impulse towards darker interpretations.[19] We would not take Oberon or Robin Goodfellow as *creating* ass-headed Bottom, and Titania has not wished for anything except having her own way. Like the men. Hermia and Helena are never in any doubt about which stupid boy they love; they are never deceived, and are finally rewarded – and the stupid boys, too. Let us look at a series of 'sot Pygmalions', in pairs: Romeo and Rosaline; Claudio and Hero; Bassanio and Portia; a blink at the aptly named Valentine and Proteus – *Proteus? Valentine?* – and, later I shall allow myself a glance at Mira Nair's wonderful *Monsoon Wedding* of 2001. But if Pygmalions can be stupid, so also are the misprising Phoebe (*As You Like It*), whose beloved is not a man, and Margaret (*Much Ado about Nothing*), whose ambition misprises a real sot. What unites the men in my examples is an acquisitive egotism in which the women's value changes as the men gradually learn to understand them not as property, not even as complements to their own status, but as fully human.

Romeo need not delay us long: the play's early mockery of his Petrarchan adoration of the haughty beauty, Rosaline, is a brief prelude to the real thing, castigated by Mercutio, his other friends and the Friar. When Romeo rejoices, publicly, in suffering the compulsory distance, the *amor de lonh* of the troubadours, the mystery of the untouched beauty, his historical position is pan-European, and pretty stupid. It is not about love at all, but about preening oneself on one's articulate suffering, probably in artistic competition with other men. In another key we mock Phoebe when she falls for another Rosaline – Rosalind, disguised as Ganymede; this female variation concerns social status, where Shakespeare's conservatism about women aspiring above their places, marrying up, is expressed as mockery, or even in Margaret's public humiliation, in *Much Ado about Nothing*. Lucio is disgusting, but he is amusing, with his misplaced wit; lack of ambition excused by cynicism; deafness to responsibility, to reciprocity. He is a masterless man; Borachio is a drunk, not capable of synthesis and certainly not of communion. Angelo would be a rapist and a cheat if Mariana had been Isabella.

Shakespeare's plays have consistent views about treating women as people, from as early as *The Two Gentlemen of Verona* to *The Merry Wives of Windsor* to the romances. In his early trip to Verona, the women are constant, but one of the gentlemen is a rapist; in his second, Love's cool image becomes a loving woman, not when she, Rosaline, is magically changed, but when Juliet instantly metamorphoses Romeo into a social being, her legitimate spouse, responsible for her and for her good, a loving husband, but not capable of keeping his temper long enough to prevent two killings. He last sees her lying still, still untouched by Death – like what? Like a tomb statue of herself – as their fathers will provide for them. And what Romeo does, with the precipitousness that has marked him from the beginning, is join her statuesque perfection (V.iii). His last kiss resembles Othello's in his readiness to punish himself, but differs from Othello's, which retains everything of egotism.

Egotism plays havoc in another Claudio, in *Much Ado about Nothing*, three or so years later, where the speedy production of mortuary sculpture again plays a role. Claudio has seen and admired Hero – unlike Browning's sublime egotist, the Ferrarese duke of 'My Last Duchess' – but like that nobleman, he is explicit in his interest in dowry and, in the company of men, toe-curlingly macho when he admits he loves Hero, 'if my passion change not shortly' (I.i.219–20). Much virtue in if, as Touchstone says, and much depends on the actor who plays Claudio, whose 'virtue' depends on his susceptibility to changing his behaviour with his context. Like Romeo. His case varies because his terrible public humiliation of his betrothed wife has a function difficult for us to recapture. Yes, he has chosen a wife who is a paragon of virtue and modest beauty, and an heiress besides, as he ascertained from the Duke in the opening scene ('No child but Hero, she's his only heir. Dost thou affect her, Claudio?') (294–5). The difficulty is that ugly public repudiation was a way of advertising to the world that the marriage was broken before it was complete. He believes there was an impediment. The fact is, given the complexities of betrothal (*verbum de futuris*) and a wedding ceremony (*verbum de praesenti*), it makes sense to consider Claudio and Hero as married from their verbal exchange and handfast. The completing step in the process is consummation, and the old men are aware that sometimes the order is not respected. Disgusting, yes, but only *wrong* because the men have been tricked. They are all willing to believe a man they know to be a criminal rather than a woman. This looks like a tragic dilemma between responsibility and guilt. But, then, that is Leonato's first reaction as well; and everyone, he agrees with the Friar, is innocent (V.iv.2–3) – but Hero is more innocent. This is an uncomfortable observation. We must think like Beatrice, that to know Hero is to *know* her innocent. This retains the medieval idea of character as something engraved in stone, immutable. So *Much Ado about Nothing* has a stone monument for the supposed Hero, and some productions put a recumbent statue on it. Claudio is willing to marry again at Leonato's bidding, though the woman be ugly as 'an Ethiope'. He calls her a 'reck'ning … I must seize upon' (V.iv.52–3). In Shakespeare's English 'a reckoning' was an enumeration or a calculation; another item in his punishment, it was not yet monetary accounting. The woman who appears, and whose face Claudio demands to see, is now almost always heavily veiled in white, and evidently not a statue, but as not-dead as Hermione. Procedural marriage is why Hero can say 'I was your other wife.' She *was* and *is* his wife: 'other', because Claudio is ambiguously a widower. She was and is also exactly what he acquired, the perfect woman with a big dowry. There is no evidence that Claudio has learnt much but none either that he will make a bad husband. Certainly money should be no problem. This is one of the happy comedies, so we must agree that he is dismissed to happiness, as Dr Johnson said of Bertram in *All's Well that Ends Well*. I will not make the related case for that wastrel Bassanio, whose inferiority to his wife is patent, except to point out that Portia's father's test is meant to address right values – that is, Portia for her endowments, not her father's.

I promised a quick comparison to finish, so let me refer to *Monsoon Wedding*, with the young American's shock when he discovers that his idealised Indian bride is in fact sexually experienced, like him, and his recovery when he is able to replace his fantasy of a chaste and obedient wife with the recognition that his reality will be a woman who shares his desires and, indeed, his flaws. 'I think', he says, 'we can make this work'. At that moment the two young people have begun to know each other, with a commitment to knowing better.

Absences

Recognition is the heart of my argument: not just the recognition of romance when a family are reunited and all is forgiven, not even just the recognition that comes when we think we 'recognise' that *The Winter's Tale* — my fourth example — alludes to Pygmalion because it contains an apparent statue that apparently comes to life. That would be a very common form of cherry-picking — as Caliban is often picked from his original context to make something new. But *The Winter's Tale* may rather make something old, in a *coup de théâtre* that is more likely to invite us to remember Pygmalion than Hero's earlier appearance. In its context, as in *Much Ado about Nothing*, we, like the characters, recognise something greater than metamorphosis: pardon's the word for all. For Shakespeare's first audience had no idea what they were watching, beyond the fact that they could see that the same boy actor was recapitulating his Hermione. And the actor playing Leontes does something almost like wooing, as he declares his love aloud. This is a recognition scene, related to *The Comedy of Errors* and *Pericles* in our desire to recognise not only the restoration of a family, but also forgiveness — among friends, spouses, parents and children, masters and servants. The regeneration of a myth is one way to make magic magic, to collapse narrative sequence into the simultaneity of recognition and recovery. The theatre is one of the few places where we see that transformative magic, that creative strength, and eight times a week. Shakespeare's plays have that advantage over Pygmalion's private bliss.

The Winter's Tale is not another riff on Pygmalion, but something new, that was not in Shakespeare's source. Apollo's oracle pronounced the queen innocent, but there is no god here. People airily compare the final scene to Ovid's *Metamorphoses*, allowing the variation that the statue that appears to be a woman metamorphoses into a woman because she *is* woman. Or perhaps it is a false metamorphosis, the impersonation of a metamorphosis rather than the real thing. So who is the sculptor? Is it Julio Romano, who Paulina claims has just finished painting it? Obviously not, since it has not been painted. Then it must be Paulina, who carved nothing but an idea of the impersonation of a statue. Romeo's statue was still warm; and the missing Hero was not cold either. Certainly Paulina suggests that she has the power to 'make the statue move indeed, descend, / And take you by the hand' (V.iii.88–9).

But let us tarry awhile. The moment Paulina predicts is the aspect of the myth most represented in the history of western art, including the allegorised medieval illuminations of the moralised Ovids. Paulina is not Venus granting a prayer; she is a loyal friend to the man who widowed her. There is no prayer, but only a kind of recapitulative declaration of love. Leontes is no 'sot Pygmalion'. He is not stupid at all – he did not worship a statue, but his wife, of whom his long knowledge and trust he forgot, in a fit of jealousy caused we know not why or how. Hermione's defence was the same argument as Beatrice's of Hero, with her coincidental name. Authenticity, communion, exchange: if you know someone you trust them against the evidence. If the person is true the evidence is, de facto, false. We know nothing of what their marriage was like, but we heard Leontes describe his earlier wooing. We know that such is Leontes's virtue as a ruler that his courtiers feel free to object, contradict, almost condemn him to his face. He is no tyrant. A moment of madness, and he, rightly, takes sole responsibility for the destruction and loss; for sixteen years he has taken his punishment and awaited the Oracle's prediction.

So might we opine that the reputable Pygmalion, the authentic artist, is not a man at all, but Paulina, who is also not an artist, but one who has used art's transforming power with love. The statue, like its model, is, Paulina says, peerless. Yet Hermione, a living woman, was not perfect, either sixteen years before or now with the addition of wrinkles. Elsewhere in this play, however, perfection is claimed by another husband for another perfect woman: Mrs Shepherd, another otherwise nameless woman.

> Fie, daughter, when my old wife liv'd, upon
> This day she was both pantler, butler, cook,
> Both dame and servant; welcom'd all, serv'd all;
> Would sing her song, and dance her turn; now here,
> At upper end o' th' table, now i' th' middle;
> On his shoulder, and his; her face o' fire
> With labor, and the thing she took to quench it
> She would to each one sip.
>
> (IV.iv.55–62)

This is perfection, a woman doing the perfect hostly thing, and the old man misses her, grieves for her, and holds her up as an example, red-faced from fire and alcohol. She does not get a lot of scholarly attention, so let us remember that she is the play's third married woman welcoming important guests, a variation hard to recognise. It is the shepherd family, with their mysterious wealth, who create '[un] lieu de synthèse et de communion', as Peyré put it. If there is supernatural machinery it was the storm that cast the unknown baby on the shore of Bohemia – first no doubt having created a shore in Bohemia – and brought her home safely.

Coda: modern Pygmalions for what?

I want briefly to end with some modern instances. Over the last century or so, many readers and theatre-goers have learned about Pygmalion from Lerner and Loewe's 1956 adaptation of an earlier play by George Bernard Shaw, and later the film: *My Fair Lady*. Shaw's revolutionary reversal seems ordinary now, but it was not, and his epilogue to his published version of the play is practically a novel with chastisements. He forbids us to be sentimental about Professor Higgins and Eliza Doolittle: at the final curtain he allowed us to ask if Higgins loves her, if she has metamorphosed *him*. Does she marry him or does she carry out her threat to go off with the penniless Freddy Eynesford-Hill? Shaw planned the latter for his *Pygmalion* of 1912.[20] He reversed Ovid's version of Pygmalion by giving love and choice to the woman, not the man – or men – responsible for her metamorphosis; this reversed centuries of the Pygmalion story from a man's point of view, in which the woman is beautiful, chaste, silent, full of desire – but only for him. From a man's point of view, historically, this is an agreed impossibility, like a black swan or, indeed, a platypus. That does not stop the idea being a motor for fiction, and not just fiction. Reinterpretations, adaptations, are a privileged category of literary criticism, because they select and extract only what they need, without having to respect the source text's coherent whole. In the context of this, my second tentacular example of a television adaptation, literary reference is a cue, an invitation to intertextuality. Like Shaw, like Shakespeare, even like Ovid himself.

Shaw's ground-breaking adaptation of the myth enjoyed great international success and set an example for other offshoots. These include a *Star Trek* episode on Valentine's Day 1969. 'Requiem for Methuselah' is usually associated with *The Tempest*, with a planet as the island and Flint/Prospero as the brilliant inventor, living alone with his well-educated 'daughter', Rayna/Miranda. Flint/Prospero, the brilliant and almost immortal inventor, aspires to create a beautiful and talented robot woman, who won't ever leave him by dying. But the prototypes of his repeated failures all share the same bug, which is why Flint has constantly to remake and improve his invention – this recalls Pygmalion's repeated statues, who remain ivory and feel nothing. It is something Prospero knew you could not hard-wire: Prospero can only hope that his daughter and his enemy's son will fall in love; Flint cannot fabricate a robot woman who will love him forever. Like all previous beta versions, this Rayna is innocent of emotion until she spontaneously feels love, the *coup de foudre* that awakens her into humanity. Alas, for Flint, he is not the object of her affection. It is not Venus, but love itself, for Captain Kirk, which arrives with the human necessity to choose; it is more than she is wired for and she blows her circuits. Gene Rodenberry, the creator of the original three-season *Star Trek* television series, liked many different literary authors, but he loved Shakespeare, and his half-hour programme is quite different from its apparent full-length feature film, *Forbidden Planet*, of 1956.[21] Flint's Rayna is a mechanical *idiote savante*, hugely learned but innocent of all passion, ego or desires of her own. Rodenberry's take on Shakespeare's story absorbed *Forbidden Planet* with a touch of E. T. A. Hoffmann's clockwork automaton. In Shakespeare's day, at the heart of all the Pygmalion stories, was a consistent inconsistency about the story's contradictions, and the nameless woman's. We are invited to marvel at Venus's generous gift, which prompts the question: when is a statue not a statue? It is clear that the inconsistent answer is that it's when a living woman *remains* a statue – which defies a basic axiom of Aristotle. But it is at the heart of much of the criticism I mentioned above for which 'Pygmalion' is a way of exploring male gaze, male desire and the deeply rooted contradictory demand for a desiring woman who desires to own the man who creates her humanity by inspiring her adoration. One might end with Milton's idea of Adam's paradise as 'he for god only; she for god in him'. Or one might conclude with the fundamental necessity in literary criticism to read a great deal, and remember. This is well said by Peyré in the fine book that lies behind the conference from which this chapter grew:

> Ce sont les décalages, les glissements et les divorces qui sont le plus richement signifiants. Ils permettent à l'image mythologique d'acquérir la force et la labilité sémantiques, la puissance créatrice du symbole.[22]
>
> (It is the displacements and the ruptures that are most richly significant. They allow the mythological image to assume force and semantic instability, the creative power of the symbol.)

Notes

1 William Shakespeare, *Measure for Measure*, III.ii.44–7 (through line-numbering 1534–7), *A New Variorum Edition of Shakespeare*, ed. Mark Eccles (New York: Modern Language Association of America, 1980). The historical annotations show puzzlement about precisely what is implied, both here and later on in the scene. For a long discussion around this passage, for the generous gift of a copy of his book and for years of good talk together, I am grateful to George T. Wright.

2 Post-classical diachronic studies of myths are popular subjects. For examples of two different kinds, see Essaka Joshua, *Pygmalion and Galatea: The History of a Narrative in English Literature* (Aldershot: Ashgate, 2001); Gail Marshall, *Actresses on the Victorian Stage: Feminine Performance and the Galatea Myth* (Cambridge: Cambridge University Press, 1998). George L. Hersey collects a range of statues that come to life as a way of thinking about artificial intelligence and whether it implies 'life': *Falling in Love with Statues: Artificial Humans from Pygmalion to the Present* (Chicago: University of Chicago Press, 2006).

3 Often 'Pygmalion' is shorthand for precisely this longing, as when Joseph Hillis Miller introduces his book as indicating from the beginning his interest in 'what is at stake when someone becomes infatuated with a statue or a painting or, for that matter, when someone reads or hears a story and thinks of its characters as "real people"'; *Versions of Pygmalion* (Cambridge, MA: Harvard University Press, 1990), p. 3. 'Pygmalion' is shorthand for Miller's argument about reader response, but leads to assertions such as that Galatea can only see Pygmalion, only have the feelings that Pygmalion has. Something similar is at work in Victor I. Stoichita's *The Pygmalion Effect: From Ovid to Hitchcock* (Chicago: University of Chicago Press, 2008), p. 1, where the introduction takes a similarly thin definition of the *simulacrum*, something constructed from the maker's imagination, rather than a copy, a definition he derives from Plato (*Sophist*, 236c).

4 In *Shakespeare's Songbook* (New York: Norton, 2004), Ross Duffin gives two references to *Measure for Measure*, one of which is to associate the song 'O, Death, rock me asleep' with Escalus's grief for the death of Claudio (II.i), although not Lucio's harangue here. However, Lucio continues to ask how Pompey likes 'this tune', which traditional annotation suggests is the chink of coins he will not use on Pompey's behalf. Duffin's song's persona is a prisoner awaiting execution, like Claudio – and now, as Elbow threatens, Pompey. The other reference is to Mariana's self-imprisonment in her moated grange.

5 George T. Wright, *Poetic Craft and Authorial Design in Shakespeare, Keats, T. S. Eliot, and Henry James, with Two Essays on the Pygmalion Legend* (Lewiston: Edwin Mellen, 2011), p. 14.

6 Pygmalion's beloved, Galathée, appears in Jean-Jacques Rousseau's *Pygmalion*, his early musical melodrama of 1762 in which Venus plays no part. Arguments

about exactly who first borrowed the name Galatea (from the story of Acis and Galathea?) for Pygmalion's statue seem to have settled finally on Rousseau's libretto. See for instance Anne Geisler-Szmulewicz, *Le mythe de Pygmalion au XIXe siècle: pour une approche de la coalescence des mythes* (Paris: Champion, 1999).

7   Wright, *Poetic Craft*, pp. 12–14. There may be some recall of John Lyly's *The Woman in the Moone* (1597) and/or John Marston's *The Metamorphosis of Pigmalions Image* (1598), in *The Poems of John Marston*, ed. Arnold Davenport (Liverpool: Liverpool University Press, 1961), pp. 47–61, but neither work illuminates Pompey's reference.

8   Yves Peyré, *La voix des mythes dans la tragédie élisabéthaine* (Paris: CNRS Editions, 1996), p. 151.

9   I quote from *Ovid's Metamorphoses: The Arthur Golding Translation 1567*, ed. John Frederick Nims (London: Collier-Macmillan, 1965). Italics and glosses are mine.

10 Stith Thompson, *Motif-Index of Folk-Literature: A Classification of Narrative Elements in Folktales, Ballads, Myths, Mediaeval Romances, Exempla, Fabliaux, Jest-Books, and Local Legends*, 6 vols (Bloomington: University of Indiana Press, 1955–58).

11 Helen Cooper, *The Structure of the 'Canterbury Tales'* (London: Duckworth, 1983); *The English Romance in Time: Transforming Motifs from Geoffrey of Monmouth to the Death of Shakespeare* (Oxford: Oxford University Press, 2004).

12 Frank Kermode, *The Sense of an Ending: Studies in the Theory of Fiction* (Oxford: Oxford University Press, 1968 [1967]), p. 39. I owe this quotation to Stefan Collini.

13 Kenneth Gross, *The Dream of the Moving Statue* (Ithaca, NY: Cornell University Press, 1992), Chapter 5, p. 79.

14 Guillaume de Lorris and Jean de Meun, *Le Roman de la rose*, ed. Félix Lecoy (Paris: Champion, 1965–70), Vol. III, pp. 125–38, lines 20787–21212 (line 21125).

15 See the chapters by Helen Cooper and Bruce Harbert in Charles Martindale (ed.), *Ovid Renewed: Ovidian Influences on Literature and Art from the Middle Ages to the Twentieth Century* (Cambridge: Cambridge University Press, 1988).

16 In fact, it is remarkable how often critics add details that are not in the originals they are discussing: even Gross, in the course of his discussion of Hermione, attributes a desire to touch the statue to all the onlookers, rather than remembering that Paulina invites Leontes alone to take it by the hand. See Gross, *The Dream of the Moving Statue*, passim.

17 In Middle English, Chaucer's Wife of Bath refers to our sex-distinguishing 'smalle things' ('Wife of Bath's Prologue', line 121): a euphemism like '*ma belle chose*' or '*faire la chose*' in Old French.

18 Peyré, *La voix des mythes*, p. 151.

19 Wright, *Poetic Craft*, pp. 15ff.

20 He had W. S. Gilbert's *Pygmalion and Galatea* of 1871 in mind, though there had been many prior retellings in English, and by Rousseau in French.

21 In an article on *The Tempest* and science fiction, I missed the Pygmalion references completely. See Ruth Morse, 'Monsters, magicians, movies: *The Tempest* and the final frontier', *Shakespeare Survey*, 52 (2000), 164–74. For a general reference, although with an excellent bibliography only to 1990, see Susan R. Gibberman (ed.), *Star Trek: An Annotated Guide to Resources on the Development, the Phenomenon, the People, the Television Series, the Films, the Novels and the Recordings* (Jefferson: McFarland, 1991).
22 Peyré, *La voix des mythes*, p. 9.

Select bibliography

This select bibliography focuses on the classical reception in the late medieval, Tudor and early modern periods. It is intended to give an idea of the availability and circulation of mythological texts and the range of the works they inspired (drama, poetry, chronicles, etc.). A more extensive bibliography of printed and online primary and secondary sources on this subject is also available and regularly updated at www.shakmyth.org. See the notes to each chapter for the wider range of references used by authors.

Primary sources

Adlington, William, *The Xi Bookes of the Golden Asse* ... (London: Henry Wykes, 1566).

Alighieri, Dante, *The Comedy of Dante Alighieri*, trans. Dorothy L. Sayers: *Cantica I Hell (L'Inferno) and Cantica II Purgatory (Il Purgatorio)* (Harmondsworth: Penguin, 1963–76 [1955–62]).

Amyot, Jacques, *Les Vies des hommes illustres* (Paris: Michel de Vasconsan, 1565 [1559]). See also North, *The Lives of the Noble Grecians*.

Aneau, Barthélemy, Charles Fontaine and Jean de Vauzelles, *La Métamorphose d'Ovide figurée* (Lyon: Jean de Tournes, 1557).

Anon., *Chronica majora*, published as *Matthew Paris's English History from the Year 1235 to 1273*, trans. J. A. Giles, 3 vols (London: Henry G. Bohn, 1852–54).

—— *Ovide moralisé: poème du commencement du quatorzième siècle*, ed. Cornelis de Boer, 5 vols (Amsterdam: Johannes Müller, 1915–36).

—— *Ovide moralisé en prose: texte du quinzième siècle*, ed. Cornelis de Boer (Amsterdam: North Holland, 1954).

Apollonius Rhodius, *Argonautica*, ed. and trans. William H. Race (Cambridge, MA: Harvard University Press, 2008).

Appian, *An Auncient Historie and Exquisite Chronicle of the Romane Warres, Both Civile and Foren. Written in Greeke by the Noble Orator and Historiographer, Appian of Alexandria ... Translated out of Divers Languages, and Now Set Forth in Englishe,*

According to the Greeke Text ... by W. B. ... (London: Ralph Newberrie and Henry Bynneman, 1578).

Apuleius, *Metamorphoses (The Golden Ass)*, trans. and ed. J. Arthur Hanson, 2 vols (Cambridge, MA: Harvard University Press, 1989–96). See also Adlington, *The Golden Asse*.

Ariosto, Ludovico, *Ludovico Ariosto's 'Orlando furioso': Translated into English Heroical Verse by Sir John Harington*, trans. John Harington, ed. Robert McNulty (Oxford: Oxford University Press, 2012 [1972]).

Barnes, Barnabe, *Parthenophil and Parthenophe*, ed. Victor A. Doyno (Carbondale: Southern Illinois University Press, 1971).

—— *Parthenophil and Parthenophe: Sonnettes, Madrigals, Elegies and Odes* (London: John Wolfe, 1593).

Barnfield, Richard, *The Affectionate Shepheard* (London: John Danger for T. G[ubbin] and E. N[ewman], 1594).

—— *The Complete Poems*, ed. George Klawitter (Selinsgrove: Susquehanna University Press, 1990).

Baron, Robert, *Mirza a Tragedie* (London: Humphrey Moseley, 1647?).

Beaumont, Francis and John Fletcher, *The Dramatic Works in the Beaumont and Fletcher Canon*, ed. Fredson Bowers, 10 vols (Cambridge: Cambridge University Press, 2008).

Boccaccio, Giovanni, *Famous Women*, trans. and ed. Virginia Brown (Cambridge, MA: Harvard University Press, 2001). See also Parker, *Forty-Six Lives*.

—— *[Genealogia deorum gentilium] Joannis Boccatii ... deorum libri quindecim cum annotationibus Jacobi Micylli* (Basel: Johann Herwagen, 1532).

Caius, John, *De antiquitate Cantebrigiensis Academiae ...* [1568], in *Three Books of Polydore Vergil's English History*, trans. and ed. Sir Henry Ellis (London: Camden Society, 1844).

Calamy, Edmund, *An Indictment against England because of Her Selfe-Murdering Divisions* (London: I. L., 1645).

Calepino, Ambrogio, *Dictionarium* (Rhegii Lingobardiae [Reggio]: Dionysius Bertochus, 1502).

Caxton, William, *Caxton's 'Eneydos' (1490): Englished from the French 'Livre des Eneydes' (1483)*, ed. W. T. Culley and F. J. Furnivall (London: Oxford University Press, 1962 [1890]).

—— *The History of Jason* [1477], ed. John Munro (London: Early English Text Society, 1913).

—— *The Recuyell of the Historyes of Troye* (Bruges: Caxton, 1473/74).

Chapman, George, *Chapman's Homer*, ed. Allardyce Nicoll (Princeton: Princeton University Press, 1998 [1956]).

—— *The Crowne of All Homers Workes* (London: John Bill, 1624).

—— *The Whole Works of Homer; Prince of Poetts: In His Iliads, and Odysses. Translated According to the Greeke ...* (London: Nathaniell Butter, 1616).

Chaucer, Geoffrey, *The Boke of Fame Made by Geffray Chaucer: With Dyvers Other of His Workes*, ed. Richard Pynson (London: Richard Pynson, 1526).
—— *The Riverside Chaucer*, ed. Larry Benson (Boston, MA: Houghton Mifflin, 1987).
—— *The Woorkes of Geffrey Chaucer, Newly Printed, with Divers Addicions ... with the Siege and Destruccion of the Worthy Citee of Thebes, Compiled by Jhon Lidgate ...*, ed. John Stow (London: John Wight, 1561).
Christine de Pizan, *The Boke of the Cyte of Ladyes by Christine de Pizan Translated by Brian Anslay [1521]*, trans. Brian Anslay, ed. Hope Johnston (Tempe: Arizona Center for Medieval and Renaissance Studies, 2014).
—— *The Book of the City of Ladies [1404/05]*, trans. Rosalind Brown-Grant (London: Penguin, 1999).
—— *Christine de Pizan in English Print, 1478–1549*, ed. Anne E. B. Coldiron, MHRA Tudor and Stuart Translations, 6 (London: MHRA, 2015).
Coke, John, *The Debate between the Heraldes of England and France [1550]*, in *Le Débat des hérauts d'armes de France et d'Angleterre*, ed. L. C. A. Pannier and Paul Meyer (Paris: Firmin Didot, 1877).
Colluthus, *Helenae raptus*, trans. and ed. Michael Neander (Basel: J. Oporin, 1559).
Colonna, Francesco, *Hypnerotomachia: The Strife of Love in a Dreame* (London: Simon Waterson, 1592).
Colonne, Guido delle, *Historia destructionis Troiae*, ed. Nathaniel Edward Griffin (Cambridge, MA: Mediaeval Academy of America, 1936).
Conti, Natale, *Mythologia*, trans. John Mulryan and Steven Brown, 2 vols (Tempe: Arizona Center for Medieval and Renaissance Studies, 2006).
Cooper, Thomas, *Thesaurus linguae Romanae et Britannicae* (London: Berthelet, 1565).
Craig, Alexander, *The Amorose Songes, Sonets, and Elegies* (London: William White, 1606).
Daniel, Samuel, *The Vision of the .12 Goddesses Presented in a Maske the .8 of January, at Hampton Court* (London: Simon Waterson, 1604).
Desrey, Pierre, *Les Croniques de France* (Paris: Galiot du Pré, 1515).
Drant, Thomas, *Horace His Art of Poetrie, Pistles and Satyrs Englished and to the Earl of Ormounte by Tho. Drant Addressed* (London: Thomas Marshe, 1567).
Drayton, Michael, *Idea in Sixtie Three Sonnets* [1605], in *Elizabethan Sonnets*, ed. Maurice Evans (London: Everyman, 1994 [1977]).
Du Souhait, Sieur, *L'Iliade d'Homere ... ensemble le Ravissement d'Helene* (Paris: Pierre Chevalier, 1620).
Elyot, Thomas, *The Dictionary of Syr Thomas Elyot Knyght* (London: Thomas Berthelet, 1538).
Eobanus Hessus, Helius, *Coluthi ... De raptu Helenes ... Epithalamion Helenes ex Theocrito. Moschi Amor fugitivus* (Erfurt: Melchior I Sachse, 1534).
Euripides, *Plays*, trans. and ed. David Kovacs, 6 vols (Cambridge, MA: Harvard University Press, 1994–2002).
Fabyan, Robert, *The New Chronicles of England and France, in Two Parts; by R. F. [1516]*, ed. Henry Ellis (London: Rivington, 1811).

Feylde, Thomas, *Contraversye bytwene a Lover and a Jaye* (London: Wynkyn de Worde, 1527).
Flaccus, Valerius, *Argonautica*, trans. J. H. Mozley (London: Heinemann, 1934).
Florio, John, *A Worlde of Wordes* (London: Edward Blount, 1598).
Foxe, John, *Actes and Monuments* (London: John Day, 1563).
Fraunce, Abraham, *The Third Part of the Countesse of Pembrokes Yvychurch: Entituled Amintas Dale* (London: Thomas Woodcocke, 1592).
—— *The Lamentations of Amyntas* (London: John Wolfe for Thomas Newman and Thomas Gubbin, 1587).
Garnier, Robert, *Marc Antoine, Hippolyte*, ed. Raymond Lebègue (Paris: Les Belles Lettres, 1974).
Geoffrey of Monmouth, *The History of the Kings of Britain [Historia regum Britanniae]*, trans. and intr. Lewis Thorpe (Harmondsworth: Penguin, 1966).
Gilles, Nicole, *Les Croniques et annales de France, depuis la destruction de Troye ...*, Vol. I (Paris: Gabriel Buon, 1566).
Gosynhyll, Edward, *Lytle Boke Named the Schole House of Women ...* (London: Thomas Petyt, 1541).
Greene, Robert, *Pandosto* (London: Thomas Cadman, 1588).
Greville, Fulke, *Poems and Dramas of Fulke Greville, First Lord Brooke*, ed. Geoffrey Bullough, 2 vols (London: Oliver and Boyd, 1939?).
Hall, Edward, *The Union of the Two Noble and Illustre Famelies of Lancastre and Yorke. Hall's Chronicle*, ed. Henry Ellis (London: J. Johnson, 1809).
Harrison, William, *The Description of England*, ed. Georges Edelen (Washington: Folger Shakespeare Library; New York: Dover Publications, 1994 [1968]).
Herrick, Robert, *Hesperides; or, The Works Both Humane & Divine of Robert Herrick, Esquire* (London: John Williams, 1648).
Heywood, Jasper, *Troades* [1559], in *Seneca His Tenne Tragedies, Translated into English*, ed. Thomas Newton (London: Thomas Marsh, 1581).
Heywood, Thomas *The First and Second Parts of King Edward IV*, ed. Richard Rowland (Manchester: Manchester University Press, 2005).
—— [*The Ages*] *The Golden Age, The Silver Age, The Brazen Age*, and Parts I and II of *The Iron Age*, Vol. III of *The Dramatic Works of Thomas Heywood*, 6 vols (London: John Pearson, 1874; repr. New York: Russell and Russell, 1964).
—— *Love's Mistress; or, The Queen's Masque*, ed. Raymond Shady (Salzburg: Institut für Englische Sprache und Literatur, 1977).
—— *Thomas Heywood's 'Art of Love': The First Complete English Translation of Ovid's 'Ars amatoria'* [London, 1598], ed. M. L. Stapleton (Ann Arbor: University of Michigan Press, 2000).
—— *Troia Britanica* (London: W. Jaggard, 1609).
—— *Troia Britanica*, ed. Yves Peyré et al., *Troia Britanica*, Cantos I–XVII (2009–19), www.shakmyth.org.
Holinshed, Raphael, *The First and Second Volumes of Chronicles* (London: Henry Denham, 1587).

―― *The Firste Volume of the Chronicles of England, Scotland and Ireland*, 2 vols (London: Henry Bynneman, 1577).

[Homer], *Batrachomyomachia* (Basel: J. Froben, 1518).

Homer, *Homeri poemata duo, Ilias et Odyssea, sive Ulyssea. Alia item carmina ejusdem* ([Geneva]: [Henri II Estienne], 1588).

―― *Iliad*, trans. A. T. Murray and William F. Wyatt, 2nd edn, 2 vols (Cambridge, MA: Harvard University Press, 1999 [1924–25]).

―― *Ilias et Odyssea. Secunda editio*, ed. Franciscus Portus ([Geneva]: J. Crispinus, 1570).

―― *Odyssey*, trans. A. T. Murray and George E. Dimock, rev. and corr. edn, 2 vols (Cambridge, MA: Harvard University Press, 1998 [1919]).

Homer et al., Οἱ τῆς ἡρωϊκῆς ποιήσεως πρωτεύοντες ποιηταί, ed. Henri Estienne ([Geneva]: H. Estienne, 1566).

Horace, *All the Odes and Epodes of Horace*, trans. Henry Rider (London: John Haviland, 1638).

―― *Q. Horatii Flacci Venusini, poetae lyrici, poëmata omnia doctossimis scholiis illustrate* (London: [J. Kingston], 1574).

Hyginus, *The Myths of Hyginus*, trans. Mary Grant (Lawrence: University of Kansas Press, 1960).

Jonson, Ben, *The Complete Masques*, ed. Stephen Orgel (New Haven: Yale University Press, 1969).

Junius, Franciscus [Francis Du Jon], *The Painting of the Ancients, in Three Bookes ...* (London: Richard Hodgkinsonne, 1638).

Juvénal des Ursins, Jean, *Ecrits politiques de Jean Juvénal des Ursins*, ed. Peter S. Lewis (Paris: Klincksieck, 1978).

La Badessa, Paolo, *Il rapimento di Helena* (Messina: heir of Petruccio Spira, 1571).

Lefèvre, Raoul, *L'Histoire de Jason: Ein Roman aus dem fünfzehnten Jahrhundert* [c. 1464], ed. Gert Pinkernell (Frankfurt: Athenäum Verlag, 1971).

―― *Le Recoeil des hystoires de Troyes* [Ghent?: David Aubert? for William Caxton?, c. 1474/75].

Linche, Richard, *Diella*, in *Elizabethan Sonnets*, ed. Sidney Lee, 2 vols (Westminster: Constable, 1904), Vol. II, pp. 297–320.

Lodge, Thomas, *Phillis, Honoured with Pastorall Sonnets, Elegies and Amorous Delights*, in *Elizabethan Sonnets*, ed. Sidney Lee, 2 vols (Westminster: Constable, 1904), Vol. II, pp. 1–22.

―― *Scillaes Metamorphosis* [1589/90], in *Elizabethan Narrative Verse*, ed. Nigel Alexander (London: Edward Arnold, 1967), pp. 33–55.

―― *The Wounds of Civil War*, ed. Joseph W. Houppert (London: Edward Arnold, 1970).

Lucan, *M. Annaei Lucani, De bello civili, libri decem argumentis illustrati ...* (London: George Bishop, 1589).

Lumley, Lady Jane, *Iphigenia in Aulis* [c. 1550–53], in *Three Tragedies by Renaissance Women*, ed. Diane Purkiss (Harmondsworth: Penguin, 1998).

Lydgate, John, *The Fall of Princes*, ed. Henry Bergen (Washington: Carnegie Institute of Washington, 1923).

Lydgate, John, *Troy Book*, ed. Henry Bergen (London: Early English Text Society, 1906–35).

Lyly, John, *Campaspe and Sappho and Phao: John Lyly*, ed. George K. Hunter and David Bevington (Manchester: Manchester University Press, 1991).

Linch, Richard, *An Historical Treatise of the Travels of Noah unto Europe: Containing the First Inhabitation and People Thereof ... Even until the First Building of Troy by Dardanus* (London: Adam Islip, 1601).

Malipiero, Federico, *L'Iliada d'Omero ... il Ratto d'Elena* (Venice: Paolo Baglioni, 1642).

Marlowe, Christopher, *The Collected Poems*, ed. Patrick Cheney and Brian J. Striar (Oxford: Oxford University Press, 2006).

—— *Dido Queen of Carthage and The Massacre at Paris*, ed. H. J. Oliver (London: Methuen, 1968).

—— *Doctor Faustus: A- and B-Texts (1604, 1616)*, ed. David Bevington and Eric Rasmussen (Manchester: Manchester University Press, 1993).

—— *The Jew of Malta*, ed. N. W. Bawcutt (Manchester: Manchester University Press, 1990).

—— *Tamberlaine the Great*, ed. J. S. Cunningham (Manchester: Manchester University Press, 1981).

Marston, John, *The Metamorphosis of Pigmalions Image* [1598], in *The Poems of John Marston*, ed. Arnold Davenport (Liverpool: Liverpool University Press, 1961).

Melanchthon, *Opera omnia*, ed. K. G. Bretschneider and H. E. Bindseil, 28 vols (Halle an der Saale/Braunschweig: C. A. Schwetschke, 1834–60), Vol. XI.

More, Edward, *A Lytle and Bryefe Treatyse, Called the Defence of Women ... Made agaynst the Schole Howse of Women* (London: John Kynge, 1560).

Moschus, *Idyll II*, in *Theocriti aliorumque poetarum idyllia* ... (Paris: Henri Estienne, 1579).

—— *Theocritus. Moschus. Bion*, ed. and trans. Neil Hopkinson (Cambridge, MA: Harvard University Press, 2015).

Musaeus, Ποιημάτιον τὰ καθ' ἡρώ καὶ Λέανδρον (Venice: Aldus Manutius, 1495–97).

Nash, Thomas, 'To the gentlemen students of both universities', in Robert Greene, *Menaphon* (London: T[homas] O[rwin] for Sampson Clarke, 1589), sigs **r–A3r.

North, Thomas, *The Lives of the Noble Grecians and Romanes Compared Together by That Grave Learned Philosopher and Historiographer, Plutarke of Chaeronea; Translated out of Greeke into French by James Amyot ...* (London: Thomas Vautroullier and John Wight, 1579).

Ovid, *Ars amatoria and Other Poems*, trans. J. H. Mozley, rev. G. P. Goold (London: William Heinemann, 1979 [1939]).

—— *Fasti*, trans. James George Frazer (London: William Heinemann, 1931).

—— *The .xv. Bookes of P. Ovidius Naso, Entytuled Metamorphosis ...*, trans. Arthur Golding, facsimile of the 1567 edition, ed. W. H. D. Rouse (London: Centaur Press, 1961).

―― *Heroides and Amores*, trans. Grant Showerman, rev. G. P. Goold (Cambridge, MA: Heinemann, 1977 [1914]). See also Turberville, *Heroycall Epistles*, and Marlowe, *The Collected Poems*.

―― *The Heroycall Epistles of the Learned Poet Publius Ouidius Naso*, trans. George Turberville (London: Henry Denham, 1567).

―― *Metamorphoses*, trans. Frank Justus Miller, rev. G. P. Goold, 2 vols (Cambridge, MA: Harvard University Press, 1977 [1916]). See also Golding, *The .xv. Bookes of P. Ovidius Naso*.

―― *Ovid's Metamorphoses*, trans. Arthur Golding, ed. Madeleine Forey (London: Penguin, 2002).

―― *The Three First Bookes of Ovid de Tristibus Translated into English*, trans. Thomas Churchyard (London: Thomas Marsh, 1580 [1572]).

―― *Tristia*, trans. A. L. Wheeler, rev. G. P. Goold (Cambridge, MA: Heinemann, 1988). See also Ovid, *Ovid de Tristibus*, trans. Churchyard.

Parker, Henry, *Forty-Six Lives Translated from Boccaccio's 'De claris mulieribus' by Henry Parker, Lord Morley*, ed. Herbert G. Wright, Early English Text Society, OS 214 (Oxford: Oxford University Press, 1970 [1943]).

Rainolds, John and William Gager, *Th'Overthrow of Stage-Playes* (Middleburgh: R. Schilders, 1599).

Robinson, Richard, *The Rewarde of Wickednesse* (London: William Williamson, 1574).

Ronsard, Pierre de, *Œuvres complètes*, ed. Jean Céard, Daniel Ménager and Michel Simonin, 2 vols (Paris: Gallimard, 1993).

―― *Selected Poems*, trans. Malcolm Quainton and Elizabeth Vinestock (London: Penguin, 2002).

Sandys, George, *Ovid's Metamorphosis Englished, Mythologiz'd and Represented in Figures [1632]*, ed. Karl K. Hulley and Stanley T. Vandersall (Lincoln: University of Nebraska Press, 1970).

Scaliger, Julius Caesar, *Poetices libri septem*, ed. Luc Deitz, G. Vogt-Spira and M. Fuhrmann, 5 vols (Stuttgart–Bad Cannstatt: Frommann–Holzboog, 1994–2003).

Seneca, *Hippolytus*, in Seneca, *Seneca His Tenne Tragedies, Translated into Englysh*, ed. Thomas Newton (London: Thomas Marsh, 1581).

―― *Medea*, in Seneca, *Seneca His Tenne Tragedies, Translated into Englysh*, trans. John Studley, ed. Thomas Newton (London: Thomas Marsh, 1581).

―― *Seneca His Tenne Tragedies, Translated into Englysh*, trans. John Studley, ed. Thomas Newton (London: Thomas Marsh, 1581).

―― *Tragedies*, trans. Frank Justus Miller (Cambridge, MA: Harvard University Press, 1998 [1917]).

Shakespeare, William, *The Complete Works*, in *The Riverside Shakespeare*, gen. ed. G. Blakemore Evans with J. J. M. Tobin *et al.*, 2nd edn (Boston, MA and New York: Houghton Mifflin, 1997).

Sherburne, E., *Salmacis ... The Rape of Helen, a Comment Thereon* (London: W. Hunt for T. Dring, 1651).

Shirley, James, *The Dramatic Works and Poems of James Shirley*, ed. W. Gifford and A. Dyce, Vol. VI (New York: Russell & Russell, 1966).

Sidney, Philip, *Astrophil and Stella; the Poems*, ed. W. A. Ringler, Jr (Oxford: Clarendon Press, 1962).

Sidney Herbert, Mary, *The Collected Works of Mary Sidney Herbert Countess of Pembroke*, ed. Margaret P. Hannay, Noel J. Kinnamon and Michael J. Brennan, 2 vols (Oxford: Clarendon Press, 1998).

Spenser, Edmund, *The Faerie Queene*, ed. A. C. Hamilton (London: Longman, 1977).

Sponde, Jean de (ed.), *Homeri quae extant omnia*, 2 vols (Basel: E. Episcopius, 1583).

Statius, *Achilleid*, in *Statii Sylvae ..., Thebais ..., Achilleis cum Maturantii commentariis* (Venice: Bartholomaeus de Zanis, 1494).

Tasso, Torquato, *Gerusalemme liberata* (Parma: Erasmo Viotti, 1581).

Thornborough, John, *A Discourse Shewing the Great Happiness that Hath and May Still Accrue to His Majesties Kingdomes of England and Scotland by Re-Uniting Them into One Great Britain* (London: R. H., 1641).

Trussell, John, *The First Rape of Faire Hellen* [1595], in M. A. Shaaber, '*The First Rape of Faire Hellen by John Trussell*', *Shakespeare Quarterly*, 8:4 (1957), 407–48.

Vergil, Polydore, *Anglica historia* [1534], in *Three Books of Polydore Vergil's English History ...*, ed. Sir Henry Ellis (London: Camden Society, 1844).

Virgil, *The Aeneid: A New Prose Translation*, trans. David West (Harmondsworth: Penguin, 1991).

—— *Eclogues, Georgics, Aeneid 1–6 and Aeneid 7–12. Appendix vergiliana*, trans. H. R. Fairclough, rev. G. P. Goold, 2 vols (Cambridge, MA: Harvard University Press, 1999, 2001).

—— *The .xiii. Bookes of Aeneidos*, ed. Thomas Phaer and Thomas Twyne (London: William How, 1584).

Walter, William, *The Spectacle of Lovers* (London: Wynkyn de Worde, 1533?).

Warner, William, *Albions England* (London: George Robinson, 1586).

Watson, Thomas, *Amintae gaudia* (London: William Ponsonby, 1592).

—— *Amyntas* (London: Thomas Marsh, 1585).

—— *Coluthi ... Helenae raptus* (London: John Wolfe, 1586).

—— *The Complete Works*, ed. Dana F. Sutton (2011), www.philological.bham.ac.uk/watson/.

—— *The Hekatompathia or Passionate Centurie of Love* [1582], in *English and Scottish Sonnet Sequences of the Renaissance*, ed. Holger M. Klein, 2 vols, Vol. I (Hildesheim: Georg Olms, 1984).

Whetstone, George, *An Heptameron of Civill Discourses* (London: Richard Jones, 1582).

Secondary sources

Adger Law, Robert, 'The Roman background of *Titus Andronicus*', *Studies in Philology*, 40:2 (1943), 145–53.

Allen, Don Cameron, *Mysteriously Meant: The Rediscovery of Pagan Symbolism and Allegorical Interpretation in the Renaissance* (Baltimore: Johns Hopkins University Press, 1970).

Allen, Walter, 'The epyllion: A chapter in the history of literary criticism', *Transactions and Proceedings of the American Philological Association*, 71 (1940), 1–26.

——— 'The non-existent classical epyllion', *Studies in Philology*, 55 (1958), 515–18.

Armstrong, Guyda, *The English Boccaccio: A History in Books* (Toronto: University of Toronto Press, 2013).

Baldwin, T. W., *William Shakspere's Small Latine and Lesse Greeke*, 2 vols (Urbana: University of Illinois Press, 1944).

Ballestra-Puech, Sylvie, *Métamorphoses d'Arachné: l'artiste en araignée dans la littérature occidentale* (Geneva: Droz, 2006).

Barkan, Leonard, *The Gods Made Flesh: Metamorphosis and the Pursuit of Paganism* (New Haven: Yale University Press, 1986).

Bartillat, Christian de and Alain Roba, *Métamorphoses d'Europe: trente siècles d'iconographie* (Turin: Bartillat, 2000).

Bate, Jonathan, *Shakespeare and Ovid* (Oxford: Clarendon Press, 1993).

Béhar, Roland, '*Musæum ante omnes* ...: la fortune critique de Musée dans la théorie poétique espagnole du *Siglo de Oro*', *e-Spania*, 2015, http://e-spania.revues.org/24615.

Bergeron, David M., *English Civic Pageantry 1558–1642*, 2nd edn (Tempe: Arizona State University Press, 2003 [1971]).

Bernau, Anke, 'Myths of origin and the struggle over nationhood in medieval and early modern England', in Gordon McMullan and David Matthews (eds), *Reading the Medieval in Early Modern England* (Cambridge: Cambridge University Press, 2007), pp. 106–18.

Boffey, Julia, 'Richard Pynson's *Boke of Fame* and the *Letter of Dido*', *Viator*, 19 (1988), 339–54.

Boitani, Piero (ed.), *The European Tragedy of Troilus* (Oxford: Clarendon Press, 1989).

Borris, Kenneth and George Klawitter (eds), *The Affectionate Shepherd: Celebrating Richard Barnfield* (Selinsgrove: Susquehanna University Press, 2001).

Bossuat, Alain, 'Les origines troyennes: leur rôle dans la littérature historique', *Annales de Normandie*, 8:2 (1958), 187–97.

Botley, Paul, *Learning Greek in Western Europe, 1396–1529* (Philadelphia: American Philosophical Society, 2010).

Boutcher, Warren, '"Who taught thee rhetoricke to deceive a maid?": Christopher Marlowe's *Hero and Leander*, Juan Boscán's *Leandro*, and Renaissance vernacular humanism', *Comparative Literature*, 52 (2000), 11–52.

Braden, Gordon, *The Classics and English Renaissance Poetry: Three Case Studies* (New Haven: Yale University Press, 1978).

Brown, Georgia E., *Redefining Elizabethan Literature* (Cambridge: Cambridge University Press, 2004).

Brunel, Pierre, *Dix mythes au féminin* (Paris: Librairie Jean Villeneuve, 1999).

Buckley, Emma, '"Live false Aeneas!" Marlowe's *Dido, Queen of Carthage* and the limits of translation', *Classical Receptions Journal*, 3:2 (2011), 129–47.

Burrow, Colin, 'English Renaissance readers and the *Appendix Vergiliana*', *Proceedings of the Virgil Society*, 26 (2008), 1–16.

——— *Shakespeare and Classical Antiquity* (Oxford: Oxford University Press, 2013).

Bush, Douglas, *Mythology and the Renaissance Tradition in English Poetry*, rev. edn (New York: Norton, 1963).

Butler, George F., 'Frozen with fear: Virgil's *Aeneid* and act 4, scene 1 of Shakespeare's *The Second Part of King Henry VI*', *Philological Quarterly*, 79:2 (2000), 145–52.

Carter, Sarah, 'Early modern intertextuality: post structuralism, narrative systems, and *A Midsummer Night's Dream*', *Literature Compass*, 13:2 (2016), 47–57.

——— *Ovidian Myth and Sexual Deviance in Early Modern English Literature* (New York: Palgrave Macmillan, 2011).

Cave, Terence, *The Cornucopian Text: Problems of Writing in the French Renaissance* (Oxford: Oxford University Press, 1979).

Cerasano, S. P. and Marion Wynne-Davies, *Readings in Renaissance Women's Drama* (London and New York: Routledge, 1998).

Cheney, Patrick, *Marlowe's Counterfeit Profession: Ovid, Spenser, Counter-Nationhood* (Toronto: University of Toronto Press, 1997).

Cheney, Patrick and Philip Hardie (eds), *1558–1660*, Vol. II of David Hopkins and Charles Martindale (gen. eds), *The Oxford History of Classical Reception in English Literature* (Oxford: Oxford University Press, 2015).

Chevallier, Raymond (ed.), *Colloque présence d'Ovide* (Paris: Les Belles Lettres, 1982).

Clark, James G., Franck T. Coulson and Kathryn L. McKinley (eds), *Ovid in the Middle Ages* (Cambridge: Cambridge University Press, 2011).

Clark, Sandra (ed.), *Amorous Rites: Elizabethan Erotic Verse* (London: Everyman, 1994).

Clauss, James J. and Sarah Iles Johnston (eds), *Medea: Essays on Medea in Myth, Literature, Philosophy and Art* (Princeton: Princeton University Press, 1997).

Clay, Jenny Strauss, '*Providus auspex*: Horace's Ode 3.27', *The Classical Journal*, 88:2 (1993), 167–77.

Clinton Woodworth, Dorothea, 'Lavinia: An interpretation', *Transactions and Proceedings of the American Philological Association*, 61 (1930), 175–94.

Coffin, Charlotte, 'An Echo chamber for Narcissus: Mythological rewritings in *Twelfth Night*', *Cahiers élisabéthains*, 66 (2004), 23–8.

——— 'Heywood's *Ages* and Chapman's Homer: Nothing in common?', in Tania Demetriou and Tanya Pollard (eds), *Homer and Greek Tragedy in England's Early Modern Theatres, Classical Receptions Journal*, 9 (2017) (special issue), 55–78.

——— 'L'impertinence du commentaire: de la mythographie à la scène dans l'Angleterre élisabéthaine', *Sillages critiques*, 9 (2009), 9–25.

——— 'The Gods' lasciviousness, or how to deal with it: The plight of early modern mythographers', *Cahiers élisabéthains*, 81 (May 2012), 1–14.

Coldiron, Anne E. B., *Printers without Borders: Translation and Textuality in the Renaissance* (Cambridge: Cambridge University Press, 2015).

Cooper, Helen, *The English Romance in Time: Transforming Motifs from Geoffrey of Monmouth to the Death of Shakespeare* (Oxford: Oxford University Press, 2004).

Cope, Jackson, *The Theater and the Dream: From Metaphor to Form in the Renaissance* (Baltimore: Johns Hopkins University Press, 1973).

Copeland, Rita (ed.), *800–1558*, Vol. I of David Hopkins and Charles Martindale (gen. eds), *The Oxford History of Classical Reception in English Literature* (Oxford: Oxford University Press, 2016).

Crowley, Timothy D., 'Arms and the boy: Marlowe's Aeneas and the parody of imitation in *Dido, Queen of Carthage*', *English Literary Renaissance*, 38:3 (2008), 408–38.

Crumley, J. Clinton, 'Questioning history in *Cymbeline*', *Studies in English Literature, 1500–1900*, 41:2 (2001), 297–316.

Crump, Mary Marjorie, *The Epyllion from Theocritus to Ovid* (Bristol: Bristol Classical Press, 1997 [1931]).

Cunningham, Jack P., 'England's Adam: The short career of the Giant Samothes in English Reformation thought', *Early Modern Literary Studies*, 16:1 (2012), http://extra.shu.ac.uk/emls/16–1/adam.htm.

Deats, Sara Munson and Robert A. Logan (eds), *Marlowe's Empery: Expanding His Cultural Contexts* (Newark: University of Delaware Press, 2002).

Demats, Paule, *Fabula: trois études de mythographie antique et médiévale* (Geneva: Droz, 1973).

Demerson, Guy, *La Mythologie classique dans l'œuvre lyrique de la 'Pléiade'* (Geneva: Droz, 1972).

Demetriou, Tania, '*Periphrōn* Penelope and her early modern translations', in Tania Demetriou and Rowan Tomlinson (eds), *The Culture of Translation in Early Modern England and France, 1500–1660* (Basingstoke: Palgrave Macmillan, 2015), pp. 86–111.

Demetriou, Tania and Tanya Pollard, 'Homer, Greek tragedy, and the early modern stage: An introduction', in Tania Demetriou and Tanya Pollard (eds), *Homer and Greek Tragedy in England's Early Modern Theatres, Classical Receptions Journal*, 9 (2017) (special issue), 1–35.

Desmoulière, Paule, 'Psyché sur la scène anglaise: *Love's Mistress* de Thomas Heywood', *Silène* (2006), www.revue-silene.com.

Dyson, Julia T., 'Lilies and violence: Lavinia's blush in the song of Orpheus', *Classical Philology*, 94:3 (1999), 281–8.

Ellis, Jim, *Sexuality and Citizenship: Metamorphosis in Elizabethan Erotic Verse* (Toronto: University of Toronto Press, 2003).

Enterline, Lynn *The Rhetoric of the Body from Ovid to Shakespeare* (Cambridge: Cambridge University Press, 2000).

——— *Shakespeare's Schoolroom: Rhetoric, Discipline, Emotion* (Philadelphia: University of Pennsylvania Press, 2012).

Ewbank, Inga-Stina, 'The fiend-like queen: A note on *Macbeth* and Seneca's *Medea*', *Shakespeare Survey*, 19 (1966), 82–94.
Felson Rubin, Nancy, *Regarding Penelope from Character to Poetics* (Princeton: Princeton University Press, 1991).
Fowler, D. P., 'Vergil on killing virgins', in Michael Whitby, Philip R. Hardie and Mary Whitby (eds), *Homo viator: Classical Essays for John Bramble* (Bristol: Bristol Classical Press, 1987), pp. 185–98.
Frontisi-Ducroux, Françoise, *L'Homme-cerf et la femme-araignée* (Paris: Gallimard, 2003).
—— *Ouvrages de dames: Ariane, Hélène, Pénélope...* (Paris: Seuil, 2009).
Geisler-Szmulewicz, Anne, *Le Mythe de Pygmalion au XIXe siècle: pour une approche de la coalescence des mythes* (Paris: Champion, 1999).
Gill, Roma, 'Marlowe's Virgil: *Dido Queene of Carthage*', *Review of English Studies*, new series, 28:110 (1977), 141–55.
Ginestet, Gaëlle, 'Les huit Dames d'Alexander Craig (*The Amorose Songes, Sonets and Elegies*, 1606)', in Armel Dubois-Nayt, Pascal Caillet and Jean-Claude Mailhol (eds), *L'Écriture et les femmes en Grande-Bretagne (1540–1640): le mythe et la plume* (Valenciennes: Presses Universitaires de Valenciennes, 2007), pp. 249–60.
Goy-Blanquet, Dominique, 'Des histoires tristes', in Marie-Thérèse Jones-Davies (ed.), *Mythe et histoire: actes du congrès 1983 de la Société française Shakespeare* (Paris: Touzot, 1984), pp. 31–49. Available online at http://shakespeare.revues.org.
—— (ed.), *Le Poète dans la cité: de Platon à Shakespeare* (Brussels: In'hui/Le Cri, 2003).
—— 'Shakespeare, Burgundy, and the design in the arras', in Jean-Christophe Mayer (ed.), *Representing France and the French in Early Modern English Drama* (Newark: Delaware University Press, 2008), pp. 49–67.
Griffith, R. Drew, 'In praise of the bride: Sappho Fr. 105 (A) L-P. Voigt', *Transactions of the American Philological Association*, 119 (1989), 55–61.
Gross, Kenneth, *The Dream of the Moving Statue* (Ithaca, NY: Cornell University Press, 1992).
Haegemans, Karen, 'Elissa, the first queen of Carthage, through Timaeus' eyes', *Ancient Society*, 30 (2000), 277–91.
Hardie, Philip, *Ovid's Poetics of Illusion* (Cambridge: Cambridge University Press, 2002).
Heavey, Katherine, *The Early Modern Medea: Medea in English Literature, 1558–1688* (Basingstoke: Palgrave Macmillan, 2015).
—— 'An infant of the house of York: Medea and Absyrtus in Shakespeare's first tetralogy', *Comparative Drama*, 50:2 (2016), 233–48.
Hersey, George L., *Falling in Love with Statues: Artificial Humans from Pygmalion to the Present* (Chicago: University of Chicago Press, 2006).
Heuzé, Philippe, *L'Image du corps dans l'œuvre de Virgile* (Rome: Ecole française, 1985).
Hirota, Atsuhiko, 'The memory of Hesione: Intertextuality and social amnesia in '*Troilus and Cressida*', *Actes des congrès de la Société française Shakespeare, Shakespeare et la mémoire*, 30 (2013), 43–56.

Select bibliography

Hirrel, Michael J., 'Thomas Watson, playwright: Origins of modern English drama', in David McInnis and Matthew Steggle (eds), *Lost Plays in Shakespeare's England* (Basingstoke: Palgrave Macmillan, 2014), pp. 187–207.

Hulse, Clark, *Metamorphic Verse: The Elizabethan Minor Epic* (Princeton: Princeton University Press, 1981).

Hutton, James, 'The first Idyl of Moschus in imitations to the year 1800', *The American Journal of Philology*, 49:2 (1928), 105–36.

Jack, Ronald D. S., 'The poetry of Alexander Craig: A study in imitation and originality', *Forum for Modern Language Studies*, 5:4 (1969), 377–84.

James, Heather, *Shakespeare's Troy: Drama, Politics and the Translation of Empire* (Cambridge: Cambridge University Press, 1997).

Jamset, Claire, 'Death-loration: The eroticization of death in the *Thebaid*', *Greece & Rome*, 51:1 (2004), 95–104.

Jones-Davies, Marie-Thérèse (ed.), *Les mythes poétiques à la Renaissance* (Paris: Touzot, 1985).

Joshua, Essaka, *Pygmalion and Galatea: The History of a Narrative in English Literature* (Aldershot: Ashgate, 2001).

Katz, Marilyn, *Penelope's Renown: Meaning and Indeterminacy in the 'Odyssey'* (Princeton: Princeton University Press, 1991).

Keith, Alison and Stephen Rupp (eds), *Metamorphosis: The Changing Face of Ovid in Medieval and Early Modern Europe* (Toronto: Centre for Reformation and Renaissance Studies, 2007).

Kingsley-Smith, Jane, *Cupid in Early Modern Literature and Culture* (Cambridge: Cambridge University Press, 2010).

Krier, Theresa M., *Gazing on Secret Sights: Spenser, Classical Imitation, and the Decorums of Vision* (Ithaca, NY: Cornell University Press, 1990).

Kuskin, William, *Recursive Origins: Writing at the Transition to Modernity* (Notre Dame: University of Notre Dame Press, 2013).

Lafont, Agnès, '"Il ne faut pas / Que le bon menestrier accorde / Toujours son chant sur une corde": Shakespeare, Ronsard et la polyphonie', *Actes des congrès de la Société française Shakespeare*, 24 (2007), 213–27. Available online at http://shakespeare.revues.org.

——— 'Métamorphoses burlesques de la *fabula* classique dans le théâtre anglais de la fin de la Renaissance', *Revue de la société d'études anglo-américaines des XVIIe et XVIIIe siècles*, 60 (2005), 25–30.

——— (ed.), *Shakespeare's Erotic Mythology and Ovidian Renaissance Culture* (Aldershot: Ashgate, 2013).

Leclerc, Jean, *L'Antiquité travestie et la vogue du burlesque en France (1643–1661)* (Paris: Hermann, 2014 [2007]).

Lotspeich, Henry Gibbons, *Classical Mythology in the Poetry of Edmund Spenser* (New York: Gordian Press, 1965 [1932]).

Lyne, R. O. A. M., *Further Voices in Vergil's 'Aeneid'* (Oxford: Clarendon Press, 1987).

Lyne, Raphael, *Ovid's Changing Worlds: English 'Metamorphoses' 1567–1632* (Oxford: Oxford University Press, 2001).

Macfie, Pamela Royston, 'Allusion as plunder: Marlowe's *Hero and Leander* and Colluthus's *Rape of Helen*', *Renaissance Papers* (2013), 31–42.

Maguire, Laurie, *Helen of Troy: From Homer to Hollywood* (Chichester: Wiley-Blackwell, 2009).

Martin, René, *Enée et Didon: naissance, fonctionnement et survie d'un mythe* (Paris: CNRS Editions, 1990).

Martindale, Charles (ed.), *Ovid Renewed: Ovidian Influences on Literature and Art from the Middle Ages to the Twentieth Century* (Cambridge: Cambridge University Press, 1988).

Martindale, Charles and Michelle Martindale, *Shakespeare and the Uses of Antiquity* (London: Routledge, 1994 [1990]).

Martindale, Charles and A. B. Taylor (eds), *Shakespeare and the Classics* (Cambridge: Cambridge University Press, 2004).

McAlindon, Thomas, *Shakespeare's Tragic Cosmos* (Cambridge: Cambridge University Press, 1991).

McKinley, Kathryn L., *Reading the Ovidian Heroine: 'Metamorphoses' Commentaries 1100–1618* (Leiden: Brill, 2001).

McLeod, Glenda, *Virtue and Venom: Catalogs of Women from Antiquity to the Renaissance* (Ann Arbor: University of Michigan Press, 1991).

Miller, Joseph Hillis, *Versions of Pygmalion* (Cambridge, MA: Harvard University Press, 1990).

Miller, Paul W., 'The Elizabethan minor epic', *Studies in Philology*, 55 (1958), 31–8.

Miola, Robert S., *Shakespeare and Classical Comedy: The Influence of Plautus and Terence* (Oxford: Clarendon Press, 1994).

—— *Shakespeare and Classical Tragedy: The Influence of Seneca* (Oxford: Clarendon Press, 1992).

Moreau, Alain, *Le mythe de Jason et Médée: le va-nu-pied et la sorcière* (Paris: Les Belles Lettres, 1994).

—— *Shakespeare's Rome* (Cambridge: Cambridge University Press, 1983).

Morris, Harry, 'Richard Barnfield, *Amyntas*, and the Sidney circle', *Proceedings of the Modern Language Association*, 74 (1959), 318–24.

Morse, Ruth, *The Medieval Medea* (Martlesham: D. S. Brewer, 1998).

—— *Truth and Convention in the Middle Ages: Rhetoric, Representation and Reality* (Cambridge: Cambridge University Press, 1991).

Morse, Ruth, Helen Cooper and Peter Holland (eds), *Medieval Shakespeare: Pasts and Presents* (Cambridge: Cambridge University Press, 2013).

Mortimer, Nigel, *John Lydgate's 'Fall of Princes': Narrative Tragedy in Its Literary and Political Contexts* (Oxford: Oxford University Press, 2005).

Newlands, Carole E., *Statius, Poet between Rome and Naples* (London: Bloomsbury, 2012).

Oakley-Brown, Liz, *Ovid and the Cultural Politics of Translation in Early Modern England* (Aldershot: Ashgate, 2006).

Panofsky, Erwin, *Renaissance and Renascences in Western Art* (London: Granada, 1970 [1958]).

Pérez, Ángel Ruíz, 'Historia editorial del *Rapto de Helena* de Coluto', in Ignacio J. García Pinilla and Santiago Talavera Cuesta (eds), *Charisterion Francisco Martín García oblatum* (Cuenca: Universidad de Castilla-La Mancha, 2004), pp. 339–61.

Peters, Julie Stone, *Theatre of the Book, 1480–1880: Print, Text and Performance in Europe* (Oxford: Oxford University Press, 2000).

Peyré, Yves (ed.), *A Dictionary of Shakespeare's Classical Mythology* (2009–), www.shakmyth.org.

—— 'Homeric voices in *Antony and Cleopatra*', in Tania Demetriou and Tanya Pollard (eds), *Homer and Greek Tragedy in England's Early Modern Theatres, Classical Receptions Journal*, 9 (2017) (special issue), 36–54.

—— 'Iris's "rich scarf" and "Ariachne's broken woof": Shakespeare's mythology in the twentieth century', in Jonathan Bate, Jill L. Levenson and Dieter Mehl (eds), *Shakespeare and the Twentieth Century* (Newark: University of Delaware Press, 1998), pp. 280–93.

—— 'Marlowe's Argonauts', in Jean-Pierre Maquerlot and Michèle Willems (eds), *Travel and Drama in Shakespeare's Time* (Cambridge: Cambridge University Press, 1996), pp. 106–23.

—— 'Niobe and the Nemean lion: Reading *Hamlet* in the light of Ovid's *Metamorphoses*', in A. B. Taylor (ed.), *Shakespeare's Ovid: The 'Metamorphoses' in the Plays and Poems* (Cambridge: Cambridge University Press, 2000), pp. 126–34.

—— *La voix des mythes dans la tragédie élisabéthaine* (Paris: CNRS Editions, 1996).

Phillippo, Susanna, '"A future for Astyanax": Alternative and imagined futures for Hector's son in classical and European drama', *International Journal of the Classical Tradition*, 14:3–4 (2007), 317–68.

Pincombe, Michael, *The Plays of John Lyly: Eros and Eliza* (Manchester: Manchester University Press, 1996).

Poignault, Rémy and Odile Wattel-de Croizant (eds), *D'Europe à l'Europe. I. Le mythe d'Europe dans l'art et la culture de l'antiquité au XVIIIe siècle* (Tours: Centre de Recherches A. Piganiol, 1998), pp. 163–72.

Pollard, Tanya, 'Greek playbooks and dramatic forms in early modern England', in Allison K. Deutermann and András Kisery (eds), *Formal Matters: Reading the Materials of English Renaissance Literature* (Manchester: Manchester University Press, 2013), pp. 99–123.

—— 'What's Hecuba to Shakespeare?', *Renaissance Quarterly*, 65:4 (2012), 1060–93.

Poucet, Jacques, 'L'origine troyenne des peuples d'Occident au Moyen Age et à la Renaissance: un exemple de parenté imaginaire et d'idéologie politique', *Les Études classiques*, 72 (2004), 75–107.

Prauscello, Lucia, 'Colluthus' pastoral traditions: Narrative strategies and bucolic criticism in the *Abduction of Helen*', in Katerina Carvounis and Richard Hunter (eds), *Signs of Life? New Contexts for Later Greek Hexameter Poetry, Ramus*, 37 (2008) (special issue), 173–90.

Pugh, Syrithe, *Spenser and Ovid* (London: Routledge, 2005).

Reid, Lindsay Ann, *Ovidian Bibliofictions and the Tudor Book: Metamorphosing Classical Heroines in Late Medieval and Renaissance England* (Burlington: Ashgate, 2014).

Rivère de Carles, Nathalie, '"The chaste Penelope": questionnement d'un modèle mythique', in Armel Dubois-Nayt, Pascal Caillet and Jean-Claude Mailhol (eds), *L'Écriture et les femmes en Grande-Bretagne (1540–1640): le mythe et la plume* (Valenciennes: Presses Universitaires de Valenciennes, 2007), pp. 131–42.

Scammell, J. M., 'The capture of Troy by Heracles', *Classical Journal*, 29:6 (March 1934), 418–28.

Seznec, Jean, *The Survival of the Pagan Gods* (London: Warburg Institute, 1940).

Sklar, Elizabeth S., 'Bassanio's Golden Fleece', *Texas Studies of Literature and Language*, 18 (1976), 500–9.

Smith, Hallet, *Elizabethan Poetry: A Study in Conventions, Meaning, and Expression* (Cambridge, MA: Harvard University Press, 1952).

Stapleton, Michael L., *Marlowe's Ovid: The Elegies in the Marlowe Canon* (Burlington: Ashgate, 2014).

—— *Spenser's Ovidian Poetics* (Newark: Delaware University Press, 2009).

Starnes De Witt, T. and Ernest William Talbert, *Classical Myth and Legend in Renaissance Dictionaries* (Westport: Greenwood Press, 1973 [1955]).

Staton, Walter F., 'The influence of Thomas Watson on Elizabethan Ovidian poetry', *Studies in the Renaissance*, 6 (1959), 243–50.

Staton, Walter F. and Harry Morris, 'Thomas Watson and Abraham Fraunce', *Proceedings of the Modern Language Association*, 76 (1961), 150–3.

Stoichita, Victor I., *The Pygmalion Effect: From Ovid to Hitchcock* (Chicago: University of Chicago Press, 2008).

Tromly, Fred B., *Playing with Desire: Christopher Marlowe and the Art of Tantalization* (Toronto: University Press of Toronto, 1998).

Tudeau-Clayton, Margaret, *Jonson, Shakespeare and Early Modern Virgil* (Cambridge: Cambridge University Press, 1998).

Valls-Russell, Janice, '"As she had some good, so had she many bad parts": Semiramis' transgressive personas'', *Anglophonia*, 29 (2011), 103–17.

—— 'Erotic perspectives: When Pyramus and Thisbe meet Hero and Leander in *Romeo and Juliet*', in Agnès Lafont (ed.), *Shakespeare's Erotic Mythology and Ovidian Renaissance Culture* (Farnham: Ashgate, 2013), pp. 77–90.

Velz, John W., *Shakespeare and the Classical Tradition: A Critical Guide to Commentary 1660–1960* (Minneapolis: University of Minnesota Press, 1968).

Walker, John Lewis, *Shakespeare and the Classical Tradition: An Annotated Bibliography, 1961–1991* (New York: Garland, 2002).

Weaver, William P., *Untutored Lines: The Making of the English Epyllion* (Edinburgh: Edinburgh University Press, 2012).

Weinfield, Henry, '"We are the Jasons, we have won the Fleece": Antonio's plot (and Shakespeare's) in *The Merchant of Venice* (what really happens in the play)', *The European Legacy*, 15 (2010), 149–58.

Williams, Deanne, 'Dido, Queen of England', *English Literary History*, 73:1 (2006), 31–59.

Wilson-Okamura, David Scott, *Virgil in the Renaissance* (Cambridge: Cambridge University Press, 2010).

Wind, Edgar, *Pagan Mysteries in the Renaissance* (London: Faber and Faber, 1968 [1958]).

Wisman, Joelte A., 'Christine de Pizan and Arachne's metamorphoses', *Fifteenth-Century Studies*, 23 (1997), 138–51.

Wofford, Susanne L., *The Choice of Achilles: The Ideology of Figure in the Epic* (Stanford: Stanford University Press, 1992).

Wolfe, Jessica, *Homer and the Question of Strife from Erasmus to Hobbes* (Toronto: University of Toronto Press, 2015).

Wright, George T., *Poetic Craft and Authorial Design in Shakespeare, Keats, T. S. Eliot, and Henry James, with Two Essays on the Pygmalion Legend* (Lewiston: Edwin Mellen, 2011).

Index

This index does not include references in the notes. Illustrations are indicated in bold.

abduction 17, 19, 42, 54, 152, 153–4, 157, 163, 165, 167, 169
Achilles 33–4, 56, 75, 103
Acteon 166
Adonis 31–2, 52, 165, 223
  see also Venus
Aeëtes 17, 110–11, 122, 128, 131, 134, 136–44
Aeneas 11, 13, 18, 27–8, 35, 68–9, 74, 75, 88, 90, 95, 99, 115, 195–210, 243–4
Aeson 116–17, 121
affect 14, 112
  see also Apsyrtus; child; grief
affection 44, 96, 140, 179, 181, 242, 255
Agamemnon 68, 87, 219
Alcides 87
  see also Hercules
Alighieri, Dante 67, 74, 79
allegory 178, 217, 229, 233
ancestry 11, 72–3
  see also Troy
Andromache 16, 86–7, 90, 93–6, 99–103
Anslay, Brian 10, 178, 198
antimasque 229–32
  see also masque(s)
Antony 13, 34–5
anxieties 17, 133, 141–2, 176
Aphrodite 45–6, 52, 55
  see also Venus

Apollo 26, 29, 165–6, 168, 187, 216–17, 219–20, 225, 230–1, 252
Apollonius Rhodius 110, 129, 133
Appian 4, 7
Apsyrtus 17, 117, 128–38, 142–4
Apuleius 18, 216–18, 220, 222–6, 229–30, 232–3
Arachne 1–2, 18, 30, 111, 155, 158–9, 165, 173–8, 183–8, 190
arbitration 218, 224–6
Argonauts 69, 111, 113, 128, 137, 166
Ariachne 1–2, 189
Ariadne 1–2, 195, 201
Aristotle 18, 50–1, 173–5, 185, 188, 255
Ascanius 68, 95, 205–8
Astyanax 16, 86, 90, 93–5, 99–103
Aurora 30, 31, 42, 58–9
Ausonius 4, 8

Barnes, Barnabe
  Parthenophil and Parthenophe 158, 161
Barnfield, Richard
  Affectionate Shepherd 44, 48–9
  Hellens Rape 41–7, 52, 54–5
Baron, Robert
  Mirza 139–40, 141–4 *passim*
Battle of the Frogs and Mice (*Batrachyomachia*) 49–52
beauty 26, 29, 33, 95, 156, 158, 160, 164, 166, 204, 209, 217–18, 249–50

bed-trick 189–90
Benoît de Sainte-Maure 10, 69
Bersuire, Pierre 248
Bible 115, 121, 245
blood 6–8, 26–9, 32–4, 65, 68–70, 74, 78, 87, 90–2, 120–1, 130, 134–5, 138, 144, 207, 225
blushing 15, 26–34 *passim*, 58, 247
Boccaccio, Giovanni 2, 3, 10, 111, 131, 157, 160, 176–8, 198–9, 202, 207
book
  as son 128–9, 142–4
  trade 5, 13–14, 198–9
Boscán, Juan 4, 49
boy actors 18, 195, 197, 205–6
Bracciolini, Francesco 222
bride 26, 154, 251
Briseis 2
Britain 16, 19, 70–4, 77–8, 87
brother 129–36
brotherhood 69, 131
Brutus (Aeneas's grandson) 65, 68–9, 72–4, 88
burlesque 18, 44, 204, 216, 214, 226, 228, 230, 233

Callimachus 47
Calypso 187
Carroll, Tim 205
Carthage 195, 201, 208, 243–4
  see also Dido
Cassandra 90, 93, 96–7
Catullus 25, 47
Caxton, William 10, 12, 69, 143
  Eneydos 18, 198, 199
  History of Jason 17, 133, 137–42 *passim*
  Recuyell of the Historyes of Troye 10, 12, 88
Chapman, George 12, 50, 222, 228
Charles I 141, 189, 216–17, 225, 230
chastity 75, 163, 167, 176–7, 180–1, 186, 209
Chaucer, Geoffrey 2, 10, 17, 198–202 *passim*, 246, 248
  Boke of Fame 200–1
  Canterbury Tales 198

House of Fame 198
Legend of Good Women 18, 198
Troilus and Criseyde 12, 163
child 17, 76, 89, 93–5, 98–104, 129, 131, 137, 140, 142–3, 167, 206, 251
children 19, 50, 68, 92–3, 103, 130–1, 135, 205, 223, 252
chorus 13, 76, 101, 103, 217, 220, 223–4, 226–8, 230, 232
chronicle(s) 5, 6, 8, 10, 72, 77, 88–9, 102–3
Chryseis 2
Churchyard, Thomas 17, 136
Circe 187
Cleopatra 13, 34–5, 78
Clovis 66, 70–1
Clown (*Love's Mistress*) 216–17, 219, 222–3, 226, 228
coercion 92, 152, 164–5
Colchis 110–12, 116, 122, 130–1, 135, 137–9, 144, 166
Colluthus
  Abduction of Helen 4, 8, 16, 44–7, 49–50, 52–5
competition 14, 16, 66, 217, 219, 250
conquest 16, 18, 65–6, 73, 76–7, 79, 112, 128, 152, 158, 169
Constance 17, 86–104
consummation 55, 162, 168, 251
Conti, Natale 3–4, 163
Cooper, Thomas 28, 157
courtiers 18, 89, 103, 217, 232, 244, 253
courtship 76, 154, 164–5, 167
Craig, Alexander 163, 168
Creon 111, 134–5
Cressida 1–2, 12, 115
  see also Shakespeare, *Troilus and Cressida*
Creusa 26, 111, 134
Cupid 8, 34, 52, 56, 149, 158, 162, 196, 198, 204–8, 219–20, 230
  and Psyche 18, 216–20, 224, 227

Danae 151, 158–9, 160–2, 227–8
Daniel, Samuel 5, 13
Daphne 31, 165
Dares the Phrygian 10

Index

daughter 27, 33, 93, 99, 110–11, 116–19 passim, 122, 131–2, 137–40, 142, 145, 153, 156, 164, 166, 187, 204, 244, 253–5 passim
Deidamia 33–4
Dekker, Thomas 11
desire 3, 4, 18, 26, 27, 29–36, 46, 55–7, 73, 110–11, 129–31, 140, 144, 151, 154, 157, 159, 166, 168–9, 187, 200, 203–6, 242, 246–7, 249, 251–2, 254–5
Diana 158, 161, 166, 208–10
Dido 13, 18, 28, 115, 195–210, 243–5
Dionysius of Halicarnassus 68
disguise 7, 30, 34, 78, 116–17, 155, 161, 166, 180, 182, 186, 189, 205, 221, 227, 250
dismemberment 74, 95, 100, 117–18, 128–9, 131, 135–7, 142–4
disobedience 18, 175–6, 186
Distaff Gospels 176
Doran, Gregory 86, 90, 92–3
Du Bellay, Joachim 200

Edward's Boys 195–6, 198, 205
Edwards, Thomas 47
Egypt 13, 42
Elizabeth I 74–5, 88, 103, 163
emotions 17, 30, 32, 99, 102, 142, 145, 168, 217
empathy 99, 157
empire 16, 27, 65, 67–8, 70, 74, 79
England
   classical reception in 49–50, 76–7, 89–91, 109, 216, 221–2
   early modern 4–6, 11, 13, 17, 77, 98, 112–14, 119, 188–9
   and France 70–2, 74
   history of 5, 65–7
   medieval 16, 248
   and Troy 11, 70–1, 74, 78–9, 88
   see also Troy
epic 11–12, 14–16, 20, 25, 27–8, 33–4, 41–54, 56–8, 66, 88, 99, 195–6, 199, 206, 210, 221, 227–8

epyllion 15–17, 41–59 passim, 153, 195, 242
Erasmus 5, 93, 100–1, 184–5
eroticism 29, 52, 161
Euripides 4, 11, 17, 68, 90, 93–8 passim, 100, 102, 111, 129, 133–5
Europa 8, 17, 149–69
exemplariness 93, 110

family 19, 65–8, 70, 87, 89, 95, 130, 134, 140, 144, 149, 182, 252, 253–4
father(s) 27, 44, 56, 65, 76, 94–6, 99–102, 111, 116–18, 121–2, 128–44, 154, 167, 189, 205, 220, 246, 250–1
Feylde, Thomas 18, 200
fire 28, 32, 35, 162, 165, 187, 206–7, 253
Fletcher, John *et al.*
   The Honest Man's Fortune 175, 180–2
Flora 166–7
Florio, John 28, 244
France 9, 13, 16, 18, 65–7, 69–71, 74, 76, 88, 218, 220–1
   see also England
Franks 68–71
fratricide 67, 128–44
Fraunce, Abraham 4, 43–4, 49, 53

Gager, William 49, 179, 188, 206
Gaguin, Robert 71–2
Galatea
   in Horace 154, 167
   in Ovid 188, 240
Ganymede 195, 197, 204–6
Garnier, Robert 12–13
gender 3, 17, 19, 27, 34, 36, 130, 142, 173, 178, 182, 189, 210, 223
genealogy 2, 10–11, 72, 76, 86, 88, 104
Geoffrey of Monmouth 10–11, 69–71, 73
Giles, David 86, 98
Golden Fleece 17, 109–23, 129, 134, 166
   Order of 69, 109
Golding, Arthur 156–7, 166–7, 247
Greece 41, 50, 68, 113, 130
Greene, Robert 165
Greville, Fulke 13, 169

Index

grief 17, 19, 29, 75, 89, 93–9, 128, 134, 136–44, 219, 223, 256
  see also mourning
Griselda (Grissel) 165
Guido delle Colonne 10

hair 2, 7, 31, 45, 53, 94, 96–7, 109–12, 139
Hall, Edward 76
Harrison, William 72–3
Hecate 121, 162
Hector 69, 75, 92–103
Hecuba 11, 75, 90, 93, 95–9, 102
Helen (of Troy) 4, 8, 16, 41–50, 54, 59, 219
Henrietta Maria (Queen) 14, 18, 216–18, 222, 230
Henry V 66, 70, 76–7
Henry VIII 67, 74, 176–7
Henryson, Robert 2, 12
Hercules 33–5, 75, 87–8, 137
  see also Alcides
Hermaphroditus 15, 26, 31–2, 36
Hero (and Leander) 55–8
  see also Marlowe, *Hero and Leander*; Musaeus (Mousaios)
hero 69, 88, 109, 111, 113, 196, 222
heroine 12, 27, 75, 198, 200–2, 203
Herrick, Robert 17, 128–9, 141–4
Hesione (Hesyone) 41, 74
Heywood, Jasper 17, 86, 93–101
Heywood, Thomas 3, 10, 12, 14, 17–18, 47, 88–90, 113, 216–38
  1 Edward IV 89–90
  Brazen Age 131–3, 228
  Golden Age 227
  Iron Age 228
  Love's Mistress 14, 18, 216–33
  Oenone and Paris 47
  Troia Britanica 10, 88, 113
hierarchy 130, 175, 183
historiography 72–3, 76, 88
history 2–20, 65–79, 86–8, 91, 102–3, 113, 128, 216, 221, 240, 245, 248, 253

Homer 4, 8, 11, 15–17, 21, 25, 29–30, 42, 46, 49–50, 52, 57, 68–9, 75, 90–1, 93, 96, 102, 173–4, 176–83, 187–8, 222, 228
Horace 4, 17–18, 152, 154–6, 158, 165, 167
humanist 3, 9, 195–6, 223
hunt 197, 208–10
Hyginus 166
Hypsipyle 111, 131

Iarbas 196–7, 206–8
infanticide 128, 132
Io 165
Italy 9, 13, 19, 77, 248

Jacob 114–16, 122
Jason 17, 69, 109–23, 128–35, 137, 139, 142, 144
Jesus Christ 4, 120, 122
Jonson, Ben 230–1
judge 224–5, 242
judgement 45–6, 50, 54, 65, 204, 224–6, 233
Jupiter 7, 17, 19, 67–8, 86, 91, 149, 151–69, 187, 195, 197, 204–6, 227–8, 231
justice 76–8, 188, 241

kiss(es)/kissing 43, 55, 138, 154, 161, 163–4, 197, 206–7, 248, 250
Kyd, Thomas 12

Laban 114–15
Lalli, Battista 222
lamentation(s) 13, 52, 96–8, 103, 154, 219
Lavinia (*Aeneid*) 27–9, 31, 33, 58, 68
Leander 55–8
  see also Marlowe, *Hero and Leander*; Musaeus (Mousaios)
Leda 151, 159
Lefèvre, Raoul 10, 69, 88, 133, 137
legitimacy 11, 67, 77, 91, 98, 104, 244
Lemaire de Belges, Jean 70, 72
lineage 87, 117
  see also Troy

Livy 67–8, 75
Lodge, Thomas 7, 47, 88, 159–62, 168
love poetry 149, 164, 166, 169, 197
love-shaft 197, 207–8
Lucan 4, 6, 8, 195
Lucian 4
Lucrece 19, 32, 75, 165, 177
lust 27, 32, 34–5, 41, 45, 156–7, 162–7, 182, 186, 205, 246
Luther, Martin 140
Luzvic, Stephanus 4
Lydgate, John 70, 131–2, 136, 143, 196
Lyly, John 12, 174, 185

magic 46, 113, 121, 162, 250, 252
Marlowe, Christopher 3–4, 6–8, 11, 12, 15–16, 18, 30, 41, 43, 47–9, 53, 55–9, 113, 195–210, 242
  1 Tamburlaine 7
  Dido, Queen of Carthage 11, 18, 195–210
  Doctor Faustus 113
  Edward II 205
  Hero and Leander 4, 14–16, 43, 47–8, 55–9, 195
Marot, Clément 49
marriage 27–8, 45, 54, 58, 66, 68–9, 73, 78–9, 122, 134, 154, 164–5, 167–8, 180, 182, 203, 218, 241–2, 244, 251, 253
Marston, John 12, 242
  Metamorphosis of Pigmalions Image 48
Martinus Crusius 51, 57
masque(s) 5, 14, 143, 218, 227, 229–33
  see also antimasque
Medea 8, 17, 27, 110–23, 128–45, 177, 195
  see also Seneca, *Medea*
Menelaus 29, 41–3, 54, 219
Mercury 48, 54, 86, 197, 205, 217, 220, 225
Michelangelo 206
Midas 217, 220, 223–33
Mills, Perry 195
Milton, John 255
Minerva 175–6, 179
misogynist 245

misogyny 12, 122–3, 145, 197, 199, 245–6, 249
monarchy 66, 69, 74, 76–7, 88, 104, 129
Montaigne, Michel de 31, 69, 244
moralisation 45, 132, 157, 173–4, 176–8 *passim*, 190, 242–3
  see also Ovide moralisé
More, Edward 200
Moschus 17–18, 152–64
mother(s) 6–7, 17, 27–8, 33–4, 67, 87, 89, 93, 97–101, 132, 136, 141, 175, 206–7
mourning 13, 93–4, 96, 100, 103, 136, 138–9, 140–2, 144
  see also grief
Musaeus (Mousaios) 4, 8, 14, 47–52, 55–7
My Fair Lady (Lerner and Loewe) 254
mythographies 3, 18, 173–8, 175, 182–3, 186, 188, 199

nakedness 57–8, 91, 149, 162
Narcissus 4, 15, 26, 47, 159–61
Nausicaa 56–7
Neander, Michael 44–5, 50
Neptune 57, 87–8, 165–6, 187
Nestor 42, 75
Noah 70, 72
North, Thomas 13, 35

Odysseus 43, 56–7
  see also Ulysses
Omphale 33–5, 87
origins 9–11, 16, 19, 50, 65–79, 88, 95, 182, 196, 202, 218, 221–2
Orpheus 131, 142–3, 168
Ovid *passim*
  Amores 29–30, 53, 195, 206, 210
  Ars Amatoria 195, 207–10
  Fasti 32, 75, 154, 167
  Heroides 29, 129, 131, 133–5, 189, 195, 198, 200–2, 207, 210
  Metamorphoses 2, 7, 13, 26, 31, 49, 74, 96, 103, 109, 121, 130–1, 133, 136, 154–6, 159, 162, 167, 174–5, 184, 200, 204, 210, 217, 240, 242, 245, 248, 252

Tristia 17, 129, 133–4, 136
Ovide moralisé 17, 120, 136, 157, 197, 200, 248

pageants 11, 111, 189, 218, 225–30, 233
pamphleteers 18, 74
Pan 168, 217, 219–20, 225–6, 230
Pandarus 75
paratexts 12, 50, 223
Paris (city) 69, 221
Paris, Matthew 66
Paris (mythology) 41, 44–5, 47, 50, 54, 65, 69, 75, 204
Parker, Henry, Lord Morley 198
parody 12, 18, 45, 49, 87, 206, 218–21, 223–4, 227–8, 231
passion(s) 13, 33, 46, 98, 158, 167, 185–7, 197, 219, 243, 250, 255
pastoral 16, 44, 49, 53, 78, 167
patron(s) 13, 44, 221
patronage 14
Pausanias 4
pedagogy 3–5, 50, 223
Pelias 121
Pelly, Laurent 86, 90–1
Penelope 2, 18, 173–90
performance(s) 5, 13–14, 18, 52, 76, 103–4, 173, 179, 195, 203, 216–18, 226
  court performance 216–17, 226, 229–32
Petrarch 248
  see also rhetoric
Pharamond 66, 69–70, 76
Philip of Burgundy 69
Philomel 19
Philostratus 185
Phyllis 195
Pictorius 3
Pizan, Christine de 10, 178, 198, 207
Plantagenets 66, 76
Plautus 14
playhouse(s) 14, 88, 226
Pliny 185
Plutarch 13, 34–5
Polydore Vergil 72, 76, 78

power
  female 116, 122–3
  of love 205, 246, 252–3
  of poetry/rhetoric 11, 46, 69, 75, 103, 161, 184, 219, 249
  political 13, 66, 68–9, 98, 178–9, 181, 183–5, 187
préciosité 218, 221–2
Priam 41, 68–70, 72, 74–5, 88, 92, 99, 103, 219
printer(s) 9, 69, 144, 197–8, 201, 221
prologue(s) 41, 50, 65, 198, 200, 204, 217, 223, 225–6, 230
Propertius 25, 30, 33
Propoetides 245, 247
Proserpina 166–7, 217, 225
Psyche 18, 216–18, 220, 224–5, 227
Pygmalion 3–4, 8, 18–19, 88, 168, 184–5, 187–8, 239–55
Pynson, Richard 200–1
Pyrrhus 103

Queen Henrietta's Men 216
queens 14, 89, 96, 103, 249
querelle des femmes 189, 195, 196, 197–9 *passim*

rape 17–18, 28, 31, 32, 34, 41, 42, 45, 50, 68, 74–5, 149–69, **151**, **152**, 187
readers 2, 4, 5, 9, 11, 28, 42–3, 46, 50, 52, 56–9, 72–3, 88, 111, 128, 132, 141–3, 156, 197, 199, 207, 225, 242, 244, 247–8, 254
recognition 15, 221, 239, 240, 243, 248–9, 252
Red Bull Theatre 216
Restoration 216, 249
revenge 27, 69, 95, 131, 217, 223, 225
rhetoric 3, 5, 11–17 *passim*, 57, 86, 90, 92, 93, 98, 103–4, 151, 152, 158, 165–8, 173, 175, 179, 185, 203
  Petrarchan 2, 109, 111, 114, 122, 162, 163–4, 196–7, 210, 248–9
Richard II 66, 140
Richard III 76
Richard the Lionheart 87, 89

282 Index

Robinson, Richard 17, 132, 136, 138–44 *passim*
Roman de la Rose 242, 247
romance 14, 15, 69, 109, 167, 246, 252
romances 5, 10, 68–9, 88, 246, 249, 250
Rome 6–7, 11, 16, 27, 58, 67–70, 74, 76–7
Romulus and Remus 68
Ronsard, Pierre de 159–62, 168
Rourke, Josie 86, 90, 95–6, 102

Saint-Amant, Marc Antoine Girard de 222
Sainte-Maure, Benoît de 10, 69
Salmacis 26, 31, 36
Salomon, Bernard 149, 155–6
salons 218, 222
Samothes 65, 72–3
Sandys, George 3, 151, 157, 247
Sappho 26–7, 31
Scaliger, Julius Caesar 50, 51, 57
Scudéry, Madeleine de 222
sculptor 240–1, 245, 248, 252
Scylla 7–8
Seneca 4, 8, 11, 17, 25, 90, 93, 95–6, 99, 102–3, 111, 129, 131, 144, 176
  Hippolytus 136
  Medea 17, 26–7, 109, 117, 129–30, 133–5, 138
  Troades 86, 93, 96
Servius 29
sexuality 13, 33–4, 177, 242, 247
Shakespeare
  2 Henry VI 5–8, 128, 131
  Antony and Cleopatra 13, 34–5
  As You Like It 166, 249
  Comedy of Errors, The 252
  Coriolanus 175, 182–3
  Cymbeline 19–20, 75, 77–8
  Hamlet 86
  King John 11, 16, 86–104
  Measure for Measure 18, 239–43
  Merchant of Venice, The 17, 109–23, 201–2
  Merry Wives of Windsor, The 164, 250
  Midsummer Night's Dream, A 249
  Much Ado About Nothing 164, 249, 250–2
  Pericles 252

Rape of Lucrece, The 32–3, 75, 165
Richard III 76–7, 95, 103
Sonnets 163
Taming of the Shrew, The 164–5, 168, 189
Tempest, The 244, 254–5
Titus Andronicus 27, 29, 74
Troilus and Cressida 1–2, 10–11, 74–5, 96–7, 164, 189, 223, 228
Two Gentlemen of Verona, The 250
Venus and Adonis 31–2, 47–8, 223
Winter's Tale, The 165–8, 175, 183–8
shame 29–33, 36, 46, 58, 87, 133, 165, 204
Shaw, George Bernard
  Pygmalion 254
sheep 41, 45, 66, 110, 114–15, 119–23
Sherburne, Edward 189
Sherburne, John 189
Shirley, James 18, 189, 233
  Gamester, The 189
  Schoole of Complement, The 143
  Triumph of Beauty, The 143
  Triumph of Peace, The 218, 231
  Witty Fair One, The 189
sibling 129–36
Sidney, Mary Herbert 12–13
Sidney, Philip 4, 53–4, 151
sister 17, 93, 96, 99, 129–36, 141–2, 145
sonnet sequences 11, 158–63, 168–9
sonnets 11, 17, 159–61, 164–6
son(s) 33, 68, 72, 73–5, 78, 87, 89, 93–103 *passim*, 119, 121, 129, 131, 136–40, 142–4, 205, 208, 209
speaker 132, 154, 160–1, 163, 167, 169, 187, 228–9, 239–40
spectators 6, 11, 92, 104, 111, 123, 202, 207, 219, 224–6, 229
Spenser, Edmund
  The Faerie Queene 30–1, 58, 74, 187
staging 3, 16–17, 89, 102, 205–6, 213, 225
Statius 8, 25, 31, 33–4
statue 4, 19, 164, 185, 239–55 *passim*
Still, Melly 19
Studley, John 17, 117–18, 135–6, 144
suicide 52, 78, 138, 154, 196–8, 207–8
Sulla 6–8
sword 7, 34, 75, 118, 134, 135, 207

Tacitus 65–6, 72
tapestry 2–3, 155, 158–9, 160, 165, 173–6, 187
Tarquin (Sextus) 19, 32, 75
Tasso, Bernardo 14, 49
Tasso, Torquato 4, 35
tears 28, 29, 32, 128, 140, 143, 203, 207
Terence 14
Theocritus 26, 47
Theseus 54, 201
Tibullus 26–9 *passim*
Titian 149, **153**, 158, 168
tragicomedy 48, 179, 181, 184
translation 4, 6–10, 12–15, 16–18, 30, 43–4, 50–1, 54, 86, 88, 93, 95, 100, 109, 117, 129, 133–7, 156–60 *passim*, 162, 176–8, 179, 195–7, 199–201, 210, 222, 228, 247
translator(s) 8, 13, 17–18, 50, 135–6, 144, 197, 200–1, 210
Trojans 65, 68–70, 75–6, 91, 101, 104, 243
Troy 1–2, 13, 33, 45, 87–8, 95, 196
  as ancestor/lineage 11, 16, 68, 70–4, 76
  battlements of 102–3
  fall of 16–17, 32, 90–3, 103
  imagery of 86, 100–4
  matter/story of 9–12, 50, 68, 93
  as medieval city 17, 88
  siege of 75, 89–90
Trussell, John 54
Turberville, George 135

Ulysses 75, 86, 98–9, 176, 184, 219
  and Penelope 176, 178, 180–2, 186–7, 189
  see also Odysseus

van Balen, Hendrick 149, 168
Venus 32, 34–5, 53–4, 68, 154, 165, 205–9 *passim*, 216–17, 220, 223, 225, 230, 243, 245–6, 253, 255

see also Adonis; Aphrodite
Veronese, Paolo 149, **152**, 168
Virgil 8, 11, 13, 16, 18, 52
  Aeneid 6, 25, 27–31, 33, 35, 68, 79, 90–1, 93, 99, 195–210
virginity 31, 34, 154, 157
virility 34, 149, 163
virtue 65, 69, 110, 140, 173, 175–7, 179–82, 190, 250, 253
Vulcan 217, 220, 229–30, 246

Walker, Timothy 205
Walter, William 200, 207–8
Warner, Deborah 86, 90
wars 6–8, 45, 68, 70, 128, 219
Watson, Thomas 16, 45, 54–6 *passim*
  Amyntas 41, 43–5, 49, 52–3
  Hekatompathia 158–9, 164, 168
weaver 2, 30, 173–90
Whetstone, George 3–4, 167
whore(s) 12, 163, 242, 245
widow(s) 89, 93–5, 101, 197, 200, 207, 208, 243–4
women 129, 133, 141, 163, 177, 245–6, 249–50
  abandoned 195
  agency of 168
  as casualties of war 92–3
  debate over 195–202, 206–8
  emasculating power of 123
  government of 183–4, 188–9
  grieving 103, 136, 138
  as patrons 14, 218
  status of 198–9, 248–9
  see also misogyny; *querelle des femmes*
wool 17, 33, 110, 113–14, 186
wound 28–9, 206–8
Wynkyn De Worde 12, 200

Zeus 42, 46, 56, 154
  see also Jupiter
Zeuxis 185

EU authorised representative for GPSR:
Easy Access System Europe, Mustamäe tee 50,
10621 Tallinn, Estonia
gpsr.requests@easproject.com